"One will seldom go wrong to attribute:
 — extreme xxx to vanity
 — moderate ones to habit &
 — petty ones to FEAR."
   — Nietzsche —

"It's better to know some/the q's than all/the answers."
   — James Thurber —

"The years teach much which the days never know."   — Ralph Waldo Emerson —

"Life is one long struggle in the dark."   — Lucretius —

"No treaty is ever an impediment to a cheat."
   — Sophocles —

"I bend & break not." — Jean de la Fontaine —

Hume, Passion, and Action

6 components of motiv'n

① purpose
② exp'tn's
③ competence
④ feedback
⑤ support
⑥ rewards

Motiv'n
  extrinsic
  intrinsic

3 elements of:
① direction
② intensity
③ persistence

Types / motiv'n:
① achievement - to pursue & gain goals (guide)
② affiliation - to relate to people on a social
   basis
③ competence
④ power
⑤ attitude
⑥ incentive
⑦ fear

Also:
① biological & homeostasis - physiologic
② hunger
③ thirst
④ - regulation of body T
⑤ - sleep need
⑥ - avoidance / pain
⑦ - elimination of waste

Hume, Passion, and Action

Elizabeth S. Radcliffe

OXFORD
UNIVERSITY PRESS

OXFORD
UNIVERSITY PRESS

Great Clarendon Street, Oxford, OX2 6DP,
United Kingdom

Oxford University Press is a department of the University of Oxford.
It furthers the University's objective of excellence in research, scholarship,
and education by publishing worldwide. Oxford is a registered trade mark of
Oxford University Press in the UK and in certain other countries

© Elizabeth S. Radcliffe 2018

The moral rights of the author have been asserted

First Edition published in 2018
Impression: 1

All rights reserved. No part of this publication may be reproduced, stored in
a retrieval system, or transmitted, in any form or by any means, without the
prior permission in writing of Oxford University Press, or as expressly permitted
by law, by licence or under terms agreed with the appropriate reprographics
rights organization. Enquiries concerning reproduction outside the scope of the
above should be sent to the Rights Department, Oxford University Press, at the
address above

You must not circulate this work in any other form
and you must impose this same condition on any acquirer

Published in the United States of America by Oxford University Press
198 Madison Avenue, New York, NY 10016, United States of America

British Library Cataloguing in Publication Data
Data available

Library of Congress Control Number: 2017960671

ISBN 978-0-19-957329-5

Printed and bound by
CPI Group (UK) Ltd, Croydon, CR0 4YY

Links to third party websites are provided by Oxford in good faith and
for information only. Oxford disclaims any responsibility for the materials
contained in any third party website referenced in this work.

"The rich have become richer and the poor " " poorer and the vessel of the state is driven between the Scylla and Charybdis of anarchy and despotism." —Percy Shelley—

For Rick,
and in memory of my parents,
Herb and Frances Schmidt

"The public demands certainties... but there are no certainties."
—H. L. Mencken—

In Greek mythology, Scylla was a monster that lived on one side of a narrow channel of water and Charybdis lived on the other side — each side was w/in the range of an arrow so any attempt to avoid one side brought one dangerously close to the other side. [sraboue comput] [compusion]

"7a does NOT SUCCEED IN CONVERTING CONSOLATION INTO T₁ " " " " F₁ NOR DOES VSN INTO CONSULATION.
compassion

Contents

Acknowledgments	ix
Hume's Texts and Abbreviations Used	xi
Introduction	1
0.1 Historical Context	3
0.2 A Sketch of Hume's Characterization of Reason and Passion	7
0.3 Method of Interpretation and Preview of the Arguments	9
1. Motives to Action	14
1.1 Motives and Reasons: Some Clarifications	15
1.2 Overview of Hume's Characterization of the Passions	17
1.3 Which Passions Are Motives?	24
1.4 Summary	28
2. Hume's Argument for the Inertness of Reason	29
2.1 What Is the Target of Hume's Argument?	29
2.2 "Reason Alone Can Never Be a Motive"	33
2.3 Does Hume's Argument Allow that Beliefs Motivate Even If Reason Does Not?	39
2.4 An Interpretation that Beliefs Alone Are Not Motives	50
3. Belief: Some Complications	65
3.1 Hume's Characterization of Ideas	66
3.2 Hume's Characterization of Belief	68
3.3 Is the "Direction-of-Fit" Argument Derived from Hume?	81
3.4 Objects of Belief and Objects of Reason	84
4. The Passions as Original Existences	89
4.1 Reason Generates No Impulses or Attractions	90
4.2 The Features of Original Existences	90
4.3 A Defense of Hume's Conception of the Passions	98
4.4 "Unreasonable" and "Reasonable" Motivating Passions	104
4.5 Has Hume Effectively Countered the Rationalists?	111
5. Morality and Motivation	112
5.1 Hume's Motivation Argument	112
5.2 Moral Internalisms	115
5.3 The Natural-Motive Interpretation	119
5.4 The Moral-Discernment Interpretation	121
5.5 Moral Sentimentalism and Moral Cognitivism	137
6. Motivational Dynamics and Regulation of the Passions	146
6.1 Strength *versus* Violence	147
6.2 Natural Influences on the Passions	151

6.3 How Others' Passions Affect Us: Sympathy and Comparison	155
6.4 Strength of Mind	160
6.5 Moderating the Passions with the Passions	167
6.6 Limits to Self-Regulation of the Passions	176
6.7 The Practical Role of Strength of Conviction	178
7. Conclusion: The Passions in Hume's Project	183
7.1 The Understanding, the Passions, and Morals as a System	183
7.2 The Passions in Relation to Tragedy and Religion	191
7.3 The Passions as an Antidote to Religious Moralizing	194
7.4 The Signature Role of the Passions	195
Appendix: The Passions and Reason in Seventeenth- and Eighteenth-Century Philosophy	197
A.1 Seventeenth-Century Theories of Passion, Reason, and Action	197
A.2 Eighteenth-Century Theories of Passion, Reason, and Action	206
Bibliography	215
Index	225

Acknowledgments

The contents of this book have evolved over very many years. I first conceived of writing a book on Hume's theory of morality back in 1996–97, with the support of an NEH Fellowship. I produced some articles that year, but they did not constitute a book. I was fortunately able to begin again with yet another such fellowship in the calendar year of 2006. In the meantime, my focus became Hume's theory of motivation; and I discovered my greatest interest was in Hume's theory of the passions and their relation to action. Here, at last, is the result.

I am beholden to many scholars whose professional work has had an impact on my thinking. I am grateful to Nicholas Sturgeon, whose teaching first inspired me to take up study of Hume and the British Moralists many years ago in graduate school. His British Empiricists course was one of the best of my life. Work on the passions by the late Rachel Kydd and the late Annette Baier, plus publications by Rachel Cohon, James Harris, Jane McIntyre, and Jackie Taylor have been very influential on the contours of my discussion here. The writings of Don Garrett, Peter Kail, and David Owen have also been important in various ways. The late David Fate Norton was an encouraging presence during many years of my career.

I am immensely indebted to Rachel Cohon for her many detailed and insightful comments on the manuscript, and to two other anonymous reviewers for Oxford University Press, whose feedback was invaluable. I am also grateful to participants and discussants at various conferences where I presented papers on which parts of chapters are based. These include many International Hume Society Conferences going all the way back to 1992. Other more recent venues, with appreciation to the organizers, include: the New Philosophical Voices on Hume Conference at the University of San Francisco (2007), organized by Jacqueline Taylor; the Hume Society Group Meeting at the Pacific Division Philosophical Association Meeting, San Francisco (2007), organized by Kathleen Wallace; the Department of Philosophy at Vanderbilt University (2009), organized by Jeffrey Tlumak; a books-in-progress workshop at the University of Toronto (2009), organized by Donald Ainslie, who also generously provided funding; the David Hume and Contemporary Philosophy Conference in Moscow (2011), organized by Ilya Kasavin; the Department of Philosophy at the College of Charleston (2011), organized by Deborah Boyle; the Harvard History of Philosophy Workshop (2014), organized by Jeff McDonough; the Virginia Philosophical Association Meeting (2015), organized by Nathaniel Goldberg; the Iowa Philosophical Society Meeting (2015), organized by Annemarie Butler and Patrick Connolly; and the Eastern Division Meeting of the American Philosophical Association (2017), organized by John Carriero.

I am grateful for the reinforcement of my work over the years from various philosophical friends. Many are members of the Hume Society, without whom scholarly life would be less productive and more solitary. Some of them I have already named; others include: Robert Audi, Donald Baxter, Charlotte Brown, Richard Dees, Karánn Durland, Lorne Falkenstein, Aaron Garrett, Michael Gill, Lorenzo Greco, Livia Guimarães, Tom E. Hill, Haruko Inoue, Tom Holden, Mike Karlsson, Lauren Kopajtic, Eugenio Lecaldano, Willem Lemmens, Tito Magri, Alison McIntyre, Miriam McCormick, Ted Morris, Katie Paxman, Terence Penelhum, Dario Perinetti, Gerald Postema, Wade Robison, Amy Schmitter, Lisa Shapiro, Rob Shaver, Neal Sinhababu, Corliss Swain, Saul Traiger, Alessio Vaccari, Rico Vitz, and Margaret Watkins. I especially thank Geoffrey Sayre-McCord, who invited me to spend time in the invigorating atmosphere of the UNC-Chapel Hill Philosophy Department in the early years of my career; Kenneth Winkler, who was a brilliant philosophical colleague (and co-editor) in years gone by; and Angela Coventry, who has been a source of much enthusiasm since we worked together as Hume Society officers some years ago. I apologize to those whom I may have forgotten; it's hard to remember all to whom gratitude is due.

Thanks to my colleagues at Santa Clara University for their warm support, especially Bill Prior, whose friendship I will always value. I appreciate my current colleagues and students, who provide a friendly and stimulating work environment at the College of William & Mary. Friends and family have, over the years, been a source of understanding and good cheer, especially: Claudia Lowder, Patricia Rohr, Corina Vaida, Frank and Doris Tillman, David and Linda Schmidt, Barbara and Kevin Urban, and Kay and Don McCarty. Thank you to Dana Radcliffe for his encouragement in the initial years of my career, and to Stephen Tramel, for inspiring me to be a philosopher.

For financial sponsorship, I am indebted to the National Endowment for the Humanities; Santa Clara University; the College of William & Mary; and Joseph Plumeri, a generous patron of William & Mary faculty endeavors. I also thank Peter Momtchiloff at Oxford University Press, who gave me the latitude to do this book in my own good time.

I want to acknowledge the following journals or volumes in which some of the material or ideas in this book appeared previously: *Journal of the History of Philosophy*, *Canadian Journal of Philosophy*, *Hume Studies*, *Res Philosophica*, *Hume Readings* (Edizioni di Storia e Letteratura), and *Thinking about the Emotions: A Philosophical History* (Oxford University Press).

Finally, this book is dedicated to Rick McCarty, who keeps the household going when I'm too busy to cope (which is much of the time), and who has for many years talked with me about my ideas as they were evolving. His advice has improved the arguments tremendously. He also read the entire manuscript and worked on footnote and bibliography formatting. I owe him more, and love him more, than I can ever say.

Hume's Texts and Abbreviations Used

Abstract *An Abstract of a Book Lately Published; Entituled* A Treatise of Human Nature &c. *Wherein the Chief Argument of that Book is farther Illustrated and Explained* (1740). In *A Treatise of Human Nature*. David Fate Norton and Mary J. Norton (Eds.) Oxford: Oxford University Press, 2007. ["Abstract" with paragraph number]

App. Appendix.

Diss. *A Dissertation on the Passions and the Natural History of Religion* (1757). Tom L. Beauchamp (Ed.) Oxford: Oxford University Press, 2007. ["Diss." with section and paragraph numbers]

EHU *An Enquiry Concerning Human Understanding* (1748). Tom L. Beauchamp (Ed.). Oxford: Oxford University Press, 1999. ["EHU" with section and paragraph numbers]

EPM *An Enquiry concerning the Principles of Morals* (1751). Tom L. Beauchamp (Ed.). Oxford: Oxford University Press, 1998. ["EPM" with section and paragraph numbers, or "EPM" with Appendix ("App.") and paragraph numbers]

Essays *Essays, Moral, Political, and Literary* (1777). Eugene F. Miller (Ed.) Indianapolis: Liberty Fund, 1987. ["Essays" with name of essay and paragraph numbers]

Letter *A Letter from a Gentleman to his Friend in* Edinburgh (1745). In *A Treatise of Human Nature*. David Fate Norton and Mary J. Norton (Eds.) Oxford: Oxford University Press, 2007. ["Letter" with paragraph number]

NHR *A Dissertation on the Passions and the Natural History of Religion* (1757). Tom L. Beauchamp (Ed.) Oxford: Oxford University Press, 2007. ["NHR" with section and paragraph numbers]

T *A Treatise of Human Nature* (1739–40). David Fate Norton and Mary J. Norton (Eds.) Oxford: Oxford University Press, 2007. ["T" with book, part, section, paragraph numbers, or "T" with Appendix ("App.") and paragraph numbers]

Introduction

Hume's theory of the passions is integral to his philosophical system. This is actually a controversial claim, since it is easy to dismiss Hume's narrative of the passions as chiefly a project of taxonomy and anatomy. Some readers regard the account as yet another mechanistic analysis in the manner of seventeenth-century science, alongside the offerings of Malebranche, Hobbes, and Spinoza.[1] Contemporary philosophers in action theory, however, regard Hume's account of the motivating passions as highly influential in current discussions, citing it as crucial inspiration for the main naturalist line on motivation and action. Proponents of the Humean Theory of Motivation, or the belief-desire model, which says that both a belief and a desire are necessary to constitute a motive, appeal to Hume's arguments as the classical rationale for their theory. Since at least this part of Hume's theory of the passions has been immensely effective, and since it is wise to judge a project by its fruits, we should surely reject the claim that Hume's narrative is merely a scheme of classifying affections! So, while this book has as its focus Hume's theory of the passions in relation to action, it is also designed to offer vindication of the theory's importance both to Hume's study of human nature and to our own thinking on motivation, action, and evaluation.

My aim in studying Hume's theory of passion and action is to defend an interpretation of his views on reason and motivation that is consistent with other theses in his philosophy, loyal to the text, and historically situated. Two arguments form the core of Hume's thinking on this matter. One is his argument on the "Inertness of Reason" directed at early modern rationalists, in which he maintains, on the basis of reason's functions, that it never, on its own, provides a motive to action. The other is the "Motivation Argument" for the origin of morality, in which Hume reasons that because moral distinctions have an effect on passions and actions (they "motivate"), they cannot be derived from a principle, reason, which has no such effect. Both have been subject to multiple readings by commentators, and discussion of these arguments can be found in Chapter 2 and Chapter 5.

Hume's first book, *A Treatise of Human Nature* (1739–40), was written in three books. The first, "Of the Understanding," contains his epistemology; the second, "Of

---

[1] For contrary views, see Buckle (2012) and Taylor (2015a).

the Passions," is his account of our emotional life, and the third, "Of Morals," concerns moral psychology and virtue. Readers regard *An Enquiry Concerning Human Understanding* (1748, "the first *Enquiry*") as Hume's more popular presentation of the ideas from *Treatise* Book 1. *An Enquiry Concerning the Principles of Morals* (1751, "the second *Enquiry*") is a more accessible version of the contents of Book 3, perhaps with some modifications (see below). Hume's brief *Dissertation on the Passions* (1757) is an edited version of Book 2 of the *Treatise*, but many commentators have found it unappealing as a guide to the passions, since it ignores many of the interesting topics of Book 2, including the psychology of sympathy and the relation of passion to action.[2] I reference it, especially in Chapter 2, as verification of some of the views I attribute to Hume.

In this project, I move fairly freely among Hume's texts, even though there are some differences in views expressed between his earlier and later works. The main differences relevant to this discussion are those between Hume's *Treatise* and the second *Enquiry*. In EPM, Hume seems to characterize moral sentiments differently, moving from a sympathy-based account of moral sentiments in the *Treatise*, to an account whereby a universally-possessed "sentiment of humanity" is the feeling by which we make moral discernments. In the *Treatise*, Hume describes us as sympathetically partaking of others' pleasures and pains, which allows us to have a sense of how agents affect the people around them. Our moral judgments depend on those sympathetic feelings when we moderate them by taking up a general or common point of view, which divests us of personal prejudices and allows moral spectators within a community to achieve an agreement in their moral judgments. That process is replaced in EPM by the simpler account, referencing the universal sentiment of humanity, which is both indicative of morality and can motivate us in accord with its demands (see Taylor 2008). In EPM, Hume offers the arguments concerning the impotence of reason in the context of discussing "the offices of reason and of taste" (EPM, App. 1.21), so the arguments are not as explicit as they are in the *Treatise*, and he retains arguments for moral sentimentalism, based on directly eliminating reason as the possible source of our moral distinctions.

Traditionally Hume's Inertness of Reason argument has been understood as an argument for the conclusion that beliefs, the products of reason, do not act as motives on their own (without passion or desire). The Motivation Argument has then been read as an argument for the conclusion that moral distinctions are not matters of belief, but of sentiment, which has sometimes led to interpretations of Hume as a moral non-cognitivist. Recent scholars, however, have defended a reading of Hume on which belief on its own may very well be a motive to action in some respect, even

---

[2] See Kemp Smith (1941: 535); Passmore (1968: 128–30); Selby-Bigge (1975: xxi); Immerwahr (1994: 225–40); Baier (2008b: 245). Baier describes the *Dissertation on the Passions* as a mutilation of the *Treatise* Book 2.

though reason is not.³ If they are correct about this, then Hume does not actually provide the support for contemporary Humeanism, as past readers have thought.

In this study, I argue against recent commentators and in favor of the traditional reading. I am convinced that Hume did *not* regard the power or impotence of reason as distinct from what its results, beliefs or enlivened ideas, can do. At the same time, I contend that the impotence of beliefs (on their own) does not imply, on Hume's view, that when we make moral distinctions, like that between virtue and vice, moral good and evil, etc., we cannot have moral beliefs. It is important to understand that Hume's thesis that moral distinctions are sentimentally-based is a thesis about the origin of ideas of morality, part and parcel of his general empiricist program, which says that all meaningful ideas must begin in experience. That moral concepts must start in experiences that are sentiments, rather than sensations, does not preclude that those concepts are cognitions, or so I argue. Additionally, I closely examine Hume's theory of motivational dynamics, the effects of conflicting passions on our psychological well-being, and the sorts of control we might exercise to regulate our passions, which cannot be controlled by reason alone. My conclusion is that there are some ways, given the principles of Hume's motivational psychology, that we can use one passion to moderate another, but there are limits to this endeavor, given human nature and individual emotional constitution.

0.1 Historical Context

As has been emphasized, Hume's theory of motivation and action has been highly influential in contemporary discussions of moral and motivational psychology. Many current philosophers profess to align themselves with the naturalistic model of motivation defended by Hume, which clearly separates conative states from cognitive states. However, present-day critics have often discussed Hume's theory of motivation (and his views on practical reason) as though they were explicitly in opposition to Kant or current Kantian thinking.⁴ This is understandable, given that present-day philosophers typically affiliate themselves with a traditional view they find most persuasive, and three centuries later, we find it instructive to pit followers of Hume against followers of Kant. However, while Kant admits to being stimulated by Hume's analysis of causal thinking to formulate his own theory of causation in response, Kant was not familiar with Book 2 of Hume's *Treatise of Human Nature*, "Of the Passions," where Hume offers his renowned views on motivation. Consequently, to interpret Hume's own views on reason, passion, and motivation in the context of a dispute with Kantian thinking can be at least misleading (although I have done the same myself). To understand the genuine context and meaning of Hume's remarks, we obviously need to turn our attention back to Hume's predecessors.

---

³ See Cohon (2008b), Kail (2007a), Owen (2016), Pigden (2009), Sandis (2012), and Stroud (1977).
⁴ For instance, see Blackburn (2000), Wiggins (1995), and Radcliffe (1997).

One of the predominant themes of philosophy in the late seventeenth and early eighteenth centuries was the relation between reason and passion and their respective effects on motivation and action. The entrenched view from Aristotle onwards, superseded gradually in later centuries, was that the passions were passive powers of the sensitive part of the tripartite soul, the part that reacts to sensible objects acting on the body (see James 1997: 40–2). The early moderns offered alternative perspectives that tried to address the relation between mind and body and provide a more unified account of the mind than that found in Ancient and Scholastic thought, while also emphasizing the activity of the passions themselves. Since the passions influence action, on the prevailing seventeenth- and eighteenth-century view, they could be useful when controlled, but harmful or misleading when not.[5] Thus, one persistent refrain in the work of philosophers prior to and around Hume's time was the governance of the passions, whether the internal authority of reason could direct the passions, or whether an external authority was necessary.

Among the philosophers who were preoccupied with this topic and with whose work Hume was acquainted are Descartes, Malebranche, Leibniz, and Clarke (see Norton 2000: *I*12, n.8), in addition to Hobbes, Locke, Mandeville, and Shaftesbury, not to mention Hume's contemporaries, Butler and Hutcheson.[6] Hume is reputed by some to be influenced by Spinoza's theory of the passions, too.[7] Several other seventeenth- and eighteenth-century thinkers were writing on the oversight of the passions as well, among them French philosophers Jean-François Senault, Nicolas Coeffeteau, and Marin Cureau de La Chambre, plus English theorists William Ayloffe, Francis Bragge (Vicar of Hitchin), Walter Charleton (M.D.), Henry Grove (English Presbyter), and Edward Reynolds. All of these thinkers contributed to some degree to the intellectual background contextualizing Hume's arguments concerning the respective roles of reason and passion in motivation.

Hume's arguments on this topic, then, are responses to prominent theses propagated by these early modern philosophers, writers, and clergy. Below, in summary, are some of their theses, to which Hume is reacting:

---

[5] See McIntyre (2006a: 200–4); Harris (2013: 270–1). The articles by McIntyre and Harris, along with work by Susan James, have been invaluable to my thinking and research.

[6] Annette Baier writes, "A great wealth of intellectual influences come together in Hume: Theophrastus, Epicurus, Cicero, Lucretius, Hobbes, Locke, Malebranche, Berkeley, Shaftesbury, Hutcheson, Butler" (Baier 1993: 250).

[7] Baier contends that the circumstantial evidence that Hume read Spinoza is "overwhelming:"

> He clearly read Malebranche and Leibniz, and they read Spinoza. He was a friend of Pierre Desmaixeaux, a known Spinozist. As Hume's correspondence documents, and as Paul Russell has emphasized, the young Hume frequented Spinozist meeting places in London (such as the Rainbow Coffeehouse, Lancaster Court, where he stayed while arranging for the publication of the *Treatise*), and surely knew Anthony Collins, as well as knowing of Clarke's disputes with him and with Bentley and John Toland. (1993: 238)

(1) Many passions, left unregulated, lead to the pursuit of unsuitable objects. Generally underlying this perspective is a teleological view of the universe, with certain objects proper to our endeavors or inclinations. On some views, God has instilled in us a desire for genuine good and an aversion to genuine evil, but the passions can derail our pursuits.

(2) Reason can overcome the pernicious influence of the passions and take control of them and of our actions. On some views (like Senault's), reason must be supplemented by the grace of God.

(3) The passions are not self-regulating: it is harmful for us to depend on one passion's opposing another in an attempt to thwart the latter's effects. (Not all agree with this, but Senault, Bragge, and Clarke do.)

(4) Passions represent good and evil, which are their objects. This means that passions are cognitions.

(5) On some versions of how the passions are regulated, for instance, Reynolds's, reason offers a suitable object for them to seize upon or pursue. On other versions, such as Descartes's, the passions misrepresent objects as good or as worthy of pursuit, and reason offers the proper representation of those objects.

(6) Reason and passions are "advisors" to the will. Thus, reason and passion can be opposed to one another over the direction of our actions.

Hume, of course, rejects teleology, for which he substitutes a mechanistic account of the passions and their relation to action. He argues that some rationalists wrongly characterize the passions as representations and that they misunderstand the functions of reason. He maintains that the passions in fact can be moderated *only* by other passions (when they can be moderated at all). His arguments for these claims are the subjects of the subsequent chapters.

A survey of theories on the passions and action by the seventeenth- and eighteenth-century philosophers and theologians further reveals that few, if any, of these major thinkers explicitly held the view that reason in any of its functions motivates action without an affective state. I provide such a survey in the APPENDIX, "The Passions and Reason in Seventeenth- and Eighteenth-Century Philosophy," which offers support for many of the claims I am making now. For those interested in the history of the passions, I offer it as valuable background to this discussion of Hume's theory of motivation. Here I present some general reflections on early-modern perspectives on the relation between reason and passion.

A prominent theme in the era was that the passions could mislead us, or mislead the will, and clash with the guidance that reason gives to the passions. So, we find in Descartes and Malebranche the thesis that the passions can misrepresent or distort our notions of the good and that their physiological manifestations can be disruptive to our rational volitions to action. Spinoza depicts reason as a motivating, but affective faculty; so, he sets up an opposition between reason and passion, but the conflict is actually between affects. He depicts knowledge of good and evil, presumably

representations, as emotions, or rational affections, which can be opposed to the passions we have for apparent goods that lead us to transient pleasures. Hobbes and Locke argue for the necessity of desire to action, with reason offering information on the means to relieve the uneasiness that desire involves.

Cudworth founds morality in immutable truths known in the way that geometry is, but argues that "speculative intellection without inclination" cannot motivate (see Passmore, 1951:53). He also emphasizes the importance to happiness of possessing certain internal conative states. Clarke argues that understanding demonstrative truths of morality on their own does not produce action and that passions and appetites are needed to "stir" people up (1724: 144). Passions require the oversight of reason, however, to prevent us from pursuing outrageous things and engaging in unreasonable action. Yet, on Clarke's view, we have the free will to act against our best judgment. Integral to both Shaftesbury's and Hutcheson's motivational psychologies are passions and affections that need to be regulated by reflection and other stabilizing influences in order to produce the best lives for agents. For Hutcheson, reasons for action only make sense in light of affectionate states.

When Hume writes about the origin of some of the motivating passions,[8] he writes that the impressions which arise directly from good and evil are "the passions of desire and aversion, grief and joy, hope and fear, along with volition." Then he adds, "The mind by an *original* instinct tends to unite itself with the good, and to avoid the evil tho' they be conceiv'd merely in idea and be consider'd as to exist in any future period of time" (T 2.3.9.2). The role instinct plays in an empiricist theory like Hume's is taken up by the God-instilled direction toward the good in philosophers like Reynolds and Malebranche, and by the propensity to self-preservation in Spinoza. These innate propensities produce various motivating passions in light of our discerning various goods by experience. Obviously, Hume does not accept the metaphysics of these rationalists, but the structure of his theory of motivation is in some revealing respects similar to theirs. In Malebranche, for instance, the propensities are in place, directing actions to the goal of the universal good, and action is caused upon the formation of beliefs about particular goods and the production of the passions that move the body. Hume, however, is clearly an opponent of many of the theses that the rationalist thinkers professed, several of which I listed earlier, and a central disagreement between Hume and many of the rationalists is over the rationalists' characterization of passions as representations. I think his argument on this matter is more important to his project than many commentators have thought (and I discuss this issue in CHAPTER 4). Why, however, does Hume so conspicuously highlight the thesis that reason alone cannot motivate action when no one professes to defend the contrary? His argument for this conclusion is also one

---

[8] I am referring to the direct passions that are not natural instincts. See the discussion of the direct passions in CHAPTER 1.

of the most prominently-featured arguments in contemporary treatments of his motivational psychology. I take up this question in CHAPTER 2.

0.2 A Sketch of Hume's Characterization of Reason and Passion

Here I present the core of my interpretation, in brief, without supporting arguments, which will be added in subsequent chapters. Hume first defends his theory of motivation at *Treatise* 2.3.3, in the section entitled, "Of the influencing motives of the will." Some of the themes in and related to this section are repeated in modified forms in the *Enquiry Concerning the Principles of Morals* and in the *Dissertation on the Passions*. At *Treatise* 2.3.3, Hume has just concluded his discussion of free will, where he rejects the traditional doctrine that has human responsibility opposed to causality or necessitation of actions. Hume argues that uncaused actions would be chance events and attributable to no one. In order for actions to have merit or demerit at all (and for actors to be held responsible for them) their actions must be caused by enduring principles of character. Hume explains the use of "will" in his discussion in the following way: "by the *will*, I mean nothing but *the internal impression we feel and are conscious of, when we knowingly give rise to any new motion of our body, or new perception of our mind*." This impression, he maintains, is not further definable or describable, but he makes it clear that this impression is an immediate effect of pleasure or pain, as are the passions of desire and aversion, grief and joy, and hope and fear (T 2.3.1.1). These latter are direct passions, on Hume's scheme, because they arise directly from the feelings of pleasure or pain, or from ideas of the sources of the pleasures and pains, with no intermediary impressions or ideas (T 2.1.1.4). Hume's point seems to be that the internal impression that we identify with willing, although the result of pleasure or pain, requires no pleasure or pain beyond that involved in the passion that causes the action.[9] Thus, just as Hobbes suggested, the will is nothing over and above the experience of an internal change, just prior to the occurrence of action.[10] It is safe to say that the will as a faculty of choice drops out of Hume's theory of action; "will" is simply a way of referring to the feeling we have of bringing forward a perception or of initiating a bodily movement.

---

[9] Hume's description makes it sound as though the will is itself a direct passion. But impressions for Hume are of two sorts: impressions of sensation and impressions of reflection. Impressions of reflection are the passions, and they arise from reflecting on our experienced pleasures and pains. My idea of the feeling of pleasure I get from the warmth of the fireplace gives me desire or hope for more of that pleasure. But the impression we feel upon our moving the body or initiating thought, Hume's "will," is not the consequence of such reflection. It simply occurs when a passion moves us. On the other hand, the will is not a sensation either, since sensations are defined as impressions arising from unknown causes, which presumably signals Hume's doubt about the existence of external objects that are said to cause our sensations (T 1.1.1.2).

[10] Hobbes defines will as "the last Appetite, or Aversion, immediately adhaering to the action, or to the omission thereof...." This, he says, is "the Act, (not the faculty), of *Willing*" (Hobbes 1651: Chapter 6, 44).

8 HUME, PASSION, AND ACTION

The real question Hume is intent on answering in "Of the influencing motives of the will" is, what are the causes of our actions, prior to that feeling?

On this topic, Hume makes the following points. (1) The prevailing view in philosophy is that our passions are often opposed to our reason in providing motives to actions, and that people are virtuous when they conform their actions to the dictates of reason. Reason is eternal, invariable, and divinely originated, according to this view, while passions are variable and deceptive. (2) This accepted view of motivation and morality is mistaken on two counts, because (a) Reason can never be a motive to any action of the will, and (b) Reason can never oppose passion in directing the will. Hence, persons cannot be told to regulate their actions according to the dictates of reason and to oppose other forces (since they cannot be required to do what is impossible—namely, to be moved by reason).

Hume's arguments turn on several key theses that will be discussed in detail later, but I want to keep in mind here his characterizations of reason and passion, respectively, on which the argument is based. Reason, he writes, serves to reveal to us conceptual connections in necessary truths or to derive inductive conclusions about the world. A large part of Book I of the *Treatise* concerns induction, or causal reasoning, and there Hume says that "all reasonings from causes or effects terminate in conclusions, concerning matters of fact; that is, concerning the existence of objects or of their qualities" (T 1.3.7.2). These conclusions are, from the perspective of the investigator, beliefs; so the products of reason are beliefs, and beliefs are enlivened ideas, as opposed to impressions. Impressions are the forceful and lively perceptions that we initially experience (sensations and passions or emotions), while ideas are the fainter copies of the impressions, which Hume says the ideas "exactly represent" (T 1.1.1.7). Our beliefs about the world purport to copy our initial experiences and to represent to us the way the world is. In Book 3 of the *Treatise*, Hume defines reason as "the discovery of truth or falshood" and defines truth and falsehood as an agreement or disagreement of our ideas to "relations of ideas" (necessary truths) or to matters of fact, following the division of types of truths in Book 1. Passions, on the other hand, make no reference to anything beyond themselves; they are "original facts and realities" (T 3.1.1.9). In other words, passions are not copies of previous experiences and so contain no content that portrays the world in one way or another. Since passions do not represent something to be the case, as reason does, passions cannot contradict reason. (This is, of course, a controversial view.)

Also crucial to Hume's argument is his point that reason alone does not generate impulses to action. This means that we are unmotivated (i.e., we feel no push or pull at all) when we engage reason, including (what some call) the use of rational intuition, the use of demonstration, and the use of probabilistic and inductive reasoning. I want to interpret Hume, contentiously, to mean that neither the comprehension of demonstrative truths nor the formation of factual beliefs through reason, with no contribution from the passions, can prompt action. This is because beliefs do not give us ends to pursue and so cannot offer direction. Since beliefs, the products of reason, produce no impulses to action on their own, they cannot move us without the passions. Hence, Hume argues that reason cannot oppose passion for direction of the will. Reason works with our ideas, copied from our impressions, to determine which of our ideas represents their objects accurately. Since only an impulse can oppose an impulse, individual passions, which provoke us, cannot be opposed to individual beliefs (or ideas), which represent but do not provoke us. To say that passion cannot oppose reason is to implicate the capacity of feeling and the capacity of reason. However, it is only because their *products* cannot be opposed, I contend, that we are justified in saying the capacities cannot be opposed.[11] In holding this, I disagree with many contemporary interpretations of Hume, in which products of reason are motivationally different from reason or the reasoning that produces them. These interpretations of Hume allow that beliefs motivate on their own, even though reason cannot.

0.3 Method of Interpretation and Preview of the Arguments

My method in defending my interpretation of Hume follows a coherentist strategy. My attempt is to present a reading of Hume's theory of the passions, motivation, and action that makes best sense of his claims (in the relevant contexts) in terms of developing a coherent and consistent theoretical picture. Since Hume's theses do not always seem entirely consistent, this method requires that occasionally claims be interpreted in ways that do not seem like the most obvious reading at first glance. (Hume may have changed his mind about some issues, or he may just be inconsistent at times, or he may be consistent and the attempt to read his claims in the less obvious way is what he really intended.) All parties to the discussion over how to best understand Hume must use the same approach and face the quandary about what claims to take at face value. Part of this approach, of course, aims as far as possible to preserve simplicity for Hume's theory, to attribute to him claims that are in themselves plausible or defensible, and to ascribe a view that makes best sense of the complex observations of human nature that he tenders. I believe I succeed in offering a way to read Hume on what each of reason, passion, motive, and belief is and that constitutes a coherent and productive picture of his theory of motivation. It gives him a credible (and, I think) correct view of the respective roles of reason and passion in motivation.

---

[11] We might also bear in mind Hume's positive view of motivation: "When we have the prospect of pain or pleasure of any object, we feel a consequent emotion of aversion or propensity, and are carry'd to avoid or embrace what will give us this uneasiness or satisfaction" (T 2.2.3.3). These aversions or propensities are the direct passions like desire, aversion, grief, joy, fear, and despair. And, although Hume does not make it explicit, he is committed to the thesis that one always acts on one's strongest passion. This is an important component of Hume's Theory of Motivation that has received little attention, and I will later explain in Chapter 6 why I think it is a view of much significance to his motivational psychology.

CHAPTER 1 sets the stage for the analysis of Hume's arguments concerning the practical impotency of reason and its inability to oppose passion. There I ask the question which passions count as motives, for Hume, and why. Hume discusses the indirect passions in Parts 1 and 2 in Book 2 of the *Treatise*, and explicitly says that pride and humility, love and hatred, the four indirect passions he analyzes in depth, are not motives to action. He introduces motivational issues in Part 3, "Of the will and direct passions," which suggests that he considers all and only direct passions as motives. I show that this reading is false. After considering his distinction between natural instincts, direct passions, and indirect passions, I confirm that some passions in each of these categories are motivating. I also add support to John Bricke's thesis that motives, for Hume, are passions that include desires as part of their descriptions—that is, they *are* desires of some sort (Bricke 1996: 36–7).

CHAPTER 2 is an in-depth discussion of Hume's "Inertness of Reason Argument" that reason alone is not a motive or does not produce motives. First, I consider why he places great emphasis on this argument, given that few, if any, of his predecessors actually professed that reason could motivate people without passion. I entertain two suggestions. One is that Hume sees the rationalist view of morality, when stripped of teleology, as committed to the idea that reason can motivate on its own. The other is that he thought (perhaps mistakenly) that any theory that has reason and passion practically opposed, as many rationalists did, is committed to the thesis that reason alone motivates. Second, I argue against the view that Hume's account of reason and motivation equivocates between two senses of reason. Third, I also argue against the commentators who defend an interpretation of Hume's argument on the inertness of reason that allows that beliefs, products of reason, can motivate, even if reason cannot. On my reading of Hume's Inertness of Reason Argument, he must identify reason with beliefs. For if he thinks beliefs motivate, the following results: (1) his thesis that reason does not originate motives, but does contribute something to motivation, will depend on the equivocation I earlier disposed of; (2) we have no explanation of how actions result from competing motives; and (3) he undermines his dictum that an active principle cannot be founded on an inactive one. Finally, I offer positive textual evidence for my reading of Hume.

In CHAPTER 3, I present a close examination of Hume's account of belief. This chapter extends my argument from CHAPTER 2, since Hume's characterization of belief is crucial in the debate over whether Humean beliefs could qualify as motives. Some commentators allege that Hume had doubts about his account of belief in the *Treatise*, made corrections to it in the Appendix, and developed the corrected view in the first *Enquiry*. At least three readings of Hume's theory of belief have been defended: (1) belief as a vivacious idea; (2) belief as a sentiment; and (3) belief as a disposition to behavioral manifestations. These varied readings have implications for the power of belief to originate action. I argue, based on the full context of Hume's remarks, that Hume's notion of belief as an idea (either vivacious, or with a particular, distinctive sentimental aspect) is not undermined by the hesitations he expresses. So, beliefs are not intrinsically motivating states. I also consider to what degree the "direction of fit" manner of distinguishing beliefs and desires in contemporary philosophy is rooted in Hume's own theory. On this popular contemporary view, beliefs aim to fit the world, and desires aim to fit the world to themselves. I then reply to some criticisms that imply Hume was confused about reason's objects.

After arguing for the Inertness of Reason thesis, Hume moves to the second step in his case for the conclusion that reason does not govern passion and action. Accordingly, he argues that reason and passion cannot be opposed to one another over the direction of the will. This thesis is the subject of CHAPTER 4, and depends on his defending two claims: (1) because reason generates no impulses to action, it cannot oppose the impulses of the passions; and (2) because passions do not represent anything, they cannot oppose reason by offering contrary representations of objects. The characterization of the passions as "original existences" that do not make reference to anything is a prominent theme in Hume and has been subject to much critique. Some readers have argued that the passions are obviously intentional and make reference to their objects; they also think Hume is inconsistent since he depicts passions, for example, in his account of the indirect passions, as having objects and subjects. I defend Hume's conception of passion and show how his account can be read consistently. Then, I discuss in what sense or senses Hume can countenance reasonableness in action.

Hume's thesis that reason is not motivating (the conclusion of the Inertness of Reason Argument) serves as the second premise in his crucial argument from motivation against moral rationalism. CHAPTER 5 examines various ways to interpret the first premise in Hume's "Motivation Argument," namely, the claim that "morals excite passions and produce or prevent actions." This claim is perplexing, given that Hume's Theory of Motivation characterizes passions, which are considered virtues or vices, as motives; yet, the thesis that "morality" is motivating is not about virtues and vices. It is actually about our recognition of moral distinctions and how they can influence us when we lack the appropriate natural virtue. I argue that, in order to make his argument valid, Hume's thesis must be considered as some form of moral internalism. I explain various forms of internalism and then examine two possible internalist readings of the second premise, both of which make Hume's argument valid. The most natural reading does not, however, give support to the ultimate conclusion Hume wants to reach after concluding that morality cannot be derived from reason—namely, that our moral distinctions come from a sensibility. What appears to be a less natural reading is, when placed in the context of Hume's general theory of motivation set out in previous chapters, the best reading. It gives Hume a valid argument and supports his ultimate position about the source of moral distinctions.

I then consider, in the same chapter, whether Hume's moral sentimentalism is compatible with moral cognitivism, the view that when we make moral utterances, we make property-attributions and say something truth-evaluable. Philosophers have defended the view that moral internalism and the belief-desire theory of motivation are together incompatible with moral cognitivism. Here I argue that Hume's sentimentalism is an answer to the question how our ideas of morality originate, which both implies that we have such ideas and leaves open the possibility that motivation can be a result of the impressions upon which our ideas are based. Moral distinctions (or any distinctions, for that matter) cannot be produced from ideas we already possess, since they would have to be generated by demonstration or by probabilistic reasoning, neither of which originates ideas. So, they originate in impressions—not in sensations, but in sentiments—although their genesis is complicated by the fact that they fall under general terms and are technically abstractions. Here I apply Hume's account of how we develop ideas that general terms cover to explain the origin of the concepts of virtue, vice, moral good, moral evil, and so on. After we have acquired these concepts, we can apply them to characters we have not experienced, by inference, given descriptions of those persons' traits. Thus, we can acquire moral beliefs by reasoning. There is nothing in Hume's account of moral motivation that prohibits us from having moral beliefs; moral distinctions are dependent on impressions of approvals and disapprovals that, when directed toward the self, can provide motives to action.

After establishing that Hume does defend a version of the belief-desire (or belief-passion) theory of motivation, I take a detailed look in CHAPTER 6 at the psychological principles in Hume's theory that explain how action results from passions and belief. Hume's naturalistic approach commits him to the thesis that we always act on the strongest desire, other things being equal. Since this thesis is a truism, it does not explain anything, but Hume's psychology of action is actually much more nuanced and interesting than this claim reveals. A study of the phenomena of conflicting passions in Hume's theory reveals that several psychological principles can explain how such passions affect each other, often making the dominant passion even stronger. Furthermore, Hume's distinction between violent passions and causally strong ones, essential to his theory of motivation and to a virtue that he calls "strength of mind," introduces numerous questions about our ability to moderate internal emotional upheaval. The person with strength of mind, the motivational prevalence of calm passions, such as concern for long-term good, over violent ones, such as intensely-felt interest in short-term good, is likely to find genuine happiness. I investigate Hume's characterization of this virtue and whether anyone who is deficient in it might develop it, drawing on the principles I extract from Hume's discussion of passionate dynamics. In other words, I explore to what degree self-moderation of the passions is possible. Contrary to many of the writers noted in this Introduction, who thought using the passions to regulate one another was ineffective or even dangerous, Hume thinks it is possible, within certain limitations.

In the CONCLUSION, I show how Hume's theory of the passions is pivotal in many respects to his philosophical system. The theory clearly serves as an analysis of that part of human nature connecting perception and cognition with morality and action. My discussion addresses several ways in which Hume's treatment of the passions has been thought to make a major contribution to his general philosophical views: (1) as a solution to the skeptical problem of the self that emerges from Book 1 of the *Treatise*; (2) as a medium for his account of morality and moral sentiment; (3) as a phenomenon that makes sociability and psychological well-being possible; (4) as an instrument to explain the psychological aspects of religious belief; (5) as a means to explain paradoxical emotions such as aesthetic appreciation of tragedy; and (6) as a naturalistic alternative to religious perspectives on human action and morality. I maintain that Hume's psychology of the passions serves all of these purposes and can only do so because the signature feature of the passions is their role in initiating action.

1

Motives to Action

Books 1 and 2 of Hume's *Treatise* were published together in January 1739. The advertisement to the publication, which immediately follows the title page of Book 1, announces, "*The subjects of the* understanding *and* passions *make a compleat chain of reasoning by themselves*" (T Advertisement). Book 3, on morality, was published alone, in late October or November of 1740.[1] In his classic work on Hume, Norman Kemp Smith complains that the reader is bewildered by Hume's *Treatise* Book 2 discussion of the passions. He says that the reader expects the doctrines of Book 1, on the contents of the mind and the function of the understanding, to be illustrated and enforced, but they are not. "Instead [Hume] finds himself faced by a quite new set of problems, but with little direct bearing on the problems of knowledge" (Kemp Smith 1941: 160). Furthermore, Kemp Smith notes that over a third of Book 2 is spent on the indirect passions, "which have no very direct bearing upon Hume's ethical problems, and play indeed no really distinctive part in his system" (ibid.: 160). Other commentators have offered analyses, however, meant to show that the passions play a central role in Hume's system—although they do not always highlight the same role. It is, ultimately, the practical forcefulness of the passions (as I claim in the CONCLUSION) that makes possible the other crucial roles they play in Hume's overall science of human nature.

In this chapter, I offer an overview of Hume's theory of the passions and broach the issue which passions count as motives and why. I first clarify what a motive is for Hume. Then I set out Hume's distinction between direct and indirect passions. Hume discusses the indirect passions of pride and humility in *Treatise*, Book 2, Part 1, and the indirect passions of love and hatred in Part 2. He argues that none of these is a motive to the will. Part 3 is entitled "Of the will and direct passions," which suggests that Hume classifies all and only direct passions as motives. I show this reading to be wrong, however. I explore the role in motivation of what Hume identifies as natural instincts. I then add support to the thesis, derived from John Bricke's study of Hume, that motives for Hume are passions that are defined in terms of desire (even though not all desires are motives). In the CONCLUSION to this monograph, I return to the broad issue concerning the objectives of Hume's theory

---

[1] Norton and Norton (2007: v); Harris (2009: 129). The former say October, and the latter says November.

of the passions in his study of human nature, where I argue for the centrality of the passions' motivational effects.

1.1 Motives and Reasons: Some Clarifications

In contemporary discussions, the Humean theory of motivation is the view that desire in combination with belief is essential to motivate action; so, beliefs are not motives on their own.[2] Whether this was in fact what Hume had in mind when he argued that reason alone can never be a motive or can never produce volition or action is a matter of contention, which I discuss in CHAPTER 2. The Humean theory of motivation is often depicted as a theory of reasons for action. This is especially so in current debates where "the Humean theory" is typically taken to refer to a certain view of practical reason—the view that an agent has a reason for action when she has a desire and a belief about how to fulfill that desire. It is important, however, in considering Hume's particular claims, to distinguish reference to reasons from reference to motives. Motives for Hume are causes or potential causes of actions. Appealing to his notion of causality, Hume writes "that as the *union* betwixt motives and actions has the same constancy, as that in any natural operations, so its influence on the understanding is also the same, in *determining* us to infer the existence of one from that of another" (T 2.3.1.14). Reasons, of course, might be causes as well, but it is difficult to see how Hume could countenance reasons for action in any sense different from motives, the mental antecedents to which the actions are causally connected. Rationalists like Descartes, Malebranche, Spinoza, Cudworth, and Clarke all countenance reasons for action, for even if they believe that conative states like passions or inclinations are necessary to motivation, their views allow that these conations can be subject to reason. Reasonable passions are those that correctly represent the good or that prompt the will in the proper direction by following reason's indication of the good.

Hume never alleges that a belief and a desire together constitute a reason for action, although he does say, as I discuss later, that many of our motivating passions arise when an aversion or propensity is created by the prospect of pleasure or pain from an object and that our concern extends to the causes and effects of those objects, causes and effects discovered by reason (T 2.3.3.3).[3] It is my view that Hume does not

---

[2] By implication, desires and beliefs are separate mental states.
[3] Bricke understands Hume's theory in terms of reasons for actions and attributes to Hume a "conativist" theory of reasons for actions, "one that assigns a distinctive and ineliminable motivational role to an agent's *desires*" (Bricke 1996: 5). He sees Hume's view as implying that reasons rationalize the actions they cause (ibid.: 10). As I say, I can see Hume's remarks developed in this direction, and Bricke's project blurs the line somewhat between interpreting Hume and developing Humean views. However, going in this direction leads to questions such as whether any actions could *not* be justified, since all have

offer a theory of reasons for action, where reasons provide *justification* for actions or for ends. Readers have often thought Hume an instrumentalist, one who holds that we are practically rational when we take the best means to our ends (for instance, Audi 1989: 43), but there are really no texts to support that ascription. Other commentators have insisted that Hume was skeptical about practical reason—that is, that his claims about the functions of reason imply that reason is theoretical and never practical.[4] I agree that he has no traditional theory of practical reason, although I think that there is a sense in which reason is practical, even on Hume's view: it delivers information with practical application, depending on one's aims (see Radcliffe 1997). This view does not imply any normative assessment of agents who do or do not act on that information, however, since reason does not actually tell us what we ought to do, among those things we can do. Furthermore, Hume does allow that passions and actions can be reasonable by an informal and improper way of speaking—that is, when they are caused by certain passions. I say more about this later as well.

Moreover, in writing about motives and motivation with respect to Hume, I mean to indicate, not the actor's movement to action, but the actor's possession of a psychological state that could or might cause movement and action (but may not be so effective).[5] Thus, to have a motive for Hume is to experience a psychological push or a pull toward an end, even if that push or pull does not, due to the competition of other motives, ultimately produce action. When Hume refers to a "motive," he is referring to this psychological state, a possible cause of action, which he identifies with a passion. In contemporary Humeanism, one is said to have a motive when one has a desire *and* a belief about how to fulfill the desire, but a motive for Hume is the passionate state, rather than a belief-desire complex. It is also important to note that, in tracing the causes of actions, Hume looks to the mind. Regardless of which objects in the person's environment might be the causes of his or her perceptions, the immediate causes of actions are one's perceptions, and, for Hume, the salient question is which perceptions cause actions. If there were no external world or if the world were not the way the agent believes it to be, she would still act on the perceptions she experiences. Thus, Hume is a psychologist in action theory, assuming as he does that psychological states, not objects in the world, ultimately explain one's actions.

---

belief-desire causes, and whether having a justificatory reason requires that the beliefs it involves be subject to evaluation.

[4] See Hampton (1995), Millgram (1995), and Korsgaard (1986).
[5] I use "actor" here rather than agent, since "agent" might implicate notions of freedom that do not apply to Hume's discussion of motivation. But I have no objection to the use of "agent" (and sometimes use it myself in discussions of Hume), as long as it is understood that the actions of an agent are caused, by either internal or external factors.

1.2 Overview of Hume's Characterization of the Passions

In Hume's philosophy, the mind is occupied with perceptions, and perceptions are divided into impressions and ideas, which are distinguished from each other by the degrees of forcefulness and liveliness with which they enter the mind. Impressions are the more forceful and lively (or "violent"), and ideas are less. Of the first type are the "sensations, passions, and emotions, as they make their first appearance in the soul" (T 1.1.1.1). Ideas are the fainter copies of the impressions that we bring to mind when we think about the original experiences, as illustrated by the thought of a bitter taste or the thought of a pain, as opposed to having a bitter taste or being in pain. Impressions are further divided into impressions of sensation and impressions of reflection, with the former including those vivid experiences we identify as coming from the five senses, which Hume describes as arising "in the soul originally, from unknown causes" (T 1.1.2.1). Impressions of reflection (or "secondary impressions," as he sometimes calls them) are derived from "reflecting" on certain ideas, namely, the sources of pleasure and pain; the impressions of reflection are "passions, desires, and emotions." This reflection is not a form of reasoning or contemplation, but a reflexive move whereby the mind returns to certain objects represented by ideas and responds to them.[6] Hume first describes how they arise in this way:

> An impression first strikes upon the senses, and makes us perceive heat or cold, thirst or hunger, pleasure or pain of some kind or other. Of this impression there is a copy taken by the mind, which remains after the impression ceases; and this we call an idea. This idea of pleasure or pain, when it returns upon the soul, produces the new impressions of desire and aversion, hope and fear, which may properly be called impressions of reflection, because deriv'd from it. These again are copy'd by the memory and imagination, and become ideas; which perhaps in their turn give rise to other impressions and ideas. (T 1.1.1.2)

Hume makes it clear later in his discussion of motives to action in "Of the influencing motives of the will" (T 2.3.3) that impressions of reflection are motives to action, while ideas are not. Yet, not all impressions of reflection serve as motives, and one goal of this discussion is to determine which are and why.

Hume's taxonomy of the passions begins with a fundamental division between calm and violent passions, which he specifies in terms of the internal upheaval with which a passion is felt: calm passions cause "no disorder in the soul," are known by their effects, and are often mistaken for reason. Among calm passions are generally

---

[6] Sometimes Hume spells "reflection" in this context "reflection," and sometimes he spells it "reflexion." He uses the latter spelling when he first introduces the distinction between ideas of sensation and ideas of reflection (reflexion), or the passions. The Norton edition has changed the spelling in all cases to "reflection." (Thanks to Donald Ainslie for pointing this out.) Perhaps, in order to avoid any invocation of reasoning, "reflexion" is the more appropriate spelling when Hume is writing about the passions. However, Hume himself is inconsistent in the spelling, even when referring to the passions.

the sentiments of beauty and morality (T 2.1.1.3) and the natural instincts of benevolence, resentment, love of life, and kindness to children (T 2.3.3.8). Violent passions usually include love and hatred, grief and joy, pride and humility (T 2.1.1.3). The passions that fall under each description can change with the circumstances, however. Resentment of someone who harms me may be felt violently and provoke a desire for revenge (T 2.3.3.8). "The raptures of poetry and music frequently rise to the greatest height; while those other impressions [love and hatred, etc.]...may decay into so soft an emotion, as to become, in a manner, imperceptible" (T 2.1.1.3). Hume calls this division a "vulgar and specious" one, yet it is crucial to his theory of motivation, as I shall explain in Chapter 6. The other major distinction central to Hume's account is that of direct and indirect passions. According to Hume, direct passions arise immediately from pleasure or pain (natural good or evil), and the indirect arise from pleasure and pain in conjunction with other qualities (including reference to the self or to others).

1.2.1 The Direct and the Indirect Passions

The Stoic classification of the passions dominated Renaissance and early-modern thought. Their account of four primitive passions—which, for Cicero, were joy, grief, desire, and fear—was modified by Descartes, Spinoza, and Malebranche (Fieser 1992: 3–4). The distinction between direct and indirect passions is entirely original to Hume (McIntyre 2000: 78), but his list of direct passions, too, reflects the Stoical primitives (Fieser 1992: 7). Hume writes:

> When good is certain or probable, it produces Joy. When evil is in the same situation there arises Grief or Sorrow.
>
> When either good or evil is uncertain, it gives rise to Fear or Hope, according to the degrees of uncertainty on the one side or the other.
>
> Desire arises from good consider'd simply, and Aversion is deriv'd from evil.   (T 2.3.9.5–7)

When explaining his distinction between the direct and the indirect passions in Book 2 of the *Treatise*, Hume gives a slightly different description of the passions than that above in T 1.1.1.2. It is not clear whether the implications of the difference may be significant. After explaining that he does not intend to explore the origins of impressions of sensation, he says that he will confine his discussion to those impressions he has called "*secondary* and *reflective*, as arising either from the original impressions, or from their ideas." He continues, "Bodily pains and pleasures are the source of many passions, both when felt and consider'd by the mind;...A fit of the gout produces a long train of passions, as grief, hope, fear;..." (T 2.1.1.2). So, it sounds as though some passions originate from the *sensations* of pleasure or pain with no intermediate thought required. Two paragraphs later, Hume distinguishes the passions into the direct and the indirect. "By direct passions I understand such as arise immediately from good or evil, from pain or pleasure. By indirect such as proceed from the same principles, but by the conjunction of other qualities" (T 2.1.2.4). The reader might think at this point that the direct passions are those that require no preceding ideas, but come directly from pleasure or pain, while the indirect require antecedent ideas. Yet, Hume names as direct passions desire, aversion, grief, joy, hope, fear, despair, and security (T 2.1.2.4),[7] and desire and aversion and hope and fear are explicitly said in the quote from Book 1 above to be caused by the *idea* of pleasure or pain. Consequently, the distinction between the direct and the indirect passions cannot be understood in terms of which has an idea of pleasure or pain as its immediate cause and which has the pleasurable or painful sensation as its immediate cause. Some direct passions seem to be caused immediately by the sensations and others seem to come immediately upon possessing the idea of the object as pleasurable or painful.

Among the indirect passions are "pride, humility, ambition, vanity, love, hatred, envy, pity, malice, generosity, with their dependents" (T 2.1.2.4). For Hume, all the passions are officially simple sensations and defy analysis, but his object is to explain the circumstances that "attend," or bring them about. To explain the origin of the indirect passions, Hume uses a series of thought experiments and draws upon a feature of human nature he has discussed earlier, in Book 1 of the *Treatise*: namely, the tendency of the mind to associate ideas by certain principles, including resemblance (contiguity and cause and effect are the others).[8] Just as the mind associates ideas based on resemblances between them (a picture of you reminds me of you), it passes from one passion, or impression of reflection, to another, based on a resemblance of the feelings to each other. For instance, "…our temper, when elevated with joy, naturally throws itself into love, generosity, pity, courage, pride, and the other resembling affections" (T 2.1.4.3). Hume explains the origin of the indirect passions in terms of a double relation of impressions and ideas, which he explicates with particular examples.

Consider the cause of pride. In the most general terms, one has pride when something reflects well on oneself. Hume observes that pride is always caused by our thinking of a subject that is related to the self and has a pleasing quality (for instance, my lovely flower garden). Both are requisite. Then Hume finds two qualities in the feeling of pride. The first is that the object of pride is the idea of the self: nature has "assigned" the idea of self to this passion, in the same respect that the idea of food always accompanies the sensation of hunger (T 2.1.5.6). The second quality of pride

---

[7] At T 2.3.9.2, when naming direct passions, Hume names all of these but despair and security, and adds volition.

[8] Discussions of the indirect passions are prevalent in the Hume literature. See, for example, Ainslie (1999: 471–3); Baier (1991: 130–45); Cohon (2008a: 161–74; 2012: 234–9); McIntyre (2000: 79–83); and Taylor (2015a: 50–9). Scholars widely agree that Hume's associationist view has its antecedents in Malebranche. Both describe the mind's tendency to associate passions, but Malebranche's associationism does not contain specific principles like Hume's, and Malebranche offers a physiological explanation of how passions infect our reactions toward related things. See Jones (1982) and Kail (2007a; 2008).

is that pride is itself a pleasurable feeling. The pleasure of pride is, of course, a separate feeling of pleasure from the pleasure one takes in the quality of the subject that causes pride. Consequently, Hume explains the production of indirect passions generally:

…the true system breaks in upon me with an irresistible evidence. That cause, which excites the passion, is related to the object, which nature has attributed to the passion; the sensation, which the cause separately produces, is related to the sensation of the passion: From this double relation of ideas and impressions, the passion is deriv'd. The one idea is easily converted into its correlative; and the one impression into that, which resembles and corresponds to it: With how much greater facility must this transition be made, where these movements mutually assist each other, and the mind receives a double impulse from the relations both of its impressions and ideas? (T 2.1.5.5)

Since the human mind is disposed to move from one perception to another that resembles it, the relationships between similar ideas and between similar impressions facilitate the formation of the passion. When I think of my lovely flower garden, my mind is transported to an idea of the self, which is the object of the passion of pride (an association of ideas); likewise, the pleasure I take in the attractive quality of the garden moves my mind along to the sensation of pleasure that is essential to pride (an association of impressions). The cause is doubly related to the effect, and both lines of mental association contribute to the generation of the passion of pride. In sum: "Any thing, that gives a pleasant sensation, and is related to self, excites the passion of pride, which is also agreeable, and has self for its object" (T 2.1.5.8). All the indirect passions presumably have such subjects (as causes) and such objects (as effects). Humility is explained in an analogous fashion to pride, substituting a displeasing subject for the pleasing subject and understanding that humility itself produces a separate displeasure. Love and hatred are analogous to pride and humility, respectively, except for the fact that their objects are ideas of other persons rather than of the self. Among the primary subjects of pride and love are virtue, beauty, and possessions; among the primary subjects of humility and hatred are vice, deformity, and poverty (T 2.1.5.2).[9]

My particular interest here is neither in the structure of the indirect passions per se, nor in the critical questions that have been raised about their production. My interest is in Hume's treatment of the indirect passions in relation to his theory of motivation.[10] Hume says explicitly that pride and humility are not motives to action;

---

[9] Some philosophers have argued that Hume's account of pride addresses the skepticism of the self that arises in Book 1 of the *Treatise*. Hume there concludes that the idea of the self is a fiction, since it depends upon a stream of perceptions associated by causality and resemblance and is not derived from an impression of a unified self (T 1.4.6). However, Hume goes on to distinguish personal identity "*as it regards our thought or imagination*" from personal identity "*as it regards our passions*" (T 1.4.6.5), and he is not skeptical about the latter. The latter is connected to his treatment of pride and humility.

[10] Among the critical questions raised about Hume's account is the question whether Hume misrepresents the relationship between pride and the idea of self when presenting it as a causal one. I discuss this issue in Chapter 4.

and that neither are love and hatred. Typically, however, they carry the mind to a thought of the happiness of the beloved and the unhappiness of the one hated, in which one takes pleasure. So love is accompanied by a desire for the happiness of the loved one and an aversion to her misery, identified as benevolence. Hatred produces a desire for the misery of the one hated and an aversion to her happiness (T 2.2.6.3), which Hume identifies with anger (T 2.2.6.3). This connection is a contingent one, however, as Hume makes clear when he says: "Love and hatred might have been unattended with any such desires, or their particular connexion might have been entirely revers'd. If nature had so pleas'd, love might have had the same effect as hatred, and hatred as love" (T 2.2.6.6).[11] Benevolence and anger are motives; pride and humility and love and hatred are not. Hume's treatment of the four indirect passions he features most prominently raises the question whether all of the indirect passions are likewise motivationally inert.

1.2.2 Direct Passions, Natural Instincts, and the General Appetite for Good

For Hume, the passions generally, but not universally, proceed from perceptions of pleasure or pain, or from the ideas of pleasures and pains. The source of these pleasures and pains are designated natural good and natural evil, respectively, in virtue of their effects. The direct passions proceed directly from these sensations, or from their ideas, without the contribution of other perceptions. As I've noted, among the direct passions are desire, aversion, grief, joy, hope, fear, despair, security, and volition (combining lists at T 2.1.2.4 and T 2.3.9.2). So, for instance, the thought of my mother's death, a painful experience, produces grief, and the idea of the end of a stressful time in my life produces joy or hope. The picture of the passions, however, is a little more complicated than this broad account suggests, since there are a few passions that Hume discusses as direct that are actually exceptions to the scheme. These he identifies with natural instincts, and discusses two sets of them.

First, in the context of describing how the work of calm passions is often confused with the work of reason, he notes that there are "certain calm tendencies and desires," which are "real passions," but "are known more by their effects than by the immediate feeling or sensation." Then he writes:

These desires are of two kinds; either instincts originally implanted in our natures, such as benevolence and resentment, the love of life, and kindness to children; or the general appetite to good, and aversion to evil, consider'd merely as such. When any of these passions are calm and cause no disorder in the soul, they are readily taken for the determinations of reason, and are suppos'd to proceed from the same faculty, with that, which judges of truth and falsehood.

(T 2.3.3.8)

---

[11] That the effects of love and hatred might have been reversed is at least curious. I explore Hume's view on this topic in Radcliffe (2004).

A few sections later, in *Treatise* 2.3.9.8, "Of the Direct Passions," Hume again lists the direct passions and then refers to instincts, but different ones:

> Besides good and evil, or in other words, pain and pleasure, the direct passions frequently arise from a natural impulse or instinct, which is perfectly unaccountable. Of this kind is the desire of punishment to our enemies, and of happiness to our friends; hunger, lust, and a few other bodily appetites. These passions, properly speaking, produce good and evil, and proceed not from them, like the other affections.

There are two noteworthy observations about these passages. In the former passage, Hume mentions the instincts apart from the general appetite to good and aversion to evil. Evidently, this general appetite is a genuine passion, but he implies here that it does not belong in the list of instincts. Yet, obviously, it is not a derived passion; in fact, passions are derived from it, when "good" and "evil" are thought of as natural good and evil, or pleasure and pain, respectively, as Hume thinks of them. Second, the latter passage is ambiguous. "Of this kind" in the excerpt could refer to impulses or instincts that are unaccountable, or it could refer to direct passions that arise from unaccountable instincts. If the former is so, then desire of punishment to our enemies and of happiness to our friends, hunger, lust, etc., are inexplicable instincts that sometimes produce direct passions. Then, some passions have more than one source, arising at times from the prospect of pleasure or pain, and at other times, from these instincts. If the latter reading is correct, however, then desire of punishment to our enemies and of happiness to our friends, hunger, lust, and so on, are direct passions themselves that arise from inexplicable instincts, and it would make sense to see them as instinctual direct passions. On the one reading, hunger causes, say, the desire for my breakfast (a desire that can also be caused by the prospect of an enjoyable meal), and on the other, hunger just is a motive to eat.[12]

My concern here is with questions related to motivational force of the passions. I think it's clear that Hume regards the instincts in both lists as motivating, regardless of whether they are themselves direct passions, or whether they give rise to direct passions that are motives. However, I want to consider the general appetite for good and aversion to evil, which Hume has not classified as an instinct in the first passage. It is different from the others in its generality. The derived passions, Hume says, originate when good or evil is presented, even just in thought, and we respond to it. The response is a passion whereby "[t]he mind by an *original* instinct tends to unite itself with the good, and to avoid the evil tho' they be conceiv'd merely in idea and be consider'd as to exist in any future period of time" (T 2.3.9.2). Here he does refer to the mind as having an instinct to seek good and avoid evil. So, the non-instinctual

---

[12] Rachel Cohon has argued that these instincts are not themselves to be counted as direct passions, but are existing states from which direct passions arise, given what Hume says about them in the quotation above (see 2008a: 164).

MOTIVES TO ACTION 23

passions motivate ultimately because of this general appetite, from which these passions derive their motive force.

We might ask, then, why the reference to any of the passions beyond this inclination, or beyond it and some of the other instincts Hume names, is necessary to action explanations. Hume's would be a simpler theory of motivation if our actions can be explained entirely by instincts, perhaps by those he names explicitly (benevolence, love of life, hunger, etc.), plus this general instinct to unite with good and to avoid evil. Why do we need a theory of the production of motivating passions (such as anger or desires for particular things), which arise upon our perceptions of good and evil *due to* our natural inclination for good and aversion to evil?

To answer this question, consider the characterization of the natural instincts, at least as described in the second passage: they cause good and evil, and are not produced by them. Surely Hume means that their presence does not depend on our experiencing which objects in particular are pleasurable or good and which are not. I think Hume intends this description to apply to the instincts in the first list as well (benevolence, resentment, love of life, kindness to children). For example, if one is benevolent, one's benevolence is an innate disposition, not a feature due to finding particular persons a source of pleasure and others not, even though we extend our benevolence most often to those close to us (and to those we love, as seen above). Even though Hume calls the inclination to good and aversion to evil a genuine passion, it is equally the disposition to form motivating passions.[13] It is not a desire for impressions of pleasure and a desire to avoid impressions of pain, since what people desire are to have the *objects* they find pleasurable and to avoid the ones they find painful. But appealing to this disposition (the appetite for good and away from evil) does not offer informative explanations of actions. We get genuine explanations of actions only when we understand what objects or events strike a particular agent as pleasurable or painful, and to what degree. So, for instance, while it is true that I run from a building on fire because the thought of being burnt to death is a horror to me, a more useful explanation of my action is that I fear injury or death by fire. A firefighter will go into the burning building that I run from. To explain the difference in our actions, we must call upon something beyond the disposition to pursue pleasurable things and to avoid painful ones. An experienced firefighter also finds it painful to suffer burns, but she does not fear the situation, or fear it as much as I do. While we need reference to a diversity of passions to explain why different people behave differently in the same circumstances, we also need such appeal to explain the same behavior done from various psychological states. My cat obviously takes pleasure in eating, and he eats a lot. But sometimes he eats from boredom and sometimes he eats from hunger. Sometimes people give to charity out of generosity and sometimes they give out of self-interest. Character evaluation depends upon the

---

[13] I think that passionate dispositions do a great deal of work in Hume's theory of action and that they count as passions as well (see Radcliffe 1999: 113–14).

ability to identify in individuals motives such as anger, fear, malice, magnanimity, pity, and so on. Thus, Hume's explanation of the motives that originate action must refer to details beyond a few instincts and the general appetite to natural good and aversion to natural evil.

1.3 Which Passions Are Motives?

I've raised the issue how Hume determines which among the passions are motivating ones and which are not. This is especially curious, given that the motivating/non-motivating distinction does not track with the direct/indirect division. Hume discusses motivation in Part 3 of Book 2 of the *Treatise*, "Of the will and direct passions," which creates the initial, false impression that only the direct passions provide impetuses to action. As I have mentioned earlier, when Hume names the indirect passions, he names pride, humility, ambition, vanity, love, hatred, envy, pity, malice, generosity, "with their dependents." As direct passions, he names desire, aversion, grief, joy, hope, fear, despair, security, and volition. Oddly enough, anger (which is not an instinctual passion) doesn't make these lists, but it receives a long discussion as the attendant of hatred, just as benevolence receives such a discussion as the attendant of love. Even though Hume notes explicitly that pride, humility, love, and hatred do not motivate, he never claims that other indirect passions cannot be motives, and it is clear that malice and pity are.

John Bricke suggests that all conative states (what I am here calling "motives") for Hume are defined in terms of desire, where desire also includes aversion (that is, desire to avoid an object) (Bricke 1996: 36–7). Thus, any passion that is defined in terms of desire by Hume is a motivating state; the other passions are affections, but not conations, on Bricke's view. Bricke names among desires for Hume benevolence (a natural instinct), anger, malice (an indirect passion), and pity (an indirect passion), "as well as desires more narrowly construed" (direct passions). Benevolence for Hume is "a desire of the happiness of the person belov'd" (T 2.2.6.3); the description of anger includes reference to "a desire of the misery and an aversion to the happiness of the person hated" (T 2.2.6.3). Malice is "the unprovok'd desire of producing evil to another, in order to reap a pleasure from the comparison" (T 2.2.8.12); the characterization of pity is as "a desire of happiness to another, and aversion to his misery" (T 2.2.9.3). Fear, which is typically experienced when evil is uncertain, clearly involves a desire to be rid of the possible object (or cause) of the passion. (See T 2.3.9.21–7 for a long discussion of fear.) This interpretation of Hume implies that whether a passion is a motive does not depend on whether or not the passion is formed directly upon the idea or perception of pleasure or pain. A second implication is that some of the direct passions actually are *not* motives or potential causes of action. For instance, grief and joy seem not to be desires of some kind, but affections felt in light of certain considerations. Yet, a third, more mystifying, implication is that even though desires are classified as direct passions, some indirect passions are characterized in terms of desires. Since I endorse this reading, I want to investigate these second two features further, starting with the last.

My proposal to make sense of the idea that some indirect passions are desires, even though Hume has said that desire is a direct passion, is to emphasize that these indirect passions are significantly different from the desire and aversion that Hume classifies as direct passions. All indirect passions have persons as their objects (the self or another), and pity and malice are desires, produced through an associative process, for certain hedonic states for another person. The production of pity and malice is particularly complicated. Pity arises when one person takes displeasure through sympathy in the condition of another and experiences concern for that person's welfare. Yet, displeasure at another's situation might have instead produced reactions like contempt, revulsion, or hatred as well. On the other hand, malice arises when one person, comparing her situation to another, is displeased and desires gratuitous harm to the other; but displeasure at another's situation is also connected with pity or compassion. So, Hume goes to great effort to explain why pity is the result in some cases, but not in others. Later, in Chapter 6, I discuss Hume's explanation of the circumstances that produce one or the other of these passions. Here, I want to emphasize that the desires that define pity and malice are desires arising out of complex psychological circumstances, with the condition of others as an aim.

I've also remarked that reading all motivating passions as desires of some sort implies that some direct passions are not motives. We might ask, however, whether grief and joy, which are not forms of desire, really never motivate. Actions often follow upon our feeling each of them, and we talk about jumping for joy or going into seclusion because of grief. But actions do often follow passions that Hume thinks are not motives. Love and hatred are cases in point, where it's tempting to say that love moves me to look after the welfare of the beloved and hatred moves me to cause pain for the person I hate (or perhaps just avoid her). These actions, according to Hume (as we've seen), are caused, not by love and hatred, but by motives constantly conjoined with love and hatred, respectively. Likewise, we might be inclined to attribute actions to pride (for instance, boasting or showing one's prized possessions to others), or to humility, but Hume explicitly thinks pride and humility, as he has defined them, are not motives. Another consideration is this. In discussing how the mind has a tendency to pass from one resembling impression to another, he writes:

Grief and disappointment give rise to anger, anger to envy, envy to malice, and malice to grief again, till the whole circle be compleated. In like manner our temper, when elevated with joy, naturally throws itself into love, generosity, pity, courage, pride, and the other resembling affections. (T 2.1.4.3)

So, an action that follows from grief or joy might well be caused by one of these resembling passions with which it is associated.

One thing that is clear about Hume's view on motives is that what determines whether a passion is motivating does not lie in whether action follows the experience of the passion, since other passions we have not considered may be present as well. Rather, the identity of a given passion—i.e., in terms of desire—is crucial to whether it can be a motive. Recall that Hume describes the circumstances of grief and joy, fear and hope this way: Desire arises from consideration of natural good and aversion from natural evil. When good is probable or certain, we experience joy; when evil is probable or certain, we experience grief. When either good or evil is uncertain, it gives rise to fear or hope, depending on which side the greatest probability lies (T 2.3.9.5–7). Hume then writes about the effect of probability on the mind:

Probability arises from an opposition of contrary chances or causes, by which the mind is not allowed to fix on either side, but is incessantly tost from one to another, and at one moment is determined to consider an object as existent, and at another moment as the contrary.

(T 2.3.10)

Applying this point to the direct passions, he says:

Suppose, then, that the object, concerning whose reality we are doubtful, is an object either of desire or aversion, it is evident, that, according as the mind turns itself either to the one side or the other, it must feel a momentary impression of joy or sorrow. An object, whose existence we desire, gives satisfaction, when we reflect on those causes, which produce it; and for the same reason excites grief or uneasiness from the opposite consideration... (T 2.3.9.11)

So, it looks as though joy and sorrow are dependent in part on our already having a desire or an aversion for an object. Desire and aversion are certainly motives, and joy and sorrow are reactions to the possibility of achieving what we desire. So, there is evidence for the conclusion that if Hume sees joy and sorrow as motives, it's because they presuppose desire or aversion for an object. These considerations make the proposal that motivating passions, for Hume, are all described in terms of desires even more plausible.

This discussion so far still leaves the question why Hume discusses motivation in the context of his treatment of direct passions, given that some indirect passions are motives. One possible answer lies in Hume's classifying volition as a direct passion. He writes, "The impressions, which arise from good and evil most naturally, and with the least preparation are the *direct* passions of desire and aversion, grief and joy, hope and fear, along with volition" (T 2.3.9.2). Volition here is set apart from the other direct passions, apparently signaling its special status, and it is sometimes mentioned in conjunction with desire (twice, at T 2.3.9.4 and T 3.3.1.2), which is distinctive as a motive for the reasons already noted. There are, however, some peculiarities surrounding Hume's treatment of volition. While Hume does not define volition in either the *Treatise* or in the *Enquiry Concerning Human Understanding* (the two works in which it receives the most attention), he uses that term to indicate the feeling of initiation of force or effort, as in, for instance: "An act of volition produces motion in our limbs, or raises a new idea in our imagination. This influence of the will we know by consciousness" (EHU 7.9). (He goes on to argue that we cannot get the idea of necessary connection from this experience, however, since the connection between volition and action is itself not experienced.) But the point I want to make here is that Hume uses volition synonymously with the will (or willing), "*the internal impression we feel and are conscious of, when we knowingly give rise to any new motion of our body, or new perception of our mind*" (T 2.3.1.2). I've referred to Hume's view of the will a bit in the INTRODUCTION. Hume says that the will is not a passion, properly speaking. So, if it is correct to think that volition and willing are the same, then volition, technically, is not a passion, even though it is mentioned in the above list of direct passions.

Tito Magri has a nice explanation of Hume's divided mind on this issue. Magri points out that we can desire or be averse to any objects or states of affairs, but we can will only what we believe ourselves to be in a position to undertake. This means that our actions are the sole effects of the will, and Hume himself writes, "the will has an influence only on present actions" (T 3.2.5.3). Then Magri explains, "Therefore, the will is nothing else but direct passion being exerted in action. In this way, it is not different from any particular kind or episode of direct passion, and thus, properly, not a passion at all" (Magri 2008: 189). I've agreed that motivation, for Hume, consists in nothing beyond passions causing actions. This point is confirmed by Hume's argument that the inner feeling of willing is *not* indicative of what philosophers have called "liberty of indifference," the ability to do anything, no matter our desires.

We may imagine we feel a liberty within ourselves; but a spectator can commonly infer our actions from our motives and character; and even when he cannot, he concludes in general, that he might, were he perfectly acquainted with every circumstance of our situation and temper... (T 2.3.2.2)

Every action is caused or necessitated by a motivating passion. Still, we call a movement of the body or change in the mind an "action" only when it seems to be voluntary, or initiated by the agent—that is to say, when it is accompanied by the (misleading) feeling of volition. This may explain, then, why Hume discusses motives "of the will" in the context of the direct passions: Volitions are the experiences that accompany these motivational episodes, and seem like direct passions (even though they are not technically passions at all). That he conjoins the discussion of motivation with the treatment of direct passions is not meant to imply that only direct passions are motives to action. Rather, the idea is that motives to action are conjoined with this "*false sensation*" (T 2.3.2.2) of willing, which is an apparent (but not genuine) direct passion.

So, being identified with a desire is necessary to a passion's being a motive, for Hume, but is it sufficient? I can have aspirations for ends that I simply could never even try to bring about (or believe I could never try), and it's hard to see how these longings could be desires. I can wish that the clouds go away or that I be taller than I am, but wishes are not desires. Desires have ends that I believe I could possibly pursue. One reason, I think, that Hume excludes pride, humility, love, and hated from the set of *motives* is that these are not passions whose objects, myself or others, are possible ends for me. They are reactive attitudes: I love or hate another as a result of features that person possesses; I feel pride or humility as a result of something I've done. If it looks like love or pride is moving me to act, it is because of an associated desire that occurs in conjunction with these feelings. The evidence suggests, then, that all and only desires are motives. The motivating passions have as their objects conditions for which I believe I can aim, where the objects are either states that produce pleasure or at whose thought I take pleasure—my eating the food I need to satisfy my hunger, another's future happiness, my child's future health, and so on. But this is just what desires are in Hume's view: affections for pleasurable circumstances that I think I can take steps to bring about, or aversions to unpleasant conditions that I think I can take steps to avoid.[14]

1.4 Summary

My arguments have been interpretative, offering an answer to the question which passions are motives for Hume and why. I have noted that Hume does not regard motives as belief-desire pairs. Rather, motives are perceptual states that exert a psychological force on the person who possesses them. Even when these perceptions are not effective in producing actions—because their force is blocked by other such perceptions (passions)—they count as motives as long as they have causal force. I have argued that the general appetite to natural good and aversion to natural evil, to which Hume refers in his discussion of the passions, cannot by itself account for the variety of motives from which different people do the same sorts of actions. Thus, Hume's theory of motivation includes that instincts, many direct passions (derived from the general appetite to good and aversion to evil), and some indirect passions are motives. What they all have in common is that each falls under the description of "desire," although not of "wish," since unlike reactive attitudes, each has objects or ends that the agent believes he or she can possibly bring about. I revisit the taxonomy of the passions in Chapter 6, where I focus on the question how passions that are motives gain the requisite causal force against other passions to be successful in action.

---

[14] This is not to say that desires include beliefs or that a belief-desire pair is after all what constitutes a motive for Hume. It is just to say that the general belief that the end is the sort of thing I'm capable of achieving is a prerequisite for an urge or inclination to count as a desire rather than as a wish. I need not have a belief about what particular thing I can do to achieve the end in order to have a desire for that end. Contemporary philosophers regard both a desire plus a particular belief about the means to the end of the desire as necessary to having a motive.

2

Hume's Argument for the Inertness of Reason

The compelling arguments that have prompted many contemporary philosophers to take seriously Hume's theory of motivation appear in *Treatise* 2.3.3, "Of the influencing motives of the will." There Hume argues, among other things, that "reason alone can never be a motive to any action of the will." Some Hume interpreters, like Annette Baier and John Bricke,[1] have attempted to squeeze as much plausibility as they can out of Hume's claims, but end up rejecting some of the main tenets of his theory of motivation as either implausible or incapable of supporting the conclusion he wants. Other contemporary Humeans, like Michael Smith (1994) and Bernard Williams (1979), who are not necessarily concerned about exactly how Hume's arguments go, have found the "Humean" view of motivation that emerges to be persuasive overall and offer their own defenses of it. This chapter offers an interpretation of Hume's eminent argument and addresses the question whether he is best read as an advocate of the belief-desire model that contemporary philosophers have attributed to him.

2.1 What Is the Target of Hume's Argument?

Hume commences his arguments concerning reason and motives in *Treatise* 2.3.3 by citing the perspective on morality and motivation prevalent in his predecessors and in common thinking: this view recognizes "the combat of reason and passion" and asserts that people "are only so far virtuous as they conform themselves to [reason's] dictates" (T 2.3.3.1). Ralph Cudworth, Samuel Clarke, and others place this view in a theological context. Hume further describes the perspective he opposes:

> Every rational creature, 'tis said, is oblig'd to regulate his actions by reason;... The eternity, invariableness, and divine origin of the former [reason] have been display'd to the best advantage: The blindness, unconstancy, and deceitfulness of the latter [the passions] have been as strongly insisted on. (T 2.3.3.1)

---

[1] Baier (1991); Bricke (1996). Some of Baier's views are discussed in subsequent chapters.

30 HUME, PASSION, AND ACTION

Hume's aim is to show the fallacy of this philosophy by proving "*first*, that reason alone cannot be a motive to any action of the will; and *secondly*, that it can never oppose passion in the direction of the will" (T 2.3.3.1).[2] As noted in the Introduction, most of the philosophers and theologians writing and sermonizing in the early modern period did not in fact promote the view that reason alone could be a motive to action, and some explicitly argued against it. Yet, Hume underscores the error of this thesis, and it is crucial as a step, or as a sub-argument, in the overall case for the conclusion he draws in Book 3 of the *Treatise* and in Appendix 1 of the second *Enquiry*: that morality cannot be derived from reason. So, there is a question that few, if any, readers have asked: Why does Hume insist on arguing that reason alone does not motivate when no one seems to have thought otherwise? It certainly has become a touchstone in discussions of Humeanism about motivation and action, but Hume would not have been able to predict that. I have two suggestions about an answer to this question.

(1) My first speculation is that Hume regards the rationalist view of morality as relying on the thesis that reason alone can motivate, that is, that it can originate motives to action, even if those defending rationalist morality do not acknowledge this commitment, or even argue against it. How might Hume's rationalist predecessors be committed by their moral theories to the notion that reason alone provides motives to action? It is not at all obvious.

If we accept the rationalist's subscription to teleology, which allows reference to an infused inclination of theological origin to goodness, then the early modern thinkers to whom Hume is opposed can trace the source of moral motivation to that proclivity, rather than to reason. French thinker Jean-François Senault and British intellectual William Ayloffe thought that all the passions include this God-instilled proclivity to good and repulsion from evil, and have the potential to be virtues because of that fact (Senault 1641: Fourth Treatise, 126–7; Ayloffe 1700: 53). The moderating effect of reason, along with God's grace, can make them worthy motivations. On Ayloffe's view, reason reveals to the passions the genuine features of objects. Motivation is initiated by passion's seeking the good, and reason is essential in identifying it (Ayloffe 1700: 47–51). The Vicar of Hitchin, Francis Bragge, expressed a similar view: the passions are essential to action, but we need reason to show to them (or, to us) the relative worth of goods. The hope is that we will be moved to turn away from the paltry pleasures of this world and toward the permanent goods of the next (Bragge 1708: 1, 6–8). One question these thinkers need to answer is how it is that passions, which all contain an inclination to good and aversion to evil, can have us act badly when reason is not in control. Perhaps passions

---

[2] Hume retains the term "will" here, but since he reduces the will to a feeling of acting voluntarily (as I've suggested), he is here referring to what might serve as a cause of action, not to what might be an "adviser."

sometimes make one misidentify the good by presenting an alternative conception of it, or perhaps they cause one to latch onto a mistaken idea of it by disrupting deliberation. Either way, however, if having a motive to any action is rooted in the original inclination to good, then it looks as though reason need not create a motive to action from scratch. Instead, it presents a conception of the good for us to pursue by our predispositions. So, the view shared by Senault, Ayhoffe, and Bragge does not presuppose that reason is a motive to action, *if* interpreted within their own teleological metaphysics.

Furthermore, Cudworth characterizes the mind as an integration of reason, imagination, passion, and appetite, all orchestrated by the will (Cudworth 1731/1838: 183) (see the APPENDIX for more detail). An incessant desire for the good is the source of motivation or the spring to action, but this desire's fulfillment requires the guidance of reason (ibid.: 173). In deliberation, we assess the degrees of goodness and evil produced by possible courses of action. When we go wrong, the fault lies in our failure to deliberate, or to deliberate well, and we end up acting on the basis of unclear and indistinct ideas. Consequently, the source of error for Cudworth is like that in Descartes's account. It lies in erroneous representations (ibid.: 179). So, the opposition between reason and passion is between representations generating contrary motivations. In this sense, reason is reputed to motivate, and yet, the origination of motivation still ultimately lies in the innate drive for the good.

On Clarke's theory of motivation, the following claims are true. The will is naturally turned to conforming itself to the fitnesses in the universe of which morality is composed, but it can be corrupted by lust, passions, and self-interest (Clarke 1706: vol. 2: 11). Comprehension of necessary truths is not by itself sufficient to motivate human beings, who (unlike God) need the passions to excite them where bare abstract understanding leaves them cold (Clarke 1724: 144). To achieve the aims of morality, the passions require the governance of reason, but reason cannot determine or cause the will. Clarke says that judging is separate from acting, and the will is always free to act against the considerations reason offers (Clarke 1716–17: 126). So, he presents the quintessential picture of the will, advised by reason and by passion, with the ability to choose freely between them. He believes that the will's innate tendency to the good can be bent and diverted by the passions, a view he shares with Senault, Ayloffe, and Bragge. The best explanation how this happens is that the passions somehow represent objects to us as better than they actually are. When an innate tendency to the good is left unfilled because of passionate diversions, given that we are not forced to act by causal strength of the passions, the resultant action must be due to the will's heeding the passions' (mis)representation of certain ends as good. That is, the passions embody judgments that are opposed to the judgments of reason. For instance, given the will's orientation to the good, I have (best) reason to obey God's commands because God's authority over me is a "fitness" in the universe that specifies a moral duty; but I also have reason to fulfill my self-interested affections and passions, which are also good, even in conflict with God's will. When I decide to follow reason, I'm not caused by reason to act, on Clarke's view, but I (freely) conform my action to its assessment of the good, rather than to passions' assessment. None of this implies that reason is originating a motive, since the will's attraction to the good is the root of the conation. It *does* imply that passion is representational, in additional to conative.

Hume, however, rejecting the metaphysical orientation of these philosophers and theologians, perhaps eliminates from his conception of their views the idea that human beings are directed by a non-natural force toward goodness. Reference to divinely-instilled inclinations is groundless when this metaphysics is removed. Any theory that purports to account for an intrinsic motive to morality has to found that motivation on the source of morality itself, since there is no justification for appealing to separate conative states mysteriously and necessarily connected to the comprehension of morality. In other words, to account for the internal, or necessary connection between morality and the will that thinkers like Senault, Ayloffe, Cudworth, and Clarke believe exists, they would, minus their metaphysics, have to ground the motivational feature of morality in morality's origin, which they claim to be reason. So, when their non-natural framework is removed, these intellectuals, believing that morality takes its content from reason and is accessed by reason, would be committed to the thesis that reason alone motivates. Hume's strategy, I am suggesting, might be to show that moral rationalism minus its unjustified references to metaphysics is committed to the false thesis that reason alone is a motive to action, or that it can originate passions that are motives to action.

(2) Another, simpler, explanation of why Hume argues against the thesis that reason can motivate on its own is that he believes it is implied by another thesis with which he disagrees: that the passions and reason can be motivationally opposed. On Hume's view, the passions interact with reason in the sense that they push us toward objects that fit particular descriptions that reason offers us, but the passions themselves are never practically at odds with reason. To be motivationally opposed, Hume thinks that both reason and passion would have to originate motives or impulses to action; if he shows that reason never does, then he has undercut the traditional picture that has reason prompting in one direction and passion in another. However, the way in which the early modern rationalists saw reason and passion in opposition was not typically in terms of generating impulses in contrary directions, but in terms of their giving us contrary ideas of the same objects, as good and as bad. So, it's not clear that Hume hits his target in this particular argument about non-opposition; but he offers another one that does, when he makes his case that passions are "original existences," and not ideas or representations. (I discuss this characterization of the passions, and his argument concerning the non-opposition of passion and reason in Chapter 4.)

2.2 "Reason Alone Can Never Be a Motive"

Regardless of Hume's intended historical target, his Inertness of Reason Argument is of great significance philosophically. Generally, for Hume, reason includes the mind's capacity to engage in reasoning in one of two ways: demonstration, which concerns relations of ideas, or causal reasoning, which concerns objects of experience. In all cases, the operations of reason involve comparison of ideas whose content has come from experience, in order to determine relationships among them. Demonstration is deductive reasoning from necessary truths; Hume says that since demonstration concerns ideas, and the will concerns reality, the two are "totally remov'd from each other." Mathematics, which Hume recognizes as a demonstrative science, is useful in "almost every art and profession," but it does not by itself have any influence on the will and action. "Mechanics are the art of regulating the motions of bodies *to some design'd end or purpose*; and the reason why we employ arithmetic in fixing the proportion of numbers is only that we may discover the proportions of their influence and operation" (T 2.3.3.2). His point is that without the person's having an established end, demonstrative operations of the understanding have no practical purpose. "Abstract or demonstrative reasoning, therefore, never influences any of our actions, but only as it directs our judgment concerning causes and effects; . . . ." So, Hume is arguing that demonstrative reasoning does not have an effect on actions by itself, but it does inform our judgments concerning causes and effects. For example, by doing mathematical calculations, an engineer can determine what design and materials are needed to build a bridge in a particular location to carry a certain kind and quantity of traffic. A chemist uses mathematics to establish the proportions of substances needed to produce certain effects, as is done by pharmaceutical researchers in their investigations on drug interactions. None of this information is sufficient for action, however, absent the desire to build a bridge or market a drug.

When Hume considers causal or probabilistic reasoning, he concludes that the process of identifying causes and effects in the world is not sufficient to produce action. The impulse toward an object does not arise from causal reasoning, but "is only directed by it."

'Tis from the prospect of pain or pleasure that the aversion or propensity arises toward any object: And these emotions extend themselves to the causes and effects of that object, as they are pointed out to us by reason and experience. (T 2.3.3.3)

Later I address what Hume must mean by the "prospect of pain or pleasure" which he contrasts with reasoning. The point here is that if an object has not first awakened or produced a passion, then knowing that object's connections with other objects has no influence on the will; since causal reasoning is the discovery of these sorts of connections, it cannot by itself produce action. Neither causal reasoning nor demonstrative reasoning is sufficient to influence action. Thus, Hume concludes that "reason alone can never be a motive to any action of the will" (T 2.3.3.1).

However, a passion of propensity or aversion without a causal belief to direct it, seems insufficient as well. An engineer cannot build an effective bridge unless she knows how wide the river is, what materials are available, what the budget is, what the traffic across the bridge will be, and so on. So, it seems as though Hume cannot give any place of privilege to passion in his account of motivation, since the conclusions of reason are just as important in getting us to action. Some commentators have observed that Hume seems to assert both that reason does not motivate and that it does. Rachel Kydd, in her classic book, *Reason and Conduct in Hume's Treatise*, offered the observation that, on reason's influence, there seem to be two distinct themes in Hume: (1) that reason, in conjunction with desire, can influence action in many ways that are important to our interests, and (2) that reason is "wholly inactive" or "perfectly inert" (Hume's terms) and so does not contribute to motivation (Kydd 1946: 140). Sixty years later, Sophie Botros revived the idea of two theses in Hume's account of the inertness of reason (although independently of Kydd's work), and has argued that, given Hume's impact on contemporary philosophical psychology, his equivocation has produced a legacy of contradiction.[3] The argument I have just sketched is his argument that reason alone can never produce action or a volition. Hume does indicate that reason plays a necessary part in the production of action, so it seems that reason does motivate, not alone, but in conjunction with a passion. In this way, it appears to make a contribution equal in influence to that of desire in causing the will's volitions, despite Hume's celebrated declaration that reason is slave to the passions. In Book 3, however, when Hume refers to the conclusion he has earlier drawn concerning reason and action, he sometimes makes the ostensibly stronger claims that "reason has no influence on our passions and actions" (T 3.1.1.7), that "reason is perfectly inert" (T 3.1.1.8) and "reason is wholly inactive" (T 3.1.1.10). If "reason alone can never be a motive to any action of the will" means that reason *could* possibly contribute to motivation in conjunction with something else (desire), and if "reason is utterly impotent" means that reason *could not* possibly contribute to motivation (even in conjunction with something else), then the statements must have opposite truth values and so are contradictory.[4] This would imply that Hume has two incompatible positions on reason and motivation. So, does Hume provide the grounds for two theories of motivation at odds with each other?

---

[3] Botros thinks that the strong thesis, on which reason contributes nothing to action, is supported in part by Hume's assertion that reason deals with the world of ideas, while passion and motivation place us in the world of realities (T 2.3.3.2) (Botros 2006: 25). She proposes that Hume's ambivalence is due to his attempt to undermine two different approaches to morality current at the time: moral rationalism, from Clarke and Cudworth, and moral sense theory, from Hutcheson (ibid.: 61–114).

[4] Without the explication, however, (1) "Reason alone does not motivate" does not contradict, on the face of it, (2) "Reason does not motivate"—that is, the two do not necessarily require opposite truth values. Consider: Negate (1), "Reason alone does not motivate." Then reason alone does motivate, which is the negation of (2). Thus, when (1) is false, (2) is false. So, (1) and (2) do not require opposite truth values. (1) and (2) are contraries, however: while they can both be false at the same time, but they cannot both be true.

It is important to note that Hume himself never talks about "motivation" per se; contemporary philosophers (including me), provide this gloss on Hume when we interpret and discuss his views. Hume writes about "motives to actions of the will," "influence on the actions (or conduct) and affections," and "preventing or producing" actions. Hume's remarks about the practical impotence of reason (either demonstrative or causal) are unambiguous in Book 2. The relevant statements there about reason are:

(a) Reason alone can never be a motive to any action of the will (2.3.3.1).
(b) Abstract or demonstrative reasoning,... never influences any of our actions, but only as it directs our judgments concerning causes and effects (2.3.3.2).
(c) ...reasoning takes place to discover...[the effects of the objects of our aversion and propensity], and accordingly as our reason varies, our actions receive a subsequent variation. But 'tis evident that the impulse arises not from reason, but is only directed by it... Where the objects themselves do not affect us, their connexion can never give them any influence... (2.3.3.3).

These three statements together indicate what Hume thinks reason can and cannot do. Reason and sentiment are capacities of human nature that lead, respectively, to conclusions we believe and to passions that we feel. To the question which capacity initiates an impulse to action, the answer is clearly sentiment: The objects must first affect us by appealing to our established passionate dispositions or by producing new passions for or against the objects. Our dispositions (some generally shared with others, some more rare or idiosyncratic) determine to what we are attracted and from what we are repelled. When Hume writes about motives, he is referring to the experience of a psychological push, pull, impulse, or attraction toward a goal (rather than, as I've noted, the belief-desire combination that is often identified as a motive in contemporary discussions of Humeanism). This attraction or impulse is something that reason clearly cannot initiate, on his view. Reason does not produce original motives, which is to say that our impulses for certain ends do not originate in reason. Once the impulse is established, we reason about how to get to (or from) the object of the impulse, and this can generate a passion derivative from the original. But to know causal connections between events does not in itself originate the drive or the force. Hume's view in Book 2 is clear.

It is in Book 3 of the *Treatise*, where Hume uses his conclusions about reason from Book 2 to argue that our moral distinctions are not derived from reason, that Hume makes three ostensibly stronger claims than those in Book 2:

(A) As long as it is allowed that reason has no influence on our passions and actions, 'tis in vain to pretend, that morality is discover'd only by a deduction of reason (3.1.1.7).
(B) ...reason is perfectly inert, and can never either prevent or produce any action or affection (3.1.1.8).
(C) Reason is wholly inactive, and can never be the source of so active a principle as conscience, or a sense of morals (3.1.1.10).

Each of the above (A)–(C) lacks a reference to any qualification on the impotence of reason, as each of (a)–(c) contains. But Hume also writes in Book 3: "Morals excite passions and produce or prevent actions. Reason of itself is utterly impotent in this particular" (T 3.1.1.6). Here he qualifies reason with "of itself." Furthermore, he signifies that he is well aware in Book 3 of the ways he has asserted in Book 2 that reason can influence behavior:

> It has been observ'd, that reason, in a strict and philosophical sense, can have an influence on our conduct only after two ways: Either when it excites a passion by informing us of the existence of something which is a proper object of it, or when it discovers the connexion of causes and effects, so as to afford us means of exerting any passion. These are the only kinds of judgment, which can accompany our actions, or can be said to produce them in any manner;… (T 3.1.1.12)

Hume shows in Book 3 how morality is neither derived from demonstration nor a conclusion of inductive or matter-of-fact reasoning, so he is concerned about both in his discussion of the origin of morality. He is asserting in Book 3, as he did clearly in Book 2, that neither demonstrative nor causal reasoning *produces* an original impulse or drive, toward or away from an end. This is just what it means to say that reason is "perfectly inert" or "wholly inactive": it cannot initiate. The only claim that raises any question, and only if taken out of context, is (A), that reason has no influence on our passions and actions. Of course, he thinks (and is correct to think) that reason can influence passions and actions, in the sense that it is a necessary component of the cause of actions and of some passions, those that are derived from original passions. For instance, if I want to drink some coffee and realize, by reasoning, that I need to brew it in order to drink it, normally, I would acquire a desire to brew some coffee. The desire to brew coffee is a secondary, or derived, passion. When Hume says that reason has no influence on passions and actions, he clearly means that reason has no *original* influence; that is, that it cannot generate non-derived passions or generate impulses to action. Reason determines no ultimate ends for us and so is not the sufficient cause or origin of our passions and actions. This view is not at odds with the notion that reason can work with a present passion to produce another passion or action.

My interpretation might elicit the reply that since we need reason to recognize the qualities of objects in the world before we can be attracted to them, reason is in fact initiating passions. Hume says that reason "excites a passion by informing us of the existence of something which is a proper object of it." This is one of two ways in which reason is said by Hume to influence conduct; the other is by discovering "the connexion of causes and effects, so as to afford us means of exerting any passion" (T 3.1.1.12). But Hume must think that to excite a passion is not to produce it "from scratch," so to speak. If my passion for chocolate is excited when I discover that the shop next to my new office is a chocolate shop, the investigation, or induction, that led to the conclusion that there is a chocolate shop next door isn't originating my passion for chocolate. Hume's point is that beliefs about what exists or about what is available to me as a possible object of desire or action would have no practical effect if I didn't also have some inclination to that sort of object. Even in the case of my tasting chocolate for the first time and discovering it is a source of pleasure to me, my passion for chocolate isn't originated by reason or reasoning. That I enjoy it, and form a passion for it, are partly a function of my non-rational dispositions. If not, everyone would react in the same way and enjoy it to the same degree, or enjoy most the same type of chocolate, and so on. Analogously, in discovering the means to "exert" a passion, it doesn't affect me in a practical way to know that there is an eight-hour time difference between my home in California and London, England, unless I have a stake in an activity connected to that piece of information. I must have a concern, an interest, an attraction, etc., that makes a piece of factual information relevant to my behavior before it can play any part in motivating me.

Consequently, that reason does not originate passions is a view defended uniformly throughout the *Treatise*. Hume writes:

An active principle can never be founded on an inactive; and if reason be inactive in itself, it must remain so in all its shapes and appearances, whether it exerts itself in natural or moral subjects, whether it considers the powers of external bodies, or the actions of rational beings. (T 3.1.1.7)

Reason cannot produce an original affection, even though the information it procures for us may influence what we do, just as I cannot lift two hundred pounds, even though I might contribute to or influence the lifting of two hundred pounds. Of course, an objection to this analogy might be that, while I am the kind of thing that can lift, and it makes sense to say that I can contribute to the lifting of two hundred pounds, reason is not, according to Hume, even the kind of thing that can motivate. However, if Hume is understood to mean that reason is not the kind of thing that can initiate (by providing ends or originating passions), reason can still be the sort of thing that contributes to motivation, since being moved to action depends both on having ends and having relevant information about how to achieve them.[5] This interpretation affords some clue why Hume writes that reason is slave to the passions, despite the fact that a person cannot act without both passion and cause-effect belief. Without the attractions provided by the passions, we cannot ascertain what rational inferences are relevant to achieving our goals, because we have no goals.[6]

Kydd ultimately argues that this is the proper way to understand Hume as well:

He grants that reason has considerable powers once it is operative, and his persistent remarks that these powers are ultimately a negligible factor in the control of our conduct can be

---

[5] When I say that reason contributes to motivation, I do not withdraw my claim from CHAPTER 1 that Hume regards passions as motives. However, my point is that, for a motive to be effective in action, the agent must form a belief by reasoning about how to achieve the motive's aim, and then act on that belief.
[6] For a different take on Hume's thesis about reason and passion, see Brett and Paxman (2008).

attributed only to the view that reason is never operative as an independent variable, but that it is both brought into operation and guided in its operation by some passion which does not itself come under its control. (Kydd 1946: 153)

Her reading, with which I concur, allows that reason can bring into being new passions in the service of original passions and in that sense be a mediate cause of action, but only under the control of another, ruling passion (see, for instance, Norton 1982: 96–101). Botros differs, however, in part because she suggests that Hume intends the claims about "the perfect inertness" of reason to be about demonstrative reasoning only.[7] This seems like a promising way to read the text, since philosophers like Cudworth and Clarke thought both that morality was discerned by rational intuition or demonstrative reason and that we are motivated to seek the good (although passions might mislead us). (This leaves aside the often-unrecognized fact, which I explain in the APPENDIX, that Cudworth and Clarke also argued that demonstrative reason was inert.) This reading allows that Hume thinks that demonstrative reasoning has no influence at all on passions and actions, while causal reasoning has the influence described in some of the passages noted, where it assists the passions in finding their objects. However, this reading does overlook the fact that Hume earlier portrays demonstration as supplementing or supporting causal reasoning in the production of action, in the way that causal reasoning supports passion in the production of action: "Abstract or demonstrative reasoning, therefore, never influences any of our actions, *but only as it directs* our judgment concerning causes and effects; ..." (T 2.3.3.2, my emphasis). So, in the same respect in which one might say that causal reasoning is not actually totally ineffective, practically speaking, one might also say that demonstrative reasoning is not totally ineffective (or else that they both are). This interpretation, in which the practicality of causal reasoning is separated from the practicality of demonstrative, might seem to gain support from the following proposal. The arguments of Book 2, all of which use the qualified language, are about inductive reasoning; the arguments of Book 3, which (except for one), using the language of "perfectly inert," or "wholly inactive," are chiefly about demonstrative reasoning. But of course, Hume refers back to the arguments of Book 2 in Book 3, treating his reiterations in Book 3 as the same arguments as those given earlier. Consequently, it makes best sense of Hume's texts to interpret his view about the inertness of reason, whether it be demonstrative or causal reasoning, to concern its inability to originate the passions that motivate. This interpretation is corroborated by the fact that Hume's argument that reason alone is not a motive to an action of the will continues with his positive account of how motivating passions (that are not instincts) arise, after distinguishing the functions of reason. I discuss this account next.

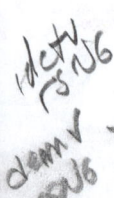

---

[7] Botros argues along these lines and tries to show that the conflicting strands are directed at different opponents.

2.3 Does Hume's Argument Allow that Beliefs Motivate Even If Reason Does Not?

It has been standard for readers to consider Hume a defender of the view that two distinct mental states, belief and desire, are both necessary to motivation.[8] Thus, it is commonly supposed that, for Hume, beliefs are not motives by themselves and do not produce motives on their own; a separate conation is necessary as well. This is the Humean Theory of Motivation in contemporary philosophy defended by many current naturalists.[9] Hume has been taken to have argued for it when he argued that reason alone is not a motive, but contributes to motivation in conjunction with a passion. But was it actually Hume's theory? Several Hume commentators have recently argued that it was not. Much of the discussion concerning this question centers on how to read Hume's description of the origin of the derived passions, which I have already referenced:

'Tis from the prospect of pain or pleasure that the aversion or propensity arises toward any object: And these emotions extend themselves to the causes and effects of that object, as they are pointed out to us by reason and experience. It can never in the least concern us to know, that such objects are causes, and such other effects, if both the causes and effects be indifferent to us. (T 2.3.3.3)

Some philosophers have argued that "the prospect of pain or pleasure" is to be understood in terms of belief, so that beliefs about prospective pleasure or pain, for Hume, produce prompts or motives to action. Hume's characterization of belief is relevant here. Recall that in Hume's psychology, the mind has perceptions of two types: impressions and ideas. Ideas are mental representations of impressions, which they copy, and are less vivid and forceful than the impressions. Beliefs are ideas—because they have representational content—but they differ from the ideas we merely entertain or imagine. Beliefs are more vivacious and forceful than imagined ideas, on Hume's view, because beliefs are acquired by experiences that transfer vivacity to the relevant idea in the process of causal reasoning. So, for instance, researchers in the 1960s entertained the hypothesis that smoking is a cause of lung cancer. After finding repeated instances of the two occurring together and collecting further data that provided evidence for a mechanism, they developed the belief that smoking is causally connected to lung cancer, and that belief is a more lively and vivacious version of the idea.

The thesis that beliefs about prospective pleasure and pain produce motives (passions) seems to be bolstered by Hume's discussion of the impact of beliefs in

---

[8] Some of the arguments in this section have appeared in various forms in Radcliffe (1999, 2008, and 2012b).

[9] See, for instance, Blackburn (1998); Schroeder (2007); Sinhababu (2009, 2013); Smith (1994, 92–129); Williams (1979).

Book 1 of the *Treatise*, in a section called, "Of the influence of belief" (T 1.3.10). This section follows his discussion of how beliefs are acquired. There Hume writes about the effect of pleasure and pain in producing motives, and connects their effect to belief. He writes first, "... pain and pleasure have two ways of making their appearance in the mind; ... They may either appear in impression to the actual feeling and experience, or only in idea, as at present when I mention them" (T 1.3.10.2). He then explains that all impressions "actuate the soul,"[10] but only some ideas do—namely those ideas that are believed:

> Tho' an idle fiction has no efficacy, yet we find by experience, that the ideas of those objects, which we believe either are or will be existent, produce in a lesser degree the same effect with those impressions, which are immediately present to the senses and perception. The effect, then, of belief is to raise up a simple idea to an equality with our impressions, and bestow on it a like influence on the passions. (T 1.3.10.3)

Hume comments that it would be very inconvenient to be influenced by fictitious ideas, since we have many imagined conceptions of pleasurable and painful objects and would never enjoy a moment's peace if we were moved by them. He concludes,

> Belief, therefore, since it causes an idea to imitate the effects of the impressions, must make it resemble them in these qualities, and is nothing but *a more vivid and intense conception of any idea*. This, then, may both serve as an additional argument for the present system, and may give us a notion after what manner our reasonings from causation are able to operate on the will and passions. (T 1.3.10.3)

Thus, there is a substantial basis for attributing to Hume the view that beliefs, because of their force and vivacity, on their own, without passions, can initiate action.

2.3.1 Recent Interpretations

Below, I sketch six recent interpretations of these texts on belief, reason, and motivation. At least five impute to Hume a view that is contrary to the belief-desire theory, which has traditionally been assumed to derive from Hume. I emphasize that these are sketches; the arguments that back up each of these views are detailed and complicated. While I cannot address all of the details, I offer some general observations about them. While I respect all of these arguments, I obviously have many disagreements with them.

1. *Non-inferential beliefs motivate, while inferential beliefs do not.* Some beliefs are derived from inference, and others are not. Hume's allegation that reason does not motivate implies that beliefs derived from inference do not give rise to

---

[10] This is a puzzling remark given that he later says, as I've noted, that some passions, like love, hatred, pride, and humility are not motives to action. They are impressions (of reflection), but, presumably, they don't actuate the soul. Of course, whether this is so depends on the meaning here of "actuate."

motivating passions, or to actions. But, as Charles Pigden argues, other beliefs are acquired immediately, or non-inferentially, simply upon our feeling pleasure or pain from an object. If I experience pleasure upon tasting a raspberry, I believe without inference that the taste of raspberries is pleasurable and this belief by itself gives rise to a motivating passion for future occasions of eating raspberries. Pigden argues that some beliefs actually are impressions and that other beliefs are ideas associated with impressions. The former, he says, are, of course, not inferred. So, non-inferential beliefs can produce motives, even if reason cannot (see Pigden 2009: 97).

2. *Beliefs about good and evil can motivate because pleasure and pain are essential values, which, when recognized in objects, produce desire or aversion ("Metaphysical hedonism").* P.J.E. Kail has argued that, on Hume's view, our beliefs that objects are good or evil contain ideas that are faint copies of pleasures and pains, which manifest the power of pleasures and pains "to actuate the will." On his interpretation of Hume, beliefs with evaluative contents motivate in virtue of those contents (Kail 2007a: 181–2). While Kail does not think that Hume explicitly intended to defend what he calls "metaphysical hedonism," he believes that it is implicit in Hume's view. Reason alone is not a motive to the will because it cannot produce these ideas of good and evil, which must come from experience and motivate by setting ends for us. Nothing in Hume's view prohibits beliefs from motivating, however; the point is that reason is inert when we are indifferent to the objects, that is, when we have no notions of them as good or bad (ibid.: 192–3).

3. *Reason is inert; the products of reasoning, namely, beliefs, are not.* On this view, beliefs about prospective pleasure and pain are inferential and so are produced by reasoning. However, this interpretation has it that the causal effects of beliefs are not attributable to the reasoning that produces them. So, if beliefs motivate by producing passions, this does not mean that the reasoning process motivates, or produces motivating passions. Rachel Cohon explicitly defends this reading by arguing that when a process produces a product, and that product produces an effect, it does not follow that the effect was produced by the process (Cohon 2008b: 74). For instance, if a manuscript produced by the process of typing falls off a desk and causes a loud noise, it doesn't follow that the typing produced the loud noise. Thus, Hume is consistent to hold that beliefs about prospective pleasure or pain are produced by reasoning, and that these beliefs produce motivating passions, even if reason itself does not motivate (ibid.: 73–7).

4. *While the faculty of reason does not have a passion or action as a product, beliefs can produce actions, even without passions.* David Owen agrees that, for Hume, the motivational force of beliefs that are products of reasoning is not attributable to reason. However, Owen adds that beliefs about prospective pleasures and pains can sometimes motivate action without producing any intervening

desires or passions.[11] He argues that there is much textual evidence in the *Treatise* for attributing to Hume the view that beliefs about prospective pleasure and pain, when they reach force and vivacity approaching impressions, can either produce volitions to action, or can produce actions directly.[12] He emphasizes that Hume means to say, not that beliefs do not motivate, but that the faculty of reason, producing only ideas, never has a passion or an action as a product (Owen 2016).

5. *Beliefs are sentiments, which are not derived from reason alone; so, while reason alone does not motivate, beliefs do.* Barry Stroud has argued that a belief, for Hume, is a sentiment directed toward a proposition.[13] Constantine Sandis notes that Hume distinguishes a mere idea from a belief in that the latter is a firm conception of what he describes as a "peculiar feeling" or "sentiment" in the Appendix to the *Treatise* and in the first *Enquiry*. So beliefs, as sentiments, can move us to act, and reason alone cannot produce the feeling that is necessary to form beliefs. On Sandis's interpretation, the conclusion of reasoning is a judgment, which is not motivating on its own. However, we can judge something to be the case without believing it, so beliefs are not judgments (Sandis 2012: 206–8).

6. *Beliefs are contingently motivating, but in themselves inert.* Mikael Karlsson argues that, for Hume, the starting points of the motivational process are a pair of cognitions (beliefs), one to the effect that something is pleasant, another to the effect that by acting in a certain way, the pleasure will be realized (Karlsson 2006; see also, Karlsson 2000, 2001). Karlsson calls these cognitions "creatures of reason," and so attributes to Hume the view that they are inert. These cognitions are nevertheless active within the context of human nature, though they would not have a motivational effect for purely rational beings. So, on this view, beliefs are contingently motivating. Since these beliefs are begotten of reason, in themselves they are inert.

All of these readings, but the last, are contrary to the Humean Theory of Motivation, even though only two of them, the fourth and fifth (Sandis's and Owen's), actually include the claim that beliefs motivate actions directly, without desire or passion. The others, by including the thesis that beliefs originate passions, are also contrary to Humeanism because of the following considerations. If beliefs can produce passions

---

[11] Owen also seems prepared to say that on Hume's view, beliefs of any content (not just those about pleasure and pain) could produce passions or action.

[12] As noted in Chapter 1, volition is oddly categorized as a direct passion. Recall that Hume writes, "The impressions, which arise from good and evil most naturally, and with the least preparation are the *direct* passions of desire and aversion, grief and joy, hope and fear, along with volition..." (T 2.3.9.2). "Thus a suit of fine cloaths produces pleasure from their beauty; and this pleasure produces the direct passions, or the impressions of volition and desire" (T 2.3.9.4).

[13] Stroud (1977: 158–61). I discuss Stroud's view in more depth in Chapter 3, in connection with the topic of belief.

that motivate, these beliefs have in themselves all the force needed to produce motives, and in turn, action. Consequently, the first five interpretations imply that Hume did not advocate the belief-desire model of motivation. The sixth, Karlsson's, suggests that beliefs only motivate in the "context" of human nature, which provides the conative elements essential to motivation. While his interpretation doesn't say that desire is necessary to motivation for Hume, I think it is sympathetic to the structure of contemporary Humeanism, which argues that the conative and cognitive elements in motivation are distinct.[14]

2.3.2 Difficulties with Recent Interpretations

I have various doubts about the readings of Hume that imply that beliefs are motivating, and here I offer four arguments for declining the first five readings listed above. My arguments are offered in ascending degrees of generality. In the end, I disagree with all five, but my case is not actually complete until I discuss the nature of Humean belief in CHAPTER 3.[15]

---

[14] For an interpretation of Hume that supports the conclusion that Hume does not subscribe to the belief-desire model of motivation, see Sturgeon (2015). Sturgeon's view is extremely nuanced, however. He defends the theses that Hume allows exceptions to the belief-desire model, that motivation by the prospect of pleasure and pain is, in a sense, motivation by reason, and that Hume is a qualified rationalist. Sturgeon's view is that while Hume denies that reason in the strict and philosophical sense is practical, in another sense, he offers a narrative of what practical reason requires of us.

[15] A question specific to the first reading, that non-inferential beliefs can motivate, even though beliefs that are inferential cannot, for Hume, is this. How are the beliefs at issue in this debate, about prospective pleasure and pain, not inferential, since they reference, not present (or not only present) pleasures and pains, but future ones as well? Such a belief requires inference to the future based on past experiences, along with the expectation that the future will continue in the same way as the past. For instance, I believe that eating a bowl of raspberries that I have not yet tasted will be pleasurable, because the ones I've eaten in the past have been sources of pleasure. So, the belief that these raspberries are a prospective source of pleasure is a belief acquired inferentially. If such beliefs are motivating, then it appears that beliefs produced by reason do motivate. Second, I'm reluctant to accept the view that the products of reason (or reasoning) might motivate, even though reason does not. Rachel Cohon argues for this thesis in part by using examples to support a general claim about causation. When an agent produces something that has an effect, the effect is usually attributable to the agent—for instance when a book contains false claims that create confusion, the confusion is attributed to the author. The claim is that this transitivity of causation does not hold when the cause is a process that has a product, and the product then causes an effect. If a statue produced by the lost-wax process causes a scandal, the process did not create a scandal (Cohon 2008b: 74). Analogously, if a reasoning process produces beliefs that in turn produce motivating passions, the reasoning process that produces the beliefs should not be seen as the cause of the motivating passions. This argument is ingenious, although not offered by Hume himself. But I question the degree of analogy between these processes and reasoning. My doubt is illustrated by the fact that it would be incongruous for a rationally-functioning person to say that a conclusion she believed moved her, but that the evidence and reasoning on which she adopted that conclusion did not.

An anonymous reader offers an attempted reply to my line of thinking here: that reference to evidence and reasoning are enabling conditions that allow us to explain why the belief motivated, but those conditions are not part of the motive. This reply calls upon the notion of "enabling conditions" that Jonathan Dancy uses to defend his (non-Humean) view that reasons for action are facts that favor acting in a certain way. Dancy says that the agent having certain beliefs is simply what allows us to explain the action, but the beliefs are not part of the motive (Dancy 2000: 127). The problem is that I don't think that Dancy's maneuver works, since an agent's beliefs about which reasons obtain are enabling conditions for

First argument. Kail and Owen say that Hume's denial that reason can be a motive applies to the *faculty* of reason (Owen 2016: 346–9, and Kail 2007a: 192). Faculties are capacities, and the faculty of reason is the capacity to engage in reasoning, which involves the activity of comparing ideas, to come to conclusions, which then produce beliefs.[16] However, to say that the faculty of reason can produce action is to say that the potential to reason, or to compare ideas, or to produce beliefs, has the capacity to motivate or to produce action. (I'm not certain that this is exactly what Kail and Owen have in mind, though.[17]) This view attributes a capacity to a capacity, which, as John Locke memorably highlights in his discussion of free will, is problematic.[18] To say that the faculty of reason motivates is to say that the potential to engage in reasoning processes produces passions or actions. However, potentials do not produce or act, although the person or thing that has the potential can exercise it. In exercising it, the subject fulfills what the potential was a potential for, which is to reason. Perhaps the rationalists, or some of them, held the confused thesis that the faculty of reason motivates, but I don't find evidence that they did. As I've already noted, most of the rationalists writing before Hume acknowledged that reason without passion was inert.[19] Furthermore, when the seventeenth- and eighteenth-century thinkers write about motivation from passion, they are referring, not to the capacity to feel a passion, but to individual passions. Both they and Hume realize that a passion, rather than the faculty of passion, is a cause of action. Analogously, anyone who thought that reason was active would hold that a particular reason or belief, not the faculty of idea comparison or belief formation itself, is a motive. Neither the capacity to feel nor the capacity to reason or to believe, etc., is the right sort of thing to motivate action. So, it is not likely that Hume felt any need to deny that the capacity or faculty of reason can motivate.

Second argument. It is also important to ask what Hume means by saying that reason "alone" cannot motivate. As I've noted, Hume does think that reason contributes to motivation. In what manner would the *faculty* of reason, as distinguished from the activity of reasoning, and from belief, contribute to motivation? In what way might it assist passions in achieving their ends? The capacity to reason, when distinguished from reasoning and from belief, is not able to offer anything to the passions, since it is not the proper sort of thing. Without reference to reasoning or the beliefs it produces, it cannot direct passions to their proper ends. Perhaps reasoning

---

rationalizing explanations only because an agent's beliefs caused the action. For more on why this move fails, see Lance and McAdam (2005: 395).

[16] Hume actually defines reason as "the discovery of truth or falshood" (T 3.1.1.9), which may indicate that he defines it in terms of its activity. He also says at T 2.3.3.3 that reason is the discovery of causal connections. Thus, Cohon thinks he intends to treat reason as a process of reasoning (Cohon 2008b: 69).

[17] If they intend to identify the faculty of reason with its processes or activities, instead, then this argument does not apply to their view. I consider the "activities of reason" view next.

[18] Locke (1690: Book II, Chapter xxi, Paragraphs 14–16).

[19] See the APPENDIX for further evidence.

can, or beliefs can, but the faculty of reason, cannot. So, on this reading—that Hume's concern is with the faculty of reason—his view on the impotence of reason has to be understood as the claim that reason is wholly inert and makes no contribution to action. Then, of course, Hume's references to reason "alone" are puzzling; and as commentators I've discussed have noted, these references would suggest a hidden equivocation between senses of reason in Hume's text: reason as the faculty is wholly inert, but reason as belief contributes to motivation.

Perhaps, however, what some commentators mean by the "faculty of reason" is reason's processes or functions. This may be what Kail and Owen actually have in mind. This understanding is also consistent with Cohon's interpretation of Hume, on which the *process* of reasoning is inert. Hume does, after all, name demonstration and matter-of-fact reasoning as the functions of reason—and discusses separately how each one is not a motive. Hume's claim, on this interpretation, is that engaging in the activity of demonstration or in reasoning about matters of fact does not produce passions or actions. The activity of reasoning is not a potential, but the exercise of one. Thus, it might make sense for someone to think it can produce a passion or an action; so, Hume would want to deny this. Even if none of the early moderns actually thought this, Hume might have believed they did, or thought they were committed to this view.

Consider now what the thesis "reason alone does not influence action" implies if reason here is understood as the exercise of reasoning, that is, as the activity. In that case, Hume's thesis is that the exercise of reasoning does not produce motives on its own, but it does assist the passions in achieving their ends. This thesis sounds more plausibly like what Hume might have had in mind. But it's important to see that this gloss on reason *as reasoning* seems to work because the activity of reasoning (i) usually comes to a conclusion and (ii) usually produces a belief in the reasoner. If the reasoning process went on indefinitely, or if an agent did not believe the conclusions she came to by inference, the activity or process of reasoning would not make a contribution to motivation. This fact is an indication that the motivational force is being supplied by the belief, not by the activity. We know that the sorts of beliefs relevant here are about means and ends, or about what objects are suited to one's passions; these are the beliefs caused by the reasoning. Since, on the interpretation under consideration, these beliefs are ontologically distinct from the reasoning that produces them, it would not be correct to say that the reasoning process is making the contribution to motivation. Another way to put my point is this. The following two theses are not compatible: (1) The activity of reasoning cannot motivate on its own, although it contributes to motivation by causing beliefs. (2) Beliefs can motivate on their own, because they are ontologically separate from the inert reasoning process that produces them. If (2) is the case, then (1) cannot be, since (1), in asserting that reasoning itself is motivating in virtue of beliefs, treats beliefs as essentially connected to the activity of reasoning. Consequently, I think the reading of Hume that identifies reason with the activity of reasoning also has difficulties in making sense of Hume's thesis that reason "alone" does not motivate. Again, it looks as though reason, as reasoning, is completely inert, even though beliefs are active, and Hume is equivocating.[20]

In sum, my second argument is this. Given that reason as a faculty, reason as an activity (reasoning), and reason as effects (beliefs) are distinguished, commentators have defended the following interpretations of Hume's thesis about the inertness of reason. (1) The faculty of reason is inert, but beliefs alone can motivate. (2) The activity of reasoning is inert, but beliefs alone can motivate. (3) Beliefs are inert on their own, but not in conjunction with a passion (the traditional reading). Theses (1) and (2) cannot explain why Hume says reason "alone" is not a motive to the will, since they cannot explain how reason, given how they have defined it, can contribute anything to motivation. All the motivational force, on those interpretations, belongs to belief, but appeal to beliefs is not an appeal to reason as described in the two views, respectively. Only thesis (3), where Hume's reference to reason is understood as a reference to belief, can explain why Hume writes that reason alone cannot motivate.

Third argument. My third argument against recent interpretations offers some logical considerations related to the explanation of action. I believe that these considerations indicate that beliefs do not produce motives to action or produce actions directly. It's easy to conceive an explanation of action in terms of belief when an agent has only one (supposedly) motivating belief at a time. But multiple possible future goods and evils present themselves to us constantly. Consequently, it is a challenge for the view that beliefs about goods and evils motivate to explain why one or another belief is effective in competition with others. One essential feature of motivation for Hume is causal strength, which determines whether a given motive is operative when it conflicts with other motives. On the proposal that beliefs originate desires, beliefs must also account for the causal strength of the desires they supposedly produce. (I focus here only on beliefs about future pleasurable or painful objects.[21]) So, consider first the suggestion that the strength of belief, or conviction,

---

[20] An anonymous reviewer suggested that Hume is referring to the activities of the faculty of reason when he argues that reason alone does not motivate. I'm not quite sure how this differs from the idea that the process of reasoning motivates, but perhaps the suggestion is that the activities of gathering evidence, making inferences, correcting what we take to be mistaken beliefs, and so on—all activities of reason—cannot or do not provide motives. However, these activities seem to contribute to the process of reasoning, and so the considerations I have offered against interpreting "reason" as reasoning apply here as well.

[21] The view that beliefs of any content might motivate for Hume is different, so what I say here does not apply to it. As one might note about Humeanism, given that beliefs and desires are distinct states, along with the proposal that beliefs motivate on their own, there seems to be no theoretical reason to posit passions (or desires) as causes of action. If the beliefs account for motivational strength as they must if they are to produce motives on their own, then there is no need to refer to desires to explain why one action rather than another results. This point applies equally to Hume's view. He clearly regards passions or desires as causes of action, and he thinks beliefs and desires are separate mental states. Being parsimonious, as he is, he would be precluded from holding that beliefs by themselves produce motivating passions. Consequently, there is just one way left to impute to Hume the view that beliefs motivate: to attribute to him the view that beliefs motivate directly, not by producing passions. On this interpretation of Hume, some actions are caused by passions and some are caused directly by beliefs.

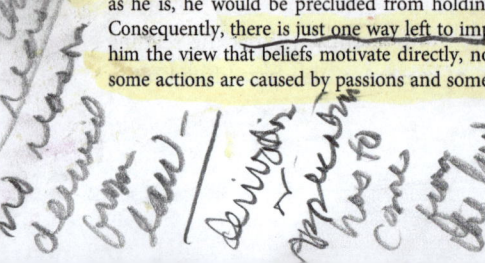

determines the strength of motive (desire)—that is, that degree of conviction determines any resulting motive's potential to prevail in conflicts with other belief-generated motives. For example, my eating a mango instead of an apple, when I believe that each is a source of pleasure, would be explained by my believing *more strongly* that the mango is pleasurable than I believe that the apple is. Here strength of evaluative belief, rather than content, is determining the relative strengths of my motivations. This position seems implausible, however, when one considers a situation like the following. I believe that eating a mango has n amount of pleasure in store for me, and I believe that eating an apple has $n+2$ amount of pleasure in store for me. But I hold these beliefs with equal strength or conviction. It follows, on the view that strength of conviction determines strength of motivation, that I would have no greater desire to eat the apple than the mango. This implication is not credible. On the proposal that beliefs about prospective pleasure produce motives, it surely matters to action how pleasurable the agent believes the various prospective objects to be. The content of beliefs matters.

Kail, for instance, thinks that the content of beliefs motivates (Kail 2007a: 97). On his view, reason alone doesn't motivate because it cannot produce the ideas of good and evil that are the content of motivating beliefs, for Hume. Those ideas depend on perceptions of pleasure and pain, which give us the ideas of things that

On this reading, when the set of the purported motivating beliefs is restricted to those concerning pleasures and pains, the best explanation of action is probably in terms of some hypothetical formula such as I earlier referred to, one which includes reference both to content (expected pleasure or pain) and to strength of conviction. But someone might in fact admit as motivating beliefs for Hume, not only those about future pleasures and pains, but beliefs with various contents, citing texts from his section on "Of the influence of belief." On the presupposition that beliefs motivate on their own for Hume, his remarks in that section seem open to the interpretation that any idea with sufficient force and vivacity could motivate action. On this reading of Hume, I could, for example, be moved to grab an umbrella by the belief (on its own) that it's raining outside or by the belief that the umbrella will keep me dry (and not just by the belief that using an umbrella will be productive of pleasure or good for me). On this interpretation, however, it's even harder to explain why one action rather than another results. That the sun is shining brightly in the middle of summer can motivate me to buy sunglasses. That sunglasses are expensive can motivate me to endure the glare of the sun. The question a proponent of this interpretation needs to answer is: what features of these respective beliefs determine why I do one action rather than another? Neither the content of belief, the strength of my conviction, nor some combination of the two seems to provide a plausible explanation here. Rather, reference to the relative strengths of the desire to protect my eyes versus the desire to save money seems to be necessary to explain why I am moved to do one thing over the other.

One more complicating factor in the proposal that, for Hume, motivation sometimes comes from beliefs and sometimes comes from passions is that, on this view, it looks like beliefs and passions can be in competition with each other. When beliefs and passions call for conflicting actions, action explanations will have to refer to some parameter on which the motivational force of belief and desires can be compared. It can be neither content nor strength of conviction, since Hume makes it clear that passions do not represent. They have no content and give us nothing to be convinced about. One suggestion is that the relevant parameter is force and vivacity, which all mental states possess, but I am at a loss to explain how the account would go from here. This is primarily because force and vivacity most naturally explain the relative violence or calmness of passions, which is a different continuum from their motivational strength or weakness. For these reasons, I am doubtful that this interpretation of Hume (that beliefs of any kind motivate action directly) can account for why we do one action rather than another.

are valuable.[22] Reason serves to make those ideas more forceful, but it cannot originate them. However, there is no explanation in Kail's account of how beliefs about valuable objects lead to action, given that we consider many objects valuable (a source of pleasure) at the same time. Do some ideas of good and evil cause desires and some not? Do some lead to desires causally stronger than other desires? If so, how? Or do some lead to action directly, and some not, and if so which ones, and why?[23]

A possible suggestion is that the relative amount of pleasure (or pain) an agent believes an object has in store, when compared to alternative objects, determines the relative strength of the passions or desires for the objects. Thus, the quantities of pleasure or pain referenced in one's beliefs about future objects are decisive to the motivational strength of desires produced. This approach implies, given that we are caused to act on the strongest desire present, that no one ever acts against his or her assessment of the greatest overall pleasure or good. This, however, is inconsistent with Hume's view; Hume certainly thought we sometimes act against our assessment of the greatest good (see T 2.3.3.10). On the supposition that beliefs produce desires, we have no reason to think that the belief that an object is for my overall greatest good will necessarily produce a desire that is causally stronger than the desire generated by my belief that the object currently before me offers an immediate, but smaller good. And on the view that some beliefs can produce actions directly, we have no reason to think that the former belief will produce action rather than the latter.

Someone, however, might say that this is too simplistic a model of action, and that degree of conviction surely does matter to action, even if it's not the whole story. We can readily make sense of a case where I neglect to act on my belief about the greatest pleasure because I have doubts or less conviction concerning it. So, given the view that beliefs produce desires, perhaps some complicated formula involving *both* strength of belief and quantity of pleasure or pain expected from an object accounts for motivational strength. It's hard to know what that formula would be. However, if this is so, there is no theoretical reason to include passions or desires in the motivational chain at all. The question why an agent did this action rather than another is (supposedly) answered completely by citing the features of beliefs just mentioned. Except for a few instincts, individual passions would play no part in the explanation of action, so reference to them becomes superfluous. So, if Hume holds that beliefs are motives, and if he can offer a narrative of how they account for motivational strength (which I doubt he can), then he undercuts a basis for the thesis

---

[22] See Kail (2007a: 189–93). Kail's argument that reason alone doesn't motivate because it cannot produce the ideas that motivate implies that both demonstration and causal reasoning are not reason alone, since ideas used in both processes, must, according to Hume, be derived first from experience. Given that episodes of reasoning depend on content, it's difficult to see how reason *alone* does reasoning.

[23] Kail's view, in fact, is that beliefs produce desires that produce action, but Owen and Sandis hold that some beliefs motivate directly.

that many passions are motives.[24] On the other hand, if Hume claims that beliefs generate passions and denies that beliefs determine the strength of the passions' motivating force, then he is committed to the denying that beliefs are the source of motivation. This is because an adequate account of motivation needs to explain what gets us to action, which is a function of causal force, when there are competing motives (and there always are). On the theory that beliefs about pleasure and pain or good and evil are motivating on their own, we have an account of how a passion forms, but no coherent explanation of how it results in action. When the beliefs are thought to motivate action directly, without the production of passions, we have an analogous problem, since beliefs are specified by content, and the content does not account for causal strength.

Fourth argument. A fourth consideration that militates against the reading of Hume that implies that beliefs alone motivate is the following. In Book 3 of the *Treatise*, Hume applies the conclusion that reason is not a motive in his argument against moral rationalism (the Motivation Argument). That argument is:

Since morals, therefore, have an influence on the actions and affections, it follows, that they cannot be derived from reason; and that because reason alone, as we have already proved, can never have any such influence. Morals excite passions, and produce or prevent actions. Reason of itself is utterly impotent in this particular. The rules of morality therefore, are not conclusions of our reason. (T 3.3.1.6)

Then he continues by saying that the only way to evade this inference is to deny the principle on which it is founded, the claim I quoted earlier:

An active principle can never be founded on an inactive; and if reason be inactive in itself, it must remain so in all its shapes and appearances, whether it exerts itself in natural or moral subjects, whether it considers the powers of external bodies, or the actions of rational beings.
(T 3.1.1.7)

So, Hume's Motivation Argument says: (1) Morality causes passions or actions. (2) Reason alone does not cause passions or actions. (3) An active principle cannot be founded on an inactive one. (4) Conclusion: Morality is not founded on reason alone. The rule in (3) implies that if something is an active or motivating principle of human nature, it cannot be founded on, or caused by, an inactive or non-motivating principle. This further implies that if beliefs are motivating, those beliefs cannot be founded on reason, which is inert in itself. Yet, on a standard reading, Hume thinks that most beliefs are founded on reason (or adopted as the result of reasoning), and it certainly looks as though beliefs about future pleasurable and painful objects are. Furthermore, if Hume were to relinquish his generalization about the derivation of

---

[24] One recourse is to say that beliefs about natural good and evil are representational, but passion-like states, which commits Hume to a view very close to the rationalists' view that desires are representations of good and evil. (None of the interpretations referenced in this discussion propose that view.)

active states and hold that beliefs are motives, even though the reason or reasoning on which they are based is not motivating, then he would be compelled to admit that "morality" could be based on reason as well. But this consequence undercuts his crucial argument against the rationalists. (On Sandis's view, beliefs are not a product of reason, so this criticism does not apply to his interpretation. I address the implications of the characterization of beliefs as sentiments in Chapter 4.)

For these reasons, and for others that I am about to offer, my view is that Hume's argument for the inertness of reason is an argument for the conclusion that beliefs do not produce passions or actions on their own.

2.4 An Interpretation that Beliefs Alone Are Not Motives

2.4.1 Historical Considerations

My argument here begins with historical considerations. The two main theses of Hume's motivational theory are that reason alone is not a motive and that reason and passion cannot be opposed for direction of the will. I discuss the second thesis in Chapter 4, but I want to note here that Hume purports to confirm it by a further consideration, namely, that the passions are not representations. Hume's arguments about the motivational impotence of reason are logically connected to the characterization of the passions that he thinks an empiricist must accept: namely, that passions are conative states that, unlike ideas, bring no content before the mind. Rationalist models have a single psychological state that serves both to represent the world and to motivate. As we have seen, Descartes explains an opposition between reason and passion in terms of representations. Clear and distinct representations of the good derived from reason are set against the obscure representations that constitute the passions. Passions have a physiological component that sets the "spirits" in motion to prompt the body to move in opposition, at times, to the volitions produced by reason's depiction of the good. This motivational opposition between reason and passion has reason initiating motivation against the motions generated by the passions. For Malebranche, we are inclined by God toward universal good, and the passions, which are meant for the preservation of the body, produce motion in the spirits, which creates confused ideas of the good that we seek.

Not all the early modern rationalists I've discussed write explicitly of passions as representational, but I think almost all are committed to this description. The idea that reason and passion can give opposing direction to the will is practically ubiquitous among these thinkers in these centuries. The one exception may actually be Cudworth, on whose theory the soul, reason, imagination, passion, and appetite are integrated by the will. On his view, there is no division between reason and passion, but instead, the mind in deliberation practices self-governance. When it is unsuccessful in governance, the problem seems to be due to lack of adequate deliberation.

However, for the other rationalists, reason and passion are sometimes in dispute, and unregulated passion is the source of disruption or misdirection of the will. But how does this happen? The explanation, I think, implies that passions are representations. Consider Reynolds: he holds that the passions are meant to enrich human nature by inclining us to good objects or by producing an aversion to bad ones. Reason gives the passions a depiction of the good to fasten onto. Obviously, however, the passions don't always fulfill this potential and can cause us to act irrationally. The only plausible explanation how this happens is that the passions perceive other ends as the goods they are seeking, rather than the ends that reason presents. Ayloffe thinks that the passions are deceived at times by the senses, and reason must reveal the true features of objects for us to be properly motivated. Here the passions and reason are at odds in their representations of the objects of pursuit. Similarly, Bragge sees passions as tendencies toward what is good and conducive to happiness, but they can get their objects wrong and need to be guided by reason to the appropriate ends. The only sense to be made of how the passions latch onto mistaken goods is in terms of their representing the wrong things as part of our happiness. For Clarke, as I suggested, some rational beings are not regularly governed by reason and morality, and they instead allow lusts, passions, sensual pleasures, and so on, to motivate them. Clarke writes of these persons: "These, setting up their own unreasonable Self-will in opposition to the Nature and Reason of Things, endeavour (as much as in them lies) to make things be what they are not, and cannot be" (Clarke 1706: vol. 2: 12). Here also is the suggestion of passions as false representations of goodness.

So, given that the majority of the seventeenth- and eighteenth-century rationalists writing on action were committed to this idea of the passions, it is no wonder that Hume offered specific arguments against this view. That the dispute over the nature of passion is integral to the debate over the source of action offers further evidence that Hume was concerned with the role of representations or ideas in motivation. When Hume argues that reason alone is not a motive, his concern is to show that ideas, which are essentially representational, cannot create motives on their own, even when they have the status of belief. Passions, on the other hand, do create motives, not because they are representations, but because they are essentially active states that derive their impetus from perceptions of pleasure and pain. I say more about this theory of the source of motivational force shortly.

2.4.2 The Treatise Account of the Origin of Motivating Passions

I want to argue that there is a way to understand the *Treatise* account of motive formation that makes the account consistent with these two theses: that beliefs are not motivating on their own and that the origination of motives depends upon sentiments or affections. In other words, that motivating passions are derived from the prospect of pleasure or pain need not be understood as implying that beliefs about objects motivate. This interpretation depends on an appeal to the instincts as real passions, as Hume emphasizes they are. Physical pleasures and pains are impressions of sensation; mental pleasures and pains are impressions of reflection. Impressions of pleasures and pains of either sort are motivating, I think, because of the instinct Hume calls "the general appetite to good, and aversion to evil, consider'd merely as such" (T 2.3.3.8). They are what Hume in the *Treatise* calls active principles, or those capable of producing affection or action (T 3.1.1.7), even though they accompany other, inert sensations. For instance, we experience impressions of heat, cold, colors, smells, and so on, as pleasurable or painful. Likewise, in the case of psychological pleasures and pains, we respond with pleasure or displeasure to our ideas of a certain movie, a friend's misfortune, a well-composed painting, and so on. These active (or perhaps, activating) responses derive from the affective or motivational aspect of the mind. (I will soon argue that this is another way of saying that pleasures and pains, both mental and physical, originate in what Hume calls "taste" in the second *Enquiry*.)

Understanding pleasure and pain as active sentiments has implications for interpreting the *Treatise* texts on motive formation. I want to suggest that the motives which develop from the prospect of pleasure or pain are derived from certain felt sentiments of pleasure and pain. This is not to say that the promise of a tasty dinner has me feeling the pleasure of eating the forthcoming meal, and that's why I desire it. Rather, I have an experience of pleasure from an object that I know has certain features. I desire those features due to having experienced their pleasantness. Observation and inference yield the belief that another object, which I have not experienced, has similar features. Since I desire those features, this object holds for me the prospect of pleasure, and I develop a desire for the new object. Desire originates from the impression of pleasure I've experienced in the past and gets transferred to future objects via reasoning. The desire isn't arising from belief or from reasoning, however. My previous impression of pleasure originates a desire for objects that are like the one that gave me the original pleasure; when I discover objects with such features, my desire is transferred to those objects. This reading of the passage concerning prospective pleasure and pain is consistent with the natural reading of Hume's remark at T 3.1.1.12, where he repeats the arguments about the impotence of reason from Book 2 and writes:

It has been observ'd, that reason, in a strict and philosophical sense, can have influence on our conduct only after two ways: Either when it excites a passion by informing us of the existence of something which is a proper object of it; or when it discovers the connexion of causes and effects, so as to afford us means of exerting any passion.

In the first way, a passion is excited by reason when we discover that an object fits the description of something we care about.

Thus, when Hume writes "when we have the prospect of pain or pleasure from any object, we feel a consequent emotion of aversion or propensity," he need not be read as saying that a belief that an object will be pleasurable or painful creates a desire. Earlier, I mentioned that Hume says that pleasure and pain are introduced into the mind sometimes as impressions and sometimes as ideas. When the pleasure or pain enters as an impression, the desire follows upon the impression, which produces it. When the pleasure or pain enters as idea, the account is the one given above. I'm not experiencing the pleasure of the object now, and perhaps I never have. For example, I've enjoyed Richard Linklater movies in the past and become convinced by reading a review that his new movie has features like the ones I've enjoyed. So, I acquire a desire to see his new movie. That desire originates in a feeling of pleasure from the past that produces a desire for an object in my future. In such cases, I become convinced, either by reasoning on my part, or by someone's persuading me, that an object has certain features that I enjoy, and I come to expect it to be pleasurable. The desire for that future thing derives from an impression of pleasure I've experienced in the past. My having an idea of an unexperienced thing as pleasurable is not the cause of my desire for it. Rather my desire for it originates in pleasure that I've felt in the past, which is conveyed to the future object. So, then I think of that future object as a probable source of pleasure.

I want to be clear about the scope of my argument. The above description applies to the cases of derived passions only. It has nothing to do with the original instincts that Hume names and to which I earlier referred. If I jump in response to a sudden loud noise, or jerk my head when the sun suddenly flashes in my eyes, I'm moved by the instinct away from pain that Hume mentions as original, with no contribution from a belief about a future object.[25] If I give my neighbor a ride to the doctor out of benevolence, I do so from an instinct, rather than from a passion derived from an impression of pleasure in conjunction with a belief about an object I have yet to experience. Likewise, hunger, or desire for food, is not acquired by a feeling of pleasure or pain and a belief about a prospective object—although my action of eating a sandwich is motivated by hunger plus a belief that eating the sandwich will relieve my discomfort. And so on for the other original instincts that Hume mentions.

2.4.3 Consistency with Other *Treatise* *Texts*

Hume's reference to the prospect of pain or pleasure as the source of aversion or propensity at *Treatise* 2.3.3.3 looks like a recounting of the origin of certain contents of the mind, which he offers in the beginning of the *Treatise*. There his description of how impressions of reflection differ from impressions of sensation says:

Impressions may be divided into two kinds, those of SENSATION and those of REFLECTION... The second is deriv'd in a great measure from our ideas, and that in the following order. An impression first strikes upon the senses, and makes us perceive heat or cold, thirst or hunger, pleasure or pain of some kind or other. Of this impression there is a copy taken by the mind,

---

[25] It's tempting to say that these cases don't actually count as cases of action, and Hume's theory of motivation need not apply to them. But I think he can account for them by reference to the instincts he names, and he never indicates that there is a restriction on the scope of action to intentional movement in the way that contemporary Humeans do.

which remains after the impression ceases; and this we call an idea. This idea of pleasure or pain, when it returns upon the soul, produces the new impressions of desire and aversion, hope and fear, which may properly be call'd impressions of reflection, because deriv'd from it... (T 1.1.2.1)

Here it looks as though ideas by themselves produce passions, which is precisely what I have been denying. I have several points to make about this passage. First, I want to note that Hume says that impressions of reflection, or passions, are derived "in a great measure" from our ideas. This is consistent with my point earlier that in cases when pleasure and pain are felt as sensations, a motivating passion can follow directly. Second, Hume says that a copy of the impression remains, but new impressions, which are the motivating passions, originate *when* the idea returns. So, I enjoy a new jasmine tea blend for the first time at a friend's house and retain an idea of that tea as pleasant. This is the point at which the text about the prospect of pleasure or pain is relevant. The "prospect of pain or pleasure" refers to the return of ideas of certain objects one previously found enjoyable, or unenjoyable. So, when I'm shopping, my thinking about the tea blend in this box, which has the same features as the tea I enjoyed, gives me a desire to buy it. Third, the crucial point in my account is that the idea of the tea as pleasant or good is not the *source* of my motive to buy it. That idea itself is dependent on having previous experiences of that kind of tea as pleasant (or of something analogous to that kind of tea), experiences which themselves are dependent on certain features of my personal constitution (since not everyone enjoys it).

Furthermore, the *Treatise* hints at the view that the motivating force of finding objects pleasurable or painful is attributable to the general inclination to natural good and aversion to natural evil. I considered this general appetite in Chapter 1 and concluded that Hume must also consider it an instinct, since he insists it is a real passion and he refers to "an *original* instinct" by which the mind "tends to unite itself with the good, and to avoid the evil" (T 2.3.9.2).[26] On the other hand, the objects of desire are pleasurable *things*, and of aversion, painful ones (rather than impressions of pleasure and pain), which implies that this instinct should not be interpreted as a

---

[26] Peter Kail argues that the general appetite for good and away from evil is not an instinct, but is contrasted with them, since Hume writes of "either instincts originally implanted in our natures... or the general appetite to good, and aversion to evil" (T 2.3.3.8). I've already explained why I think this appetite is an instinct nonetheless. Furthermore, Kail claims, "such general appetites are acquired from encounters with particular instances of good and evil... Pleasure and pain are causally prior to the general appetite" (Kail 2007a: 197). In other words, Hume's reference to the appetite for good and away from evil is a way of referring to the fact that we form desires for things, upon finding them pleasurable, and avoid bad ones, upon finding them painful. I think this reading is appealing, and agree with it to a large degree. But Hume does call this appetite a real passion, often confused with reason. The various desires we form for good things and away from bad ones, the appetites acquired from experiences in Kail's account, encompass many passions that would not be mistaken for reason. Many such desires are violent ones. So, I think Hume means to treat this appetite as a disposition to form particular passions; given that it is a passionate disposition (rather than, say, an intellectual, one), it also counts as a passion.

desire for impressions of pleasure and an aversion to impressions of pain. Rather, I suggested that it is more plausibly seen as the disposition to acquire passions for particular objects that are sources of pleasure and pain. Likewise, the other instincts can contribute to the formation of motivating passions and so are dispositions as well. The instinct of benevolence, for instance, might participate in the production of generosity when we have ideas of things that contribute to the good of others. Our love of life can produce prudential passions or desires when we bring to mind ideas of things that are in our long-term good, like exercise and healthy eating, and so on. Therefore, it makes sense to infer that ideas of pleasurable and painful things do not produce impressions like desire and aversion or hope and fear in isolation from natural instincts, which are dispositions to form other passions. Hume sees the instincts as passions in their own right, as well, which is consistent with his view that passions can cause other passions. These non-representational, conative states are essential to Hume's picture of the production of motivating passions. Thus, the suggestion that beliefs are motivating on their own is not the only way to read what is happening when we are motivated by the prospect of pleasure or pain, and the reading I offer avoids the logical problems I described earlier.

My interpretation does raise questions about Hume's remarks on belief in *Treatise* 1.3.10, "Of the influence of belief," and in *Treatise* 2.3.3, "Of the influencing motives of the will," where he seems to offer examples of motivating beliefs. He describes two ways in which passions appear to be controlled by beliefs:

First, When a passion, such as hope or fear, grief or joy, despair or security, is founded on the supposition of the existence of objects, which really do not exist. *Secondly*, When in exerting any passion in action, we chuse means insufficient for the design'd end, and deceive ourselves in our judgment of causes and effects. (T 2.3.3.6)

In the paragraph after, he writes, "The moment we perceive the falshood of any supposition, or the insufficiency of any means, our passions yield to our reason without any opposition." Consider some examples. A mother feels despair and grief over the kidnapping of her daughter, partly on the supposition that the girl has been killed; but the police bring the mother news that her daughter is living in another country. The despair and grief vanish upon the belief that her daughter is alive and are replaced by the passions of hope and joy. In another case, my desire to go out to dinner at a new restaurant tonight is quashed when I read a bad review by a reliable critic. It looks as though belief is causing passions (motives) to go in and out of existence in these cases.[27] How can I reconcile this with the interpretation of Hume as arguing that beliefs do not contribute to motivation without prior passions?

Earlier, I quoted parts of a passage from "Of the influence of belief," where Hume says that ideas influence actions, but only when they approximate the force and

---

[27] I borrow these examples from a previously published article (Radcliffe 1999).

56 HUME, PASSION, AND ACTION

vivacity of impressions, which is to say, when they become beliefs. More of that discussion is here:

> Nature has... neither bestow'd on every idea of good and evil the power of actuating the will, nor yet has entirely excluded them from this influence. Tho' an idle fiction has no efficacy, yet we find by experience, that the ideas of those objects, which we believe either are or will be existent, produce in a lesser degree the same effect with those impressions, which are immediately present to the senses and perception. The effect, then, of belief is to raise up a simple idea to an equality with our impressions, and bestow on it a like influence on the passions. This effect it can only have by making an idea approach an impression in force and vivacity... Belief, therefore, since it causes an idea to imitate the effects of the impressions, must make it resemble them in these qualities, and is nothing but *a more vivid and intense conception of any idea*. This, then, may both serve as an additional argument for the present system, and may give us a notion after what manner our reasonings from causation are able to operate on the will and passions. (T 1.3.10.3)

Hume says here that an idea that has been raised in vivacity to the status of a belief has an "influence on the passions" akin to the influence of our impressions, and this remark seems to imply that beliefs can create passions or cause actions. However, it is important to note that, in the last sentence of the excerpt, Hume tells us that his remarks give us a notion how "our reasonings from causation are able to operate on the will and passions." He has been talking about beliefs throughout, so here he clearly identifies beliefs with reasonings from causation. No matter how Hume's argument that reason alone doesn't motivate is read, interpreters agree that he clearly denies the possibility that reasoning from causation by itself produces passions. So he can't be taken here to mean that beliefs produce or generate passions, since he here clearly takes them as reasonings from causation. His point has to do with the way in which reasoning or belief can *influence* action, even though it does not originate motivation.

Hume's phrases like "actuating the will" and "influence on the passions" are vague. I take Hume to be saying that beliefs actuate the will and influence the passions in the way mere ideas don't, either by the beliefs giving direction to the already-existing motivating passions, or by the beliefs concerning the existence of objects for which we have a passionate attraction or repulsion, and so causing actions when they are paired with those passions. It is fortunate that ideas of idle fictions don't have this influence, according to Hume, because, having various thoughts about all sorts of good and bad things in the world, we would never be at rest (T 1.3.10.2). We would find ourselves acting in ways to pursue things that don't exist or in ways that simply cannot achieve the ends we really want. Dennis desires a career as a singer and envisions himself in idle moments as having an excellent voice when he actually has a mediocre one. Acting on his imaginings will likely lead to frustration, but the point is that if Dennis is only entertaining ideas, he will not be moved to pursue the actions that lead to a singing career, since the ideas have not reached the force and vivacity to qualify as belief and influence action.

Hume's next paragraph says:

> As belief is almost absolutely requisite to the exciting our passions [sic], so the passions in their turn are very favourable to belief; and not only such facts as convey agreeable emotions, but very often such as give pain, do upon that account become more readily the objects of faith and opinion. A coward, whose fears are easily awaken'd, readily assents to every account of danger he meets with; as a person of a sorrowful and melancholy disposition is very credulous of every thing, that nourishes his prevailing passion. When any affecting object is presented, it gives the alarm, and excites immediately a degree of its proper passion; especially in persons who are naturally inclined to that passion. This emotion passes by an easy transition to the imagination; and diffusing itself over our idea of the affecting object, makes us form that idea with greater force and vivacity, and consequently assent to it, according to the precedent system.
>
> (T 1.3.10.4)

Hume describes here a causal interaction between passions and beliefs. To say that belief is requisite to excite a passion doesn't mean that the belief creates the motivating passion, but that it brings to mind an object appropriate for a passion one possesses. For instance, my liking for Belgian chocolate is not created by my belief that there are Belgian chocolates in this box, but my liking is excited by my coming to believe that there are chocolates here in this box. This is an example of what Hume means when he says that reason contributes to motivation when it "excites a passion by informing us of the existence of something which is a proper object of it." Similarly, beliefs excite passions by producing motivation to particular actions in view of passionate dispositions one possesses; so, for instance, a belief activates a person's disposition to fear, when a particular event is brought before the mind. A timid person is disposed to fear public speaking and that disposition is awakened when she is called upon to give a presentation on her work. Passions also can excite beliefs by contributing to the boosting of force and vivacity in an idea. What this means is that the point at which one accepts an idea as a belief, the point at which the vivacity of the idea becomes strong enough to constitute belief, can be influenced by the passionate dispositions one possesses. So, the cowardly or fearful person needs less evidence to be convinced that something bad is about to occur, while the brave or confident person requires more evidence before assenting to beliefs about present or future dangers. Furthermore, what one takes pleasure in and the degree to which one finds it pleasurable are also a function of one's passions, or what I have elsewhere called one's "passionate nature."[28] Someone disposed to be fearful of heights may not

---

[28] Some years ago, I argued that the passages here discussed from T 1.3.10. show us that Hume takes seriously the notions of personality, character, passionate nature, and dispositions of an agent. The opening phrase, "belief is almost absolutely requisite to exciting our passions" can be read in this context as indicating that our passionate nature, when coupled with beliefs, generates individual passions, which are motives for particular objects. Beliefs alone don't produce motives, but beliefs in conjunction with the dispositions of the person, do. The relevant texts (from 1.3.10 and 2.3.3), considered together, support the conclusion that Hume's theory of motive formation contains the following elements.

enjoy the view from the top of a cliff in the way that someone with no such fearful tendency will.[29] This view, I will show, is supported by the second *Enquiry* and the *Dissertation*.

Hume also writes that the passions of admiration and surprise affect beliefs in the way the other passions do and that

> among the vulgar, quacks and projectors meet with a more easy faith upon account of their magnificent pretensions, than if they kept themselves within the bounds of moderation. The first astonishment, which naturally attends their miraculous relations, spreads itself over the whole soul, and so vivifies and enlivens the idea, that it resembles the inferences we draw from experience. (T 1.3.10.4)

Surprise is produced by an idea of something unexpected or fantastic (highly unusual) being presented to the mind, an idea which Hume thinks we find agreeable. The feeling of surprise enlivens the initial idea and makes it resemble beliefs acquired by inference ("the inferences we draw from experience," here again, synonymous with beliefs). The admiration of which Hume here writes is not the feeling of calm admiration of character that he describes in connection with our moral sensibilities,

> The production of motivating passions requires, first, a representation with a belief in its truth: I have the idea of standing at the edge of a steep cliff; this could be an idea of imagination, but experience and reason in some cases turn this idea into a belief. The production of a motivating passion requires, second, a particular disposition on the part of the believer: Since I am disposed to be fearful of heights, susceptible to vertigo, etc., the representation of standing at the edge of the cliff is for me associated with the idea of discomfort. As a consequence of this association, when I come to the belief that I am actually standing at that location, I feel fear. But if I don't have these tendencies, but others, I might associate the idea of being at the cliff's edge with pleasure. Then I would feel joy at the view or at the sense of freedom I get standing there. Alternatively, I could be the sort of person who has no particular association with this experience and, therefore, little emotional reaction at all to the belief, considering my situation all very calmly and coolly, matter-of-factly, as we might say, as though I were only gathering information. *The representation of the situation without a contribution from my emotional constitution doesn't affect me.* (Radcliffe 1999: 113)

I have not changed my mind about this, but I have changed my emphasis. Our natural dispositions do enter into a determination of what each of us finds pleasurable or painful and how much. I have also argued here, however, that Hume's theory of the influence of belief and passion goes like this. The idea of a pleasurable or painful object originates a passion when coupled with the natural instincts, a passion that can, on the occasion that one comes to believe there is a means of acquiring that object, be aroused and thus lead to action. Reference to idiosyncratic background dispositions explains why we take pleasure in what we do.

[29] The astute discussion in Saul Traiger (2005) of Hume's analysis of the case of the man hung in an iron cage from a high precipice is relevant here. Even though the man ought to feel secure with the support provided by the cage based on past experience with iron, Hume says that the "circumstances of depth and descent strike so strongly upon him, that their influence cannot be destroy'd by the contrary circumstances of support and solidity..." (T 1.3.13.10). The imagination "runs away" and "excites a passion proportion'd to it." And the passion then enlivens the imagined idea of descent and danger, which influences the passion, which increases the vivacity of the idea, and so on. Traiger explains this case not as an opposition between reason and passion, but as a case where the passions influence ideas of the imagination, so that passions plus imagination are set against reason (2005: 108–9). Traiger's interpretation of the case is consistent with my reading on the influence of passions on belief.

but instead refers to our reaction to those about whom or by whom fantastic and wonderful claims are made. So, a person may acquire a lively idea of the wonders of a new anti-aging cosmetic as its purported virtues are detailed in an advertisement accompanied by "before" and "after" pictures. Another may be caught off-guard by the vague image of a specter in the allegedly haunted house and believe all of a sudden that she has seen a ghost.[30]

So, we do have some beliefs that are not products of reason. That an idea can be enlivened by astonishment and "resemble the inferences we draw from experience" Hume calls a "mystery" that he intends to explore (T 1.3.10.4). This circumstance doesn't settle the debate over what Hume means when he argues that reason by itself cannot motivate, as far as I can see. Even if there are some beliefs not produced by reasoning that resemble those that are produced by reasoning, the products of reason are still beliefs, that is, enlivened ideas. So, it is still plausible to think that in saying reason on its own is not a motive, Hume means that the products of reason are not motives on their own. Furthermore, I think the evidence suggests that on Hume's theory, no beliefs motivate, produced by reasoning or not, because beliefs are representations, and representations are inert without conations. So, for instance, my belief that I have seen a ghost motivates me because of fear, which is likely intensified by the element of surprise.

2.4.4 Later Hume Texts: Taste as the Source of Motivation

My argument so far has been that beliefs, for Hume in the *Treatise*, require either instincts, which are general in human nature, or background dispositions, which are specific to persons, to generate the passions that motivate (see Radcliffe 2008: 269–70, and Radcliffe 1999). This interpretation is corroborated by the *Enquiry Concerning the Principles of Morals* and the *Dissertations on the Passions*. In the second *Enquiry*, what Hume writes in Appendix 1 about the acquisition of ends confirms this understanding of the *Treatise*:

It appears evident, that the ultimate ends of human actions can never, in any case, be accounted for by *reason*, but recommend themselves entirely to the sentiments and affections of mankind, without any dependence on the intellectual faculties. Ask a man, *why he uses exercise*; he will answer, *because he desires to keep his health*. If you then enquire, why he desires health, he will readily reply, *because sickness is painful*. If you push your enquiries farther, and desire a reason, *why he hates pain*, it is impossible he can ever give any. This is an ultimate end, and is never referred to any other object. (EPM App 1.18–19)

---

[30] Don Garrett usefully analyzes Hume's discussion of miracles from the first *Enquiry* in such a way as to emphasize the "passionate mechanisms" that incline us to belief and to action; among them is "the direct tendency of the pleasant feelings of surprise and wonder associated with miracles to encourage belief in them" (Garrett 1997: 149). In the context of his discussion, Hume remarks how "the spirit of religion"—certainly a description of a type of passionate nature—can lead to loss of common sense and the discarding of human testimony which otherwise would have produced more credible beliefs (*Enquiry* 10.2).

Here Hume advances a positive description of the source of motives: they are produced by ultimate ends that are given by natural affections or instincts. He says explicitly in the next paragraph that "taste" is "the first spring or impulse to desire and volition:"

> Reason, being cool and disengaged, is no motive to action, and directs only the impulse received from appetite or inclination, by showing us the means of attaining happiness or avoiding misery: Taste, as it gives pleasure or pain, and thereby constitutes happiness or misery, becomes a motive to action, and is the first spring or impulse to desire and volition. From circumstances and relations, known or supposed, the former leads us to the discovery of the concealed and unknown: After all circumstances and relations are laid before us, the latter makes us feel from the whole a new sentiment of blame or approbation. (EPM, App. 1.21)

In the last sentence, Hume is referring to the origin of morality, which he thinks parallels the origin of ends valued in themselves. Reason reveals to us causal relations in the world, to which taste responds. Of course, we acquire beliefs when we comprehend these causal relations, but Hume doesn't say that therefore belief is productive of motives. Rather, he makes it clear that what he here calls "taste," whose products are affections or sentiments, is the pertinent capacity.[31]

The *Dissertation on the Passions* opens with the topic of how motivating passions are produced. We experience an immediately pleasurable or displeasurable physical sensation, or we experience a sensation agreeable or disagreeable to an already-existing passion. Upon these experiences we denominate objects as good or evil:

> 1. SOME objects produce immediately an agreeable sensation, by the original structure of our organs, and are thence denominated GOOD; as others, from their immediate disagreeable sensation, acquire the appellation of EVIL. Thus moderate warmth is agreeable and good; excessive heat painful and evil.
>
> Some objects again, by being naturally conformable or contrary to passion, excite an agreeable or painful sensation; and are thence called *Good* or *Evil*. The punishment of an adversary, by gratifying revenge, is good; the sickness of a companion, by affecting friendship, is evil. (Diss. 1.1–2)[32]

Then, Hume explains, "All good or evil, whence-ever it arises, produces various passions and affections, according to the light in which it is surveyed" (Diss. 1.3). Shortly after, he writes, "DESIRE arises from good considered simply; and AVERSION, from evil. The WILL exerts itself, when either the presence of the good or absence of the evil may be attained by any action of the mind or body" (Diss. 1.6).[33] The *Dissertation*'s explanation of what we find good and evil appeals either to the

---

[31] "Taste" is usually associated with the affective faculty by which qualities are judged in terms of beauty. See, for example, Costelloe (2013: 430). Here, however, Hume is using it in a broader sense, to include value judgments of all kinds that depend upon pleasurable and painful human responses.

[32] Although most of the *Dissertation* is extracted from *Treatise* Book 2, this passage is unique to the *Dissertation*.

[33] This point is also made at T 2.3.9.7.

"original structure" of our organs or to passions that we already possess. The examples Hume gives of passions already possessed are instances of the original instincts mentioned in the *Treatise*. Because what we find good or evil depends upon a prior physical or emotional constitution that determines the impressions we experience, it would be an inaccurate description of Hume's account here to say that the *original* source of the motivation consists in ideas of good and evil, or that these ideas produce motives on their own.

So, in the *Dissertation*, when Hume traces good and evil either to the structure of the organs or to passions we already possess, he means to trace our perceptions (of good and evil) to a sentimental capacity, a capacity to feel pleasure and pain. When that capacity is actualized and pleasure or pain is experienced, motives are generated. Ideas of good and evil appear to be consistently motivating because our sentimental responses to objects or to our ideas of objects determine whether they are good or bad for us. But there is no reason to think that the ideas are motivating. The force originates with the feelings of pleasure and pain themselves, which yield passions for the objects that cause these impressions.

To summarize, Hume's argument that reason is not a motive to any action of the will is not an argument that the faculty of reason or the activity of reasoning is not a motive (although neither is, and it's not clear that anyone thought they were). Rather, it is an argument that representations, or ideas and beliefs, are not motives—productive of passions or actions—on their own. Beliefs do play a role in the production of motivation, but they cannot generate motives without instincts, which are actual passions on Hume's view, or without passionate dispositions. The *Treatise* account emphasizes the role of instincts general to human nature—for instance, the inclination to natural good and away from natural evil, benevolence, and love of life—as essential to the production of motives. Hume also references there, however, passionate tendencies particular to individuals, which also interact with belief to produce passions and actions. The second *Enquiry* and the *Dissertation* stress taste as the source of motivation, which determines in what individuals take enjoyment or find disagreeable. The reference to taste is akin to the particular passionate tendencies of persons that are discussed in the *Treatise*. Hume, however, is not offering different accounts in his different texts, as far as I can see. The narrative in the later works is simply an account of motivation that focuses on why individuals with the same instincts have differing motivations and do different actions.

2.4.5 Some Further Observations on this Interpretation

1. Is the view I have attributed to Hume plausible as a theory of the source of motivation? The theory that motivation requires a contribution from our sensibility or taste seems plausible when the beliefs to which we respond motivationally concern facts that cause psychological pleasures or pains, like that an object is a certain color, or that an action improves the quality of life for a child. For example, because gray appeals to me and not to you, I have a desire

to buy the gray coat rather than the green one, but you do not. Because we both have concerns for the quality of life of children, we're both disposed to contribute to the United Nations Children's Fund. In these cases, it's plausible to think that motivation has an origin in taste, since original affections (in addition to factual beliefs) are necessary to produce motivation one way or another. Beliefs with such content seem different, however, from beliefs that concern physically pleasant or unpleasant objects. At first glance, feeling physical sensations seems to require no appeal to anything that could be called "taste" (instincts, dispositions, or prior sentiments), in the way feeling mental pleasures or pains—that is, passions—does. This fact makes it plausible to think that what Hume means to say is what he appears to say in the *Treatise*: that our beliefs about which objects will be sources of pleasure and pain are motivating *on their own*, with no appeal to other affectionate states. But this appearance is misleading. It is misleading because our *tolerance* for the intensity of physical sensations is a matter of individual physical constitution, which *is* analogous to taste. At what point the intensity of heat, for instance, becomes uncomfortable can vary from person-to-person. This consideration explains Hume's attributing in the *Dissertation* the formation of a motive to the structure of the organs, or to our passions. And then it does make sense to say that something like taste plays a part in determining even when physical sensations become pleasurable or painful.

2. This interpretation of Hume on why reason alone does not motivate explains the differences in actions among people who each take pleasure in the same thing. People may desire the same object, but find it differentially pleasurable; those who find it more pleasurable desire it more strongly. The explanation does not end there. Some persons find an object a greater source of pleasure than others, or some persons develop a stronger desire for the appealing object than others, these are explained by further principles. The explanation makes reference to other variations among persons that are variations in the non-cognitive, affective sides of their natures. Your and my differing degrees of affection for cilantro is due to our respective dispositions to taste it differently (it tastes soapy to you, but not to me) or to our respective dispositions to react differently to the taste. So, I am motivated to use cilantro in my cooking and you are not. As I've said, an adequate interpretation of Hume's theory of motivation must explain not only how motives originate, but how some motives lead to action and others do not, and this interpretation provides that.

3. Hume's reference to "active principles" is clearly a reference to those features of human nature that are capable of initiating action.[34] Passion and "morality" are

---

[34] One suggestion is that "active" in this discussion means simply to have some kind of causal power. This option cannot be right. To be active can't mean simply to have a causal power, if reason is inactive. Even reason has a causal power—to boost the vivacity of an idea and so cause belief. Furthermore, that an

active principles for Hume. My suggestion has been that, on Hume's theory, all activity derives ultimately from the natural instincts, which prompt us to pursue things that fall under certain descriptions—hunger motivates acquiring food; benevolence motivates action for the good of another person; love of life motivates self-preservation; the instinct for pleasure motivates us toward objects that are pleasurable; and so on. An idea or belief coupled with an instinct can produce another passion, which can also motivate to action, but an idea or belief without an active principle like an instinct or another passion is simply inert. Why, however, would Hume say that the ancestry of an active principle must always include active principle? I think the answer is that experience has shown us that an animating power does not originate on its own. Its source is consistently in something that is essentially dynamic by nature. To argue that motivation can arise on its own without an active source in nature requires appeal to another active source or agency beyond nature, which is not countenanced by Hume's approach.

4. An advantage of this reading of Hume on inert reason is that it emphasizes clearly Hume's disagreements with the moral rationalists, against whom his *Treatise* Book 3 arguments concerning morality's derivation are directed. Clarke and Cudworth saw the content of morality as necessary and immutable and so discerned by reason as opposed to the senses or feelings. Cudworth depicted human motivation toward the Good as an exercise of reason, passions, and free will at the same time (Cudworth 1731/1838: 171–5). Clarke described morality as dependent on certain necessary relations in the universe, such as God's superiority to humans. Certain actions are fit and others unfit in light of these relations; so, for instance, there is an eternal obligation to worship God. Clarke also thought that morality provides reasons for action, although he didn't believe that human beings would be moved by those reasons, without passions (Clark 1724: 145). I have also argued that the rationalists were committed to depicting passions as representations of goodness and evil.

Part of Hume's answer to the rationalists is to argue that representations do not motivate on their own. Another part of his response is to say, as he does in the *Dissertation on the Passions*, that we are motivated toward good and repelled by evil, *only* because our representations of what is good and what is evil (and so, what in fact is valuable for us) are founded upon sentiments determined by the human physical constitution, or by human psychology. Our ideas of good and evil (moral or natural) generate passions for certain objects because an internal capacity, taste, constitutes what is good or bad for us (and because we are naturally disposed to good and away from evil). So, the

---

inactive principle cannot be founded on an active is trivially true, if to be active means to cause something and to be inactive means to cause nothing. For then nothing at all could be founded on an inactive principle.

dispute between Hume and the moral rationalists is not just over how we are motivated, for example, whether we are motivated by reason, whether we are motivated by beliefs about objects as sources of pleasure, or whether we are motivated only by sentiments. The dispute between Hume and the moral rationalists is over whether morality is constituted by necessary rational relations or by contingent internal taste. This is a point highlighted by the reading of Hume I have offered here, on which beliefs about sources of pleasure and pain do not have motivating force in themselves, but trace their force to sentiments that depend on taste.[35]

---

[35] I have been asked (more than once) how my interpretation can be squared with Hume's claim that "any thing may produce any thing" (T 1.3.15.1). First, of course, not anything *does* produce anything, on Hume's view, or we'd never be able to sort out any causal connections, and Hume would not be able to make the claim that reason alone does not produce passion or action. However, I take it that the question is more pressing for my interpretation because I include logical considerations—that a representation is not a conation, for instance—among the claims of my argument. Hume continues at T 1.3.15.1, "Creation, annihilation, motion, reason, volition; all these may arise from one another, or from any other object we can imagine." Yet his declaration that an active principle can never be founded on an inactive is a general principle about possible causes of action or volition. It surely looks at odds with his claim that motion and volition can arise from anything. However, when something is defined functionally, as mental states are, we can make non-experiential claims about some of their causal relations, since functions *are* causal relations. I say more about this in CHAPTER 4.

3

Belief
Some Complications

I have argued that beliefs are not motivating on their own, for Hume, in part, because they are ideas, which are representations, and representations do not initiate impulses. My argument is predicated, of course, on Hume's view of beliefs as ideas and of ideas as representations. But a reader might wonder whether my characterization of a Humean idea, as distinct from a passion (or impression of reflection) in virtue of its representational function, anachronistically imposes upon Hume a theory of mind familiar in contemporary philosophy. Furthermore, Hume himself shows an ambivalence in his characterization of belief, emphasizing the vivaciousness of the believed idea in one account, and the sentiment that belief involves in another. Some commentators speculate that Hume changed his position after writing the *Treatise*, and some suggest, further, that the change shows that he came to regard belief as a sentiment. Moreover, on a third reading of Hume, belief can be understood as a disposition to action, which accounts for the durability of beliefs over time. Naturally, the respective implications of these readings are important for Hume's practical philosophy.[1]

In this chapter, I defend my reading of ideas in Hume's philosophy as mental representations distinct from impressions of reflection. I also argue that Hume changes his characterization of belief from the *Treatise* to the first *Enquiry*, but in neither account does he identify belief with a sentiment. Rather, belief in the *Treatise* is a vivacious idea, and, in the *Enquiry*, it is an idea or conception with a unique sentimental feature ("solidity"), which is important to the contribution it makes to the production of action. I also consider the way in which many contemporary Humeans distinguish belief and desire—by their opposite "directions of fit"—and to what degree this view is derived from Hume. Finally, I address some difficult objections that have been directed at Hume's argument, that reason, considered as belief, does not motivate. These criticisms concern what it is to be an "object of reason" in Hume's discussion.

---

[1] As I noted earlier, if belief is a sentiment, then it is possibly a motive (see Sandis 2012: 206–8, and Stroud 1977: 158–61).

3.1 Hume's Characterization of Ideas

I have suggested that Humean ideas are representations, but passions, impressions of reflection, are not. This sounds uncontroversial, but it raises questions about what sorts of mental states represent, and why. Often, for Hume, a mental representation signifies something by being a mental copy of what it signifies. Hume is most precise about representation early in Book 1, where he sets up the distinction between ideas and impressions and explicitly holds that simple ideas are *exact* representations (copies) of the simple impressions that precede them (T 1.1.1.7). He seems to imply that representation depends upon, or occurs through, resemblance:

> When I shut my eyes and think of my chamber, the ideas I form are exact representations of the impressions I felt; nor is there any circumstance of the one, which is not to be found in the other. In running over my other perceptions, I find still the same resemblance and representation. Ideas and impressions appear always to correspond to each other. (T 1.1.1.3)

And he asks, "For how can an impression represent a substance, otherwise than by resembling it?" (T 1.4.5.3).

Furthermore, when an idea represents an impression, he suggests that it does so by copying:

> Now since all ideas are deriv'd from impressions, and are nothing but copies and representations of them, whatever is true of the one must be acknowledg'd concerning the other... An idea is a weaker impression; and as a strong impression must necessarily have a determinate quantity and quality, the case must be the same with its copy or representative. (T 1.1.7.5)

At times, Hume suggests that ideas represent objects in addition to representing impressions. He writes, for example, that "Ideas always represent the Objects or impressions, from which they are deriv'd, and can never without a fiction represent or be apply'd to any other" (T 1.2.3.11). He also writes that "Ideas always represent their objects or impressions; and *vice versa*, there are some objects necessary to give rise to every idea" (T 1.3.14.6; see also T 1.3.7.5, T 1.3.9.12).[2]

However, the distinction between objects (external objects) and impressions may not carry much weight here, since Hume says that we cannot comprehend the difference between the two:

> ...as every idea is deriv'd from a preceding perception, 'tis impossible our idea of a perception, and that of an object or external existence can ever represent what are specifically different from each other. Whatever difference we may suppose betwixt them, 'tis still incomprehensible

---

[2] Further note: "When you wou'd any way vary the idea of a particular object, you can only encrease or diminish its force and vivacity. If you make any other change on it, it represents a different object or impression" (T 1.3.7.5). "The words or discourses of others have an intimate connexion with certain ideas in their mind; and these ideas have also a connexion with the facts or objects, which they represent" (T 1.3.9.12).

to us; and we are oblig'd either to conceive an external object merely as a relation without a relative, or to make it the very same with a perception or impression. (T 1.4.5.19)

When writing about the origin of the idea of space, he says that a compounded impression from sight and touch "represents" extension:

The idea of space is convey'd to the mind by two senses, the sight and touch; nor does anything ever appear extended, that is not either visible or tangible. That compound impression, which represents extension, consists of several lesser impressions, that are indivisible to the eye or feeling, and may be call'd impressions of atoms or corpuscles endow'd with colour and solidity.
(T 1.2.3.15)

In the same context, Hume talks once of the senses representing, which might be read as the notion that impressions represent: "The only defect of our senses is, that they give us disproportion'd images of things, and represent as minute and uncompounded what is really great and compos'd of a vast number of parts" (T 1.2.1.5). What is clear from these various remarks is that at least some mental states represent by copying and resembling their original sources. (Copying and resembling are themselves concepts requiring some de-mystification, but I do not think I need pursue those notions here.)

The details of how representations come about are actually more complicated, however. Rather surprisingly, impressions of sensation appear to be representations, as evidenced in several of Hume's claims above. Hume insists more than once that impressions and ideas resemble in every other particular except in their degree of force and vivacity (T 1.1.1.3, T 1.1.7.5, T 1.3.7.5). This thesis about impressions and ideas seems to imply that if one is a representational state, then so is the other. However, *if* representation on the part of perception occurs by copying its perceptual source, and thereby resembling it, impressions cannot be representations. Hume says as much when he says that impressions are "original or copied from no precedent perception" (EHU 2.9, n. 1).[3] It might seem that impressions of sensation copy and thereby represent non-perceptual, external causes. But this is problematic, since Hume notes: (1) that impressions of sensation arise from unknown causes; and (2) that we are unable to make out any coherent distinction between ideas of external objects and ideas of perceptions. Nevertheless, Don Garrett offers a rationale on Hume's behalf for the notion that impressions can be representations. He suggests that Hume recognizes representation without exact resemblance and without causal derivation, and that perceptions can represent not only by resemblance, but also in virtue of causal or functional roles that they play within the mind. So, for instance, inaccurate ideas can represent without exactly resembling, as when I have an idea of Mount Hood, without an idea of its particular terrain. And an idea of a future event

---

[3] See Cohon and Owen (1997: 54–5) for an argument that impressions are not representations.

represents the event, even though experience of the event has not directly caused the idea. Garrett also cites examples in Hume's writings of non-mental representations to show his commitment to a functional account of representation; so, for example, words represent facts, objects, and impressions (T 1.3.9.12, T 2.1.2.1) (Garrett 2015: 72–3). Applying Garrett's account to the case of impressions of sensation, Hume could consistently say that simple sensations represent the qualities of objects (color, shape, odor, etc.) and that complex sensations represent objects, not by copying, but by functioning in ways that signify the presence of those qualities or objects, whether or not those qualities or objects cause the sensations. Of course, when we think of those objects or their qualities, we have ideas of them, and those ideas either represent the impressions or the qualities of the things that have them.

My point here is that there is a way to see a continuity between impressions and ideas that makes sense (almost) of the thesis that impressions and ideas differ no other way, but in force and vivacity, since both can be representations. (I say "almost" because impressions will always differ from ideas in that impressions are not derived from other impressions, as ideas are.) Crucial to the distinction between belief (vivacious ideas) and passions is that beliefs function as representations that are true or false, while passions function as conations, which do not represent and are not true or false. Yet, given that impressions sometimes function as representations, and given that ideas are representations, does it follow that truth and falsity apply to non-believed ideas and impressions? No: being a representation is necessary, but not sufficient to being assessable as true or false. First, Hume's discussion of truth invokes representation by copying, as when he says that passions cannot be true or false because to be opposed "to truth and reason" consists in "the disagreement of ideas, consider'd as copies, with those objects, which they represent" (T 2.3.3.5). Second, truth makes reference to belief: "the act of the mind exceeds not a simple conception; and the only remarkable difference, which occurs on this occasion, is, when we join belief to the conception, and are perswaded of the truth of what we conceive" (T 1.3.7.5, n. 20).

3.2 Hume's Characterization of Belief

3.2.1 Belief as a Lively Idea

Following upon the discussion of probability, and within the discussion of causal reasoning in the *Treatise*, Hume includes a section entitled, "Of the component parts of our reasonings concerning cause and effect" (T 1.3.4). In three subsequent sections, he discusses the impressions involved in causal reasoning, the transition from impression to idea, and the ideas themselves. The third of these sections, on ideas, is entitled, "Of the nature of the idea or belief" (T 1.3.7), and is immediately followed by a section, "Of the causes of belief." Discussing the causes of belief at this point seems odd, given that Hume has already discussed in detail the causal process that produces belief, in the first six sections of Part 3 of Book 1.[4]

I think the question Hume aims to answer in his *general* account of belief formation (T 1.3.4) is how we come to have beliefs in matters of fact about the world, when they obviously require evidence from experience, and impressions are momentary, but beliefs concern enduring circumstances. I continue to believe that eating raw broccoli will cause me indigestion, even though I have not recently tried it. I believe that the leaves will turn colors and fall off the trees this autumn, even though I have not experienced the future. Hume's psychological theory explains what prompts us to adopt beliefs whose scope is wider than the experiences on which they are based. He argues that only one of the three philosophical relations of objects known by experience—identity, relations of time and place, and causation—can take us beyond present experience, namely, causation (T 1.3.2.2, T 1.3.6.7). In his analysis of causal reasoning, Hume focuses on a non-rational principle of human nature that moves us beyond present experience, which is custom and habit. The explanation why a person with no experience, brought full-grown into the world, has no grounds on which to predict how one rolling billiard ball will affect another is that she has no basis for forming a habit of association between the one event and any other. Custom and habit allow the human mind to forge a mental connection between ideas that have no conceptual connection, and sometimes habitual connections lead to belief. Therefore, the disposition to rely on custom is a prerequisite to causal reasoning. Causal inferences include moving from the present to the past, but in belief formation, the mind moves beyond the present moment to the future—not because deductive-style reasoning finds the connection between ideas, but because custom creates the association. The roles of custom and imagination in this process suggest that the process of causal reasoning is non-rational. However, for Hume, it qualifies as a process of reasoning, since it involves inference. Both demonstration and causal reasoning are, for Hume, inferential processes of reason, even though the latter draws upon non-rational elements.[5] This point is reinforced in Book 3 of the *Treatise* when Hume argues that morality is not derived from reason, and he proceeds by showing that it is neither a relation of ideas known by demonstration nor a matter of fact discovered by causal reasoning. Both kinds of inferential thought, then, come under the purview of "reason" in the sense relevant to the discussion of motivation.

I think that the more particular account of the causes of belief that occurs in T 1.3.8, after Hume has discussed the nature of belief in T 1.3.7, is designed to emphasize a certain feature in the process of belief formation: the feature referenced

---

[4] As I discuss what goes on in the main text of the *Treatise*, I exclude the Appendix, which was written a bit later, and which I consider after discussing the main text.

[5] See Owen (1999: Ch. 6), for a nuanced view of probable or causal reasoning. Owen argues that probable reasoning is not an activity of the "faculty of reason, conceived of as the discovery and use of intermediate ideas which explain the transition" (ibid.: 132). I agree with this interpretation, of course, but Hume does not always mean by "reason" the faculty so defined.

in Hume's definition of a belief as "... *a lively idea related to or associated with a present impression*"... (T 1.3.7.5). Hume has previously written that "The idea of an object is an essential part of the belief of it, but not the whole. We conceive many things, which we do not believe..." (T 1.3.7.1); and,

> When I think of God, when I think of him as existent, and when I believe him to be existent, my idea of him neither increases nor diminishes. But as 'tis certain there is a great difference betwixt the simple conception of the existence of an object, and the belief of it, and as this difference lies not in the parts or composition of the idea, which we conceive; it follows, that it must lie in the *manner*, in which we conceive it. (T 1.3.7.2)

Since what an unbelieved idea and what a believed idea represent can be the same, the only way a belief can be distinguished from an idea merely entertained is by a phenomenal dimension:

> When you wou'd any way vary the idea of a particular object, you can only encrease or diminish its force and vivacity. If you make any other change on it, it represents a different object or impression."... [B]elief... can only bestow on our ideas an additional force and vivacity. (T 1.3.7.5)

Hume's account is a response to the theory of belief defended by other early moderns, such as Descartes and Locke, according to which a belief has a different content and structure from an idea merely conceived.[6] Hume aims to persuade readers that belief is an idea enlivened or vivified by an impression or experience; that the present impression is necessary to the production of belief; that it (typically[7]) operates after a number of past conjunctions of impressions; and that once the impression enlivens the idea, nothing more is needed.[8] A belief, according to this account in the *Treatise*, is a vivacious complex idea formed as a result of a mental habit of associating experiences. Hume also insists that the relation to a present impression is integral to belief because beliefs are triggered by experiences or impressions after the mental habit is acquired. To borrow his own example, a person who walks to the edge of a deep river stops immediately; she needs no further experience to know that if she takes another step, she will fall into the water and drown. The current impressions trigger her belief that walking into deep water causes people to drown, although the belief itself is actually the product of causal associations already well entrenched.

---

[6] See Owen (1999: 147–74), and Bell (2002: 175–6). On Descartes and Hume on belief, see also Ainslie (2015b: 30–1).

[7] Hume countenances another way of coming to belief, which happens when emotions of wonder and amazement at fantastic claims boost the vivacity of an idea to the point of belief. This is the way Hume thinks people come to believe in miracles. I will briefly discuss this phenomenon in CHAPTER 6.

[8] Noting Hume's insistence on belief as a lively idea is another consideration explaining why Hume does not treat motivating passions as though they contain ideas of their objects. If they included ideas of their objects, they simply would *be* vivacious ideas, given that they are impressions and have more vivacity than ideas. Thus, some passions would be identified with beliefs. But Hume never suggests that passions might be beliefs.

When I look out the window to see what sort of day it is, and I find it pouring rain, I need no further information to conclude that I will get wet if I go out without an umbrella or a raincoat. The sight of the rain is a catalyst to my belief, but only because I am primed or disposed by prior experience to have the belief. So, when Hume defines a belief as a lively idea associated with a present impression, he has in mind that, even though all beliefs depend on prior conditioning, they can come to mind spontaneously in response to current experience. Custom, he says, operates in practical situations before we have time to reflect (T 1.3.8.7–17).

The liveliness of the idea we call belief is an essential feature in Hume's definition provided in the *Treatise*. A present impression is also crucial, since Hume explains that the present impression associated with an idea boosts the vivacity of that idea to the intensity of belief (T 1.3.8.1–17). Experiences always give a lift to their associated ideas. Consider the relation of contiguity that might hold between an impression and an idea. I have all sorts of ideas, vague much of the time, of my hometown, located half a continent away from where I now reside. When I get on a plane headed for that town, as I progress on the trip and look out the window of the plane, the ideas of the town I am soon to visit acquire a vivacity and detail that they typically lack in the life to which I am accustomed. The experience of locations contiguous to my hometown boosts the forcefulness of my ideas of the town as I reminisce. Resemblance has a similar effect: my seeing a picture of the Golden Gate Bridge enlivens my ideas of that bridge, and my travels across it.

The relation of causality does the same. Past experience has produced in me an association of cherry trees with white blossoms. When I am out on a walk in the springtime and see a tree in the distance arrayed in white blossoms, the vivacity of my impression is transferred to the associated idea of the cherry tree. The idea that this tree with white blossoms is a cherry tree, or that cherry trees have white blossoms, is lifted in vivacity to the status of belief. I still might entertain the idea that cherry blossoms are violet, perhaps in writing a science fiction tale about a world where nature behaves differently from nature in our world; but this fictional idea is less lively than my idea that cherry blossoms are white. The former is an idea of the imagination, according to Hume, and the latter is a belief. This explains how beliefs are the most vivacious ideas we experience, and only pale in comparison to impressions, from which they derive their vivacity.

I want to make two observations about Hume's treatment of belief in the main text of the *Treatise*. First (and this is not a new point), it is obviously an illustration of the principles of associationist psychology at work in Hume's theory of human nature. Hume writes elsewhere in the *Treatise* of mental states

changing phenomenological dimensions and converting into other perceptions. When we sympathize with others, our ideas of their pleasures and pains are converted into our own impressions of pleasure and pain—that is, the idea is infused with increased vivacity and transformed into an impression. (T 2.1.11.8)

The conversion of these ideas into impressions is explained by the force of the resembling relationship between ourselves and others, a relationship which Hume thinks intensifies our notions of others' feelings in proportion to the degree of similarity. Hume also writes about the transformation of one passion into another: " 'Tis a remarkable property of human nature, that any emotion, which attends a passion, is easily converted into it..." (T 2.3.4.2). (I address the topic of conversion of passions in CHAPTER 6.) Second, when Hume refers, in the text of the *Treatise*, to the "manner" in which we conceive an idea, he implies that he is referring to the force and vivacity of the idea, since he also claims that the only way to vary an idea of a particular object is by increasing or diminishing force and vivacity. Thus, ideas have representational content *and* force and vivacity. To believe is to increase the latter feature of an idea, and Hume's definition of belief as "a lively idea" is reinforced.

3.2.2 Belief as the Manner of Conception

As commentators have observed, by the time Hume writes the Appendix to the *Treatise* (21 months later), he already displays doubts and expresses second thoughts about his account of belief in the main text.[9] In the Appendix, Hume professes to improve upon the way he has presented some of his theses, and he immediately revisits the topic of belief. He writes there that few have asked about the nature of belief that "arises from the relation of cause and effect." "Either the belief is some new idea, such as that of *reality* or *existence,* which we join to the simple conception of an object, or it is merely a peculiar *feeling* or *sentiment*" (T App. 2). He eliminates the former possibility, as he earlier did in the text, and then concludes,

> that belief consists merely in a certain feeling or sentiment; in something, that depends not on the will, but must arise from certain determinate causes and principles, of which we are not masters. When we are convinc'd of any matter of fact, we do nothing but conceive it, along with a certain feeling, different from what attends the mere *reveries* of the imagination. And when we express our incredulity concerning any fact, we mean, that the arguments for the fact produce not that feeling.   (T App. 2)

To the question whether this feeling of belief is unique and original or whether it can be explained in terms of more general principles, Hume responds that the feeling of belief approaches near to impressions in force and vivacity. Presumably, then, the sentiment of belief can be understood in terms of the force and vivacity possessed by other mental states; it is not original. He continues that there is no way to evade this conclusion, except to assert "that belief... does not modify the conception, and render it more present and intense: It is only annex'd to it, after the same manner that *will* and *desire* are annex'd to particular conceptions of good and pleasure" (T App. 4). But, Hume continues, belief is not a separate, distinct impression attending

---

[9] See, for instance, Bell (2002); Broackes (2002); and Owen (1999: 147–74).

"every distinct idea or conception of matter of fact"; it is instead a modification of the manner in which ideas are conceived (T App. 4–7).

Hume's argument that this is so contains four considerations, the first of which is most important: experience shows us that reasoning is an operation of thoughts or ideas; "and however those ideas may be vary'd to the feeling, there is nothing ever enters into our *conclusions* but idea, or our fainter conceptions" (T App. 4). Upon hearing a voice with which I am acquainted coming from another room, as it were, the impression of the person's voice conveys my thoughts to the person and all of the surrounding objects.

> I paint them out to myself as existent at present... These ideas take faster hold of my mind, than the ideas of an enchanted castle. They are different to the feeling; but there is no distinct or separate impression attending them... Their customary connexion with the present impression, varies them and modifies them in a certain manner, but produces no act of the mind distinct from this peculiarity of conception. (T App. 4)

Here, Hume affirms that this belief is a product of inductive reasoning, which results in the promotion of the vivacity of ideas, but not in an additional, distinct sentiment.[10] I also want to note that although Hume says in the passage from T App. 2 that belief "consists in a feeling or sentiment," it is clear from the context and the considerations he notes at T App. 4 that he takes belief to be a firm conception, or an idea that feels a particular way. I think he does not mean to classify belief as a sentiment, but to say that it is distinguished from other ideas by its sentimental aspect.

So, Hume concludes that belief is distinguished from the simple conception of an idea by a sentiment, and this sentiment is "*a firmer conception, or faster hold, that we take of the object*" (T App. 8). Thus far, it looks as though his account in the Appendix does not differ significantly from the main text in emphasizing that believing is the manner of conceptualizing an object, not a feeling that can be separated from the concept believed. It would be credible to think that the kind of mental state with which Hume identifies belief is an idea and that the distinguishing feature of belief is the idea's firmness, which ideas that are not beliefs lack. It would also be reasonable to think that the "firmness and faster hold" of belief are still to be identified with what is typically called "force and vivacity." However, Hume's additions and corrections to the main text of the *Treatise*, which appear in the Appendix following his clarifications, do indicate a change of heart about certain details, and reveal a reversal within the Appendix itself. In his corrections, he implies that the manner or feeling of belief is something *other than* his ordinary notion of force and vivacity at work elsewhere in his psychology. He professes to have "considerable

---

[10] The other three considerations in Hume's argument include: (2) that there is no need to multiply suppositions to explain the difference between belief and conception; (3) that we can explain the causes of the firm conception, and this exhausts the whole subject of belief in a matter of fact; and (4) that the firm conception by itself explains the effects of belief on the passions and imagination.

difficulty" explaining the manner in which a believed idea feels differently from other ideas, although he still maintains that a belief *is* an idea. He inserts the following into the section of the *Treatise* entitled, "Of the nature of the idea or belief":

> ... an opinion or belief is nothing but an idea, that is different from a fiction, not in the nature, or the order of its parts, but in the *manner* of its being conceiv'd. But when I wou'd explain this *manner*, I scarce find any word that fully answers the case, but am oblig'd to have recourse to every one's feeling, in order to give him a perfect notion of this operation of the mind. An idea assented to *feels* different from a fictitious idea, that the fancy alone presents to us: And this different feeling I endeavour to explain by calling it a superior *force*, or *vivacity*, or *solidity*, or *firmness*, or *steadiness*. This variety of terms, which may seem so unphilosophical, is intended only to express that act of the mind, which renders realities more present to us than fictions, causes them to weigh more in the thought, and gives them a superior influence on the passions and imagination. Provided we agree about the thing, 'tis needless to dispute about the terms. (T 1.3.7.7)[11]

It now sounds as though the feeling of belief *is* original, rather than something explainable in terms of more general principles.[12] Even though Hume references "force and vivacity," he indicates that his terms may not capture the distinctive feeling of belief. The conjecture that Hume has altered his view here is corroborated when, toward the end of the Appendix, he corrects a few errors. In one case, he writes:

> where I say, that two ideas of the same object can only be different by their different degrees of force and vivacity. I believe there are other differences among ideas, which cannot properly be comprehended under these terms. Had I said, that two ideas of the same object can only be different by their different *feeling*, I shou'd have been nearer the truth. (T App. 22)

In the *Enquiry Concerning Human Understanding*, after Hume sets up the skeptical problem in Section 4 concerning how the understanding, or reason, can yield conclusions about causes in nature, he proceeds in Section 5, Part 1, to explain that custom is the source of these beliefs. At the end of that part, he tells the reader that he is about to consider the nature of belief, but that his remarks will be speculative and uncertain. He writes that this part is not for those whose tastes run contrary to the speculative sciences, and that such readers can neglect this discussion if they like. Evidently, it is not necessary to broach the topic of belief in order to understand the skeptical solution to doubt about causal connections. It is natural for the reader to take the tentativeness of Hume's presentation on belief in the *Enquiry* as evidence that his second thoughts in the *Treatise* did not resolve his concerns. Some have thought that Hume backs away from the associationist psychology on which the

---

[11] In the Norton and Norton edition, the Appendix additions are added to the main text, with the notation that they first appeared in the Appendix.

[12] The *Abstract* to the *Treatise* (1740) can be read consistently with this interpretation. There Hume concludes, "This belief joins no new idea to the conception. It only varies the manner of conceiving, and makes a difference to the feeling or sentiment. Belief, therefore, in all matters of fact arises only from custom, and is an idea conceived in a peculiar *manner*" (*Abstract* 22).

account of belief formation detailed in the *Treatise* depends, and that his diffidence is due to the fact that he has no satisfactory alternative to offer.[13]

Martin Bell argues, however, that Hume's bracketing of the belief discussion in the first *Enquiry* is part of an argumentative strategy designed to solve a problem created by the definition of belief as a vivacious idea, and to appeal to a broader, practically-minded audience (Bell 2002: 178–85). As Hume notes at T 1.3.9, resemblance and contiguity, as well as causality, might be sources of belief, since they also produce lively and forceful ideas by transference. His explanation why only the relation of causality is evocative of belief involves the notion that only impressions, ideas of memory, and what we associate with these ideas via causality are taken to indicate "realities" (T 1.3.9.3). "[T]he relation of cause and effect is requisite to perswade us of any real existence" (T 1.3.9.6). Yet, in a rather lengthy discussion somewhat later, Hume acknowledges that resemblance and contiguity do have some effect in augmenting conviction (T 1.3.9.8–15). Hume also indicates in this context that believed ideas, because they are indicative of existence, have a special feel: "a precise idea...takes its place in the imagination, as something solid and real, certain and invariable" (T 1.3.9.7). Bell notes, then, that there is a difference between "the conviction of any opinion," and "the vivacity of any conception." Again, it seems that Hume's theoretical attribute of force and vivacity does not capture what it is to believe (Bell 2002: 182). Thus, Bell persuasively argues, Hume's approach in the *Enquiry* is designed to avoid the question why resemblance and contiguity do not give rise to belief, and to emphasize the particular, indefinable feeling of belief with which we are all familiar by experience.

What does this approach in the first *Enquiry* involve, besides bracketing the discussion of the nature of belief? Hume writes there that "the difference between *fiction* and *belief* lies in some sentiment or feeling, which is annexed to the latter, not to the former..." (EHU 5.11). I want to make two observations about his claim. First, in referring to the difference in terms of "some sentiment or feeling," Hume reaffirms that the feeling of belief is distinctive, and not merely a version of force and vivacity—although he still observes that it is analogous to force and vivacity. On Bell's interpretation, this feeling is the product of connecting two instincts: instinctive belief in the real existence of the objects of ideas produced by causal inference, and the instinctive attitude of the mind toward the impressions of sense. Thus, the "instinctive manner of conception of the conclusion of causal inferences is also belief in real existence and matter of fact."[14] Second, the description here of the difference

---

[13] See, for instance, Millican (2002: 42–3). Stephen Buckle, who argues that many of the differences between the *Treatise* and the *Enquiry* constitute a significant change in Hume's philosophy, thinks that Hume downplays associationism in the *Enquiry*, in part because it had become "rather old hat to his readers" (2001: 147).

[14] Bell (2002: 182). As Bell notes, this instinct is not actually discussed until Section 5. There, it is subject to theoretical scrutiny, which it cannot withstand. Bell thinks that Hume should have discussed the second instinct where the bracketed section occurs.

between belief and non-belief as a sentiment "annexed" to an idea might suggest at first glance that belief is not an idea, but is actually a feeling contingently attached to an idea, a feeling that fictions lack (where "fiction" refers to a mental state, not to the fictitious object entertained). Hume has explicitly denied in *Treatise* App. 4 that belief consists in a special impression annexed to an idea, so the view expressed in EHU seems a significant change from the *Treatise*. I think, however, that the interpretation that Hume sees belief as a detachable feeling is unfounded.

A survey of Hume's references to "annexing" is helpful here. In Book 1 of the *Treatise*, Hume writes of ideas annexed to terms: "all general ideas are nothing but particular ones, annex'd to a certain term" (T 1.1.7.1); "we do not annex distinct and compleat ideas to every term we make use of" (T 1.1.7.14); "All abstract ideas are really nothing but particular ones, consider'd in a certain light; but being annex'd to general terms, they are able to represent a vast variety,..." (T 1.2.3.5). In Book 2, affections are annexed to each other: "I see no contradiction in supposing a desire of producing misery annex'd to love, and of happiness to hatred" (T 2.2.6.6). A sampling of uses from Book 3 include ideas annexed to ideas: "We come now to the second question we propos'd, viz. *Why we annex the idea of virtue to justice, and of vice to injustice?*" (T 3.2.2.23); "we annex the idea of property to the first possession, or to *occupation*" (T 3.2.3.6). Book 3 also has mental acts annexed to verbal acts, as in "*there is a peculiar act of the mind, annext to promises*" (T 3.2.5.7) (that is, an act of mind attending the words "I promise"); and there are sentiments annexed to action and character, as in, "*nature has annex'd a certain sentiment of pleasure to such a conduct*" (T 3.2.6.4) (that is, we react with certain sentiments to the behavior of others). In the first *Enquiry*, apart from the discussion of belief, Hume also has ideas annexed to terms (EHU 2.9) and meanings annexed to words (EHU 7.29, note 17). In all these cases, Hume is referring to contingent attachments or relations, where relata many times remain distinct, but associated.

However, it is important to recognize that *sometimes* the relata become co-mingled. In the case of promising, for instance, the act of the mind and the words are *together* constitutive of promising; yet, the words could be uttered without the mental act attending it (as when a deception occurs). Hume treats belief in this way: the sentiment *along with* the idea are together constitutive of belief, but the idea can be conceived without the sentiment (as when the person is not convinced). When Hume explains in the *Enquiry*, as he did in the *Treatise*, that believing could not consist in our annexing an idea to an idea, his argument is that because "the mind has authority over all its ideas, it could voluntarily annex this particular idea to any fiction, and consequently be able to believe whatever it pleases; contrary to what we find by daily experience" (EHU 5.10). He concludes that it must be a sentiment that tells the difference between believing and merely entertaining an idea, since sentiments cannot be commanded as we please (EHU 5.11). The emphasis here is on the involuntary nature of belief, as opposed to imagination, by which simple ideas can be assembled in any configuration we choose. The point is not that the idea and the sentiment are distinct in belief, but that we cannot conjure the vivacious sentiment of belief at will. In fact, Hume repeats in the *Enquiry* that "the sentiment of belief is nothing but a conception more intense and steady than what attends the mere fictions of the imagination." He again calls it a manner of conception, explains how it arises from the relation of cause and effect, and argues that the enlivening of ideas by natural relations or principles of association is a general law (EHU 5.14–20).

To summarize my conclusions on Hume's view of belief to this point: his departures from the text of the *Treatise* in the Appendix and the first *Enquiry* do not consist in a modification to the classification of belief as an idea. Rather, he presents a change from the characterization of belief as a vivacious idea, with vivacity on a continuum with impressions, to belief as a steady conception or idea whose feeling cannot be captured in theoretical terms. He sometimes expresses this latter characterization of belief as a difference in "the manner of conception." Earlier in the *Treatise* text, Hume eschews the suggestion that belief is an idea annexed to an idea and, in the Appendix, that belief is an impression annexed to an idea. However, in the *Enquiry*, he seems to reverse course and writes that belief is a sentiment annexed to an idea. I have argued that this sentiment is not, however, separable from the idea and thus attachable at will to other ideas. A belief is an idea with a particular sentimental aspect. In earlier arguing that a belief is not a product of annexing an idea or a sentiment to another idea, Hume was emphasizing the non-voluntary aspect of belief, and that view remains in the *Enquiry*.[15]

3.2.3 More on Belief and Sentiment

Hume calls belief a "sentiment," both in the Appendix to the *Treatise* and in the first *Enquiry*, but what he means in so doing, I have argued, highlights the fact that the vivacity necessary to belief is involuntary. Still, I want to pursue this issue a bit further. Hume does, at times, in colloquial contexts rather than in technical ones, use "sentiment" to indicate a view, opinion, or belief, as in "as extension is always a number, according to the common sentiment of metaphysicians" (T 1.2.2.3). We often do the same in conversation, without actually thinking that views consist in feelings. If Hume does mean to say that belief is a sentiment (as opposed to an idea), then beliefs *might* be motives. Hume's argument (T 3.1.1–2) that morality must be derived from sentiment and not from reason—because reason alone does not motivate—implies, of course, that sentiments do motivate. However, as I have shown in CHAPTER 1, not all passions, which are sentiments, motivate; so, even if Hume were to classify belief simply or solely as a sentiment, this would not establish

---

[15] Justin Broackes points out that Hume says at times that belief is a sentiment; at other times, that it is an idea; and at other times, that it is a conception of an idea. The last characterization is ambiguous between the view that belief is a conception of an object and a conception of an idea of an object (2002, 195–7). I do not deal with this complication here, but see Broackes for further discussion.

that beliefs are in fact motives. Nonetheless, I have suggested that I do not think that Hume does mean to classify belief in this way, and here I add some additional considerations to my argument.

Hume never explicitly defines what a sentiment is, but his usages show that "sentiment" indicates those mental states consisting in reactions to, or feelings provoked by, ideas and experiences of objects and people. Hence, Hume frequently references the sentiment of morality, of beauty, of humanity, of pleasure, of approbation, and sometimes the sentiments of pride (T 2.3.9.4; Diss. 2.13), of humility (Diss. 2.13), of benevolence (EPM 2.22, App. 2.3), of disgust and hatred (EPM 5.1), of friendship and regard (EPM 5.43), of regard and esteem (EPM 5.47, 6.23), of desire and aversion (EPM 9.5), of affection and hatred (EPM 9.5), and of self-love (EPM 9.8). It looks as though sentiments are impressions of reflection, but at one point in the first *Enquiry* Hume refers to "outward or inward sentiment" (EHU 2.5), implying that sensations may be sentiments as well. In the *Treatise*, when Hume contrasts reason with sentiment, the contrast is between the function of the mind that deals with ideas and the function that produces impressions. Hume writes early in Book 3 that he will open his investigation concerning morality with the question, "*Whether 'tis by means of our ideas or impressions we distinguish betwixt vice and virtue, and pronounce an action blameable or praise-worthy?*" (T 3.1.1.3).

Obviously, if belief were identified with a sentiment, it would officially be an impression. Indeed, one might think Hume means to say this when he writes at T 1.3.8.12: "Thus all probable reasoning is nothing but a species of sensation. 'Tis not solely in poetry and music, we must follow our taste and sentiment, but likewise in philosophy." However, he continues:

When I am convinc'd of any principle, 'tis only an idea, which strikes more strongly upon me. When I give the preference to one set of arguments above another, I do nothing but decide from my feeling concerning the superiority of their influence.

The point here is that probable reasoning is dependent on an impression, but this dependency does not imply that the belief *is* the impression. Belief is actually dependent on impressions in several ways. First, a series of successive impressions of objects must condition an observer to expect one impression to follow another. Second, a feeling of anticipation or expectation, which is an impression of reflection, must be excited in the observer when the one type of impression has constantly followed the other (EHU 7.28–30).[16] Third, a new present impression of the first type

---

[16] This impression of reflection gives rise to an idea of necessary connection, a component idea in the idea of causation, which underlies any matter-of-fact belief. It is common to think that Hume's view is that there is no impression from which the idea of necessary connection arises, but he actually says that there is no single instance or experience (of an object or a mind) that produces the idea of necessary connection (EHU 7.30). It hails instead from a repeated conjunction of experiences that produces a feeling of connectedness in the observers. Don Garrett also describes the impression of necessary connection in Hume's account as an impression of reflection (Garrett 2015: 133).

that was experienced in the succession brings to mind the idea of the associated object, and that impression transfers its vivacity to the associated idea. Hume identifies belief with the resulting forceful idea, and not with the impressions or sentiments involved.

3.2.4 Belief as Dispositional

Some commentators have offered evidence that Hume's account of belief is, at least implicitly, a dispositional one. For instance, Louis Loeb argues that the dispositional reading is necessary to make sense of Hume's views on the justification of belief. He admits that Hume uses terms like "vivacity" and "liveliness" when describing beliefs, but at the same time, he also uses terms like "firmness," "solidity," and "steadiness" to typify them. Loeb argues that justification is a matter of the latter, rather than the former. His diagnosis of this ambivalence is one he takes from Stroud: that Hume uncritically accepts a theory of ideas from Locke, onto which he grafts his associationism, and thereby offers the "vivacious idea" view of belief (Stroud 1977: 9). Yet, says Loeb, he also moves toward a new, dispositional account, as he emphasizes the settled and steady nature of a belief state (Loeb 2002: 66–7). One puzzle in Hume's account of belief is that he writes as though all beliefs acquired by causal inference are justified, which seems to undermine the notion of justification altogether. On Loeb's reading, a belief for Hume is always steady and infixed, but not all beliefs have a consistent, steady influence on thought and action (ibid.: 60). Loeb argues that the answer to this puzzle lies in understanding a distinction between types of justification that Hume calls upon. To establish that a psychological mechanism produces beliefs, whether steady or infixed states, is to determine that they are justified, other things being equal (ibid.: 73–4). In another sense, however, not all beliefs are justified, even if causally acquired. Only those that fulfill the natural function of belief to have a steady influence on will and action are justified, all things considered. So, Loeb argues, the influence of first-order beliefs can become undermined, often by the presence of second-order beliefs that question their truth, and by other psychological circumstances as well (ibid.: 81).

Jennifer Smalligan Marušić argues that Hume needs the characterization of beliefs as occurrent ideas with a particular phenomenal dimension in order to explain how they exert their influence on action (2010: esp. 167–75). In some of the passages quoted above, Hume references firmness (or solidity) as a feeling, not as a dispositional feature, as when he asks, "*Whether this feeling be any thing but a firmer conception, or a faster hold, that we take of the object?*" (T App. 8). Furthermore, the similarity to impressions in terms of the phenomena of "forcefulness," "vivacity," "liveliness," "solidity," and "firmness" is crucial to Hume's explanation why beliefs have an effect on the direction of the passions and behavior, while mere conceptions do not. Marušić's account emphasizes that the defining features of beliefs for Hume must be detectable by introspection, since the identification of *which* belief explains an action must be a matter of correlation between the idea and the effect to which it contributes. Hence, the belief must be perceptible to the agent by its phenomenology in the way that a disposition, which consists of a complex of powers, could not be discernible by the way it feels (Marušić 2010: 163–7).

For the purposes of defending my interpretation on the role of beliefs in causing action in conjunction with a passion, it makes no difference whether beliefs are characterized as ideas or as dispositions. If beliefs are dispositions, for Hume, then they are dispositions to produce action under appropriate conditions, including when the appropriate desires are present. However, I think the evidence in favor of the reading that beliefs for Hume are occurrent states is strong, and is supported further by the fact that Hume never explicitly defines a belief dispositionally. The phenomenal features of belief highlighted in Marušić's account are crucial to understanding the dynamics of action causation, as I illustrate in Chapter 6. Furthermore, Hume's references to "solidity" and "firmness," on the one hand, as opposed to "liveliness," "force," and "vivacity," on the other, could be indicative of the point that I have already discussed: that belief involves a unique feeling not describable in the same terms Hume uses to describe distinctions between other mental states. Thus, the solidity or firmness of belief need not be cashed out in dispositional terms. Granted, it does seem desirable to say that I continue to believe that George Washington was the first President of the United States, even when I have no vivacious or "solid" ideas with that content, and am wondering instead whether I locked the door to my office. However, if someone were to ask me whether George Washington was the first President, those impressions would be a catalyst to the feeling of belief, and under normal conditions, I would experience the relevant ideas with the appropriate sentiment at that moment.

As I have argued in Chapter 2, Hume is willing to ascribe to individuals dispositions to believe certain matters of fact, and dispositions to feel certain passions. These dispositions explain why some people more readily believe matters of fact that others do not believe in the same circumstances. They also explain why, under the same set of conditions, some people experience hope and others fear. Here again, Hume's remarks in "Of the influence of belief" are relevant:

A coward, whose fears are easily awaken'd, readily assents to every account of danger he meets with; as a person of a sorrowful and melancholy disposition is very credulous of every thing, that nourishes his prevailing passion. When any affecting object is presented, it gives the alarm, and excites immediately a degree of its proper passion; especially in persons who are naturally inclined to that passion. This emotion passes by an easy transition to the imagination; and diffusing itself over our idea of the affecting object, makes us form that idea with greater force and vivacity, and consequently assent to it, according to the precedent system. (T 1.3.10.4)

On my reading, beliefs are not dispositions; but dispositions contribute to the production of particular beliefs and particular passions.

3.3 Is the "Direction-of-Fit" Argument Derived from Hume?

John Bricke suggests that Hume's arguments for the belief-desire model of human action are consistent with, or can be seen as some version of, the direction-of-fit argument offered in contemporary discussions of Humeanism (Bricke 1996: 27). Michael Smith defends the difference between belief and desire in terms of "direction of fit," a characterization originally offered by G. E. M. Anscombe (1957: 256–7). What I variously refer to as the direction-of-fit "argument," "criterion," "distinction," "view," "interpretation," etc., concerns the way beliefs and desires can be decisively distinguished. On this view, beliefs aim to fit the world and are true when they do; false beliefs fail and are defective. On the other hand, desires aim to have the world conform to them, and it is not a failing of a desire when the world does not change to fit it. Of course, crucial to the contemporary Humean view is that beliefs and desires are separate mental states, and the direction-of-fit criterion is meant to demonstrate their respective uniqueness. Smith writes in a now-classic defense of the Humean theory of motivation:

> The Humean says that we understand what it is for someone to have a motivating reason at a time by thinking of her as, *inter alia*, having a goal at that time ('*alia*' here includes having a conception of the means to attain that goal). That is, having a motivating reason just is, *inter alia*, having a goal. But what kind of state is the having of a goal? Which direction of fit does this state have? Clearly, the having of a goal is a state with which the world must fit, rather than vice versa. Thus having a goal is being in a state with the direction of fit of a desire. But since all that there is to being a desire is being a state with the appropriate direction of fit, it follows that having a goal is just desiring. (Smith 1994: 116)

So, Smith maintains that goal-directed explanations of behavior require making reference to states of mind distinct from those that describe the world. He develops the distinction in terms of the functional roles of belief and desire, emphasizing that a belief that *p* tends to go out of existence in the presence of a perception with the content *not-p*, but a desire that *p* has the propensity to endure, and disposes the subject to bring about that *p*.[17]

One notion behind the direction-of-fit distinction is that a belief and desire can have the same content (a belief that *p* and a desire that *p*), but be distinguished from each other by their respective relationships to the world. In fact, to discern that direction of fit is doing the work in determining the difference between a belief and desire, the two must be alike in all other particulars. The other feature in virtue of which each exists, on this view, is their having mental content. That I teach a class in ethics can be the content of a belief or of a desire, depending on whether it purports to reflect the way the world is or whether it prompts me to make the world conform

---

[17] (Smith 1994: 115). Smith's account of the justification of desire is unlike Hume's, however, since Smith has a theory whereby desires are subject to rational assessment (see ibid.: Ch. 5).

to it.[18] One question to ask about this way of articulating the belief-desire distinction is what conception of "fitness" might be common to both belief and desire, such that we can apply "direction-of-fit" in the same sense to each. A belief that succeeds in fitting the world is a true belief, but a desire that succeeds in fitting the world to itself is not evaluated as a "true" desire. Conversely, a desire on which a person acts and succeeds in fitting the world to the desire is a fulfilled desire, but it would be mistaken to think of a belief as fulfilled when its content matches the world. My suggestion is that the direction-of-fit distinction seems problematic, given that the condition of fitting itself to the world, at which beliefs aim, is a different sort of state from the condition of having the world fit with it, at which desires aim.[19]

While the direction-of-fit distinction might be inspired by Hume, it is not, I think, the distinction Hume was outlining in his characterization of belief and passion. Hume does reference truth, and the way in which he does adds some credibility to the notion that he is concerned with the fitness of ideas to the world in the case of belief. For instance, he writes, "Truth is of two kinds, consisting either in the discovery of the proportions of ideas, consider'd as such, or in the conformity of our ideas of objects to their real existence" (T 2.3.10.2). And in EPM, he writes:

---

[18] The direction-of-fit argument obviously has implications for some rationalists' theories of motivation that generally share the notion that we are motivated by passionate representations of instances of the good. Translated into the contemporary vernacular, their proposal is that we are motivated by a mental state with both directions of fit, what have been dubbed "besires" (see, for instance, Smith 1994: 118–25; and van Roojen 1995: 40). The direction-of-fit argument implies, however, that a representation of goodness attempts to represent or depict accurately the good it finds; so, on this argument, it is impossible that that representations of goodness could also try to fit the world to themselves. The direction-of-fit view does not preclude the possibility that representations produce or cause motivating states, however. But this is problematic in other ways for the rationalist. For then, she needs to argue that beliefs about particular goods necessarily cause desires for those goods—and, of course, the empiricist would counter by saying that causal relationships are not necessary ones. If the relevant beliefs and desires are necessarily connected, the implication is that they are the same state, but the direction-of-fit argument makes this impossible. Thus, the belief about the good and the desire for the good, if causally connected, are contingently connected. This means that some agents could identify goodness in an object or situation and have no motive toward it—but that is just what the rationalists deny.

[19] The direction-of-fit argument has been subject to other critique as well. David Sobel and David Copp argue that there are some belief states that do not tend to go out of existence under the circumstances in which we would, according to Smith's distinction, expect them to; and there are some desires that do not endure where Smith's account alleges they would (Sobel and Copp 2001: 47–8). Obstinate beliefs, such as someone's belief in God, may not be affected when one acknowledges evidence to the contrary, such as the problem of evil. And a desire for a state of affairs might actually be diminished when the absence of that state of affairs persists. "Sue says that she desires that the 49'ers do well. But their not doing well tends to drive out of existence this desire" (ibid.: 48). Furthermore, Sobel and Copp argue that direction of fit cannot be distinctive of belief and desire, since the functional test is not definitive. On the functional test, if an acquired psychological state with the content *not-p* drives a background psychological state with the content *p* out of existence, then the latter state is a belief. However, they argue, other psychological states exhibit this same relationship, and they are not beliefs. For instance, a new desire that *not-p* can drive out an intention to *p*; a desire to stay home for my summer vacation can drive out the intention to make a plane reservation (ibid.: 50). Al Mele likewise thinks the direction-of-fit distinction is undermined by counter-examples: My waiting at the airport for a friend's plane to arrive might make me want it to have left on time, but I am not disposed to bring it about that it left on time because I cannot be disposed to bring it about to change the past (Mele 2003: 26).

Thus the distinct boundaries and offices of *reason* and of *taste* are easily ascertained. The former conveys the knowledge of truth and falsehood: The latter gives the sentiment of beauty and deformity, vice and virtue. The one discovers objects as they really stand in nature, without addition or diminution: The other has a productive faculty, and gilding or staining all natural objects with the colours, borrowed from internal sentiment, raises, in a manner, a new creation. (EPM App 1.21)

So, true ideas reflect existence or the way things are in nature.

Furthermore, even though he holds that the natural function of belief for Hume is stability, Loeb argues that it would be mistaken to think that Hume rejects the idea that belief aims at truth. Hume notes that reflecting on the degree to which a faculty is unreliable undermines a belief's influence, which Loeb regards as evidence that Hume thinks belief aims at truth. For instance, Hume writes that, in addition to the uncertainty found in every subject, reason obliges us "to add a new doubt deriv'd from the possibility of error in the estimation we make of the truth and fidelity of our faculties" (T 1.4.1.6). On Loeb's reading, the second-order disposition to moderate belief by evidence of truth is generally characteristic of believing for Hume, and the regulative disposition of aiming at truth operates by impacting stability (Loeb 2002: 84). So, for Hume, reason is engaged with the discovery of truth and gives rise to beliefs, and truth portrays things as they are in nature. This set of claims gives support to the direction-of-fit interpretation of belief.[20]

However, if differentiating belief and desire by direction of fit requires that desires be cognitive, Hume cannot subscribe to it. Granted, there is nothing in Smith's description of the distinction that would preclude Hume from agreeing with it. As I argue in CHAPTER 4, Hume holds that desiring is having a goal, even though the idea of the goal is not part of the desire. The person who desires necessarily has an end, in Hume's view, which makes desiring a motivating state. On the other hand, Smith himself defends a cognitive conception of desire and criticizes Hume's phenomenal conception. So, Smith evidently thinks that the direction-of-fit distinction does entail commitment to a cognitivist notion of desire.

If so, Hume's view of the belief-desire (or belief-passion) model cannot be a version of it. Furthermore, on Hume's theory, a belief and a motivating passion are

---

[20] The criterion for justifying beliefs, for Hume, is obviously not how well a belief corresponds to the world, but concerns the circumstances under which we judge that a cause-effect connection underlying any particular belief obtains. In T 1.3.15, "Rules by which to judge of causes and effects," Hume enumerates eight rules by which we can ascertain that a cause and effect are really connected. For instance, among those rules are that the cause and effect are contiguous in space and time; the cause precedes the effect; the cause and effect are constantly conjoined; and the same cause always produces the same effect, and no other cause produces that effect (T 1.3.15.3–6). The first three rules are generalizations upon the psychology of belief formation, based on instances in which persons normally form beliefs in matters of fact, while the latter is a generalization upon the causal connections people have normally made. Hume notes four other rules of this latter kind as well. So, Hume's evaluation of belief is in terms of the experiential circumstances under which causal connections are typically drawn and in terms of the features these beliefs reveal about the way causes and effects are naturally configured. Frederick Schmitt (2014) argues that truth, for Hume, is a matter of reliable truth-forming mechanisms.

not alike in all features but one. They are different "species," so to speak, with belief being an idea, and passion being an original existence. Original existences are motivators because, as "modifications of existence," they have causal force and impart impulses. But because they are such modifications, it would be false to say that the impulses they impart are to arrange the world in such a way as to fit their content. They have no content.

3.4 Objects of Belief and Objects of Reason

The foregoing discussion of belief allows me to address two challenges to Hume's position on reason and motivation. The first is Barry Stroud's allegation that Hume's conclusion that reason cannot motivate does not follow from his own characterizations of reason and passion (see Stroud 1977: 141–70). The second is from Rüdiger Bittner, who charges that Hume is dogmatic about his use of "reason" (Bittner 2001: 28). Both critiques involve Hume's notion that the objects of reason are the bearers of truth, and not entities or existences with the potential to motivate.

Hume's argument that reason cannot oppose passion depends on the claims that passions are original existences, which have causal powers and cannot be assessed as true or false, and that products of reason are not original existences. Stroud contends that Hume is right to think that propositions, which are the bearers of truth value, cannot impart any force against passions, since they "are at best abstract entities with no location in time and space." They can cause nothing. However, Stroud claims that Hume's description of reason as the discovery of truth and falsehood indicates that reasoning involves both reason's objects—which Stroud takes to be propositions—and the believer taking a certain attitude toward those objects. In other words, Stroud holds the interpretation of Hume that I earlier addressed, that believing is to be identified with a sentiment. Since that attitude *is* "a modification of existence" (a state of a person's mind), it is a potential cause of action (Stroud 1977: 158–61).

More importantly, Stroud suggests that if Hume's argument actually shows that passions cannot be in accord with or contrary to reason, it would also show that beliefs cannot be reasonable or unreasonable. Believing is not a proposition; it is rather to be in a certain state or condition, just as being 5-ft high or being angry is, and such conditions have no truth-value (ibid.: 161–2). Ultimately, Stroud concludes that Hume has no real argument for the conclusion that reason alone cannot motivate. The claim that passions in addition to belief are necessary to produce action is not even substantiated by introspection, since we cannot find the requisite passions in the case of calm motivating passions (ibid.: 163–7).

As I have already suggested, even if beliefs *were* sentiments, this would not show that they motivate, in Hume's view. I have also argued that the texts simply do not support the notion that beliefs are to be identified with sentiments. The point I want to make here is a different one. The distinction that Hume draws between original existences and non-motivating states is not a distinction between entities in the world (including mental states) and abstractions. Imagined or unbelieved ideas do not contribute to action, but the reason they do not is not because they are abstractions. They exist in the mind, just as attitudes, sentiments, and passions do; yet, Hume clearly contrasts them with original existences. As I will argue in CHAPTER 4, original existences are distinguished by Hume from ideas, because the latter are copies of impressions and the former are not. As copies, they have cognitive content, but lack the power of originating an impetus toward an object. Hume never writes about "propositions" as the objects of reason.

Now, I take up a second critique that has to do with objects of reason in Hume's discussion. Rüdiger Bittner, in his 2001 book, *Doing Things for Reasons*, also addresses Hume's case that reason cannot motivate on its own. Bittner takes Hume's main argument to be the argument that includes the claim that passions are original existences and make no reference to other passions, volitions, and actions. Thus, they cannot be true or false; they cannot conform to reason or be contrary to it. Hume concludes then that reason is inert and cannot present or produce any action or affections (see Bittner 2001: 25). Bittner holds, however, that the natural way to read Hume here is:

An object of reason must be capable of being true or false, since truth and falsity are qualities that reason discovers. Thus actions, incapable of being true or false, are not objects of reason, either. Now in order to prevent or produce an action reason would have to judge correctly that the action is contrary or conformable to reason. Since all such judgments are false, reason cannot prevent or produce an action. (ibid.: 26)

Hume's argument is a bad one, he maintains, since it depends on understanding "objects of reason" not in the natural sense of what one judges about, but in the non-standard sense of what figures in the deliberations of reason. Only statements, propositions, judgments, and so forth are premises in reasoning; but the objects are what the premises concern. On the common usage of "objects of reason," an object of reason need not be something that has truth value: actions are objects of reason, as is the weather, or one's diet, or any other thing one might think about.

Earlier, I characterized Hume as arguing in two stages: first, he considers what is necessary for something to be opposed to passion and argues that reason does not have this feature (it must initiate an impetus); second, he considers what is necessary for something to be opposed to reason (it must represent), and argues that passions and actions do not have this feature. Bittner's discussion centers on the second stage of the argument, but he puts this argument in terms of "objects" of reason in the way that Hume himself does in Book 3, when Hume rewrites the argument this way:

Reason is the discovery of truth or falshood. Truth or falshood consists in an agreement or disagreement either to the *real* relations of ideas, or to *real* existence and matter of fact. Whatever, therefore, is not susceptible of this agreement or disagreement, is incapable of being true or false, and can never be an object of our reason. Now 'tis evident our passions, volitions, and actions, are not susceptible of any such agreement or disagreement; being original facts and realities, compleat in themselves, and implying no reference to other passions, volitions, and actions. 'Tis impossible, therefore, they can be pronounced either true or false, and be either contrary or conformable to reason. (T 3.1.1.9)

It is correct to think that objects of reason for Hume must be whatever is capable of truth and falsity. However, Hume works with an implicit distinction between "objects of reason" and "objects of belief," which is unaccounted for in this critique. Objects of *belief*, for Hume, are states of affairs or the things about which we think. For instance, Hume writes:

'Tis evident, that poets make use of this artifice of borrowing the names of their persons, and the chief events of their poems, from history, in order to procure a more easy reception for the whole... The several incidents of the piece acquire a kind of relation by being united into one poem or representation; *and if any of these incidents be an object of belief, it bestows* a force and vivacity on the others, which are related to it. (T 1.3.10.7; my emphasis)

And in his discussion of the formation of belief in the Appendix to the *Treatise*, Hume writes:

These ideas take faster hold of my mind, than the ideas of an enchanted castle. They are different to the feeling; but there is no distinct or separate impression attending them. 'Tis the same case when I recollect the several incidents of a journey, or the events of any history. Every particular fact is there the *object of belief*. Its idea is modified differently from the loose reveries of a castle-builder: But no distinct impression attends every distinct idea, or conception of matter of fact. This is the subject of plain experience. (T App. 4; my emphasis)

To believe is to have in mind a solid, vivacious representation of the way things are, with "the way things are" as the object. Beliefs are a product of the use of reason in "the strict and philosophical sense," and it is also in this sense that objects of reason (and only objects of reason) are the bearers of truth values. This is exactly why the non-representative nature of passions is important to Hume's case. When Hume maintains that passions and actions are not objects of reason, he does not mean that we cannot think true and false thoughts of them; rather, even though we can think true and false thoughts about them, they are not reasonable or unreasonable themselves (our thoughts about them are). Hume's argument ultimately denies that actions and passions can sensibly be called or judged reasonable or unreasonable, as is the case for the weather or biology or any object of investigation. Being an object of belief (something one can have reasonable or unreasonable beliefs about) does not imply that the thing is evaluable by reason (that it can be called reasonable or unreasonable), even though the belief is.

Bittner offers another reading of Hume's argument, however. Again, using the version Hume gives at T 3.1.1.9, Bittner reconstructs it this way:

It must be a matter of the real relations of ideas or of real existence and matter of fact that an action has the quality by virtue of which it is contrary or comfortable to reason. This is so because reason is the discovery of truth and falsehood, and there is nothing for true or false statements to be about but real relations of ideas and real existence and matter of fact. On the other hand it cannot be a matter of the real relations of ideas or of real existence and matter of fact that an action has the quality by virtue of which it is contrary or conformable to reason. This is so because the examination of any action by reason fails to make out such a quality. Thus the assumption that actions are contrary or conformable to reason leads to a contradiction and is false. (Bittner 2001: 27)

Bittner maintains that the claim that the examination of an action by reason cannot turn up a quality that makes it contrary or conformable to reason requires further support. He thinks that the defense Hume intends to use to support it is analogous to that which Hume gives when he argues that virtue and vice are not facts in the world. Hume challenges the reader, upon examining a vicious act, like that of willful murder to, "see if you can find that matter of fact, or real existence, which you call *vice*." And he continues, "...you find only certain passions, motives, volitions, and thoughts. There is no matter of fact in the case. The vice entirely escapes you, as long as you consider the object" (T 3.1.1.26). Bittner thinks that Hume must have a similar challenge in mind when he argues that actions do not have qualities that make them reasonable or unreasonable. But Bittner sees this as a dogmatic assertion, perhaps merely a reflection of the fact that it is simply harder to justify the claim that this murder is vicious (or unreasonable)—and thus find the quality that makes it so—than it is to justify the claim that the murder was committed by a gun or at midnight, etc. So, Bittner concludes that Hume's argument is a weak one and writes:

These passages contain all the positive argument Hume offers for saying that reason is perfectly inert and that it takes desire to produce action. They contain all of Hume's positive argument for the belief/desire thesis... it is difficult to imagine that the arguments just discussed could lead anyone to accept the desire/belief thesis, if he had not believed it before. (Bittner 2001: 28)

Is this second reading of Hume's argument a fair one? Is Hume's argument tantamount to the claim that the problem with subjecting actions to rational evaluation is that the examination of an action by reason fails to find a quality that makes it reasonable or unreasonable? Recall Hume's statement that " 'tis evident our passions, volitions, and actions, are not susceptible of any such agreement or disagreement [to relations or matters of fact]; being original facts and realities, compleat in themselves, and implying no reference to other passions, volitions, and actions." They are not susceptible to such agreement or disagreement because they are not mental states that purport to represent, and the judgment of being conformable or not to reason can only be made of states that are representational. Judgments of reasonableness are assessments made of other judgments, like the judgment how or when the murder was committed. If one draws a hasty conclusion about how the killing was done, then that conclusion is an unreasonable one. Judging rationality is not a matter of looking for a quality like the time at which the act was done, only one harder to find. What Bittner has in mind here is that reason might very well intuit the irrationality of murder or discover its irrational quality inductively, and Hume begs the question by dogmatically ruling these possibilities out.

It looks like what is really "dogmatic" in this whole debate consists in the characterizations of reason that come from opposing sides, Humeans and non-Humeans alike. Philosophical theories always have axioms. However, an even more fundamental issue that separates the sides here is methodology. Hume's empiricist method in his philosophy of mind commits him to an introspective project, one in which he identifies individual mental states and processes (or faculties) by their feelings, by their functions, or by their causal origins. All of these states or processes consist in the mind's experiencing or functioning in a certain capacity. Impressions are distinguished from ideas by force and vivacity. Passions or impressions of reflection are distinguished from impressions of sensation by their origins: passions originate as reactions to ideas of pleasurable and painful objects, and sensations originate from unknown causes outside of us. Passions are distinguished from ideas not only in force and vivacity, but in that the latter represent and the former do not. Reasoning is a process of reason, and reason is identified by its function of detecting truth and falsity, which produces beliefs. But why could Hume not say that beliefs are vivacious representations that also originate action, so that reason motivates as well as produces beliefs? Or why could he not say that passions are motives that also represent vivaciously? The consequences of so doing are that passion and belief collapse into each other: passions are motivating beliefs; or beliefs are representing passions. On a naturalistic psychology, which approaches investigations empirically, the reason/passion distinction seems undermined when the hypothesis is advanced that reason both produces belief and motivates. The next move is to hold back on some beliefs and say that only some beliefs motivate.

That the products of reason do not motivate is a logical consequence of Hume's methodology, as is the conclusion that a belief cannot also be a desire. If Hume is dogmatic in his methodology, so are his opponents in theirs, but such a charge is hardly a criticism of either view.[21]

---

[21] I also want to mention that Bittner then takes up the origin of the dogma he takes Hume to have accepted, and traces the belief-desire model to Plato's theory of the soul. On Plato's theory, the soul consists of the calculating, the desiring, and the spirited parts. The spirited part often joins forces with the calculating part (reason), but "reason is the lord of the soul" and can thwart the impulse of desire (Bittner 2001: 32). Bittner thinks the Platonic account is in Hume, despite Hume's protestations that reason and desire cannot be opposed. The fact that Hume recognizes that reason can direct the impulse of desire shows that he is committed to their being in conflict: "There is no directing where forces never diverge... Thus reason directs desire because desire on its own goes astray" (ibid.: 33). And "... if reason directs desire, then it sometimes thwarts desire" (ibid.: 34).

I think the claim that a necessary condition for reason's ability to direct desire to its end is that reason being able to oppose desire is based on a false analogy. Certainly, a teacher directs a 5-year-old to the bathroom, since the child could go astray on her own, but desire is not like a child, complete with all the elements for action in place. Bittner, of course, understands reason and desire in ways very different from Hume, and Bittner's own understanding is closer to Plato's than Hume's is.

4

The Passions as Original Existences

In "Of the influencing motives of the will," after arguing that reason is not a motive in the sense that it cannot initiate action, Hume defends the thesis that reason cannot oppose passion over the production of action. As we have seen, it was a prevalent notion among the early modern rationalists that reason could act as an adviser to the will and oppose the direction of a passion, which often misrepresents what is noxious as good. Even given that the common view was that passions are necessary to produce action, philosophers like Reynolds, Senault, Malebranche, and Clarke portrayed reason as an arbiter between good and bad passions, with the power to show the "true colors" of the ends to which each inclines us. So, Hume goes on to argue that reason and passion can never be opposed, not even in the sense that reason and passion offer contrary judgments about the good. His argument seems simple, explaining what is necessary for something to be opposed to any passion (T 2.3.3.4). Matters become more complicated, however, when he introduces considerations about the passions that are meant to affirm the conclusion of the simple argument (T 2.3.3.5).[1]

In this chapter, I examine the details of Hume's argument for the conclusion that reason and passion cannot be practically opposed. That argument depends on Hume's particular characterizations of reason and of passion, respectively. Reason functions to deliver representations that are true or false, but it does not originate impulses; passions are original existences that do not represent, but they do generate impulses. Most of this discussion explores Hume's portrayal of passion and its plausibility. Hume seems to offer two descriptions of the passions, treating them at times as simple sensations and at other times as complex functional states. I address what prompts each characterization and their consistency with one another. Then I analyze the senses in which Hume says a passion might be *considered* unreasonable, although technically, passions are not subject to rational assessment. Finally, I consider to what degree Hume's argument that reason and passion cannot be opposed over the direction of the will actually undermines the early modern rationalists' view.

---

[1] Some of the material in this chapter first appeared in Radcliffe (2012a).

4.1 Reason Generates No Impulses or Attractions

In arguing that reason and passion cannot oppose each other in their influence on the will, Hume invokes his view that passions produce an impetus, or internal force, to movement. So the only way something can be opposed to passion influencing the will is by initiating a motivation in a contrary direction. However, it follows from Hume's characterization of reason that reason by itself cannot initiate a motivation at all, since without the influence of taste or sentiment, it does not determine ends toward which an action can be directed. If reason cannot originate an impetus to action, it is equally incapable of opposing an impetus that comes from a passion. As Hume argues:

> Nothing can oppose or retard the impulse of passion, but a contrary impulse; and if this contrary impulse ever arises from reason, that latter faculty must have an original influence on the will, and must be able to cause, as well as hinder any act of volition. But if reason has no original influence, 'tis impossible it can withstand any principle, which has such an efficacy, or ever keep the mind in suspence a moment. (T 2.3.3.4)

While most of Hume's predecessors agreed that reason has no original influence, I have suggested that Hume likely thought they were committed to the view that it does. Certainly many of Hume's successors, including contemporary neo-Kantians, believe that reason can be motivationally opposed to passion, although they might shun causal accounts of motivational opposition. Their view includes the internalist assumption that a rational judgment of goodness involves a motive to act in accord with that judgment, which may be contrary to the motivational impulse of a passion.

Hume concludes his simple argument in the *Treatise* 2.3.3.4 with his metaphorical exclamation, "Reason is, and ought to be, slave of the passions, and can never pretend to any other office but to serve and obey them." My interpretation of Hume in CHAPTER 2 is in part meant to clarify what this remark means. Even though reason and passion make equal contributions to motivation, since both belief and desire are necessary to generate action, reason is still in a practical sense subsidiary to passion. Its work matters for action only when the passionate dispositions of the person determine her desires. But here I am more interested in what Hume has to say next about the prospect that reason and passion may be opposed. That discussion constitutes his answer to the many philosophers who thought that reason offers proper representations of the good to counter those offered by certain passions.

4.2 The Features of Original Existences

Hume's argument makes the proper assumption that if two mental states are to be opposed, they must have common parameters along which the opposition can happen. So far, he has shown that the opposition is not one of impulse. The second part of Hume's argument is designed to show that neither can that opposition be one of contrary representation. Hume defines reason as the discovery of truth and falsity (here referring to reason's activity), which indicates that reason deals with mental states that have cognitive content, and it judges whether the representations before the mind signify truly or falsely. The operation of reason is the process whereby an idea, introduced by sensation or reflection and at first entertained, becomes a belief. An idea's force and vivacity are increased in the process whereby causal reasoning associates that idea with a lively present impression and thus ascertains that the idea is veracious. Since the ideas with which reason deals have cognitive content, anything that might oppose those ideas must also have cognitive content that is contrary to beliefs produced by reason. Hume's argument proceeds, then, to appeal to his characterization of the passions as non-representing, which distinguishes his view from that of Descartes, Malebranche, Spinoza, and other early modern thinkers already discussed above and in the APPENDIX.

Before looking at this aspect of the passions, which meant to confirm Hume's argument that reason and passion cannot be opposed, I want to emphasize, again, as I did in CHAPTER 2, that "reason" in the context of discussing opposition cannot refer to the *faculty* of reason, nor to the *function* of reasoning, but must instead refer to reason's product (i.e., beliefs, or vivacious ideas). Hume's argument here focuses on why individual passions cannot be opposed to reason because of the passions' non-representative nature. Given that, it would be implausible to think that his intent is to say that passions and the faculty of reason cannot be opposed. Perhaps the faculty of reason might sensibly to said to oppose the faculty of passion (although I'm not sure how the opposition of faculties would be explained apart from reference to their products); but only the products of the former, the passions themselves, could sensibly be thought contrary to the products of the latter, the enlivened ideas or beliefs. The same point holds for the function of reason, and for the reasoning process. Since reasoning is a mental association that deals with representations, but does not itself represent, Hume's target in highlighting the non-representational nature of the passions cannot be reasoning, but its products. So, Hume's argument that reason and passion cannot be opposed because passions are original existences, and not representations, reinforces the crucial point I defended in Chapter 2: that Hume's argument about the inertness of reason concerns beliefs.

Hume writes:

A passion is an original existence, or, if you will, modification of existence, and contains not any representative quality, which renders it a copy of any other existence or modification. When I am angry, I am actually possest with the passion, and in that emotion have no more a reference to any other object, than when I am thirsty, or sick, or more than five foot high. 'Tis impossible, therefore, that this passion can be oppos'd by, or contradictory to truth and reason; since this contradiction consists in the disagreement of ideas, consider'd as copies with those objects, which they represent. (T 2.3.3.5)

And in a passage in Book 3, he says:

Reason is the discovery of truth or falshood. Truth or falshood consists in an agreement or disagreement either to the *real* relations of ideas, or to *real* existence and matter of fact. Whatever, therefore, is not susceptible of this agreement or disagreement, is incapable of being true or false, and can never be an object of our reason. Now 'tis evident our passions, volitions, and actions, are not susceptible of any such agreement or disagreement; being original facts and realities, compleat in themselves, and implying no reference to other passions, volitions, and actions. 'Tis impossible, therefore, they can be pronounc'd either true or false, and be either contrary or conformable to reason.   (T 3.1.1.9)

Simple ideas copy impressions gained from experience, and the mind can organize these simples into complex ideas that may represent truly or falsely. Reason discerns relations of ideas, or necessary truths, and it judges whether the ideas before the mind agree in their representations with what exists or what is factual or taken to be fact. So, non-representations cannot be subject to the jurisdiction of reason. Assembling the descriptions Hume offers of the passions reveals that, as "original existences" or "modifications of existences," (1) they are complete in themselves; (2) they have no representative qualities that indicates they are copies of other existences; (3) they make no reference to any object; (4) they do not agree or disagree with anything; (5) they imply no reference to other passions, volitions, and actions; (6) they cannot be called true or false; and (7) they cannot be contrary or conformable to reason. Presumably these features are true of volitions and actions, too, although Hume only mentions volitions and actions in conjunction with some of them.

All of the propositions (1)–(7) are necessary features of original existences, or original "facts and realities." Hume's description of the passions in this manner has a general precedent in Hobbes's and Locke's accounts, but the detailed description of the passions in these terms is original to Hume. Hobbes derives the passions that produce action from our appetites and aversions, and describes reason in terms of its deductive function (see the APPENDIX). Locke argues that sensations of uneasiness at an absent good, which are necessary to motivation, cannot oppose ideas. This is because the ideas that would oppose desires would be ideas of absent goods. However, according to Locke, ideas of absent good cannot be causes because they are not *present* goods. Presumably, no ideas, even of present goods, are causes, since ideas of present goods are *also* not present goods.[2] Hume, however, is the first to offer systematic particulars in an empiricist vein on the nature of the passions, portraying them with features that show reason (or reason's products) to be unopposable to them. Hume's analogy to sickness is instructive here. A feeling of nausea might be caused by a disgusting idea, and the nausea has effects; but the cause—even if an idea—and the effects are not part of the nausea itself. Nausea can motivate the person who has it to take a remedy, but thinking of the remedy is not a constituent of the nausea, or necessarily connected to it. The feeling of nausea does not make reference

---

[2] Locke (1690: II. XXI. 37). See the APPENDIX to this volume for further discussion.

to objects or states of affairs, even though it prompts thoughts of object or states of affairs, and behavior that may involve them. The feeling does not represent or copy anything, and is neither subject to the assessment of reason nor opposed to reason. Rather, it is a phenomenal or experiential state of a person, "complete" in itself.

4.2.1 Critique of Hume's Characterization of the Passions as Non-representations

However, detractors reject an analogy between the passions and the feeling of sickness, questioning Hume's portrayal of the passions over all. Passions seem, unlike nausea, to be intentional states—that is, directed toward specific objects. Hume himself presents the indirect passions as having subjects as their causes, and the self or another as their objects. In the case of desire, which is a direct passion and the paradigm motivational passion, it is not typically thought to be an undirected sensation. Rather, it is thought to have intentionality, to be a desire *for something* in particular. Hume himself writes this way; for instance: "a desire of fame, and aversion to infamy" (T 2.1.11.11); and "man... has the most ardent desire of society" (T 2.2.5.15); and again, "I may desire any fruit as of an excellent relish" (T 2.3.3.7); and so on. Furthermore, as the modern rationalists suggested, passions seem to represent their objects in a certain light, as good or as bad, which, on Hume's view, could be thought to depend upon whether the object of the passion is pleasurable or painful. Annette Baier argues that Hume's characterization of the passions as object-less is both "unfortunate" and inconsistent with his treatment of the passions in other places. She writes:

Anger, as discussed by Hume earlier in Book Two [that is, in a section earlier than the passage from T 2.3.3.5. quoted above], is always directed at someone for some perceived insult, injury, or harm... it has an object of its own, namely the person with whom one is angry, and has also a "subject" or cause, the perceived injury that person is thought to have done one. So, like all passions, it does seem to refer us to at least one intentional "object" of the passion, and it involves the ideas of its object or objects.   (Baier 1991: 161)

Since Baier believes that the passions involve ideas of their objects and that Hume sees them in this way, her view implies that passions, on Hume's characterization, are representational states. Terence Penelhum agrees with Baier's criticism (see Penelhum 1992a: 142–3). Moreover, many contemporary philosophers, for various reasons, think the representational view is the only plausible theory of the passions. Some base their view on the intentional nature of the passions, but others believe that passions impart information about the factual or evaluative dimensions of the world. For instance, anger presents an assessment of fairness, and shame informs a person of her subordinate status.[3]

---

[3] Keltner and Haidt (1999: 509–10) offer a description of the following representationalists, who think that emotions present information:

John Bricke attempts a defense of Hume's characterization of the passions against the critics by arguing that while desires have representational content in the way that Baier conceives them, they do not actually represent—that is, they do not represent in a sense crucial to Hume's argument that desires are always prior to reason, practically speaking. Bricke interprets Hume's argument that reason is subsidiary to the passions in influencing action in one of two ways: as an argument from the claim that desires have no truth value supporting the claim that "only desires can provide the major constituent in a reason for action"; or alternatively, as an argument from the claim that beliefs *do* have truth value supporting the conclusion that beliefs alone cannot constitute reasons for action (Bricke 1996: 5).

To make sense of these arguments, Bricke calls upon the contemporary notion of direction of fit. I have argued that Hume's way of distinguishing beliefs from desires is not in terms of direction of fit, but that is not the point I want to make here.[4] Proponents of this characterization think beliefs and desires can have the same content, but differ insofar as beliefs aim to fit the world, and desires aim to fit the world to themselves. So, beliefs succeed when they represent accurately and, under these circumstances, we denominate them true. Desires succeed when they change the world to fit what they represent, though we do not call them true or false. Hence, Bricke thinks that Hume's notion that desires do not represent can be understood as the view that desires are not true or false, rather than as the claim that they lack representational content (ibid.: 25–6). He writes that the contrast between the directions of fit "follows him [Hume] in focusing on truth-evaluability and in linking talk of representation with talk of truth" (ibid.: 27). Moreover,

> It provides a route to his anti-cognitivist thesis that beliefs, alone, cannot constitute a reason for action. As cognitive states, beliefs have the mind-to-world direction of fit. Their function is accurately to represent the way the world is. That being so, how can they serve the practical or goal-setting task that, as conativist and standard cognitivist agree, the major constituent in a reason for action must perform? (ibid.: 27)

And, of course, the answer is that they cannot; rather, psychological states with the world-to-mind direction of fit are necessary to setting goals for action.

Bricke's approach at first looks like a promising way to save Hume from criticisms like Baier's. Yet the success of this tack depends upon Hume's ability to distinguish a psychological state that possesses representational content but does not attempt to represent, from a psychological state that possesses representational content and does attempt to represent. Cass Weller follows a track similar to Bricke's, writing,

---

Theorists have proposed that the feeling of anger provides an assessment of the fairness of events (Solomon, 1990), love informs the individual of the level of commitment to another (Frank, 1988), happiness may signal the reproductive potential of certain social actions (Nesse, 1990), and shame informs the individual of his or her lower social status (Tangney, Miller, Flicker, & Barlow, 1996).

[4] My critique of Bricke is taken from Radcliffe (2012a: 225–8).

"A passion might well have an ingredient idea, propositional or otherwise, just so long as the passion itself weren't the propositional attitude of belief" (Weller 2002: 197). I think it is safe to say that Bricke and Weller have in mind a distinction between an intentional state that merely contains an idea, and a belief, which is also an intentional state, but has a truth value. On their interpretation of Hume, beliefs are the only psychological states that represent, or purport to represent, even though ideas have representational or cognitive content.

While their distinctions do make sense, I have doubts that Bricke's and Weller's line can work as a way of defending Hume.[5] For one, Hume says that ideas represent: "Ideas always represent the objects or impressions, from which they are derived, and can never without a fiction represent or be apply'd to any other" (T 1.2.3.11; see also T 1.3.14.6). But I will put that point aside for now and ask whether Hume could have meant that ideas have representational content but only beliefs actually represent. For Hume, beliefs are forceful and vivacious ideas. Thinking of my winning the lottery and believing I have won the lottery feel differently to me, even though both states are complex ideas with the same contents. When someone tells me an incredible story, in order to understand it, I have to form the ideas with the same content as the other person's, but I may not believe the story. The difference between my belief and disbelief does not lie in any idea or ideas added to the one that the other lacks, but rather, in my attitude, that is, how I experience the story ideas. Since what the imagined idea represents and what the believed idea represents are the same, the only way a belief can be distinguished from an idea merely entertained is by a phenomenal, or feeling, dimension. Hume defines a belief as "A LIVELY IDEA RELATED TO OR ASSOCIATED WITH A PRESENT IMPRESSION" (T 1.3.7.5). If representation is a function of beliefs, which are true or false, and is not a function of ideas, even though ideas have representational content, then the function of representation depends on the vivacity of the idea: on how it is experienced by the agent. So far, Bricke and Weller would agree, I think. But this implication seems problematic. Passions, as impressions of reflection, are livelier than ideas, but, of course, the point of this discussion is that they are not representations. If passions are more vivacious than ideas, but contain ideas, and if belief is a function of the increased vivacity of an idea, it is hard to see how passions include ideas, but do not include those ideas as beliefs. In short, it is hard to see why passions are not beliefs. On Bricke's interpretation, copying gives an idea its cognitive content, but does not render the idea a representation. But if the passions contain ideas, then, while they are original existences, which are not copies, they are also partly copies, which is at least enigmatic.

Furthermore, this way of reading Hume seems to present a question-begging characterization of the difference between belief and desire. One feature of beliefs

---

[5] Don Garrett (2006: 303) also writes, "Hume seems clearly committed to the view that all ideas, whether of memory or imagination, represent; for he remarks that 'ideas always represent their objects or impressions.'" (See T 1.3.14.6; see also T 1.2.3.11.)

that makes them representations is that they have content, a content that they contain *because*, as ideas, they have content copied from their preceding impressions. The question at issue here is whether having such content is merely necessary to representation or whether it is both necessary and sufficient. Bricke's analysis implies that such content is necessary but not sufficient. The other condition that must be met for representation, on his view, is that the state with representational or cognitive content be experienced with the force and vivacity of belief, which makes the state evaluable as true or false. Also, since being true or false implies having cognitive content, being truth evaluable is necessary and sufficient for representation. But surely the reason passions are not true or false is because they don't have cognitive content in the first place. (It cannot be a matter of their having insufficient force and vivacity.) That they don't have cognitive content must be ascertainable apart from whether they can be true or false, since whether they can be true or false depends on their having such content. Consequently, it seems problematic, given Hume's own philosophy of mind, to justify a distinction between representation and representational content. Hume is committed to the view that all ideas represent.[6]

What I have argued, then, is that because passions clearly do not represent, for Hume, they do not have representational content. In other words, ideas are representations, so we cannot consistently attribute to Hume the view that passions contain ideas of their objects, however plausible this view seems by itself. I don't think, however, that this conclusion implies that the critics of Hume's account are correct when they argue that his characterization of the passions cannot account for their obvious intentionality. Before I present a defense of Hume's description of the passions, though, I consider a related objection to his theory.

4.2.2 Critique of Hume's Characterization of the Passions as "Sensations"

Hume is also criticized for having an implausible, "phenomenal" conception of passion. Since passions do not include ideas of their objects, and cannot be distinguished by their content, so goes the criticism, they have to be distinguished from one another by how each feels, as though they are sensations. Hume himself intimates that this is so in scattered contexts:

---

[6] One question that arises for the view I have defended, that all ideas are officially representations, is how we can evaluate the success of these attempts to represent, if not in the same terms as belief, which can be evaluated as true or false. I want to say here that there are no grounds in Hume's epistemology on which to think that all representations are subjects of evaluation. (I made this point in CHAPTER 3.) Some of my complex ideas may be sets of simple ideas that are recombined in ways not found in my original experience. But only if I take these ideas to be memories (and so reflective of previous experience), or only if I believe them, are they subject to assessment in terms of how well they represent. Ideas of the imagination are attempts at representation that are not subject to evaluation. My imagining going to the movies, for example, involves representing a possible future state of affairs to myself. If motivating passions contain ideas of their objects, as some critics of Hume contend they do, the ideas they contain would be ideas of imagined future states of affairs, which are not beliefs.

'Tis altogether impossible to give any definition of the passions of love and hatred; and that because they produce merely a simple impression, without any mixture or composition... these passions of themselves are sufficiently known from our common feeling and experience.

(T 2.2.1.1)

And, as we have seen, he says that from the prospect of pleasure or pain from an object, "we feel a consequent emotion of aversion or propensity" (T 2.3.3.3). Michael Smith, for one, argues that on a phenomenal conception of desire, as a motivating passion, desire must be treated parallel to pain; just as we say that one is in pain only when one believes one is in pain, so too, one can desire an object x only when one believes one desires x. This, he says is problematic, since an agent can be deceived or mistaken about his or her own desires. He argues for this claim by pointing to examples where a person's behavior belies what she professes to care about. For instance, John's mother has drummed into him the value of music and has great hopes for his having a successful career as a musician. John himself claims to have an interest in music, and he also admits that he does not want to disappoint his mother. He studies music and practices his piano. Then, when his mother dies, he no longer seems interested in the piano, and pursues a different career. Under these circumstances, Smith argues, we would want to say that John had previously been mistaken about his own desires (Smith 1994: 106–7).

I think this example need not be interpreted as a counterexample to the phenomenal characterization of desire, however. It is as plausible to think that John had an interest in music subsidiary to his interest in pleasing his mother as it is to understand this example as showing that he had no interest in music at all. The goal of pleasing his mother vanishes upon her death, and so do the desires subsidiary to that end. However, we can probably come up with examples in which the best explanation of a person's behavior appeals to desires the person denies having. Smith offers the case of John's going out of his way to buy a newspaper each morning at a particular stand, when there are others more convenient (ibid.: 106). The stand he favors has a mirror that allows him to see his reflection, and yet John denies that his route is affected by the desire to see how he looks. What no one can deny is that John wants a newspaper and that he wants to go by that particular stand. He surely offers some competing explanation why—that the salesperson is friendlier, or the neighborhood is attractive. So, how do we know what he desires? Both explanations—that wants to see his image and that he wants to interact with a pleasant salesperson—explain the action equally well. Debating whether a person always knows what he or she wants, by using examples, ends with a draw.

Barry Stroud also criticizes the phenomenal interpretation of desire as Hume's:

...there is a way of understanding Hume's quite reasonable claim that no belief alone would lead me to act *unless* I also had a certain desire or preference, without taking it to imply the existence of two distinct items or events, in the mind or elsewhere....

I am suggesting that the intuitive idea from which Hume derives his theory of action is quite compatible with a non-Humean theory of desires or propensities.

...wanting, preferring or having a propensity need not be understood as a matter of a certain perception's being before the mind. Having a propensity will be nothing more than there being a disposition for certain things to occur in the mind when certain others occur there. (Stroud 1977: 167–8)

Stroud's notion is that Hume's characterization of desire as passion is largely due to his concern with showing that action cannot be produced by reason on its own; this, Stroud maintains, can be accomplished without regarding passions as feeling. Hume need only argue that reason by itself cannot account for our ultimate ends, and that we must appeal to a want or propensity for that. Hume makes this move when he writes in the *Enquiry Concerning the Principles of Morals* that when we ask a person why he desires something, the person will ultimately have to appeal to a sentiment or affection as an explanation. A person desires health so that he can work at his job, which she desires to do so that she can make money, which she desires to have because money is the instrument of pleasure. "And beyond this it is an absurdity to ask for a reason... Something must be desirable on its own account, and because of its immediate accord or agreement with human sentiment and affection" (Appendix 1.19). So, Stroud argues that Hume has all he needs here to argue that reason alone cannot produce action: "All that is required is that, for each action, there be at least one want or propensity in its causal ancestry that is not arrived at by reasoning" (Stroud 1977: 170). Stroud is right to think that Hume can defend his thesis that reason alone does not motivate without characterizing motives (passions) as particular feelings, and Hume does appeal to dispositions at times to explain belief and behavior (as in the case of the cowardly and the melancholic person).[7] However, Hume's phenomenal conception of the passions, in terms of particular feelings, does other work for his theory.

4.3 A Defense of Hume's Conception of the Passions

4.3.1 The Phenomenal Conception

I have earlier argued that motivating passions are all characterized as desires for Hume. While it might not matter whether desires feel like anything in particular, since they can be described dispositionally insofar as they motivate, it does matter that the passions feel differently when it comes to certain principles of our psychology. For instance, as I noted in CHAPTER 1, the mind associates passions according to how the feelings resemble one another: "...our temper, when elevated with joy, naturally throws itself into love, generosity, pity, courage, pride, and the other resembling affections" (T 2.1.4.3). Hume uses resemblances among the feelings to

---

[7] "A coward, whose fears are easily awaken'd, readily assents to every account of danger he meets with; as a person of a sorrowful and melancholy disposition is very credulous of every thing, that nourishes his prevailing passion" (T 1.3.10.4).

explain the indirect passions as well; for instance, it is important that the feeling of pride be related to a pleasurable feeling, and the feeling of humility be related to a displeasurable one.[8]

However, the point that I want to defend here is different from my qualified disagreement with Stroud. I want to contend that Hume has a phenomenal conception of passion (and so of desire) in one sense, and a structural conception in yet another, and each is appropriate in a certain context. The defense of the phenomenal conception is tied to the non-representative nature of the Humean passions. On his account, passions are akin to sensations, but are distinguished from impressions of sensation by the fact that they originate in a reflexive operation, with the mind's recurring to objects that have been sources of pleasure or pain. Thus, they are impressions of reflection. Passions do have objects, and Hume recognizes this; for instance, in his account of the indirect passions. However, I want to argue on his behalf that a passion's possession of an object is distinct from its representing that object, just as a sensation's possessing a cause is distinct from its representing that cause. A passion can be complete in itself, have no representative quality, copy nothing, make no reference to another thing, and be neither true nor false, while still having an object.

I think it makes sense for Hume to say that the passions *have* objects, but do not represent their objects, for the following reason. The mind displays "object-directedness" in virtue of a motivating passion; however, the passion need not (and does not) represent (or copy the content of) the objects or ideas of the objects toward which it directs the mind. No one would say that pleasure or pain represents the object that causes the feeling of pleasure or pain, and yet, it is plausible to think that we can be motivated by those feelings toward and away from those objects. This is not an antiquated view; it is alive in contemporary discussion. Fred Dretske, for instance, writes in his book, *Explaining Behavior*: "Desires, though they are not representational states, do have an object, something they are a desire *for*, that gives them a special status. This special status is often acknowledged by saying that desires, like beliefs, are intentional states or attitudes" (Dretske 1988: 127). Furthermore, even though not all the passions are motivating, even some of the non-motivating ones produce mental directedness insofar as they focus the mind on an object or idea connected to the passion as its cause. This is quite clear in the cases of the indirect passions, many of which are not motivating, but which direct the mind to the self or to others.

On the account I have offered of the development of motivating passion, a person has an experience of pleasure or pain from an object with certain features. She subsequently either desires the features she has experienced as pleasant, or is averse

---

[8] In another recent article, Mark Collier defends Hume against the charge that his theory of the passions is a version of "feeling" theory, where emotions or passions are nothing more than introspective states, a view which is discredited in some contemporary circles (Collier 2011: esp. 7–12).

to those features she has experienced as unpleasant. Further observations and inference yield the belief that another object, which she has not experienced, but has similar features, offers her the prospect of pleasure or pain, as the case may be. Thus, desire originates from the impressions of pleasure or pain she has felt in the past and gets transferred to future objects by reasoning. Consider the passion of fear, which is clearly a motivating passion. Let's say that, while driving, I get lost on a dark street in a seemingly unsafe neighborhood, and my fear of being assaulted is stimulated when I see a stranger walk up to my car. My fear and the thought of an attacker (or the belief in one's presence) prompt me to lock my doors. On the contemporary critics' line, the passion of fear includes a vivid idea (a representation) of an assailant, along with a "hedonic"—painful—reaction to that idea, and Hume is wrong to ignore the fact that the idea of the assailant is part of the state we identify as my fear. Baier says that Hume treats the passion as though it is an impression of sensation, rather than an impression of reflection: a criticism that implies that impressions of sensation do not represent, but impressions of reflection do (Baier 1991: 164). But why must the fear be identified with a complex state that includes both an idea and a feeling?

Not only does Hume's narrative of the passions not allow that they include ideas of their objects, but his account of causation yields the same conclusion. I've remarked that Hume's explanation of the production of a motivating passion is a disjunctive one: the passion is caused either by the impression of pleasure or pain that arises upon perceiving the object, or it is caused by the idea of the object as pleasurable or painful that arises *upon* the impression of pleasure or pain received from the object. Hume believes that causes and effects are distinct existences, and that there is no necessary connection between distinct existences (T App. 21). So if ideas of objects are in the causal chain that leads to passions, those ideas cannot be contained in the passions themselves. That would amount to the cause being contained in the effect. In the example, the idea of a possible assailant, the idea causing my fear, cannot be a part of my fear.[9] I think this is the key to understanding Hume's view on the non-representative nature of the passions. What "fear" refers to is the feeling resulting from the idea, and it IS like a sensation insofar as it is a forceful and vivid feeling, or an impression. It is not merely reactive, however, because it has a motivating force—that is to say, it imparts an urge away from an object that the agent conceptualizes. While we define "fear" in terms of the feeling we have under certain circumstances, a feeling that gives us a motive *away* from the object or cause of the feeling, the fear itself does not contain the idea of the object or the circumstances. Nonetheless, the passion does have an object. Here I agree with Rachel Cohon, who has argued that a passion has an object in virtue of its causal relations to beliefs, whose ideas provide

---

[9] I think that if we are precise about it, we will find that when ideas cause passions, the idea that causes the passion is actually different from the idea of the object or goal of the passion. In the example, the cause-idea is the idea of the unsafe neighborhood, while the idea of the object is the imagined idea of an assailant.

the passion with its object.[10] I would add to this point that our definitions or concepts of particular passions may include reference to the causes and effects of these passions, but the passions themselves, identified phenomenologically, stand in contingent relationships to their causes and effects. I defend this view further below.

A question this way of reading Hume raises is how passions come to be connected to objects if they don't represent them. If my anger at another's behavior does not contain a representation of her, then how is it directed toward her, rather than toward someone else, or rather than toward no one, especially if it is like my being sick? The answer implied by the interpretation for which I've argued is that the connection of a passion with a particular object is provided by reasoning. If the possibility of being attacked or mugged is a source of fear for me, then of course, I want to avoid persons who might perpetrate an assault. When I believe that a stranger who is approaching my car in an unknown neighborhood may be an assailant, my fear is connected with that person. So, while the passion of fear doesn't stand for or represent anything by itself, it becomes connected to an object or person nevertheless, by reasoning or belief.[11]

4.3.2 The Structural Conception

Hume's treatment of the difference between the direct and the indirect passions relies on structural and causal accounts. How is this approach compatible with the phenomenal conception described above?[12]

---

[10] Cohon (1994: 190 ff). Weller (2002) argues against Cohon's interpretation by claiming that it undermines Hume's argument that reason and passion cannot be opposed. Weller says that the view that passions get their objects through the beliefs that cause the passions commits Hume to the following argument. What is not intrinsically either true or false cannot be opposed by or contradicted by what is intrinsically either true or false. Judgments of the understanding, beliefs, are intrinsically true or false, but passions are not, since they get their objects contingently. So, passion cannot oppose reason. Then Weller says of the first claim, "The only ground for accepting it is the assumption that only acts that are intrinsically intentional are intentional at all. But acceptance of this assumption directly undermines the causal account of intentionality at issue" (2002: 217). I don't see how this is the case, although I admit I am uncertain how to understand Weller's point. I take it that he reads, "isn't intrinsically either true or false" to mean "is extrinsically true or false," so that the claim reads, "What is extrinsically true or false cannot be opposed by or contradicted by what is intrinsically true or false." That does seem correct, but to deny of passions that they are intrinsically true or false is not to assert that they are thereby extrinsically true or false, even if they do have objects given to them contingently. Instead, the view I am defending is the view that passions have objects but they do not represent their objects, nor are they true or false in virtue of having them.

[11] Lilli Alanen has a different perspective on Hume's view of the passions and intentionality. She argues that his view is actually not at odds with the received view of intentionality, "the one expressed by the usual roundabout references in discussions of cognitive science and philosophy of mind to Brentano and 'aboutness'" (Alanen 2005: 123), which excludes sensations and emotions from the domain of the intentional.

[12] Amyas Merivale suggests that because of tensions Hume saw in his own view of the indirect passions, which officially treats them as simple impressions, but which offers the double relation account, Hume changed his mind about them by the time he wrote the *Dissertation on the Passions*. Merivale thinks that, there, he purposely depicts them as complexes (Merivale 2009: 196–202). While this hypothesis might be correct, I find it fairly speculative.

Hume offers his own reconciliation in this way:

> The passions of PRIDE and HUMILITY being simple and uniform impressions, 'tis impossible we can ever, by a multitude of words, give a just definition of them, or indeed of any of the passions. The utmost we can pretend to is a description of them, by an enumeration of such circumstances, as attend them: But as these words, *pride* and *humility*, are of general use, and the impressions they represent the most common of any, every one, of himself, will be able to form a just idea of them, without any danger of mistake. (T 2.1.2.1)

Hume recognizes that the feelings of pride and humility are simple impressions and admit of no analysis themselves; but he also suggests that we can describe the conditions under which such phenomena occur, and that this is another way to portray them accurately. He says the same when he introduces his examination of the feelings of love and hatred (T 2.2.1.1). So, it looks as though we can identify passions in two ways: phenomenally, by how they feel, and structurally, by the circumstances that attend them, including their causes and effects. The structural conception of the passions, is, I suggest, our public and scientific conception of them. The feelings persons experience as, say, love, compose the referent of "love," that is, they are instances of the feeling, but are only privately accessible.

As noted in CHAPTER 1, Hume explains that the indirect passions are caused by a double relation of impressions and ideas. "That cause, which excites the passion, is related to the object, which nature has attributed to the passion; the sensation, which the cause separately produces, is related to the sensation of the passion" (T 2.1.5.5). The particular double relation of impressions and ideas that attends each type of indirect passion is distinctive to it. So, "Any thing, that gives a pleasant sensation, and is related to self, excites the passion of pride, which is also agreeable, and has self for its object" (T 2.1.5.8). As we've seen, humility has a parallel, but opposite, structural origin to pride, and love and hatred follow suit. Earlier I wrote that, even though not all the passions are motivating, the non-motivating ones produce a "directedness," not in action, but insofar as they bring to mind an object or idea connected to the passion as cause.[13] In the case of non-motivating passions, as pride and humility are, the mind is pointed to an object already present. In the case of the

---

[13] Páll Árdal thinks that Hume misrepresents the relationship between pride and the idea of self when presenting it as a causal one:
> Whenever one is proud, one's thought is drawn to oneself, but according to Hume, it could have been otherwise. It just so happens that the feeling of pride makes one think of oneself, that when you are already proud, your thought turns to yourself. (Árdal 1989: 388)

Terence Penelhum contends that Hume's description of indirect passions is implausible because of
> [his] rigid separation of the emotion and its object, and the consequent impossibility of their relationship being other than contingent and external. To describe the relationship as internal would probably force us to introduce the notion of the intensional object, which if I am right, has not made an appearance in Hume's text. (Penelhum 1975: 99–100)

I see no reason why Hume cannot define pride in terms of its causal relationships, and indeed, this is exactly what he does in his discussion of the differences among pride, humility, love, and hatred. What

motivating passions, the mind is directed to an absent object. When the direction is accompanied by volition, the body is moved to action by the passion in regard to the absent object.[14]

Hume's offering his structural accounts of the passions does not, I think, undermine his phenomenological account, since these characterizations serve different purposes. The phenomenological account picks out the mental states or referents that are identified by the terms love, hatred, desire, benevolence, and so on. The structural account gives us descriptions of the passions, that is, it explains the various concepts of love, hatred, desire, benevolence, respectively, and so on. Our definitions of particular passions may refer to their causes, effects, and circumstances under which they occur, but the passions themselves stand in a contingent relationship to these causes, effects, and circumstances. It makes sense to identify the passion with the impression itself, but the impression of reflection has an object in virtue of its cause. Donald Davidson, in writing about whether Hume can take such a line, says:

> But whatever we decide about Hume, there is not a good argument to show that causal relations rule out necessary connections. According to my dictionary, snowblink is a white luminosity on the underside of clouds caused by the reflection of light from a snow surface. This is a necessary truth, though a truth about a causal relation. (Davidson 1976: 755)

Likewise, I understand Hume, in his structural account, as offering defining characterizations of the passions by referring to their causal relations to other perceptions.[15]

Lilli Alanen speculates that Hume's "youthful, rough-and-ready" classification of beliefs as either relations of ideas or as representations of matters of fact left no room for more subtle distinctions among cognitions, and that his theory has no place for emotive states defined by characteristic functions or for particular objects (Alanen 2005: 137). However, her disagreement with the interpretation I here defend is tempered by the following analysis. She points to the fact that passions as impressions of reflection have no antecedents to copy; so, for Hume, the only class to which they can belong is "simple existents." Still, they are "acts of perception" and so each is about an object related to each perception by natural association, in the way that

---

"just so happens" is not that when I feel pride, I think of myself, but rather, when I take pleasure in something related to me, I think of myself. This state of affairs is indicative of the feeling of pride.

[14] Amy Schmitter (2009: 235) suggests that the sense in which a passion like pride is about its object is that the passion "turns our view" to the object (as Hume says); thus, the object is an object of attention, not the subject of a proposition or the reference of a representation. In general, the indirect passions exhibit intentionality in the whole train of perceptions, which are causally linked.

[15] Hsueh Qu has argued for a different interpretation: that a passion can be both simple and intrinsically intentional because the intentionality of the passion is constituted by the qualitative character or phenomenal feeling of the passion. For instance, the directedness of anger at another is "part and parcel of its particular feel" and cannot be separated from it (Qu 2012: 110). I think his view is worthy of consideration, but I wonder how it explains the allegation that intentionality involves directedness toward a *particular* object. It seems that my anger at my friend, my anger at my sister, my anger at my neighbor, etc., would each have a distinctive feeling on this view, and yet somehow each must be identifiable as anger.

sensory perceptions are related to their objects. For instance, one perceptual smell is related to coffee and another to fried bacon. Analogously, even though inner sensations like lust and thirst are caused by physiological conditions, they always appear with ideas of objects that satisfy them. And likewise, passions—impressions of reflection—do not occur without the idea reflected, but each also has its own characteristic feeling and bodily expression, which do not depend on the objects (see ibid.: 134–6). "We can, by analysis, separate... the impressions... from the ideas that cause them, as well as from their objects—the ideas to which they turn the mind" (ibid.: 136). One kind of impression, like anger, can have many kinds of objects, and one idea can cause different passions; yet, the passion never occurs without the ideas between which it is placed. I find her interpretation compatible with the functional narrative of the passions I have suggested.

4.4 "Unreasonable" and "Reasonable" Motivating Passions

After Hume confirms his conclusion about the non-opposition between reason and passion by his discussion of original existences, he suggests a way in which passions might be considered "unofficially," or "non-technically," contrary to reason: when they are accompanied by a judgment or opinion ("a judgment of the understanding") that itself is false or contrary to the evidence. That passions could be thought unreasonable is possible only because the judgments with which they are associated are assessed by reason, rather than the passions themselves. Accordingly, he describes two ways in which a passion ("affection") may be *called* unreasonable, although technically, it is not: (1) when it is founded on the supposition of objects that do not actually exist; and (2) when, in being moved by the passion, we make bad causal judgments about the means to the end (see T 2.3.3.6–10). Here I take a close look at each case to ask what the source of alleged irrationality really is.

In the case of (1), more specifically, Hume describes it in this way: "When a passion, such as hope or fear, grief or joy, despair or security, is founded on the supposition of the existence of objects, which really do not exist" (T 2.3.3.6). I start with a point of clarification. I have argued that motivating passions are for objects or states of affairs that can be brought about. So, there is a sense in which we always desire what is non-existent. In the cases Hume is describing here, however, his point is that it is "unreasonable" to feel a motivating passion in response to an object or a state of affairs that does not exist, *when that passion is caused by the false belief that the object or state of affairs does exist*. So, for instance, if Romeo feels grief at the death of Juliet, when in fact she is not dead, but in a deeply drugged state, his passion is, in the sense under consideration, unreasonable. In this case, his own desire to take his own life, which follows upon his grief, is also unreasonable. So, he, of course, is aiming to bring about a state of affairs that did not previously exist—his own death—but it is based upon the mistaken supposition of another state of affairs, that Juliet is dead. Now, we might assess two different circumstances under which a person might have a passion based on the supposition of an object or circumstance that does not exist. One is when the agent doesn't know that the object or circumstance does not exist, or has no evidence about it one way or the other, so she believes it exists and has a motivating passionate response to it. The second circumstance is when the agent knows that object or circumstance doesn't exist, but still claims to experience a motivating passion connected to the idea that it exists. Since Hume thinks the passion derives its unreasonableness from the false belief with which it is associated, he cannot have in mind the second circumstance. Either that person is mentally ill (that is, we have no explanation for her state of mind), or she has misidentified her passion as desire when it is really a wish. Hume reinforces this point a paragraph later when he says that:

The moment we perceive the falsehood of any supposition [about the existence of objects] ... our passions yield to our reason without any opposition. I may desire a fruit as of an excellent relish; but whenever you convince me of my mistake, my longing ceases. (T 2.3.3.7)

So, let's return to the first instance, the case of someone desiring an end that depends upon believing something to exist when it does not. Here we might raise the question whether we would ordinarily call a passion based on false beliefs unreasonable. If I desire to order the salmon on the restaurant menu, not knowing that the kitchen has run out of it this evening, are we really tempted to say that I'm unreasonable in my desire? The desire is based on supposing something is available that actually is not, but ordinary assessments of reasonableness in affections and desires seem to be relative to the beliefs of the agent. If Romeo thought his life without Juliet would be miserable and he mistakenly thought she was dead, was the motivation to kill himself irrational? Perhaps Hume has misidentified just what circumstances lead us to call passions contrary to reason.

We can, however, say this on Hume's behalf. He would technically reject this notion of reasonableness in passions as well, since his point is that the passions are neither reasonable nor unreasonable, even relative to an agent's beliefs. The assessment of a passion relative to belief is actually an assessment of predictability, not one of reasonable motivation: given what the agent believes and given what we know about her (her dispositions and character), what would we expect her to desire? If I believe I've been deceived by a friend, given that I have certain (widely-shared) dispositions, I can be expected to feel anger; and so it seems reasonable that I do. But this has nothing to do with rational justification: we have no rational standards of appropriate feelings, given Hume's arguments about the jurisdiction of reason. Since the only mental states subject to rational justification in this scenario are beliefs, the assessment of reasonableness must derive from them. Thus, for Hume, the genuine sense in which we can say that a desire for an end is unreasonable is when it is based on unreasonable beliefs about the end.

In the case of (2), there are some complications in the second way in which Hume says a passion could be called unreasonable: the case in which we are moved by the passion to take insufficient means to our ends, due to mistakes in causal judgment. The irrationality in that case actually seems to lie in unreasonable action, and not in a defective passion. For I may have a desire for an end based on proper information about the end, and even if I make a mistake about how to achieve that end, nothing has changed about the assessment of the original desire. If the original desire, in conjunction with a false belief about how to satisfy it, generates an auxiliary desire that does not actually contribute to achieving the originally-desired end, then the auxiliary desire might be called unreasonable, but the status of the original desire seems not to change. The action, then, might be called irrational, because it does not achieve the end the agent aims for. For instance, a graduate student wants to do well on her modern philosophy comps, but mistakenly believes that the exam will emphasize works from the 1600s. She forms the goal of studying the writings of Descartes, Hobbes, and Locke more intensely than those of Berkeley and Hume. We might call the desire formed in light of the original desire unreasonable because in fact the exam does not emphasize the texts she aims to study. This is what Hume seems to have in mind when he writes, a paragraph later:

I may will the performance of certain actions as a means of obtaining any desir'd good; but as my willing of these actions is only secondary, and founded on the supposition that they are causes of the propos'd effect; as soon as I discover the falshood of that supposition, they must become indifferent to me. (T 2.3.3.7)

But an unreasonable belief about the means to the end of a desire does not by itself make us call the original desire unreasonable. While it is not clear that Hume intended to say this, he certainly leaves it open to interpretation that this is what he means when he says that the second way in which a passion could be regarded as unreasonable is "[w]hen in exerting any passion in action, we chuse means insufficient for the design'd end, and deceive ourselves in our judgment of causes and effects" (T 2.3.3.6).

Hume's second imputed notion of unreasonableness in a passion may make sense in another way, however. If I act on a mistaken belief about the means to my ends, it may be common to say, at least in some cases, that my desire or end has become unreasonable in light of the circumstances. That is, the end is unreasonable in cases in which the action I take actually undermines achieving that end. If I want to make it to an appointment on time, miscalculate how long it will take me to get there, and consequently, I leave much too late to arrive on time, my desire to make it to the appointment on time does seem now to be unreasonable. I can still wish I would arrive on time, but that wish is not reflective of an end on which I can now act; so it's not rational to sustain the desire. Instead of desiring the end, we now expect that

I experience feelings of regret because I didn't allow enough time. However, there are cases of my miscalculating the means to my end that simply result in my taking a less efficient means over a more efficient one, but do not undermine my end altogether. If I want to get to the emergency room quickly, and I mistakenly choose a route that has more traffic on it than I expected, my desire to get there quickly is not unreasonable, even though my means is not as efficient as it might have been if I had gone another way. Just because my means are less than optimal doesn't indicate that taking them undermines the point of my desire. So, the most charitable reading of Hume's second imputed sense of unreasonableness in passion is best understood as a case in which the passion (desire) is unreasonable when the agent takes a mistaken means to the end that makes the desire pointless, or impossible to fulfill—and this action is due to a faulty belief.

A third way in which one might call a desire unreasonable is when the end of the desire requires means that are impossible or out of reach, and the agent is mistaken about the feasibility of the means. Perhaps Hume doesn't mention this as a third notion of unreasonableness because it can be seen as an instance of the second. This is plausible, given the reading of the second for which I have argued above—namely, that the mistaken means would in practice undermine achieving the end. If the means is an impossible one for the agent, then the corresponding end is impossible to achieve, and we could say it is undermined as an end from the beginning. For instance, I desire to buy a huge house for which I will never be able to get a loan, or for which I will never be able to make the payments if I do get the loan. We can assume that I've made no mistakes about the qualities of the house that make me desire it, so there are no faulty beliefs about the end. I do have fantastic beliefs about what I can handle financially, however. So, in that sense, I have mistaken beliefs about the means, that is, not about what they are, but about whether they are within my reach. I'm rightly thought unreasonable for desiring an end when there are, though unbeknownst to me, insurmountable problems for me in taking the means.

After explaining the two ways in which passions might be "called" unreasonable, Hume emphasizes, using three memorable examples, that in no other way than those he has explained, can passions be regarded as contrary to reason.[16] The examples are presumably cases in which we are tempted to think a desire or passion involved is unreasonable. Obviously, Hume intends that none is a case where the passion in question is founded on the supposition of objects that don't exist or where the agent has mistaken judgments about the means:

'Tis not contrary to reason to prefer the destruction of the world to the scratching of my finger. 'Tis not contrary to reason for me to chuse my total ruin, to prevent the least uneasiness of an *Indian* or person wholly unknown to me. 'Tis as little contrary to reason to prefer even my own

---

[16] See Weller (2004) for a very detailed and interesting discussion of these cases. I don't agree with all of Weller's analysis and will note a couple of points of departure between us as I go.

acknowledg'd lesser good to my greater, and have a more ardent affection for the former than the latter. (T 2.3.3.6)

One question Hume's discussion of unreasonable passion raises is whether he intends to say that passions founded on properly-formed or true beliefs are reasonable. In the technical sense, passions are neither reasonable nor unreasonable, but if Hume allows that they can be unreasonable in a non-technical sense, then he surely is committed to saying that they can be reasonable in the same way. So, presumably, the preferences highlighted in these three examples are, in that sense, reasonable ones. Then he adds an explanation of how one actually could prefer the lesser goods referenced in each of these examples over the apparently greater goods:

A trivial good may, from certain circumstances, produce a desire superior to what arises from the greatest and most valuable enjoyment; nor is there any thing more extraordinary in this, than in mechanics to see one pound weight raise up a hundred by the advantage of its situation. In short, a passion must be accompany'd with some false judgment, in order to its being unreasonable; and even then 'tis not the passion, properly speaking, which is unreasonable, but the judgment. (T 2.3.3.6)

The examples of course concern comparative goods (which, in some sense, all ends are) for self and for others. The first two are "extreme" cases, chosen, of course, so that there is no doubt about the dramatically different statuses of the two goods at stake in each example. I take it that, in the first and third cases, to prefer is not simply to have an attraction for the one, but it is to desire the one more strongly than the other. This is made clear in Hume's follow-up paragraph where he explains how a lesser good could produce "a superior" desire. In the first example, preferring the destruction of the world to the scratching of my finger, I desire more strongly a great evil for others in order to have a trivial good for myself. Of course, this assumes that I'm aware that destroying the world means destroying myself, and so I ensure my survival in some way, perhaps as Annette Baier (1991: 165) suggests, by blasting off in a spacecraft the moment before destruction. In the second example, choosing my entire ruin to save a slight pain for a person in another country unknown to me, I sacrifice the greatest good for myself, my life, in order to produce a trivial good for another person unconnected to me. In the third example, preferring my lesser good to my greater, I have a stronger desire for an insignificant good for myself than I have for a significant good for myself. This third instance is, in fact, quite common, and what we generally call imprudence.

The reason we're tempted to think of these cases as exemplifying unreasonable passions is this. The fact that the agent considers the good more strongly desired greater than a lesser good implies that he or she has made an evaluation of the ends at hand. The evaluation is a deliberate process, resulting in a reflection of the agent's values. If the causal strength of the agent's passion for an end doesn't correspond to the evaluation of that end, we conclude that the passion is faulty, or that the person is at fault insofar as she doesn't react in the proper ways to her own evaluations. It looks as though there is a failure of rationality when this happens. Because we consider judgment a function of reason, we are apt to say that reason has been overcome by emotion or appetite. Consider the case of a person's having the fourth glass of wine at a dinner gathering, knowing that he will surely drive home physically and mentally impaired for having it. In that moment, he has a stronger desire for the drink than he has for his and others' safety, even though he values safety more highly than he values drinking nice wines. What Hume goes on to say is that the phenomenon of preferring a lesser good to a greater is not at all unusual. (This is not in itself an argument that it is not contrary to reason, though.) By means of its proximity and immediacy to the agent, the less-valued good can have a greater influence on the person's passions than the more-valued good. This is a naturalistic explanation of the occurrence, consistent with earlier arguments in Hume concerning the mind's principles of operation. The production of a passion is a causal process, caused by the prospect of pleasure or pain. We might think that the greater the pleasure anticipated by the good, the stronger the desire for it. But the generation of a passion is a matter of the impression of pleasure or pain, or an idea of a source of pleasure or pain (caused by the impression), acting causally upon the mind; and a current impression of pleasure or pain, or one just felt, is more vivid than an idea of one that is distant. The vivacity of the cause will influence the strength of the effect. So, we have no grounds on which to believe that the good assessed by the agent as the greatest good will produce the strongest desire.

We thus have a naturalistic explanation of how it is that the thought of the most valued good among those at stake does not always produce the strongest desire. We have already seen the logical argument for this claim, based on Hume's characterization of reason and its function of discerning truth and falsity. If passions are called rational or irrational derivatively from beliefs associated with them, and none of the agents in the examples above holds false beliefs about their ends, or the means to them, the passions involved are not unreasonable. I have already noted that, by inference, they must therefore be reasonable (but only in the same nontechnical sense in which they are not unreasonable). It may sound incredible to say that these sorts of desires and the behaviors they cause are reasonable, even if one does know all the pertinent facts—that, for instance, it's reasonable for me to risk my life to avoid a very unpleasant medical treatment, instead of enduring the discomfort and perhaps ensuring my survival. However, for Hume at least, evaluations of reasonableness are not all we can say critically about passions and actions, and they are certainly not—especially in this derivative sense of reasonableness—the most significant evaluations we can make. His theory of moral evaluation, for which he has not argued at this point in the *Treatise*, will imply that in all three cases, the agent is exhibiting a moral deficiency. All three motives would be disapproved generally by observers taking an unbiased perspective and sympathizing with those directly affected by the actions, the criterion of vice at the heart of Hume's moral theory. Imprudence is generally a vice, even when the actions it causes are based on accurate information, and its moral deficiency is highly visible to all persons with normal sensibilities.

I have mentioned two ways in which Hume writes about reasonableness: (1) the official and technical sense in which only beliefs can be reasonable (rational), when they are true or assessed by reason as based on proper evidence and inference (and unreasonable when they are false or not properly founded) and (2) the derivative sense in which Hume allows that passions can be reasonable (or unreasonable), depending on whether they are based on true beliefs about ends or about means. There is a third sense of reasonableness that Hume acknowledges, although he thinks it technically involves a mistake: (3) the sense in which people talk about certain passions as reasonable because they *feel* like reason. Reason operates with little emotional upheaval for most people (except philosophers, according to Hume!), so the calm passions are tranquil states that are sometimes thought to be determinations of reason. So, when one is motivated by a calm passion like benevolence or love of life, that passion is often thought reasonable by those who "judge of things from the first view and appearance" (T 2.3.4.8). Likewise, affections that become settled dispositions of character are experienced with little consternation or excitement because they have become commonplace for the agent. Thus, acting "in character" may also be regarded as reasonable in this sense. This point raises the question whether any character traits, regardless of their content, might be considered reasonable in this sense—selfishness and imprudence, for instance, when I act on these desires regularly. I think the answer is no, but I also think that Hume himself rejects this sense of reasonableness in any case. It certainly has nothing to do with his analysis of the three striking cases. Hume's argument is not this: preferring the destruction of the world to a scratch on my finger, choosing my ruin to give a small good to a stranger, and preferring my lesser to my greater good are not contrary to reason because they are indicative of settled traits of the agent. This is not his argument because even if any or all of these is a settled preference, consistent with past choices, this "settled-disposition" sense of reasonableness is not the sense in which Hume has said passions can be reasonable or not.[17] Hume himself sees calling calm passions reasonable the result of a failure to make fine distinctions and to investigate beyond the appearances. His point is that none of those preferences is causally connected to misinformation or faulty belief, and so none of them is contrary to reason in that sense.

Hume concludes his discussion in "Of the influencing motives of the will" with a brief treatment of how the will may sometimes be determined to action by calm passions and sometimes by violent ones. People are often moved by a calm passion for their long-term self-interest, and sometimes they are moved by a violent passion for the nearer pleasure. He mentions that we admire people who are consistently

---

[17] Weller (ibid.) argues that the passions in the first two cases ought to be understood as settled dispositions.

moved by the calm and settled dispositions, calling the virtue "strength of mind." This is a notion of Hume's that I will discuss in CHAPTER 6. I mention it here because it has been argued that strength of mind is a notion of reasonableness in action that Hume accepts (see Weller 2004). I hope it is clear for reasons I have already given that this is not a sense of reasonableness in *passions* that Hume himself accepts.

4.5 Has Hume Effectively Countered the Rationalists?

Hume's characterization of reason and the passions constitutes a direct reply to the thesis that reason and passion can oppose one another over motivation to action. Whether it also undermines the notion that reason can be a "counsellor" to the passions, guiding them to their proper ends, depends on what the guidance of reason is alleged to involve. It might mean:

1. Reason originates proper ends that compete with the ends of passion when they are improper.
2. The distorted representations of good embodied in the passions are countered by proper representations of good offered by reason.
3. Reason offers a description of the means to achieve the ends of the passions.
4. Reason identifies ends that are good, or particular objects that are instances of the Good, and "shows" them to the passions, which are naturally directed toward good or the Good.

Hume's argument concerning the functions and purview of reason and passion, respectively, refutes claims (1) and (2), since he shows that reason does not originate (motives to) ends, and that passions are not representations of anything outside themselves. Hume's view is consistent with (3), but (3) is a very weak notion of guidance, and not likely to satisfy anyone who thought that reason was needed to correct or modify the ends that the passions at time fix us on.

This leaves (4). Nothing in Hume's arguments to this point undermines the idea that reason could identify particular instances of "the Good," given a general description. From what source, however, is this description to come? If it hails from the passions in the sense that they are instinctively motives to an un-cognized Good, then (4) is simply a version of (3). If the description hails from the passions in the sense that they somehow offer it to us as a cognition, Hume has addressed and rejected that possibility in his characterization of the passions. So, the one option left is that reason is a source of the Good. It is apparent that the sense of "good" at stake here for the rationalists is moral good, not just natural good. Hume's argument against the possibility that reason could be the source of moral good comes later, in his discussion of the origin of our moral distinctions. If he succeeds in making that case, then he has effectively overturned the early modern moral and motivational rationalist psychology.

5

Morality and Motivation

In CHAPTER 1, I discussed Hume's identification of passions as motives, some of which are virtues and others vices. How motives become one or the other is a matter that Hume takes up in both the *Treatise* and the second *Enquiry*, when he argues for the view that our moral distinctions depend upon sentiments or feelings we experience toward those who exhibit behavior typical of a particular trait. We approve of actions that benefit people generally, or lead to agreeable circumstances, and so the motives behind such behaviors are regarded as virtues, such as benevolence and gratitude. Actions that undermine happiness, or produce disagreeable circumstances, are met with disapproval, and their causes are thought to be vices, such as malice and ingratitude. The relevant approvals and disapprovals are the product of spectators' sympathizing with the persons directly affected by the agent showing the behavior under consideration. The principle of sympathy, which I discuss more in CHAPTER 6, is our natural capacity to experience feelings similar to those around us, when our ideas of others' pleasures and pains are converted into impressions or sentiments of our own (T 2.1.11.3). But these sentiments count as moral sentiments only when they are experienced from what Hume calls a "general" or "common" point of view, since sympathies can vary, given personal perspectives, but moral judgments do not. My personal feelings favor family and friends, but genuine moral judgments of character do not. In a general or common viewpoint, personal connections and relations are disregarded, and approvals and disapprovals are felt with consistency and near uniformity among spectators (T 3.1.2.4, T 3.3.1.16–17). Hume defends this theory of moral sentiment after he presents the argument that reason cannot be the source of our moral distinctions. That argument regarding reason invokes a thesis about the motivational power of "morality," which is the focus of my discussion here. So, to talk about "morality" and its motivational effect is not to focus on the motivation produced by the virtues and vices themselves, which is the subject of CHAPTER 6, but is instead to focus on our comprehension of the difference between virtue and vice, and how it might have a practical influence.

5.1 Hume's Motivation Argument

In Book 3 of the *Treatise*, Hume argues against the rationalist account of the origin of moral distinctions, and for his sentimentalist explanation of their derivation.[1] He applies his previously-defended thesis regarding the impotence of reason from Book 2. First, Hume notes the natural, practical effect of "morality," which is used by educators and moralists to influence persons' behavior: "If morality had naturally no influence on human passions and actions,'twere in vain to take such pains to inculcate it; and nothing wou'd be more fruitless than that multitude of rules and precepts, with which all moralists abound" (T 3.1.1.5). He observes that morality is always discussed under practical philosophy, rather than speculative, since it influences our passions and affections, while the judgments of the understanding do not. "And this is confirm'd by common experience, which informs us, that men are often govern'd by their duties, and are deter'd from some actions by the opinion of injustice, and impell'd to others by that of obligation." Then Hume adds his observation about the influence of morality to his thesis concerning the inability of reason alone to motivate, and derives his anti-rationalist conclusion, an argument which I have already referenced in CHAPTER 2:

Since morals, therefore, have an influence on the actions and affections, it follows, that they cannot be deriv'd from reason; and that because reason alone, as we have already prov'd, can never have any such influence. Morals excite passions, and produce or prevent actions. Reason of itself is utterly impotent in this particular. The rules of morality, therefore, are not conclusions of our reason. (T 3.1.1.6)

To fill in an assumed premise in the argument, recall that he adds: "An active principle can never be founded on an inactive; and if reason be inactive in itself, it must remain so in all its shapes and appearances..." (T 3.1.1.7).

I have indicated that the early moderns writing on the passions did not generally portray reason as a motivator on its own, but many held the view that reason could and should be a guide to the passions, in matters moral and prudential, and that passions and reason could oppose one another over the direction of action. Some of the seventeenth- and eighteenth-century thinkers regarded the discernment of moral norms or their constitution as lying with reason, which in some cases included an intellectualized conception of the passions. So, for instance, in Descartes (1649: article 45), reason can correct the passions' representations of the good; in Ayloffe (1700: 47–51) and Burghope (1701: 4), reason has to show the passions their proper objects; and in Bragge (1708: 6–16), reason assesses the relative worth of goods. Among other targets for Hume are: Ralph Cudworth, who treats morality analogously to geometry in their being composed of necessary, immutable truths[2]; John

---

[1] Some of the discussion of this chapter is based on Radcliffe (1996, 2006), but with many important modifications.

[2] Hume refers to Cudworth, along with Malebranche (who gets credit for starting "this abstract theory of morals") and Clarke, at EPM 3.34, note 12. There Hume criticizes the rationalists for their inability to account for the virtue of justice.

Locke, who regarded moral truths as demonstrable[3]; Samuel Clarke (1705), who held that there are eternal fitnesses among things in nature that determine goodness and are obvious to us; and William Wollaston (1724), who took virtue to be conformity of action to reason or truth.[4] It is not clear who in the modern period fits the description of philosophers who held that moral facts are discerned inductively, although certain contemporary naturalists do (e.g., utilitarian theorists, depending on their metaethics). Nonetheless, Hume makes it clear that he also intends to undercut any suggestion that moral distinctions might be discerned in the way that contingent facts about the world are known.

I have also suggested that a credible explanation why Hume argued fervently against the thesis that reason alone can motivate, even though it was rarely explicitly defended by any writer, is that he regarded the views of many of the early moderns to imply it, after their theories were purged of teleology. So, Hume's argument from motivation against moral rationalism (The Motivation Argument), in outline, is:

(1) Morals have an influence on the actions and affections. (Morals excite passions and produce or prevent actions.)

(2) Reason alone can never influence actions and affections. (Reason of itself cannot excite passions and produce or prevent actions.)

(3) An active principle can never be founded on an inactive.

(Conclusion) The rules of morality are not founded on reason alone.

He repeats the argument in EPM, in slightly different terms:

The end of all moral speculations is to teach us our duty; and, by proper representations of the deformity of vice and beauty of virtue, beget correspondent habits, and engage us to avoid the one, and embrace the other. But is this ever to be expected from inferences and conclusions of the understanding, which of themselves have no hold of the affections, nor set in motion the active powers of men? They discover truths: But where the truths which they discover are indifferent, and beget no desire or aversion, they can have no influence on conduct and behaviour. What is honourable, what is fair, what is becoming, what is noble, what is generous, takes possession of the heart, and animates us to embrace and maintain it. What is intelligible, what is evident, what is probable, what is true, procures only the cool assent of the understanding; and gratifying a speculative curiosity, puts an end to our researches. (EPM 1.7)

Here the argument goes:

(1) Representations of morality (what is fair, noble, generous, etc.) animate (motivate, influence) us to embrace and maintain what they represent.

---

[3] See *An Essay Concerning Human Understanding* (1690) and *Essays on the Law of Nature* (1694). Hume refers to Locke's views on epistemology at scattered places in the *Treatise*, of course. He criticizes Locke's "selfish system of morals"—that is, his defense of psychological egoism—in EPM App. 2; Locke is mentioned by name at EPM App. 2.2.

[4] Hume criticizes Wollaston's view in particular at T 3.1.1.15.

(2) Conclusions of the understanding, about what is probable, true, etc., do not animate us.

(Implicit conclusion) Representations of morality are not conclusions of the understanding.

I have defended in depth an interpretation of premise (2), and my focus in this chapter is on the meaning and implications of premise (1). An acceptable interpretation must meet two constraints. First, it should make Hume's Motivation Argument valid. Second, it should explain how it is reasonable for Hume to move from the conclusion here, that the rules of morality are not founded on reason alone, to the conclusion he defends in the second section of T 3.1.1, that the rules of morality are founded in moral sentiments of approval and disapproval. Of course, either requirement is defeasible if it turns out that a preponderance of Hume's texts support a reading that cannot meet it. In that case, there would be a consistency problem in Hume's own view. But I think there is not.

5.2 Moral Internalisms

Here I rely on the version of the Motivation Argument from the *Treatise*; I discuss the version from the *Enquiry*, which differs in certain ways, in Section 5.5. In order for Hume's Motivation Argument against rationalism to be valid, the first premise must be taken to mean that morality *on its own* motivates—that is, without the assistance of a passion or motive outside of it. For if moral concerns motivate only in conjunction with a separate passion—for instance, in conjunction with our propensity to long-term self-interest, which perhaps is served by morality—then there is nothing to prevent morality's being derived from reason. Considerations derived from reason are inert by themselves, but presumably, they could motivate in conjunction with a propensity to long-term self-interest, as well. So, if morality motivates by conjoining with a separate passion, and if reason cannot motivate alone, but it can motivate by conjoining with a passion, then morality could very well be derived from reason.[5]

That "morality" motivates on its own is a thesis that has been labeled in contemporary philosophy "moral internalism," although it is also sometimes called "motivational" internalism.[6] But the thesis so stated is vague. Thomas Nagel writes of internalism:

---

[5] For a different reading of the premise, see Sayre-McCord (2008). On Sayre-McCord's interpretation, the disposition to be moved by the thought that an action is one's duty requires the conventions that make possible the thought that something is a duty:

> Hume's acknowledgement of the essential role of the passions is compatible with thinking that morality *alone* can influence action precisely because the dispositions upon which the actions depend are the dispositions the having of which constitutes one as being a moral person. In noting that these are required, we are thereby not appealing to something that is not part of morality. (2008: 313)

[6] The terms "internalism" and "externalism" were first introduced by W. D. Falk (1947–48: 492–510).

On this view the motivation must be so tied to the truth, or meaning, of ethical statements that when in a particular case someone is (or perhaps merely believes that he is) morally required to do something, it follows that he has a motivation for doing it. (Nagel 1970: 7)

Thus, the thesis, on Nagel's characterization, is a conceptual or semantic one. Korsgaard describes internalism as the view that "the reason why" an action is right and "the reasons why you do it" are the same (Korsgaard 1986: 316). (More precisely, I think she should say that the reasons why an act is right and the reasons a person *has* for doing it, although she may not act on them, are the same.) The reason why an act is justified, for Korsgaard, is the same as the motive; so the point is that internalists see justifications as among motivating states. For the externalist, justification and motivation are logically separate, and the factors that make an action right need have nothing to do with whether or how they motivate. Korsgaard and Nagel agree that Hobbes's theory is a paradigmatic internalist view, since Hobbes maintains both that people ought to do what is in their enlightened self-interest, and that concern for the self is the fundamental motive of human nature. Mill is the paradigmatic externalist, maintaining as he does, that morality consists in maximizing happiness, while admitting that humans are naturally motivated by other concerns, and so need to be subject to the inculcation of utilitarian aims by education and upbringing.

It's important to note that the "motivation" referenced in the internalist thesis is motivation in the sense of possessing a motive to act on moral justification, but that motive need not be the causally strongest motive. In other words, internalism is not the implausibly strong view that every time a person makes a judgment about moral duty or justice, etc., she acts in accord with that judgment. Another germane issue is whether the thesis must be presented as a semantic (or conceptual) one, in the way that Nagel presents it. Hume indicates that the fact that persons are motivated by moral concerns is supported by experience, but a conceptual connection cannot be so supported. Hume says that it is the "nature" of morality to motivate; he does not put the claim in terms of what an ethical statement means. Nonetheless, I think Hume intends his claim to be one about which we have practical or "moral" certainty. In his *Letter to a Gentleman* (1745), Hume defends his *Treatise* views on religion and morality from various misunderstandings. Writing about the status of the claim that everything that begins to exist must have a cause, Hume says:

It is common for Philosophers to distinguish the Kinds of Evidence into *intuitive, demonstrative, sensible,* and *moral*; by which they intend *only* to mark a Difference betwixt them, not to denote a Superiority of one above another. *Moral Certainty* may reach as *high* a Degree of Assurance as *Mathematical*; and our Senses are surely to be comprised amongst the clearest and most convincing of all Evidences. (Letter 26)

Hume says that the claim about causes is not founded on demonstrative or intuitive evidence, but it "is supported by *moral Evidence,* and is followed by a Conviction of the same Kind with these Truths, *That all Men must die*, and that *the Sun will rise*

To-morrow" (Letter 26). Hume's thesis about the motivating effect of morality is also, I think, of the sort that would be incredible to deny. While others' motives are not matters of direct observation, their actions, which are signs of their strongest motives, are. We can also introspect many of our own motives, although perhaps not the calmest ones. So, there is substantial cumulative evidence that acceptance of moral judgments affects passions and actions, and Hume calls such data "moral evidence," that is, the evidence used to derive conclusions about actions "from considerations of motives, temper and situation" (T 2.3.1.15) and which "cements together" with natural evidence "to form only one chain of argument" (T 2.3.1.17). The character of moral evidence allows Hume's thesis about the motivational effects of morality to be the sort of assurance that we accord to other experiential claims about nature. So, I think he is an internalist of a non-standard sort: the thesis is true, not in virtue of the concept of morality, or in virtue of the meaning of moral terms, but in virtue of the constitution of morality, which he explores after the motivation argument. Some contemporary philosophers also argue for understanding moral internalism as a psychological thesis, for which we can muster empirical evidence.[7]

Stephen Darwall, in his study of obligation in the philosophies of the early modern period, offers a useful distinction (Darwall 1995). (1) "Judgment" internalism (also sometimes called "appraiser" internalism) is the view that if one is convinced that one should *x*, then one would under the appropriate conditions have some motivation to *x*. This is the sort of internalism connected to views about the status of normative claims and, as Darwall notes, a view that has led philosophers to adopt non-cognitivism in metaethics.[8] (2) The other sort of internalism, "existence" internalism (also sometimes called "agent" internalism), is the view that it is a necessary condition of some person's having an obligation to *x* that that person would, under appropriate conditions, have a motive to *x* (ibid.: 10). Darwall distinguishes two sorts of existence internalism. (2a) On the first, it is a necessary *consequence* of perceiving or knowing what one ought to do that one is motivated to do what one ought. Having the motive is not part of the moral facts themselves, but persons who comprehend the facts necessarily experience the motivation to conform their behavior to them.[9] (2b) On the second existence internalism, the existence of a motive is

---

[7] See Prinz (2015) for a defense of this way of understanding moral internalism (or motivational internalism, as he calls it). Prinz cites psychological evidence in favor of motivational internalism from many sources, among them: Eskine, et al. (2011); Greene, et al. (2001); Heekeren, et al. (2003); Moll, et al. (2002); Nichols (2002); Schnall, et al. (2008); and Wheatley and Haidt (2005).

[8] For if my conviction that I ought to do *x* necessarily motivates me, then that conviction has the nature of a motive. On many theories of action, a motive is not cognitive in the way beliefs are, since motives are presumably not true or false. So, a moral judgment is not cognitive. See C.L. Stevenson (1944).

[9] Clarke appears to hold this view when he writes, "And by this Understanding or Knowledge of the natural and necessary relations, fitnesses, and proportions of things, the Wills likewise of all Intelligent Beings are constantly directed, and must needs be determined to act accordingly...." (Clarke 1706: 11). Here it looks as though the wills of reasonable persons are determined by these persons' discernment of their obligations, which consist in natural and necessary relations. Furthermore, facts about the persons' psychology do not enter into the determination of the obligations themselves. But since Clarke elsewhere

part of what it is for a person to be obligated or for a moral proposition to be true. In this case, obligation consists in something internal to the agent. This latter is the most interesting kind of internalism since, on it, the content of morality is informed by facts about human motivation (ibid.: 9–11). (I here refer to this version as the "informative version" of existence internalism.) In Nagel's and Korsgaard's discussion, this is the sort of internalism they must be referencing when they point to Hobbes as an example.[10] My aim here is to use this classification of views to shed light on the following question. Which interpretation of Hume's premise "Morals have an influence on the actions and affections" is most plausible?

The claim that morals influence actions and affections translates into talk of the practical effects of obligation quite easily, since "morals" in this context concern what one ought to do or become. Even though Hume gives central moral importance to the possession of virtuous traits of character, he acknowledges that persons who lack virtues can be motivated by a sense of obligation to do the actions that persons with those virtues would do. Hume's discussion of obligation occurs early on in his treatment of the topic of justice in Book 3 of the *Treatise*. It is helpful here to note the structure of Book 3. Part 1 is on the derivation of our moral distinctions in general, in which Hume argues first, in Section 1, that morality is not derived from reason, and second, in Section 2, that morality is derived from moral sentiments. He suggests the view, which he develops later, that virtues and vices are discerned, respectively, by approval (a sort of pleasure) and disapproval (a sort of pain) that we feel toward actors by observing their actions. Part 2 of Book 3 is on justice, and includes a discussion of the mechanism by which we come to respect property, promises, and government, and by which the traits of chastity and modesty become virtues. Early on there, Hume raises the question how being just can be a virtue when acts of justice seem to be done from a regard to the rules of justice, rather than from a natural motive. His answer involves an explanation why justice is an artificial virtue. Hence, in this context, Hume addresses the topic how motivation by a regard for duty or obligation is possible, but I want to emphasize that he means this question to apply generally, not simply within his theory of justice. This is clear from his explanation of obligation:

All morality depends upon our sentiments; and when any action, or quality of the mind, pleases us *after a certain manner*, we say it is virtuous; and when the neglect, or nonperformance of it, displeases us *after a like manner*, we say that we lie under an obligation to perform it. (T 3.2.5.4)

---

writes about the necessity of the passions to agitate people (see APPENDIX), he has to be supposing a teleology whereby the will contains a passionate inclination toward obligation.

[10] This is the case, even though Darwall's discussion shows that Hobbes's theory is actually very nuanced (Darwall 1995: Ch. 3).

Then, in Part 3 of Book 3, he discusses the natural virtues, and develops in some detail the general rules under which observers' reactions to others' characters count as indicative of the moral distinctions we generally accept.

5.3 The Natural-Motive Interpretation

So, it makes sense to look to the discussion of obligation in *Treatise* 3.2 to uncover a plausible interpretation of the claim that morals influence actions and affections. There Hume poses a problem for any theorist who wants to maintain that actions done from duty or obligation are meritorious. He argues that when we praise an action we do so because of the motive that produced it; actions are only signs of character and their value is derived from the traits that cause them. Then he writes:

> All virtuous actions derive their merit only from virtuous motives, and are consider'd merely as signs of those motives. From this principle I conclude, that the first virtuous motive, which bestows a merit on any action, can never be a regard to the virtue of that action, but must be some other natural motive or principle. To suppose, that the mere regard to the virtue of the action, may be the first motive, which produc'd the action, and render'd it virtuous, is to reason in a circle ... And consequently the virtuous motive must be different from the regard to the virtue of the action. A virtuous motive is requisite to render an action virtuous. (T 3.2.1.4)

For instance, we blame a father for neglecting his child because it demonstrates lack of a natural affection for his offspring: "Were not natural affection a duty, the care of children cou'd not be a duty" (T 3.2.1.5).[11] Hume pronounces it an "undoubted maxim" "*that no action can be virtuous, or morally good, unless there be in human nature some motive to produce it, distinct from the sense of its morality*" (T 3.2.1.7). This means, on Hume's account of obligation, that no act can be obligatory unless it be produced by a natural motive whose lack in a character we pronounce vicious.

Hume's undoubted maxim is a possible representation of premise (1) of the Motivation Argument. The argument, using Hume's maxim, could be understood in this way (the Natural-Motive Interpretation) (NM):

(NM1) One cannot be obliged to an action unless there is some motive in human nature that can produce that act.

(NM2) Reason alone is not a natural motive, nor cannot it produce natural motives.

(NM3) An active principle cannot be founded on an inactive principle.

(Conclusion) Morality (obligation) cannot be derived from reason alone.

---

[11] Of course, one might argue that feeding one's children is morally required because of the intrinsic value of one's children, or because of the importance to the general good of each person's caring for his or her offspring, or because it prevents suffering and suffering is a bad thing, and so on. But Hume's point is that while we can talk of the natural goodness or badness of actions, only virtues and vices are morally good or bad. Thus, the moral quality of actions must be derived from the traits from which they are done.

While (NM1) does not seem a very straightforward rendering of the claim that morality influences the *affections* (rather, it has morality *dependent* on the affections), it is a plausible understanding of "Morality influences actions" or "Morality is motivating." On this reading, morality is motivating in the sense that what we ought to do is derived in part from what people generally can do, that is, from motives that are natural to human beings. If the first premise is so understood, then Hume's internalism is close to the informative version of existence internalism, since the content of obligation is determined (approved) by motives commonly existing in human nature. Yet, one important feature of existence internalism is that *the person* who is so obliged necessarily has a motive to the action to which she is obliged; but on Hume's version, it seems, the obligation is based on a motive common in human beings, although not necessarily possessed by that person. Individual persons so obliged can lack the particular motive at stake and in fact would only act from obligation *when* the natural motive was absent. So, I am obliged to be grateful for my neighbor's help on my house painting project, but the obligation does not diminish if I happen to be an ungrateful person. That I ought to be grateful can be a motive to grateful actions (like saying "thanks") when gratefulness is absent from my character.

But the Natural-Motive Interpretation of premise (1) turns into the interesting form of existence internalism if we understand the lack of virtuous behavior in terms, not of the complete absence of the naturally virtuous motive, but of insufficient strength of motivation. Suppose Hume were to claim that all persons possess the virtues to some degree, but that sometimes they have them to a degree insufficient to produce the appropriate action. In that case it would follow that for every obligation there exists in each person a natural motive to the obligated behavior, even if it is weak. Hume does not put it this way, however. He writes of cases in which a virtuous motive is common in humans, and a person "feels his heart *devoid* of that principle" [emphasis mine] (T 3.2.1.8) and so performs the act from a sense of duty. So, he does believe that people are obligated to do actions for which they themselves have *no* natural motive whatsoever, and that they can be moved by their sense of obligation to do the right thing: the action that most others would do from natural virtue.

Whether the first premise of the Motivation Argument qualifies as a variety of existence internalism is less important than whether the Natural-Motive Interpretation is the best way to understand that premise and make sense of the argument overall. I think that it meets the first desideratum for an acceptable interpretation—that is, it makes Hume's argument against moral rationalism valid. The second desideratum is that the Motivation Argument be read in a way that allows Hume to move from its conclusion, that morality is not derived from reason, to his own position that morality is founded on moral sentiments; and here there seems to be a problem. The Natural-Motive Interpretation does not allow this move: its explanation why morality is not founded on reason alone—that it depends upon motives in human nature—can justify only the conclusion that morality is derived from or dependent on natural human motives in the sense that such motives are the objects of our moral evaluations. These are passions like benevolence, gratitude, and kindness toward children, which are distinct from the sentiments of approval and disapproval by which, Hume goes on to argue, we make our moral distinctions. The latter are reactive attitudes, not pre-existing passions. Hume's undoubted maxim, that no action can be virtuous unless there be some motive in human nature, distinct from its sense of virtue, to produce it, is different from the thesis that moral judgments have their foundation in sentiments of approval and disapproval. The latter is about spectator feelings' conferring normative status on natural traits,[12] while the former establishes that natural traits are the subjects (and the only genuine subjects) of such moral distinctions. (The force of "genuine" here is to allow that actions can have moral qualities, but derivatively from the character traits that motivate them.)

This discussion highlights an ambiguity in the phrase "derived from," as it appears in Hume's conclusion that morality cannot be derived from reason alone. The same is true of synonymous expressions used in the claims that morality is not a "product of" reason alone, or that morality is not "founded on" reason alone. Hume's anti-rationalist conclusion might concern the *object* of moral evaluation: what we call virtuous or vicious is not from or of reason. The Natural-Motive Interpretation makes the argument from motivation about this matter. But Hume's anti-rationalist conclusion might also concern the way in which we *discern* the difference between virtue and vice. Presumably, the object of moral evaluation might not be from or of reason because it is a motive, and motives are passions and not produced by reason alone; but the moral evaluation of the object might still be one made by reason. That is, the object of moral evaluation might be a passion, but its virtuousness or viciousness would be determined by reason. Hume thinks *both* that the objects of moral evaluation and the moral evaluation itself are not from reason, but in Part 1 of Book 3, he is ultimately defending the conclusion that moral evaluation is not done by reason, but by sentiments (forms of pleasure and pain): "Thus...virtue is distinguished by the pleasure, and vice by the pain, that any action, sentiment or character gives us by the mere view and contemplation" (T 3.1.2.11). Because the Natural-Motive Interpretation of Hume's premise that morals influence actions and affections has no evidential connection to the conclusion that morality is discerned or distinguished by sentiments, it is not the best reading of Hume's thesis about the practical effect of morality.

5.4 The Moral-Discernment Interpretation

A natural way to understand Hume's claim that "morals" excite passions and influence actions is that the making of moral judgments, or the discerning of moral distinctions (on its own), originates motives to behaviors that typically reflect virtue

---

[12] Hume writes in the second *Enquiry* that taste gilds and stains natural objects with the colors of "internal sentiment" (EPM App. 1.21).

and away from those that indicate vice. On the Moral-Discernment (MD) Interpretation, the Motivation Argument says:

(MD1) The discerning of moral distinctions on its own influences affections and actions.

(MD2) Reason alone does not influence affections and actions.

(MD3) An active principle cannot be founded on an inactive one.

(Conclusion) Morality (moral distinctions) cannot be derived from reason alone.

I want to emphasize that the first premise is not about the moral judgments we make, but about the means of making them. This reading looks like a form of judgment internalism, since it has it that the person who judges that a trait or an action is virtuous or vicious has some kind of motivation, presumably to pursue the virtue or to avoid the vice. This reading easily meets the second stipulation for an acceptable interpretation—that it allow a reasonable connection between the conclusion of the Motivation Argument and Hume's view that morality is derived from moral sentiments. It does so because it turns the Motivation Argument into an argument centered on how we make the moral assessments we do. Thus, Hume can move from the conclusion that reason alone is not the source of our moral distinctions, to a discussion of the mental phenomena by which we make moral distinctions (not by ideas, but by impressions).

There is an interesting wrinkle in Hume's view here. For the sentiments of the judge actually enter into the *constitution* of morality, in the sense that a trait would not be a virtue unless it was generally approved under the proper conditions; and another trait would not be a vice unless it was generally disapproved under the proper conditions. Hume makes this point very forcefully when he writes of a deliberate murder, which is presumably a sign of a motive that is the object of judgment:

The vice entirely escapes you, as long as you consider the object. You never can find it, till you turn your reflection into your own breast, and find a sentiment of disapprobation, which arises in you, towards this action. Here is a matter of fact; but 'tis the object of feeling, not of reason. It lies in yourself, not in the object. (T 3.1.1.26)

I do not want to discuss in detail what Hume means when he says that the vice lies in the observer rather than in the object. He certainly doesn't mean that the observer is vicious and the murderer not. I note this passage in order to make a point about Hume's purported internalism. If the sentiments by which we make moral distinctions enter into the constitution of virtue and vice itself, and if Hume also thinks these sentiments are motives, then his internalism goes beyond appraiser internalism and looks more like a version of existence internalism after all. His is a view that ultimately defies categorization. Typical existence internalism has obligation dependent upon what motives a person has, and so informs us of the content of morality (that, for instance, it consists in self-interest or in benevolence, depending on the psychological theory one accepts). Hume's view that morality depends on spectator feelings of approbation and disapprobation does not give us information about what traits might be considered virtues and vices.

It's not so important that we are able to place Hume's theory of moral motivation into a standard scheme from contemporary philosophy; the crucial question is what he means when he makes the claim that morals influence actions and affections. The Moral-Discernment Interpretation of that claim ("The making of moral distinctions on its own influences affections and actions") makes the Motivation Argument valid. The obstacles to its acceptance as the best reading of Hume's first premise are of a different sort, namely, the questions it provokes about its plausibility and its fit with other texts from Hume. Since Hume argues that the making of moral distinctions is done via the sentiments of approval and disapproval, and the validity of Hume's Motivation Argument requires that motivation not be provided by anything outside of morality itself, Hume is committed to the view that the sentiments of approval and disapproval can themselves be motivating. So, even though they are reactions to the motives we observe in people, it appears they can be motives themselves.[13] It sounds at least puzzling that reactions of pleasure and pain toward observed character traits could also be motives to action. One problem with this view, when put specifically in the context of Hume's theory, is how pleasure or pain can be motives, when, as I have argued earlier, motives for Hume are passions that involve desires. Another problem is that Hume's own explanation of how moral sentiments can be motivating looks like an externalist explanation, where the sentiments motivate in connection with other feelings outside of themselves, rather than on their own. I will first set out evidence for this externalist reading of the Moral-Discernment Interpretation. Second, I will consider the evidence for understanding the Moral-Discernment Interpretation of Hume's claim about morals and their influence as about the motivating effect of the moral sentiments themselves, even though they are types of pleasure and pains (thus, an internalist reading). This is a view I once defended, and that I now think has some problems.[14] Finally, I will propose an alternative reading to both that is internalist (and so retains the validity of the Argument from Motivation against the rationalists) and is consistent with Hume's overall theory of motivation from Book 2 of the *Treatise*.

---

[13] Such a reading has been advocated by Philippa Foot and J.L. Mackie. Foot writes that Hume "seemed to have shown the necessary connexion between morality and the will. For the moral sentiment...was a pleasurable sentiment, by which we were inclined toward those actions whose contemplation gave rise to it" (1978: 79). J. L. Mackie says:

> Hume's...premiss, that morality is practical, that "morals...have an influence on the actions and affections", must...be read as meaning or entailing something like this: the state of mind which is the making of moral judgments and moral distinctions has, by itself, and just because it is that state, an influence on actions. (1980: 52–3)

[14] Radcliffe (1996). See also Ainslie (2015a: 288–90) for a critique of this interpretation.

5.4.1 An Externalist Account of How Moral Discernment Motivates

Hume's own story of how moral judgments motivate comes with his discussion of the undoubted maxim in Section 1 of Part 2 of Book 3 of the *Treatise*. As I have detailed, he explains first how being motivated by the consideration that an action is virtuous cannot make the action virtuous, since the criterion of virtue would in that case be circular. He then moves on to explain that "the sense of morality or duty" can still produce an action, even if the virtue of any action must derive from a virtuous character, and he describes how this happens in the following way:

> When any virtuous motive or principle is common in human nature, a person, who feels his heart devoid of that principle, may hate himself upon that account, and may perform the action without the motive, from a certain sense of duty, in order to acquire by practice, that virtuous principle, or at least, to disguise to himself, as much as possible, his want of it. A man that really feels no gratitude in his temper, is still pleas'd to perform grateful actions, and thinks he has, by that means, fulfill'd his duty. Actions are at first only consider'd as signs of motives: But 'tis usual in this case, as in all others, to fix our attention on the signs, and neglect, in some measure, the thing signify'd. (T 3.2.1.8)

According to this passage in which Hume describes what happens when the sense of duty (the judgment that we ought to perform an action) motivates, we perform acts that appear virtuous, but do so without the virtuous motive. Just how we are caused to act in such cases isn't clear. Perhaps we are motivated by the actual feeling of self-hatred that arises from the realization that we lack affections common to human beings. Perhaps we are motivated by the desire to avoid that feeling. Since we develop the habit of taking acts as signs of characters in others, we are tempted to focus on a single action of our own as though it were a sign of our own character. This fact about us makes it possible for us, by doing the act a virtuous person would do in a particular situation, to thwart the hatred we would feel if we considered the general deficiency in our character. Hume affirms that this is the case when he says that a man without gratitude is still pleased by his own grateful acts; the appearances are satisfying at least for the time being, despite his lacking the virtue. If we are trying to forestall self-hatred, then it looks as though the motivational state here is the desire to avoid the unpleasantness of self-hatred, rather than the self-hatred itself. This is an externalist interpretation of moral motivation, since the desire that motivates the action has nothing to do with the morality of the action, or with the feelings (of approbation and disapprobation) whereby we assess morality.[15]

Other features of Hume's view support this externalist analysis. First, it is consistent with his view to say that we are motivated by a desire of some kind, but it is not actually consistent with his view to say we are motivated by hatred. He explains elsewhere that hatred is not a motivating passion, but is connected to anger, which is

---

[15] This is essentially Charlotte Brown's line in Brown (1988).

(T 2.2.6.3). Second, Hume emphasizes that it is important to human happiness to have the ability to undertake "a satisfactory review of our own conduct" (EPM 9.23),[16] so it is plausible to read the desire to avoid the self-hatred that comes over us when we fail the "self-survey" as a component of our general desire for happiness. Third, at the end of his discussion of "Why we annex the idea of virtue to justice, and of vice to injustice" (T 3.2.2.23), Hume describes how our moral sentiments are reinforced and given motivational strength by factors external to them. There he notes that the persuasive force of politicians extends natural sentiments and may on some occasions produce approbation of a particular action; that "public praise and blame encrease our esteem for justice," as do "private education and instruction" (T 3.2.2.26). Finally, he says, "There is nothing, which touches us more nearly than our reputation, and nothing on which our reputation more depends than our conduct, with relation to the property of others" (T 3.2.2.27). Each of these remarks seems to bolster the general conclusion that, for Hume, when an agent lacks natural virtue, the motivation to behave morally is external to moral considerations themselves. If this is so, then Hume's Motivation Argument cannot succeed.

5.4.2 Are the Moral Sentiments of Approval and Disapproval Motives?

Can Hume instead be best read as offering an explanation of motivation directly by a moral sentiment, so that the judge who experiences the sentiment also has a motivation to conform her behavior to it? On this view of the text, the self-hatred Hume describes is a justifying perception of the moral sense; that is, it is the displeasure produced when my moral sense is turned upon myself as an actor, a type of self-disapprobation or self-reproach, which signifies a character deficiency. This interpretation is supported by the fact that whatever this feeling of "self-hatred" is, it cannot be a genuine species of hatred, as Hume describes that passion in Book 2. There he says:

> Our love and hatred are always directed to some sensible being external to us; and when we talk of *self-love*, 'tis not in a proper sense, nor has the sensation it produces any thing in common with that tender emotion, which is excited by a friend or mistress. 'Tis the same case with hatred. We may be mortifi'd by our own faults and follies; but never feel any anger or hatred, except from the injuries of others. (T 2.2.1.2)

Consequently, the self-hatred to which Hume refers in the account of what he calls moral sense motivation cannot qualify as the indirect passion of hatred, since it has the wrong object. One might then ask whether this mortification "by our own faults and follies" might be a kind of humility, since pride and humility, as distinguished from love and hatred, do have the self as their object (T 2.1.2.2). One suggestion is

---

[16] "Inward peace of mind, consciousness of integrity, a satisfactory review of our own conduct; these are circumstances, very requisite to happiness, and will be cherished and cultivated by every honest man, who feels the importance of them" (EPM 9.23).

that "self-hatred" in this context is a feeling unique to the moral sense, a kind of self-disapprobation, rather than a passion of humility. This conclusion depends upon the claim that disapprobation can itself sometimes be a motivating sentiment, while pride and humility never are.

Hume does not explicitly address the question whether approbation and disapprobation are motivating sentiments. It is evident that Hutcheson thought moral approbation and disapprobation were not motives, since he argued that exciting or motivating reasons (what moves one to act) come from desires, while moral sentiments serve only to justify action.[17] However, there is no compelling reason to think Hume agreed with Hutcheson on this point. Some points in Hume's theory of the passions might be construed as indirect support for the notion that the moral sentiments are themselves motives. Both calm and violent passions determine the will, and it is plausible to regard the general appetite to good and aversion to evil to which Hume refers in discussing the influencing motives of the will as "the moral sense."[18]

Moral approbation and disapprobation are distinctive sorts of pleasure and pain on Hume's view (T 3.1.2.4); hence, if they do motivate, it must be the case that pleasure and pain motivate directly. Actually, for the purposes of this argument, it need only be the case that self-disapprobation, or pain, motivates directly, without reference to any pre-existing desire for happiness or pleasure, since moral obligation is discerned by moral disapprobation. (That is, I am not obliged to do everything the moral sense approves, but I am obliged to avoid those actions it disapproves.) There is a precedent in early modern philosophy for regarding pain as a motive, which might make the suggestion more palatable as an understanding of Hume. Consider Locke. Unlike perceptions of secondary qualities (which correspond to certain physical senses—color to sight, odor to smell, sound to hearing, etc.), pleasure and pain come, he says, "by all the ways of sensation and reflection" (Locke 1690: II.VII.1 and II.XX.1). This, of course, is due to the fact that pleasure and pain are the perceiver's subjective reactions to the perceptual experiences themselves; we have no tendency to separate them from our experiences and project them onto external objects in the way that we, say, attribute heat to a fire (see ibid.: II.VIII.16). Thus, it makes sense for Locke to say that at least some pains just are motivational states that indicate the subjective character of a perceiver's experience:

The uneasiness a Man finds in himself upon the absence of any thing, whose present enjoyment carries the Idea of delight with it, is that we call Desire, which is greater or less, as that uneasiness is more or less vehement. Where by the by it may perhaps be of some use to

---

[17] *Illustrations on the Moral Sense* (Hutcheson 1728: Section I, 137–55).

[18] The most plausible competing interpretation is to understand the phrase "appetite to good and aversion to evil" as preference for pleasure over pain, since Hume often equates pleasure with good and pain with evil. This reading, however, ignores his inclusion of the moral sense among the calm passions at T 2.1.1.3.

remark, that the chief if not only spur to humane Industry and Action is uneasiness. For whatever good is propos'd, if its absence carries no displeasure nor pain with it; if a Man be easie and content without it, there is no desire of it, nor endeavour after it...[19]

Prior to Locke, Hobbes held a similar view:

This motion, in which consisteth pleasure or pain, is also a solicitation or provocation either to draw near to the thing that pleaseth, or to retire from the thing that displeaseth; and this solicitation is the endeavour or internal beginning of animal motion, which when the object delighteth, is called appetite; when it displeaseth, it is called aversion, in respect of the displeasure present.[20]

Hume might share the view that a motivating effect is attributable to the discomfort itself. He also says that passions (many of which are motives) arise either directly or indirectly from pleasure and pain (T 2.1.1.4), and he writes explicitly that the "chief spring or actuating principle of the human mind is pleasure or pain" (T 3.3.1.2). So, on this interpretation, the sense of morality or duty motivates when a person becomes spectator of her own actions and experiences the discomfort of self-disapprobation at the realization that she lacks certain motives. This painful feeling (of self-disapprobation) is itself a motivating passion because it prompts the person, as agent, to perform an action that a virtuous actor would do in that situation, either, as Hume says, to acquire a certain motive by practice, or to hide from herself the lack of that motive insofar as she can. Either outcome—acquisition of a virtuous character or disguising one's lack of virtue—relieves the displeasure only because we have cultivated the habit, as observers of others, of focusing on the action and taking it as a sign of character. The motivation to do an act a virtuous person would do naturally derives from the moral sentiment which is the source of moral justification. Thus, this is an internalist account of moral motivation. No appeal to a preexisting desire for pleasure or concern for personal happiness or any other concern external to the moral feelings is necessary to explain how a person is motivated by duty, on Hume's view. Consequently, the passage at the beginning of the discussion of justice, in which Hume explicitly describes how the sense of duty motivates, becomes an account of how the moral sentiment of disapprobation is a conative state of mind. The moral sentiment would be classified as a direct passion on this view.

The above explains the case in favor of thinking that Hume regards the moral sentiments of approbation and disapprobation as motives to moral behavior when natural motives are lacking. However, one major obstacle for this reading is the

---

[19] (1690: II.XX.6). Locke makes the same point at II.XXI.34, where he also makes it explicit that pain is a much more forceful motive than the prospect of pleasure. Citing St. Paul, who writes, "It is better to marry than to burn [with passion]" (I Cor. 7:9), Locke comments, "A little burning felt pushes us more powerfully, than greater pleasures in prospect draw or allure."

[20] *Human Nature* (Hobbes 1650: Chapter VII, Section 2). In *Leviathan* (1651), pleasure is the appearance of good, which accompanies all desire (Part I, Chapter VI). A contemporary account of pleasure and desire similar to these is Brandt's (1979: 38–42).

question how Hume can depict motives as desires (as I have argued in an earlier chapter), while also allowing that sometimes pain itself motivates. One answer suggested in the above-sketched argument is that desires are all versions of (psychological) pain, the view represented in Hobbes and Locke. It is not obvious that Hume accepts this view and he never clearly suggests it. Hume maintains that desires arise after the mind takes a copy of an impression that was painful or pleasurable, thus, producing an idea of the source of the pleasure or pain, which then "produces the new impressions of desire and aversion, hope and fear, which may properly be call'd impressions of reflection, because deriv'd from it" (T 1.1.2.1). If pleasures and pains do motivate directly, it is puzzling why the original pleasurable and painful impressions would not be motives, and why appeal to the production of impressions of reflection is necessary to explain the genesis of motives. So, if desires are not forms of pain, and if moral disapprobation, a form of pain, is a motive, then Hume's theory of motivation is not so elegant, since it allows an exception to the generalization that motives are desires.

5.4.3 Moral Discernment and Hume's Theory of Motivation

I have argued that the claim that morals influence actions and affections (premise 1 of the Motivation Argument) is best understood as the thesis that the making of moral distinctions (Moral Discernment) has an effect on our motivating passions and our actions. When put in the context of Hume's discussion of acting from duty, the point is that when a person lacks a natural virtue, she can be motivated by a moral sentiment—disapproval of her own character—to do the action that a person with the virtue would do. The issue is how to put this interpretation, which makes good sense of Hume's Motivation Argument, and preserves its validity, within the context of his theory of motivation from Book 2 of the *Treatise*. In that theory, desires, a subset of direct passions, are motives to action, but disapproval is not a desire.

At the heart of Hume's theory of motivation is his thesis that motives arise from the prospect of pleasure or pain. In Chapter 2, I argued that this thesis is simply a consequence of his account of the origin of impressions of reflection, rather than an expression of the view that beliefs about sources of pleasure and pain are motivating beliefs. The principle that motives derive from the prospect of pleasure or pain is a summary of Hume's account of the origin of motivating passions, at least for those passions that are not among the natural instincts (T 2.3.3.8, T 2.3.9.8). These motivating passions are produced, as I have just mentioned, when we bring to mind an idea of a pleasurable or painful experience and react to it. So, my suggestion is that the case of motivation by moral discernment follows the same principle. When I am pained, or feel disapprobation, at my lack of a virtuous motive commonly found in other persons, I retain an idea of my character deficiency as a painful experience, and react to it with a new impression of reflection: a desire to correct the deficiency. The desire to change one's character is a desire that one's motives be different, and so it counts as a second-order desire, or a desire about one's desires. If my corrective desire is strong enough to overcome opposing motivation, it will move me to do what a virtuous person would do in the particular situation. Yet in that case, the best I can achieve is to "disguise" to myself my lack of the virtue, or to "practice" behavior that leads to acquisition of the virtue, since I cannot acquire by a single action the trait whose absence is causing me distress. Of course, I might be moved to take other action instead of, or in addition to, doing the required action, such as employing psychological methods that might change my desires.

This account borrows from the previous interpretation the notion that the self-hatred to which Hume refers in describing motivation by duty is actually self-disapprobation. (The textual evidence that Hume cannot actually mean this sentiment to be hatred of the self is very strong, as I have already shown.) This account makes motivation derivative from moral sentiment in the way motives are generally derived from pleasures and pains, but without regarding the sentiment itself as the motive. Nonetheless, moral sentiments here are "motivating" in the same respect that it is correct to say this of pleasures and pains in general. Just after Hume uses the example of murder to illustrate that we find virtue and vice by attending to our feelings, rather than to features of the action, he writes:

Nothing can be more real, or concern us more, than our own sentiments of pleasure and uneasiness; and if these be favourable to virtue, and unfavourable to vice, no more can be requisite to the regulation of our conduct and behaviour. (T 3.1.1.26)

On this account, the moral sentiment is motivating on its own, even if it is not itself the motive to right action, because it produces a motive without calling upon a pre-existing desire, like self-interest or the desire to be moral. It produces the motive in virtue of the experience of disapprobation only. So, this interpretation retains the internalist character of the first premise in Hume's Argument from Motivation, which is necessary to the argument's validity. This account works as well for cases in which I have in the past felt self-approval toward my own motivations. The correlative proposal that an occurrent feeling of approval functions as a motive is not very persuasive, but it is plausible that when reflecting on my own character I can be motivated by the desire for future feelings of approval like those I've experienced in the past.

As I've noted, approbation and disapprobation are themselves impressions of reflection on Hume's scheme, which divides impressions into those of sensation and reflection, and includes as the former "all the impressions of the senses, and all bodily pains and pleasures" and among the latter, "the passions and other emotions resembling them" (T 2.1.1.1).[21] The moral sentiments are dependent on reflection

---

[21] There is a complication here. When Hume opens his discussion of pride and humility, he repeats his distinction between impressions of sensation and impressions of reflection that he set out in the beginning of the *Treatise*. He writes that impressions of sensation are those acquired through the physical senses and that impressions of reflection arise from the original sensations either directly or by interposition of an idea of the sensation (T 2.1.1.1). This allows that approbation and disapprobation arise from reflection on the

since they depend on ideas of character to which we react. That a motivating passion then arises out of reflection on a previous impression of reflection, such as a feeling of disapprobation toward oneself, is not a problem for this account. Hume acknowledges that impressions of reflection "again are copied by the memory and imagination, and become ideas; which perhaps in their turn give rise to other impressions and ideas" (T 1.1.2.1); and this iteration can go on. So, certainly approbation and disapprobation can generate further ideas and passions beyond themselves.

It is also important to note in this context that while the connection between a feeling of pleasure or pain and a motive toward or away from the object that provoked it is a causal one, it is also the case that the identity of pleasure and pain is necessarily tied to their motivational effects. Many feelings, both physical and psychological, are regarded as pleasures and pains. Hume believes that various pleasures and pains have different phenomenal qualities, as illustrated by his remark explaining why we don't call the wine "harmonious" or the music "of a good flavour" (T 3.1.2.4), but he also requires some account of how these diverse sensations are comprehended under a single category. We find objects attractive for their features and thereby take pleasure in them. When we think of them, we form desires. Consistent with the theory of motivation I attributed to Hume in Chapter 2, we form desires for objects *because* of their features, which also cause pleasurable reactions in us. Likewise, we find some objects uninviting for their features and thereby find them painful; the idea of such an object provokes an aversion to, or a desire away from, the object. It is a fact about individuals that they are attracted to certain objects and repulsed by others, and that people generally find certain sorts of things attractive or other sorts of things not; but it is not a fact that human beings acquire motives toward objects they find pleasurable and away from those they find painful, as though it could have been otherwise. That is, Hume does not pose a contingent connection between approbation (pleasure) or disapprobation (pain) and the motive to virtue and away from vice.

---

idea of a character and count as impressions of reflection for that reason. But in his initial description of the distinction at T.1.1.2.1, he seems to indicate that impressions of reflection have to arise upon ideas of painful or pleasurable experiences. He explains how impressions of reflection arise this way:

> An impression first strikes upon the senses, and makes us perceive heat or cold, thirst or hunger, pleasure or pain of some kind or other. Of this impression there is a copy taken by the mind, which remains after the impression ceases; and this we call an idea. This idea of pleasure or pain, when it returns upon the soul, produces the new impressions of desire and aversion, hope and fear, which may properly be call'd impressions of reflection, because deriv'd from it.

In saying that the ideas of pleasure or pain return upon the soul to produce passions, Hume seems to be implying that all passions depend on physical pleasures and pains, since he describes impressions of sensations as having physical causes (or sometimes he says "unknown" causes, since perceptions from the senses cannot be explained by reference to external objects as their causes). But approbation and disapprobation do not depend on pleasures and pains received through the physical senses; rather, they are akin to sensations of pleasure and pain that then give rise to other passions.

Some readers have argued that the moral sentiments are identical to the indirect passions of love and hatred and of pride and humility, a view that would problematic for my reading.[22] Hume identifies virtue and vice among the causes of pride and humility: "Every valuable quality of the mind, whether of the imagination, judgment, memory or disposition; wit, good-sense, learning, courage, justice, integrity; all these are the causes of pride; and their opposites of humility" (T 2.1.2.5) Later he writes:

The very essence of virtue, according to this hypothesis, is to produce pleasure, and that of vice to give pain. The virtue and vice must be part of our character in order to excite pride or humility. What farther proof can we desire for the double relation of impressions and ideas?
(T 2.1.7.4)

One's virtue and vice enter into the relations that produce pride and humility, which are pleasurable and displeasurable impressions, respectively. Virtue and vice in oneself also clearly cause self-approbation and self-disapprobation, which are likewise pleasurable and displeasurable impressions. So, it seems a small inference from these claims to the conclusion that self-approbation is pride and self-disapprobation is humility. There are parallel textual reasons to regard approbation of another's character as love and disapprobation of another's character as hatred.

Love is followed by a feeling of benevolence, a motive to promote the happiness of the person loved and to avert her misery, and hatred is followed by a feeling of anger, a motive to promote the misery of the person hated and to thwart her happiness. If the moral sentiments are identified with love and hatred, then they are indirect passions that motivate via the motives of benevolence and anger. Motivation so characterized, however, looks unlike motivation by morality in the relevant respect, since it gives the spectator who experiences moral approbation a motive to promote the happiness of virtuous persons, or the unhappiness of the vicious, rather than a motive to become virtuous. However, if pride and humility are the relevant moral sentiments, then there is a different sort of problem: Hume says they are "pure sensations, without any direction or tendency to action" (T 2.2.9.2). So, if approbation and disapprobation of self were pride and humility, respectively, there would be no evident way to make sense of motivation by moral sentiments, and no straightforward reading of Hume's thesis that morals excite passions and influence actions.

The evidence gathered here indicates that there are strong reasons for considering closely the intent of any of Hume's statements that might suggest an identity between the moral sentiments and love and hatred. For instance, Hume writes:

Now since every quality in ourselves or others, which gives pleasure, always causes pride or love; as every one, that produces uneasiness, excites humility or hatred: It follows, that these

---

[22] As I note in CHAPTER 6, Páll Árdal maintains that the moral sentiments are indirect passions (Árdal 1966: 11, 109–23), while Norman Kemp Smith (1941: 167–8)—and Thomas Hearn, Jr. (1973: 288–92)—argue that they are direct passions. Louis Loeb holds that moral sentiments are not passions at all (1977: 395–403).

two particulars are to be consider'd as equivalent, with regard to our mental qualities, *virtue* and the power of producing love or pride, *vice* and the power of producing humility or hatred.
(T 3.3.1.3; see also T 3.1.2.5 and T 3.3.5.1).

This passage is by no means decisive with respect to the question how moral approbation and disapprobation fit into the classification of the passions. It is consistent both with this passage and the interpretation of the moral sentiments as direct passions to understand the love or pride and the humility or hatred which attend the perception of virtue and vice as presupposing the moral sentiments rather than constituting them. Consequently, this debate can only be negotiated on other grounds (see also Cohon 2008a).

My view, instead, is that when my character is the subject, Hume identifies the initial pleasure or pain involved in the production of pride or humility as a moral sentiment. The indirect passions involve a relation of two ideas, the idea of the cause of the passion (for instance, my character) and the idea of the object of the passion (self), and a relation of resembling impressions (the passion and another impression), both forms of pleasure or both forms of pain. When Hume puts the elements of his system of the production of these indirect passions together, he writes:

If I compare, therefore, these two *establish'd* properties of the passions, *viz.* their object, which is self, and their sensation, which is either pleasant or painful, to the two *suppos'd* properties of the causes, *viz.* their relation to self, and their tendency to produce a pain or pleasure, independent of the passion; I immediately find, that taking these suppositions to be just, the true system breaks in upon me with an irresistible evidence. That cause, which excites the passion, is related to the object, which nature has attributed to the passion; the sensation, which the cause separately produces, is related to the sensation of the passion: From this double relation of ideas and impressions, the passion is deriv'd.   (T 2.1.5.5)

Among the properties of the causes of an indirect passion is the ability to produce a pain or pleasure "independent of the passion," that is, independent of pride or humility. In the case of my observing my character and feeling disapproval of it, the cause is my idea of my deficient character, and the pain it produces is the disapprobation; but on Hume's system, this pain is independent of the passion being produced, humility. So, the idea of my character is related to the idea of myself: this is the relation of ideas. The thought of my character produces disapprobation or pain, which resembles the sensation of the humility, the product of the whole process: this is the relation of impressions. Humility is not identified with the disapprobation here. It would be extraordinary for Hume to discuss virtuous and vicious character as a prime cause of pride and humility (when self is the object) and of love and hatred (when others are the objects) and to neglect to mention that these passions, when provoked by thoughts of character, are identical to the approbation and disapprobation that constitute our moral distinctions.

The moral sentiments can also produce multiple passions at once. It is important to note this, because, given what Hume says in his discussion of pride and humility, it is tempting to draw the conclusion that, if self-disapprobation is not identical to humility, humility is *the* passion to which disapprobation of self gives rise. If self-disapprobation causes humility only, then it could not be motivating in any respect, since humility is not a motive and apparently causes no motivating passions. As I have mentioned, Hume depicts it as akin to a sensation. Hume does affirm that the moral sentiments enter into the genesis of pride and humility:

> To approve of a character is to feel an original delight upon its appearance. To disapprove of it is to be sensible of an uneasiness. The pain and pleasure, therefore, being the primary causes of vice and virtue, must also be the causes of all their effects, and consequently of pride and humility, which are the unavoidable attendants of that distinction. (T 2.1.7.5)

However, there is no reason to think that humility is the *only* effect of self-disapprobation, and pride the *only* effect of self-approbation. Hume allows that one set of circumstances can produce multiple passions and that one passion can give rise to a variety of others.[23] Joy, for instance, is produced when an agreeable object acquires a relation to ourselves (T 2.1.6.2), but further circumstances must obtain for a person to experience pride as well. Hume writes of the chef who produces a wonderful feast that "beside the same joy [that others at the feast experience], [the chef] has the additional passion of self-applause and vanity" (T 2.1.6.2). The chef has both joy and pride (or self-applause) because in her case, the idea of the lavish dinner evokes the idea of herself. Likewise, my agreeable character can be a source of joy to me *and* it can give rise to pride. Thus, there is no reason to think that my disagreeable character, when I reflect upon it as a source of displeasure, cannot generate multiple emotions, including humility, sorrow, and a desire to change the source of the pain.

5.4.4 Further Considerations

I have argued in this section that the first premise in Hume's argument from motivation, "Morals have an influence on the actions and affections," is best understood as the claim that the moral sentiments by which we discern or judge virtue and vice produce motives. They do so when we find in ourselves a deficiency of a morally-approved trait generally possessed by others, or when we anticipate the pleasure of self-approval for exhibiting motives that are regarded as virtues. These motives are produced by self-approbation and self-disapprobation in the same way that motives are typically generated in Hume's theory of motivation: a person retains an idea of a source of pleasure or displeasure and reacts to it with an impression of reflection. This reading of the premise makes the argument valid, has textual support, and fits Hume's view of moral motivation into his broader theory of motivation. There are four points to observe in connection with this interpretation.

---

[23] "Now 'tis evident, that the very same qualities and circumstances, which are the causes of pride or self-esteem, are also the causes of vanity or the desire of reputation; and that we always put to view those particulars with which in ourselves we are best satisfy'd" (T 2.2.1.9).

First, in arguing for this reading of Hume, I am not promoting the view that Hume has a robust theory of deliberation and moral agency. Rather, the account of how one experiences satisfaction or dissatisfaction of one's own character follows the moral spectator line: I become a spectator to my own behavior and find myself in approval or disapproval when I look to those around me. I sympathize with the feelings of those who are affected by what I do, including with their own moral sentiments toward me. To focus on the case of disapproval, which is probably more common. I might also feel displeasure regarding myself when, as Hume says, I find myself lacking a virtuous motive that others generally possess. But disapproval I feel, to be moral disapproval, needs to be the result of my realization of a deficiency of approved traits, rather than a feeling of discomfort due simply to my being different from those around me. My understanding of Hume here does not imply that an agent deliberates from a first-person perspective about what she ought to become and acquires a motive to change her character in light of such reflection. Rather, the agent acquires a motive to change the source of dissatisfaction in the way other motives are caused by sources of pleasures and pains. Granted, one might thwart the discomfort of disapproval by avoiding reflection on one's own character altogether, but people could avoid all sorts of uneasy feelings by avoiding the circumstances that produce them. I could circumvent certain pains by refusing to expose myself to others' suffering; in that case, I won't be inconvenienced through sympathy with the unpleasantness of their distress. I could avoid making moral judgments altogether, so as to avoid the unpleasantness caused by encountering vicious people. None of this means that the psychological mechanisms do not exist, and that people are not naturally subject to them. On any moral theory, a person could refuse to engage in the sort of thinking or practice that involves reference to duty, morality, "oughts," or virtue. This doesn't make the issue of moral motivation beside the point, and it does not make internalism a false thesis. The fact of the matter is that people naturally acknowledge morality, even though they are not always moved to action by it.

A second point to address regarding this interpretation of Hume's premise that morals have an influence on the actions and affections is this. In his discussion of the question why justice is a virtue, and following the discussion of motivation by duty, Hume writes that sympathy is too weak to control our passions, even though our moral sentiments depend upon it. Thus, the suggestion that moral sentiments can provide motives to action, or at least motives that could credibly compete with other passions, looks inconsistent with this claim about the motivational weakness of sympathy. However, I believe that the context is crucial here. Here is what Hume writes:

Nay, when the injustice is so distant from us, as no way to affect our interest, it still displeases us; because we consider it as prejudicial to human society, and pernicious to every one that approaches the person guilty of it. We partake of their uneasiness by *sympathy*; and as every thing, which gives uneasiness in human actions, upon the general survey, is call'd *vice*, and whatever produces satisfaction, in the same manner, is denominated *virtue*; this is the reason why the sense of moral good and evil follows upon justice and injustice. And tho' this sense, in the present case, be deriv'd only from contemplating the actions of others, yet we fail not to extend it even to our own actions. The *general rule* reaches beyond those instances, from which it arose; while at the same time we naturally *sympathize* with others in the sentiments they entertain of us. Thus *self-interest* is the original motive to the *establishment* of justice: but a sympathy with *public* interest is the source of the *moral* approbation, which attends that virtue. This latter principle of sympathy is too weak to controul our passions, but has sufficient force to influence our taste, and give us the sentiments of approbation or blame.   (T 3.2.2.24)

The passage ends with reference to "This latter principle of sympathy," which indicates that Hume offers a contrast between types of sympathies, or perhaps between the circumstances under which sympathy is felt. When the injustice or harm done is remote, we sympathize with those affected by the agent and feel the disapprobation indicative of the agent's vice, but the disapprobation does not have the power to move us to assist those who are so distant. I earlier noted that, on Hume's view, approbation is part of the cause of love, and love is followed by benevolence; disapprobation is a factor in the production of hatred, which is followed by the motive of malice. Actually, however, the motivation of which Hume writes in the passage has to do with being moved to perform beneficial actions toward those suffering injustice. In other words, he here invokes his account of pity. Pity, for Hume is a sort of imitation benevolence produced by sympathy with others' afflictions when the persons are strangers to us. It requires an extended sympathy by which we imagine vividly the persons' past, present, and future experiences (T 2.2.9.3–T 2.2.9.20).[24] This is psychologically difficult when we are unacquainted with those affected by the unjust perpetrator, and Hume seems to indicate that sometimes pity is simply too weak to move us. By contrast, the sort of motivation featured in Hume's second premise from the Motivation Argument is the sort that develops when the moral approbation or disapprobation is directed toward the self. In the preceding excerpt, he affirms that we apply the moral sentiments to ourselves, when we sympathize with the feelings others have toward us. But this form of sympathizing does not require an extension of feelings to those who are extremely removed from us, and it does not require us to envision a stranger's past and future situations. So, the psychological problem that produces sentiments too weak to originate motives is absent from these circumstances.

In this connection, in a passage from T 3.3.1., "Of the origin of the natural virtues and vices," Hume also writes that there is no contradiction (I take it he means motivational conflict) between extensive sympathy, upon which the moral sentiments depend, and our natural limited generosity. These are very different feelings. My feeling of disapproval at an ugly, awkward wall that I imagine is insecure, but I am assured is safe, is different from the feeling of fear I have when I believe that the wall is actually likely to fall upon me.

---

[24] I discuss this involved account in CHAPTER 6.

Nay, these emotions are so different in their feeling that they may often be contrary, without destroying each other; as when the fortifications of a city belonging to an enemy are esteem'd beautiful upon account of their strength, tho' we cou'd wish that they were entirely destroy'd.

Extensive sympathy is like the former feeling, a sentiment produced by the imagination, which takes "the *general* views of things," rather than like "those which arise from our particular and momentary situation" (T 3.3.1.23). However, I think it's credible to understand the sentiments we experience when we reflect on our *own* behavior as like those that arise from our particular situation, which "touch the heart" and, at least at times, "controul our passions" (T 3.3.1.23).

The third consideration I want to highlight is what to make of the seemingly external incentives to morality that Hume discusses at the end of his explanation of why justice is a virtue. After he concludes that what we call justice is the result of convention, but the sense of its morality is natural, Hume comments on the effects of the speeches of politicians, of public praise and blame, and of private education, on the natural sentiments: they all encourage our esteem for justice (T 3.2.2.25). Moreover, he maintains that our reputation, which depends most on how we behave with respect to the property of others, is our deepest concern (T 3.2.2.27). Yet, it is clear that when the entire context of Hume's remarks on this topic is examined, these external incentives by themselves will not originate our moral distinctions, nor the motivation that accompanies them:

Any artifice of politicians may assist nature in the producing of those sentiments, which she suggests to us, and may even on some occasions, produce alone an approbation or esteem for any particular action; but 'tis impossible it should be the sole cause of the distinction we make betwixt vice and virtue. For if nature did not aid us in this particular, 'twou'd be in vain for politicians to talk of *honourable* or *dishonourable*, *praise-worthy* or *blameable*. These words wou'd be perfectly unintelligible, and wou'd no more have any idea annex'd to them, than if they were of a tongue perfectly unknown to us. The utmost politicians can perform, is, to extend the natural sentiments beyond their original bounds; but still nature must furnish the materials, and give us some notion of moral distinctions. (T 3.2.2.25)

I think it is significant that the discussion of these external motives to virtue noted above comes at the conclusion of Hume's account of the origin of justice and artificial virtue. There, I think, Hume is occupied with the question how the motive to justice is strengthened so that people are in fact moved to do the actions that they already naturally have a motive to do. My general concern has been with whether there is a way in which the moral sense directly produces a motive to morality (whether a case of natural or artificial virtue), not with whether it produces the strongest among competing motives. Since acts in keeping with the rules of justice do not have beneficial results in every instance, the moral sense is, in the case of the artificial virtues, approving of a general principle or attitude of regulating our behavior by rules. Thus, in such cases, Hume's references to the external inducements to morality don't indicate that the internal motivation is absent, but that it may not always be sufficient to produce the desired action.

Fourthly, I want to emphasize, finally, that when an agent is moved by her own benevolence or gratitude or courage, etc., she is "morally" motivated in the sense that her actions are caused by dispositions that we approve of from a general point of view. That is, her actions are caused by virtues. One might want to say that this sort of case is the typical case of moral motivation in Hume's account, perhaps more properly called "virtuous" motivation, but nothing I have said is contrary to this point. One is motivated by the Humean sense of morality or duty I have been discussing when the virtuous dispositions are not present. This is moral motivation in what might be called the "strict" sense: being motivated by the awareness (thought or sentiment) that something is the moral thing to do, even though one is not naturally disposed to do it. People who are regularly motivated in this way are not, on Hume's view, virtuous persons; if they were, their own dispositions, instead of the sense of duty, would motivate them to act morally. This is the sense of being motivated "by morality" that is needed, as I showed earlier, to make his argument against the moral rationalists valid. Consequently, my discussion of being motivated by self-approbation or self-disapprobation doesn't imply that Hume considers these cases more prominent or more prevalent than those instances in which agents are motivated by virtuous dispositions.

5.5 Moral Sentimentalism and Moral Cognitivism

Moral non-cognitivists allege that claims about morality are not propositional, do not make property attributions, and cannot be true or false. When persons utter such claims, they are thought to express attitudes like satisfaction or dissatisfaction, approval or disapproval, desiring, and so on. Moral cognitivists typically argue that claims about morality make assertions, do attribute properties, and, thus, are truth-evaluable. In contemporary philosophy, Michael Smith has pressed the case that the internalist thesis, coupled with the belief-desire theory, is incompatible with moral cognitivism. The incompatibility of these three defensible views comprises "The Moral Problem" (Smith 1994). Given that belief and desire are separate mental states, and that moral judgments are intrinsically motivating, but beliefs are not, moral judgments could not be beliefs. It follows that they must be desires or sentiments, which are intrinsically conative, and non-cognitive. I have argued that Hume is a moral internalist who holds that a passion describable as desire is necessary to produce motivation. Beliefs, distinct mental states from passion, cannot originate motives on their own, but are necessary, in conjunction with desires, to produce action. Consequently, it looks as though Hume is committed to some kind of identification of moral judgments with sentiments, rather than with cognitive states, and many commentators have attributed to him some form of moral non-cognitivism.[25]

I am sympathetic to the view that the theories of classic philosophers should not be expected to answer questions that their theories were not designed to deal with. The distinction between cognitivism and non-cognitivism was not formulated until the 1920s.[26] However, it is instructive to ask the question whether Hume's empiricist, naturalistic account of morality can countenance the cognitivist line, especially since his theory, as I have argued, provides the basis for the contemporary Humean theory of motivation. Furthermore, the question of whether Hume's theory is consistent with, implies, or denies cognitivism can be translated into his own vocabulary. Ultimately, I argue that Hume's theory of motivation and his internalism do not commit him to a non-cognitivist theory.

Hume scholars may disagree over the question whether impressions, for Hume, are representational (or intentional), but there is no debate about ideas. Hume says that they represent the impressions from which they come, and he sometimes says that they "represent their objects or impressions" (T 1.3.14.6). When Humean ideas are affirmed as beliefs, they are truth-apt, since they are taken to signify something to be so. Consequently, it seems that the question whether Hume's theory allows for moral cognition is a question about whether his theory allows that there are moral beliefs: that is, vivacious ideas that portray something about morality. Hume opens the discussion of morality with the question, "*Whether 'tis by means of our ideas or impressions we distinguish betwixt vice and virtue*," and his unambiguous answer is that we distinguish virtue from vice by impressions, a thesis which is the basis of his moral sentimentalism. This answer, however, does not settle the matter concerning whether we possess moral beliefs. It is a claim about the origin of the distinctions, but it does not address the issue whether there might be representative mental states about morality, perhaps somehow independent of the originating impressions.

5.5.1 Ideas of Morality

The rationalists allow that at least some ideas, and some knowledge, are innate and accessible by reason, either by the comparison of ideas or by rational intuition. For Hume, all meaningful simple ideas must start in experience, in simple impressions, which the simple ideas copy (T 1.1.1.5, T 1.1.1.7; EHU 2.3–4). Complex ideas, likewise, are significant only if the simples from which they are composed can be traced to preceding impressions (T 1.1.1.6; EHU 2.5, EHU 2.9). Beliefs, as we have

---

[25] Philippa Foot (1978: 74–80) and J.L. Mackie (1980: 52–3) see Hume as an internalist and non-cognitivist. Simon Blackburn aligns Hume with the expressivist view (1980, 1993). Nicholas Sturgeon (2008) emphasizes that there is textual evidence for a non-cognitivist reading of Hume, but he also writes at times as though moral judgments are about feelings. So, the evidence does not tell whether he is a moral non-cognitivist or a moral subjectivist.

[26] Mark van Roojen (2015) writes that non-cognitivism was first developed as a theory about the nature of moral judgments by Ogden and Richards (1923: 125) and Barnes (1933).

seen, are vivacious complex ideas, portraying states of affairs, or objects and their features. The dispute over the origin of moral distinctions, I think, is a manifestation of this larger disagreement between Hume and the rationalists over the origin of ideas in general. If we understand ideas like virtue, vice, obligation, good, evil, and right, how have we come to comprehend them? Hume writes:

> All ideas, especially abstract ones, are naturally faint and obscure: The mind has but a slender hold of them: They are apt to be confounded with other resembling ideas; and when we have often employed any term, though without a distinct meaning, we are apt to imagine it has a determinate idea, annexed to it. (EHU 2.9)

Moral concepts are of course abstractions; so do we employ them with no distinct meaning?

Initially, I want to consider our ideas of the descriptive traits of a person, and our attributions of them to individuals. Our idea of Hitler's character is composed of notions like that he desired the extermination of a race, that he deliberately inflicted suffering and death on large numbers of people, that he valued a certain sort of ethnic purity, and so on. We attribute these desires, intentions, and dispositions to him on the basis of someone's consistent observations of his behavior, since no one can observe another's motives directly (see T 3.3.1.4). The simple ideas that make up the idea of Hitler's character are traceable to impressions. When we believe that Hitler possessed one or the other or all of these features (and are not just hypothesizing that he does), we move beyond present experience and make a causal inference that results in, for instance, the belief that he was in fact someone who could purposely inflict anguish and death on large numbers of people, and so on. But the crucial question here is: how do we come to think of him, or of someone who intentionally behaves this way, as vicious? Analogous to the case of Hume's willful murderer example, when making observations of the object alone, "In which-ever way you take it, you find only certain passions, motives, volitions and thoughts." From where does the idea of vice come, and how do we apply it? Hume's answer is that "The vice entirely escapes you, as long as you consider the object. You never can find it, till you turn your reflection into your own breast, and find a sentiment of disapprobation, which arises in you, towards this action" (T 3.1.1.26). This theme is repeated and emphasized in EPM:

> Crime or immorality is no particular fact or relation, which can be the object of the understanding: But arises entirely from the sentiment of disapprobation, which, by the structure of human nature, we unavoidably feel on the apprehension of barbarity or treachery.
> (EPM App. 1.16)

Our reaction to the intention to starve persons and to cause all manner of torment and death is a feeling of displeasure, disapproval, or disgust, which gives rise to such normative ideas as viciousness, moral depravity, and immorality. However, the process of deriving ideas of morality, on Hume's view, is a bit more complicated than this example suggests. As Don Garrett has emphasized, ideas of morality—vice, virtue, obligation, right, wrong, good, evil, and so on—are abstract ideas, since the terms that refer to them are general and cover a range of instances (Garrett 1997: 96–7). Abstract ideas are the result of our noticing the commonalities among particular impressions or groups of impressions, and using a general term to capture what they share. So, "redness," "length," "tree," "giraffe," and so on, are terms that convey abstract ideas, since they each describe a class of particular impressions or complexes of impressions that have something in common. On Hume's theory, the mind cannot represent abstractions; so when we use general terms, we bring before the mind an idea of a concrete instance, a determinate idea, from the set of ideas the general term covers. That idea readies us to recall other resembling instances of that class:

All general ideas are, in reality, particular ones, attached to a general term, which recalls, upon occasion, other particular ones, that resemble, in certain circumstances, the idea, present to the mind. Thus when the term *horse* is pronounced, we immediately figure to ourselves the idea of a black or a white animal, of a particular size or figure: But as that term is also usually applied to animals of other colours, figures and sizes, these ideas, though not actually present to the imagination, are easily recalled; and our reasoning and conclusion proceed in the same way, as if they were actually present. (E 12.20, n. 34)

As Garrett explains it, a determinate idea "achieves a general *signification*—and hence serves *as* an abstract idea—because the term also revives the custom or disposition to call up ideas of other particular instances" (Garrett 1997: 101). So a successful definition of an abstract term must be able to call up in others what Garrett calls the term's "revival set," the ideas of particular instances associated with the general term (ibid.: 104).

Likewise, the notions of virtue and vice and other moral concepts are derived from the observation of many cases with shared features. I feel disapproval upon contemplating other instances of murderous behavior motivated by tyrannical dispositions, instances of thievery motivated by greed, instances of violence motivated by narrow self-interest, and so on. As noted earlier, our approvals and disapprovals can differ, depending on our circumstances and situations relative to the object; so, in order to avoid different spectators' applying general moral terms to different sets of particulars—which creates an inability to communicate and interact with one another—we focus on "some *steady* and *general* points of view." We frame our notions of morality, then, in terms of the approvals and disapprovals that arise out of, or would so arise, when we take up those points of view (T 3.3.1.15).

So when Hume argues that moral distinctions are based on sentiment, he is making a point about how ideas of morality originate. Certainly, for Hume, no ideas originate in reason, since reason can only be applied to ideas we already have. Of course, the sentiments of approval and disapproval that are the bases for ideas of morality are different from other impressions to which ideas can be traced.

Through the moral sentiments, we acquire concepts that add a new feature or dimension to our descriptive ideas. This is the force of the famous assertion in EPM:

[Reason]...conveys the knowledge of truth and falsehood:...[taste] gives the sentiment of beauty and deformity, vice and virtue. The one discovers objects as they really stand in nature, without addition or diminution: The other has a productive faculty, and gilding or staining all natural objects with the colours, borrowed from internal sentiment, raises, in a manner, a new creation. (EPM App. 1.21)

Of course, all passions can produce ideas, as, for instance, when I think of my own fear. My thought of my fear is the thought of what it is like to feel an impression.[27] However, when I disapprove, say, of the traits of a sexist supervisor in my office workplace, the moral idea generated upon my disapproval is an idea of that person's bad character, not an idea of my own feelings of disapproval. Consequently, when Hume writes that the chief question about morality is whether we make moral distinctions by impressions or by ideas, he is referencing alternate accounts of the origin of our ideas of morality. Any idea that originates from another idea must be generated by a deduction, or an induction. Neither operation produces ideas we didn't have before: deduction reveals logical relationships, and induction reveals causal ones. Only impressions originate new ideas.

This interpretation of Hume as concerned with the generation of our abstract ideas of morality is confirmed by a telling passage in the second *Enquiry*, where he remarks on the difference between the sentiment of humanity and narrowly-focused, self-interested sentiments like avarice and ambition. As I observed in the INTRODUCTION, Hume in EPM characterizes the source of morality as the universal sentiment of humanity, rather than as sympathy experienced from a general or common viewpoint. He writes:

The distinction...between these species of sentiment [humanity and avarice] being so great and evident, language must soon be moulded upon it, and must invent a peculiar set of terms, in order to express those universal sentiments of censure or approbation, which arise from humanity, or from views of general usefulness and its contrary. VIRTUE and VICE become then known: Morals are recognized: Certain general ideas are framed of human conduct and behaviour: Such measures are expected from men, in such situations: This action is determined to be conformable to our abstract rule; that other, contrary. And by such universal principles are the particular sentiments of self-love frequently controuled and limited. (EPM 9.8)

We develop general ideas of human behavior that include the thought that persons should conform to principles that we derive from this universal sentiment of morality. While the *Treatise* discussion of moral concepts emphasizes generality, rather than universality, the point I make here is that Hume's account in EPM

---

[27] When I am fearful at a sudden noise and think of danger, the idea of danger is not originated by the fear. It is an idea that I already possess, which is brought to mind by association.

indicates that moral sentimentalism is about how we originate normative concepts or rules, a claim that is compatible with our deriving other moral beliefs by reason, once we have those concepts.

5.5.2 Judgments, Beliefs, and Motivation

After we have acquired concepts, we are able to apply them to instances we have not experienced, based on descriptions. I can infer that Pol Pot, who tortured and killed 1.5 million Cambodians in order to create an agrarian communist society and eliminate modernization, was a vicious person, once I understand what vice is and comprehend this description of him. I add my idea of him to the class of morally vicious people who serve as members of the revival set for the term "vice," or "viciousness." However, my notion of Pol Pot as a wicked person is not a moral *judgment I make* if I am not affected sentimentally by the description. So, I can acquire beliefs about morality by reason; these beliefs are not necessarily my judgments. Likewise, I might infer that some of my own motivations are morally disrespectable, but if I do not experience any disapprobation at my own character traits, I do not make a normative assessment of myself, and I will not be motivated to improve my character. Hume writes about "judgments" concerning causes and effects (e.g., T 1.3.8.13, T 1.3.13.8, T 1.3.13.20), which are "judgments of the understanding" (T 3.1.1.5). These also involve sentiments: in this case, expectations of a type of experience following upon another type of experience. Judgments in themselves, are not motivating, although the feelings by which we make them can be, depending on the sentiment. So, for instance, the expectation of an experience, which is involved in causal judgments, is not intrinsically motivating unless the expected type of experience is pleasurable or painful.

Earlier I distinguished moral discernment, the mechanism of judging, from the moral judgment, which is the outcome of discernment. Discernment or judging in general is non-cognitive, on Hume's theory, in the sense that it always involves the experience of a sentiment, or, in judging causes and the existence of objects, intensifying the force and vivacity of an idea. In the formation of causal judgments about two objects, we feel an expectation that adds the idea of necessity to the complex idea of their relation, while also enlivening that idea. Judging that an object exists in the external world is not an attribution of a quality, but a change in the manner of conceiving of an object; there is no change in content, but a change in attitude, which alters the quality of the idea and the intensity with which it is felt. In both causal judgments and judgments concerning the existence of objects, we start with ideas we already possess and end up with more vivacious versions of those ideas.

Moral discernment is a similarly non-cognitive process. As in causal and "existence" judging, when we discern morally, we start with ideas, this time of a person's character traits. Then we acquire new ideas, normative ideas, which are indicative of the value of those traits. We expand the set of determinate ideas encompassed by the abstract idea to which the moral term refers—virtuous, vicious, obligatory, wrong, etc.[28] This reading of Hume does not commit him to moral non-cognitivism, since moral motivation is a product of the sentiment of approbation or disapprobation, in those special cases where it is directed toward the self. The moral sentiments prompt us to add the idea of the normative character trait to the relevant revival set, if it was not there before, and the complex idea gets a boost in forcefulness and vivacity. We also have beliefs about morality that can be acquired by inference from the ideas we already possess: if I have the concept of virtue or of vice (or other ideas of morality), I can infer from a description of someone's character traits whether he or she is virtuous, saintly, vicious, wicked, etc. But the moral belief is not a source of motivation; the moral sentiments are. Consequently, there is no incompatibility on this account among the theses of internalism, the belief-desire model of motivation, and moral cognitivism.

Now I return to the version of the Motivation Argument that Hume offers at EPM 1.7, quoted earlier. The argument, in outline, is:

(1) Representations of morality (what is fair, noble, generous, etc.) animate (motivate, influence) us to embrace and maintain what they represent.

(2) Conclusions of the understanding, about what is probable, true, etc., do not animate us.

(Implicit conclusion) Representations of morality are not conclusions of the understanding.

Applying points from the foregoing discussion, the way to understand premise (1) is this: When preachers, teachers, authorities, writers, poets, and so on, bring before our minds ideas of virtue, our disapprobation of our own characters—insofar as we lack these traits—or our approval—insofar as we possess them—can motivate us to attempt to acquire or maintain these features.[29] Premise (2) asserts that the conclusions or ideas from reasoning (ideas of causal connection, of what exists) do not motivate us. The conclusion, then, is that our ideas of morality, what we encompass in the revival set for virtue, vice, rightness, wrongness, etc. do not originate by reasoning. Hume's next step, as we have seen, is to conclude that representations of morality originate from impressions instead.

5.5.3 Are Ideas of Morality Fictions?

Causal beliefs, beliefs in an enduring self, and beliefs in the existence of external enduring objects, among many others, all involve fictions, for Hume. What exactly

---

[28] In cases where the determinate idea is already part of the set—as, for instance, when I think once again of the motivations of a Hitler or a Hitler-like character and experience disapproval all over again—it makes sense to say that I affirm my earlier judgment.

[29] Of course, reference to the mechanism of approval and disapproval is left out of the statement of premise (1), since to state it here would beg the question. That motivation depends on sentiment is defended after the conclusion that representations of morality are not conclusions of the understanding.

fictions are is subject to debate, but one reasonable interpretation is that they are ideas that we take to depend on impression of sensations, but that really have no source in our sensations. In other words, they are not purported experiences of an external world, even though we take them to be (see Traiger 1987: 381–99). Instead, they are fabricated by the imagination due to certain normal psychological principles and our reactions to our own experiences. The imagination has a tendency to follow a train of thinking once started, even when present experience doesn't bear it up. Take, for instance, our belief in independent and enduring objects. Our perceptions have some degree of coherence in their patterns of occurrence, and that coherence is magnified when we suppose objects to have a continued existence. The idea of a continuing object is actually a fiction of the imagination, by which the unchanging object is supposed to participate in the changes of our perceptions (T 1.4.2.22–T 1.4.2.24). Coherence alone does not produce the idea of the distinct existence of the entire world, which also requires the principle of constancy. The constant reappearance of resembling perceptions makes for an easy transition of the mind along the ideas of the interrupted perceptions, and this feeling is almost the same as that of one constant and uninterrupted perception (T 1.4.2.31–T 1.4.2.35). While my perceptions of the moon or of the ocean come and go, if I were to regard these objects as destroyed when I am not perceiving them, and newly created each time I perceive them again, I would encounter irresolvable psychological conflicts. So, Hume suggests that we disguise the interruption in our perceptions, by supposing a fiction of continued existence (T 1.4.2.37).

It is therefore appropriate to wonder whether the ideas of morality produced by moral sentiments are also among such fictions. They are, after all, dependent on impressions of reflection, rather than on impressions of sensation, and they originate new elements, which are added to our complex ideas of persons. Feelings of approbation and disapprobation seem to provide a legitimate basis for ideas of approbation and disapprobation, respectively, rather than for ideas of virtue and vice and other related notions. Perhaps unaware, we purport to represent something we cannot (Mackie 1980: 71–2). The evidence, however, is indeterminate.

Hume does not express skepticism about morality in the way in which he expresses it about causality, the external world, the self, and some other ideas. Even if one emphasizes that he is a naturalist about these matters, describing the way the mind works in causal belief formation, and so on, his analysis still has it that something is hidden from the ordinary person in the process of belief formation. We are not aware that our ideas of necessary connection, independent enduring objects, and the self were invented by our mind's tendencies and feelings. But Hume does not seem to indicate that something in the process of moral evaluation is hidden from the ordinary person making moral discernments. We realize that we don't find virtue and vice in the world, but that we instead find it when we look inside ourselves. When we pronounce an action or character to be vicious, we mean that from the constitution of human nature, we "have a feeling or sentiment of blame from the contemplation of it" (T 3.1.1.26). Furthermore, "Nothing can be more real, or concern us more, than our own sentiments of pleasure and uneasiness" (T 3.1.1.26). And of the conclusion that virtue and vice are distinguished by the pleasurable and painful sentiments a character trait causes in spectators, Hume writes:

> This decision is very commodious; because it reduces us to this simple question, *Why any action or sentiment upon the general view or survey, gives a certain satisfaction or uneasiness?* in order to shew the origin of its moral rectitude or depravity, without looking for any incomprehensible relations and qualities, which never did exist in nature, nor even in our imagination, by any clear and distinct conception.
> (T 3.1.2.11; see also EPM App. 1.10, where Hume expresses a similar thought)

So, it looks as though we are not searching for imaginary ideas, nor obscure metaphysical qualities, behind our moral conceptions. In EPM, he calls those who deny the reality of moral distinctions "disingenuous" (1.2). And he implies that the crime of ingratitude is real, but "is not any particular individual *fact*; but arises from a complication of circumstances, which, being presented to the spectator, excites the *sentiment* of blame, by the particular structure and fabric of his mind" (EPM App. 1.6).

Nevertheless, it is hard to say whether Hume intends ideas of morality to be regarded as fictions, since he does not address the topic directly. There are striking parallels between moral belief formation and the elements of non-moral belief formation, whether beliefs in causes or in independent and enduring objects. A strong argument that Hume did not regard the former as fictions would have to offer a systematic reason for the difference, and I am not prepared to offer that here. Still, there very well may be one.

6

Motivational Dynamics and Regulation of the Passions

Agents experience an array of passions and affections competing for control of their actions. As Annette Baier points out, Hume depicts the conflicting tendencies between self-concerned and other-concerned passions as alternating, "wheeling us about from love of undeserved praise to contempt for our flatterers, from disinterested benevolent love to a 'great partiality in our own favor'."[1] Hume's naturalistic theory of motivation implies the thesis that a person whose various passions are directing her to differing, conflicting ends will take the action prompted by the strongest passion at the time, other things being equal. This claim is a truism: given the competition among causal forces, the outcome of such a rivalry is necessarily determined by the cause with the greatest power. This perspective raises questions about which principles determine the motivational strength of individual passions, whether and why their strengths vary from person to person, and whether there are means at an agent's disposal to alter the causal efficacy of their own passions. Obviously, Hume rejects the prevalent early modern view espoused by thinkers like Reynolds and Senault, that reason can counsel the passions, or subdue and moderate them. But what can he offer, if anything, in its place?[2]

In this chapter, I address the motivational dynamics of Hume's theory of the passions and belief—the phenomenal features that affect motivational strength of the passions and that affect the way beliefs impact action. I discuss Hume's important distinction between strength and violence of a passion, the effects of conflicting passions on one another and on action, and the effects of others' passions on us. Hume suggests that the prevalence of calm over violent passions, which helps us to avoid being moved by a trivial, proximal good over genuine self-interest, allows for a happier life. Those who possess this motivational balance of calm over violent passions have a virtue he calls "strength of mind." Here I investigate the nature of this virtue and whether there are principles of Humean psychology whereby we might cultivate it. I maintain that, even though reason cannot control the passions, and despite all the sources of conflict endemic to our emotional psychology, there are

---

[1] Baier (1991: 145–6). The Hume quote is from T 2.1.11.9.
[2] Much of the discussion in this chapter appears in Radcliffe (2015a and 2017).

resources in Hume for establishing some degree of order, harmony, and psychological health. However, this project of moderation runs up against limits. Finally, since actions are products of both passions and beliefs, this chapter also studies the role of strength of conviction in the causation of action.

6.1 Strength *versus* Violence

Hume's distinction between the calm and violent passions (noted earlier in CHAPTER 1) is crucial to understanding aspects of his motivational theory, and to identifying an unusual virtue he calls "strength of mind." Strength of mind is the motivational prevalence of the calm passions over the violent. (Why Hume considers it a virtue is an issue I address later.) As I've mentioned, Hume defines the division between calm and violent passions in terms of the internal upheaval with which a passion is felt. He says that calm passions cause "no disorder in the soul," are known by their effects, and are often mistaken for reason (T 2.3.3.8). Violent passions, by contrast, evidently create internal disorder, are known by their internal feeling, and are clearly identified as passions.[3] The details of the distinction are puzzling, however, given that Hume offers it as a fundamental division of the passions right at the beginning of Book 2 of the *Treatise*, and immediately calls it a "vulgar and specious" distinction. Then, two Parts later, the difference becomes important to Hume's theory of motivation—both in explaining the seeming combat of reason and passion, and in explaining how we can make sense of a person's doing something that she "doesn't want to do."

The calm/violent distinction may have a long history, with its roots in the Stoics, who regarded passions as perturbations causing emotional upheaval (see Fieser 1992: 3–4). Francis Hutcheson, writing prior to Hume, distinguishes "affections," which are calm or reflective passions, from non-reflective passions. The latter are composed of a "natural propensity" attended with "confused" sensations or prolonged by bodily motions. These passions can arise without any notion of good, either private or public, and can obscure our practical reasoning (Hutcheson 1728: 28–9, 60). So Hume was obviously aware of a traditional philosophical characterization of certain unreflective passions as disturbances to reason. He regards this as a false portrayal of the relation between reason and passion, given his argument that the two cannot be at odds with one another over the direction of action (T 2.3.3.4).[4] Perhaps one reason

---

[3] Louis Loeb opens his book with a discussion of calm and violent passions in order to make the point that calm passions are associated with stability, which is a predominant theme in Hume, both with regard to emotion and belief (Loeb 2002: 6).

[4] On one interpretation of Hume, all passions are "reflective," since they are sensations of reflection. This then explains Hume's rejection of the traditional way of treating the calm/violent distinction, which presumes that some passions are unreflective. However, I do not wholly agree with this depiction of Hume's view of the passions insofar as it seems to imply that they are all intellectual or contemplative in some sense. Rather, they are reflective in the sense that they recur to the sources of our pleasures and pains (i.e., they can be called "reflexive," emphasizing reflex). As I have noted, Hume writes that they arise from our

Hume calls this distinction vulgar and specious is due to his dispute with the way the traditional distinction is described, but it may also be due to the fact that he sees the designation as fluid. Recall that immediately before offering this judgment of the distinction's status, he writes:

> This division [calm/violent] is far from being exact. The raptures of poetry and music frequently rise to the greatest height; while those other impressions, properly call'd passions, may decay into so soft an emotion as to become, in a manner, imperceptible.   (T 2.1.1.3)

Hume then goes on to make four significant points related to calm and violent passions. First, he divides all reflective impressions into the calm and the violent. Second, he names among each class the following: among the calm passions are the sentiments of morality and beauty; the violent include love and hatred, grief and joy, pride and humility. Third, as I've noted, he says this division is not exact. Fourth, he says he will use this distinction, vulgar and specious as it is, to organize his discussion, and so will begin by explaining the origin and effects of the violent passions.

However, the distinction is much more than a principle of organization. After the beginning of Book 2, in his general classification of the passions, the calm/violent distinction is invoked again in T 2.3; specifically, in the discussion of motivation in T 2.3.3, "Of the influencing motives of the will," and in the subsequent section in which he explains the causes of violent passions. In T 2.3.3, in the discussion of motivation, the calm passions are called upon to explain why it appears that reason can oppose passion over the determination of action. Hume says that any mental activity that operates with calmness and tranquility is confused with reason. So where it may appear that reason and passion are in conflict, the reality is that passions are opposing other passions (T 2.3.3.8). In this section, Hume offers further details on the calm passions. He calls them "real passions," but ones that "are known more by their effects than by the immediate feeling or sensation." He offers as examples two kinds of desires (discussed earlier in CHAPTER 1): original natural instincts, such as benevolence, resentment, love of life, kindness to children; and the general appetite to good and aversion to evil. He adds that we can feel violent versions of these passions as well; I might feel a violent passion of resentment toward someone who hurts me and then desire that some evil befall that person (T 2.3.3.8–T 2.3.3.9). But what makes the distinction between calm and violent passions crucial to Hume's theory is that it explains how his causal theory of motivation makes sense of our conventional understanding of motivational psychology. Hume emphasizes the distinction between a violent passion and a causally strong one, and between a calm passion and a causally weak one (T 2.3.4.1). This distinction allows that we can act on passions that, in a phenomenal sense, we hardly feel, even when having an intense experience of a contrary passion. Hence, calm passions can have greater causal strength than violent

---

sensations or from our ideas of sensations, so some impressions of reflection originate directly out of sensations of pleasure and pain, with no ideas interposed.

ones, and so be effective in action, even though felt much less powerfully than the violent ones.

It is not clear how Hume intends the distinction between the calm and violent passions to be situated with regard to the other categories in his theory. I take seriously Hume's division of all impressions of reflection into calm and violent—at least into the generally calm and generally violent—although not all commentators agree on this.[5] On Louis Loeb's interpretation of the schema, with which I generally agree, impressions of reflection are emotions, and the violent emotions are the passions.[6] The passions, as noted in CHAPTER 1, divide into the direct and indirect, depending on whether they are produced directly from an idea of a pleasurable or a painful object (as a desire for a particular pastry is), or indirectly, by the interposition of another idea (as pride in my tasty soufflé is) (T 2.1.1.4). Loeb argues further that neither a direct nor an indirect passion *could* be calm, given the psychological mechanism by which each is produced. The indirect passions are produced by a double relation of impressions and ideas, which increases the feeling of the resulting passion. Suppose the birth of a child gives the parents pleasure. This pleasure immediately causes the direct passion of joy. When the parents are mindful of the child as their offspring, their idea of the child is associated with their ideas of themselves. Since joy is agreeable, it resembles the feeling of pride. This double relation of ideas and impressions causes the indirect passion of pride. Hume states that this indirect passion in turn gives "new force," or "additional force," to the initial joy (T 2.3.9.2–T 2.3.9.4). So, both the direct passion of joy and the indirect passion of pride are experienced with an internal commotion that makes them violent passions. The direct passions, when they play a role in producing the indirect, are reinforced by the latter, and therefore tend to be as violent (see Loeb 1977: 398).

However, this account overlooks that some of the instinctual passions are generally calm.[7] Hume writes at T 2.3.3.8, in his discussion of motivation, "Now 'tis certain, there are certain calm desires and tendencies, which, tho' they be real passions, produce little emotion in the mind." Then he names the instincts I've mentioned (benevolence and resentment, the love of life, kindness to children, and the general appetite to good, and aversion to evil). There are violent versions of at least some of

---

[5] On this point, I follow Loeb (1977). Norman Kemp Smith interprets Hume's scheme as dividing all passions into two classes: instincts (primary passions) and those derived from pleasure and pain (secondary passions). The derived or secondary passions then divide into direct and indirect, with direct passions being further divided into calm and violent (see Kemp Smith 1941: 164–8). But, as Páll Árdal notes, the indirect passions of pride, humility, love, and hatred are (generally) violent passions for Hume; hence, Kemp Smith's interpretation cannot be correct. Árdal suggests instead that every class of passions should be further sub-divided into calm and violent: primary, secondary, direct, and indirect passions (see Árdal 1966: 10–11). Terence Penelhum (1975: 89–97) agrees with Árdal.

[6] Loeb (1977). Árdal thinks that all impressions of reflection are passions (Árdal 1966: 8–11).

[7] James Fieser notices this and suggests that generally violent passions divide into direct and indirect, with direct passions further divided into primary (instincts) and secondary (derived) (Fieser 1992: 10–11). But I have to disagree with Fieser, for reasons I discuss here.

these instincts. As I've noted, resentment is one: "When I receive any injury from another, I often feel a violent passion of resentment, which makes me desire his evil and punishment, independent of all considerations of pleasure and advantage to myself" (T 2.3.3.9). A little farther on, Hume adds these to the list of instincts: desire of punishment to our enemies and of happiness to our friends, hunger, lust, and a few other bodily appetites (T 2.3.9.8)—a list which surely includes some generally calm *and* some generally violent passions. Since the primary passions, or instincts, include both types, we cannot infer that all non-derived passions are calm.

In sum, the passions, for Hume, divide into primary (instincts) and secondary (derived); the secondary are derived either from pleasures and pains or from the primary, by interposition of an idea (which copies the primary impression). Primary passions can be either calm or violent, but the generally calm, primary passions include at least the moral and aesthetic senses (which encompass certain calm pleasures and pains), benevolence, resentment, love of life, and kindness to children. I agree with Loeb that as a matter of psychological fact, all the secondary passions are *initially* violent, due to their manner of derivation.[8] However, there is logical space for calm secondary passions, and Hume makes it clear that even if they originate with some violence, these passions can change:

when a passion has once become a settled principle of action, and is the predominant inclination of the soul, it commonly produces no longer any sensible agitation. As repeated custom and its own force have made every thing yield to it, it directs the actions and conduct without that opposition and emotion, which so naturally attend every momentary gust of passion. (T 2.3.4.1)

By distinguishing a calm passion from a weak one, and a violent from a strong one, Hume clearly indicates that passions have a distinctive phenomenal dimension that does not correlate precisely with motivational force. This distinction indicates that the passion felt with the most internal turmoil among those present is not necessarily productive of action:

'Tis evident passions influence not the will in proportion to their violence, or the disorder they occasion in the temper; but on the contrary, that when a passion has once become a settled principle of action, and is the predominant inclination of the soul, it commonly produces no sensible agitation.... We must, therefore, distinguish betwixt a calm and a weak passion; betwixt a violent and a strong one. (T 2.3.4.1)

---

[8] Haruko Inoue (unpublished) has suggested recently that the division between calm and violent passions in T 2.1.1 is not entirely consistent with that of T 2.3.3, unless the two are interpreted differently. The first discussion is to be read as offering a type distinction between the calm passions—i.e., the moral and aesthetic sentiments—which are not properly passions, and the violent passions exemplified by love, hatred, etc., which are properly passions. The second discussion concerns only the proper passions. There Hume makes the point that tokens of the genuine passions can also be either calm or violent; hence, resentment, love of life, and so on, are proper passions that can be experienced tranquilly or violently. While I don't subscribe to this reading, I want to acknowledge it.

Hume makes the point that some passions are felt so calmly as to be mistaken for conclusions of reason, and yet among these calm passions are ones upon which we can act. Calm passions, on Hume's account, are either passions evoked by distant goods and evils (pleasures and pains) or passions that are settled or habitual principles of action. They are calm, as I've already noted, because they are barely perceptible, being produced with little "sensible agitation." Violent passions are evoked by near or immediate goods and evils and are felt with some disturbance or force. The psychological state of the person who experiences violent passion is described as "disordered."[9] Since the calm passions are not necessarily motivationally or causally weaker than their rivals, and the violent passions are not necessarily motivationally or causally stronger than theirs, a person cannot determine by the experienced feeling of her passion whether it will be effective in action. The sense in which I don't want to go to the dentist is the sense in which I violently feel aversion to going to the dentist; while the desire to take care of my dental health is felt calmly, but can motivate me despite my aversion.

6.2 Natural Influences on the Passions

Hume calls upon several basic principles of associationist psychology in order to explain how passions are generated, intensified, and transformed into other passions. He argues in Book 1 of the *Treatise* that we naturally associate ideas by their resemblance, contiguity, and cause and effect. These tendencies are carried into the passions. Hume writes in his discussion of the passions that resembling impressions (of which passions are a subset) follow the same principles of association:

All resembling impressions are connected together, and no sooner one arises than the rest immediately follow. Grief and disappointment give rise to anger, anger to envy, envy to malice, and malice to grief again, till the whole circle be completed.... Changeableness is essential to ... [the human mind]. (T 2.1.4.3)

Hume indicates that the association of ideas and of impressions "assist and forward each other," so that the intensity of a passion is increased when that passion involves both an association of ideas and impressions, as is the case with an indirect passion. Contiguity comes into play when the situation of an object affects the intensity of passion, so that "The same good, when near, will cause a violent passion, which when remote, produces only a calm one" (T 2.3.4.1). In fact, the effect on the passions of spatial and temporal contiguity of goods can be profound, as evidenced in Hume's discussion of justice, in which he analyzes why people so frequently act against their genuine self-interest. People prefer the trivial, immediate advantage to the benefits

---

[9] Katharina Paxman (2015) argues that the crucial distinctions between the calm and violent passions is not the "feeling" of the respective passions, but the presence or absence of disruption and the disordering of natural or customary ways of thinking.

that are remote; so acts of inequity are frequent, given that the advantages of following the rules of justice are distant (T 3.2.7.3). The effects of contiguity are evident throughout Hume's discussion of the dynamics of the passions, and present a major obstacle to restraint and moderation of certain passions, as I discuss in SECTION 6.6.

6.2.1 Conversion of One Passion into Another

Hume's discussion of how the violence and forcefulness of passions are increased occurs in the part of Book 2 of the *Treatise* that deals with the will and the direct passions. While some indirect passions are motives, the direct passions seem to have the closest connection with action, since they arise immediately from the perception of pleasurable or painful objects. One principle at work in magnifying the violence of the passions is what I call "conversion." When two passions are produced by separate causes, they "mingle and unite," even if they have no relation to one another. "The predominant passion swallows up the inferior, and converts it into itself" (T 2.3.4.2), with the prevailing passion determining the direction of action. The prevalence mentioned here must be in terms of violence (the phenomenal dimension), rather than in terms of causal strength (its motivational dimension). Hume's examples verify this point. A man's love for his mistress is intensified by the jealousy and quarrelsome affections her faults give rise to; a politician raises a question that he delays in answering in order to heighten curiosity on the part of the public. In the former case, jealousy intensifies love, and in the latter, anxiety intensifies curiosity. Even when two passions pull in contrary directions, the connection between them is more intimate than the connection between a passion and indifference.

6.2.2 Contrariety and the Role of the Understanding

Hume's account of the psychology of the passions reveals that we are subject to many forms of contrariety in our emotions and passions. Annette Baier writes, "The sorts of 'contrariety,' opposition, and hostile coexistence that human passions exhibit is one of Book Two's recurrent themes" (1991: 145). If the same object excites contrary passions, then the agent will experience internal upheaval or disorder, which will increase the violence of whichever passion is dominant. So, Hume thinks this explains why we naturally desire what is forbidden and are sometimes more desirous of doing what is wrong just because it is contrary to duty (T 2.3.4.5). The dominant passion turns out to be more violent than it would have been had it met with no opposition at all, and the effect is the same whether the opposition is internal or external. Our reactions to fictional tragedies illustrate this principle as well. The sorrow, indignation, and compassion we feel increase our appreciation of the beauty of the performance.[10]

---

[10] Hume, "Of Tragedy," in *Essays* (1777/1987), paragraphs 9–10.

The understanding or reason affects the production of passions insofar as it reveals information about unknown objects. That is, it tries to determine whether these unfamiliar objects are similar to other objects that have brought us pleasure or displeasure ("reason in a strict and philosophical sense...excites a passion by informing us of the existence of something which is a proper object of it").[11] When the understanding is uncertain about the outcome of an event or an action, the mind jumps from one reaction to another (hope, fear, etc.), which has the overall effect of increasing the vivacity of the dominant passion. The same happens when there is uncertainty about the nature of an object:

> 'Tis certain nothing more powerfully animates any affection, than to conceal some part of its object by throwing it into a kind of shade...the effort, which the fancy makes to compleat the idea, rouzes the spirits, and gives an additional force to the passion. (T 2.3.4.9)

Furthermore, absence can increase or diminish passions depending on the circumstances: "absence destroys weak passions, but encreases strong; as the wind extinguishes a candle, but blows up a fire" (T 1.2.4.10). This point is illustrated by the familiar experience of missing an absent loved one. The imagination, with which we bring ideas of sources of pleasure and pain before the mind, also intensifies the passions, and the more specific the goods or evils we imagine, the more violent the responses we experience.

Contrariety can increase the force or violence of the predominant passion, but it can have other effects as well. In Hume's treatment of the direct passions, he names as contrary pairs of passions: desire and aversion, grief and joy, hope and fear. He spends good deal of space on the effects of probability, which not only increases vivacity, but also determines the particular passion one experiences, depending on the degree of certainty or uncertainty of good or evil. Desire arises from simple consideration of prospective good and aversion from evil. When good is certain or probable, it produces joy; when evil is certain or probable, it produces grief or sorrow. Uncertain good or evil gives rise to fear or hope, according to the degrees of uncertainty on the one side or the other (T 2.3.9.5–T 2.3.9.7). When there is uncertainty about the existence of an object, the understanding fluctuates between two opposite views, just as it does when the nature of an object or its effects are unclear. Thus, if the object is an object of desire, the mind fluctuates between joy and grief as it considers the contrary points of view (T 2.3.9.11). Then Hume adds:

> Now if we consider the human mind, we shall find, that with regard to the passions, 'tis not of the nature of a wind-instrument of music, which in running over all the notes immediately

---

[11] Recall:

> It has been observ'd, that reason, in a strict and philosophical sense, can have an influence on our conduct only after two ways: Either when it excites a passion by informing us of the existence of something which is a proper object of it; or when it discovers the connexion of causes and effects, so as to afford us means of exerting any passion. (T 3.1.1.12)

loses the sound after the breath ceases; but rather resembles a string-instrument, where after each stroke the vibrations still retain some sound, which gradually and insensibly decays.

The imagination can quickly change its views, but the passions are slower to change and so they are mixed with each other.

According as the probability inclines to good or evil, the passion of joy or sorrow predominates in the composition...the grief and joy being intermingled with each other, by means of the contrary views of the imagination, produce by their union the passions of hope and fear.
(T 2.3.9.12)

Although Hume has earlier emphasized that contrary passions increase the violence of the dominant passions, which happens when they first clash, he observes other possible effects of contrariety. First, both passions may exist successively, at short intervals; second, they may sometimes destroy each other, so that we feel neither of them; and third, sometimes both remain united in the mind. Consistent with his aim of finding the ultimate tenets in human psychology, he asks to what basic principles the other effects can be attributed. The first happens when the contrary passions arise from completely different objects, with no relation to one another. Hence, they can neither mingle nor be opposed to one another. "If the objects of the contrary passions be totally different, the passions are like two opposite liquors in different bottles, which have no influence on each other" (T 2.3.9.17). Thus, a man distressed for the loss of a law suit and joyful for the birth of a son will feel one affection and then the other, and neither can provoke or moderate the other. The second situation, where the passions cancel each other and leave the mind in a state of tranquility, happens when a single object, because of its mixed character, provokes two reactions. So, if a play is both funny and sad, the spectator leaves in a state of equanimity. "If the objects be intimately connected, the passions are like an *alcali* and an *acid*, which, being mingled, destroy each other" (T 2.3.9.17). In the third instance, when an object, either good or evil, is uncertain, then contrary passions will occur together, but neither destroys nor neutralizes the other. Instead, the two unite and produce a new affection. Hume thinks this is so because the opposition between passions in the case of probabilities is not a constant and perfect opposition in terms of sensation and direction. The imagination must alternate between two views, each of which produces a passion that "vibrates" as it fades by degrees into the other. "If the relation be...imperfect, and consist in the contradictory views of the same object, the passions are like oil and vinegar, which, however mingled, never perfectly unite and incorporate" (T 2.3.9.17). This last situation is illustrated by the examples of grief and joy and hope and fear, discussed above. When the existence of good and evil is uncertain, there is both grief and joy, with hope for good and fear of evil. As the preponderance of evidence grows on the side of evil, fear increases and hope and joy diminish. Fear becomes grief when evil is certain. On the other hand, if the probabilities favor the existence of good, hope increases, as fear and grief decline. Hope eventually becomes joy, when good is certain (T 2.3.9.10–T 2.3.9.19).[12]

6.3 How Others' Passions Affect Us: Sympathy and Comparison

Hume draws on two principles of the human mind to explain the varied effects of other people's feelings and situations on our passions. Sympathy is connected to passions oriented toward the good of others—passions like pity and compassion (some readers add benevolence).[13] The principle of comparison, on the other hand, is the source of the asocial traits, such as contempt, malice, and envy, which incline us away from others' well-being. So, Hume's theory identifies two capacities fundamental to human nature that produce passions often at odds with one another. I begin with sympathy.

The mechanism of sympathy, which plays a crucial role in his moral philosophy, is introduced when Hume discusses the passions of pride and humility. He remarks that our character, reputation, beauty, and riches are causes of pride, but would have little effect on us if not "seconded" by the opinions and sentiments of others. Sympathy accounts for the influence on us of others' feelings and views. Hume notes that we feel hatred, resentment, esteem, love, courage, mirth, and melancholy more from communication by others' behavior than from our own natural temperaments (T 2.1.11.1–T 2.1.11.2). He comes close to defining sympathy when he writes:

When any affection is infus'd by sympathy, it is at first known only by its effects, and by those external signs in the countenance and conversation, which convey an idea of it. This idea is presently converted into an impression, and acquires such a degree of force and vivacity, as to become the very passion itself, and produce an equal emotion, as any original affection.

(T 2.1.11.3)

I notice another's laughter, which gives me an idea of that person's cheer, and when I sympathize, that idea is converted into a jovial feeling of my own. Hume attributes national character and citizens' uniformity of thinking to sympathy. This feeling is said to be affected by the same associative tendencies that facilitate the passions, and he remarks that among people, "where, beside the general resemblance of our natures, there is any peculiar similarity in our manners, or character, or country, or language, it facilitates the sympathy" (T 2.1.11.5).

---

[12] These points about the contrary passions are repeated in Section 1 of Hume's *Dissertation on the Passions*, in *A Dissertation on the Passions and the Natural History of Religion* (1757/2007).

[13] Philip Mercer (1972: 44) argues that Hume's view of sympathy is egocentric and doesn't leave room for concern for others, but this seems clearly false to me. I agree with Jacqueline Taylor, who argues that the self is not the object of passions derived from sympathy (Taylor 2015b: 191). It's just that, as Hume says, others' sentiments "can never affect us, but by becoming, in some measure, our own ... as if they had been originally deriv'd from our own temper and disposition" (T 3.3.2.3).

Hume does not explicitly argue that sympathy gives rise to benevolence. That would be inconsistent with his view of benevolence as an instinct. He writes that the desire of happiness or misery for another, which is "an arbitrary and original instinct," may be "counterfeited" on certain occasions and so arise from "secondary principles." Then he goes on to explain how pity, concern for the misery of others, and malice, joy in others' misery (without friendship, on the one hand, or enmity, on the other[14]) are derived from other affections. So, he seems to indicate that the passion derived from sympathy is not benevolence, but pity, which he says, imitates the effects of love. Love, as I showed in Chapter 1, for Hume, is not a motive, but is causally connected to a motive, namely, benevolence for the beloved. Nor is hatred a motive, but it is connected to the motive of anger for the one hated. So, in this sense, pity is counterfeited benevolence. In his classic study of Hume on sympathy, Páll Árdal asks, "But why, even if I am affected through the process of communication, should I be concerned about the other person's suffering or sorrow?" Why don't we hate the person who makes us feel uncomfortable, or why don't we just turn our attention away? (see 1966: 51–5). I address this question after examining Hume's account of the origin of pity in sympathy and of malice in comparison.

Others' "affliction and sorrow" strike us in a livelier manner than any enjoyment does, and they produce in us an analogous feeling, which is pity. This must happen by sympathy, Hume thinks, since spectators to tragic plays experience a train of passions—grief, terror, indignation, and then joy, as the characters undergo reversals of fortune. It makes most sense to think that these passions are felt by the spectator through a general principle of sympathy, rather than by each originating from a distinct cause. And the fact that our feelings of pity depend on the contiguity to or distance from us to the object (person) is further corroboration that the imagination, which is an integral part of sympathy, is at work in producing pity (T 2.2.7.3–T 2.2.7.4). Then Hume recognizes "a pretty remarkable phaenomenon of this passion," that pity (and some other passions conveyed by sympathy) are sometimes stronger when the feeling in the subject is weaker, or even non-existent.

> [W]hen a person... inherits a great fortune, we are always the more rejoic'd for his prosperity, the less sense he seems to have of it, and the greater equanimity and indifference he shews in its enjoyment. In like manner a man, who is not dejected by misfortunes, is the more lamented on account of his patience; and if that virtue extends so far as utterly to remove all sense of uneasiness, it still farther encreases our compassion. (T 2.2.7.5)

Few commentators have discussed the principle of comparison, the complement to the principle of sympathy, whereby we experience certain passions, notably contempt, malice, and envy, upon comparison of our situations with others. Gerald Postema writes:

---

[14] Desire of ill-will for another that comes from injury of us would instead produce revenge (T 2.2.7.1).

Hume, like Montaigne and Mandeville, thought the dark passions to which we are susceptible are deeply rooted in human nature, as deeply in fact as the fellow-feeling and sociality championed by Shaftesbury... The key to unlocking the mystery of human passions, according to Hume, lay in the interaction between two fundamental psychological mechanisms or principles: sympathy and comparison. Both our sociality and our asociality find their psychic origins in the complex interaction between them. (Postema 2005: 251)

Malice, for Hume, imitates the effects of hatred. Hatred, he argues earlier, is followed by anger; so, malice is a sort of imitation anger, as pity is an imitation of benevolence (although Hume does not put it that way). The general principle at work here is that objects appear greater or less by comparison with others. A sizable object looks greater next to a tiny object; an ugly one even uglier when put next to a beautiful object. So,

As we observe a greater or less share of happiness or misery in others, we must make an estimate of our own, and feel a consequent pain or pleasure. The misery of another gives us a more lively idea of our happiness, and his happiness of our misery. The former, therefore, produces delight; and the latter uneasiness.

Hume calls this "a kind of pity reverst, or contrary sensations arising in the beholder, from those which are felt by the person, whom he considers" (T 2.2.8.8–T 2.2.8.9).

Postema argues that there are actually three principles of comparison in Hume's discussion. First, the "contrast" principle enhances the features of objects when the items around them are sharply different, which is illustrated in the examples above of size and beauty. Second, on reversal comparison, we sympathize with others, but instead of acquiring feelings like theirs, we experience feelings that are contrary to theirs, taking pleasure in their pain or pain in their pleasure. Thus, as already noted, such feelings can take the form of envy or malice when the other person experiences advantages to which we react by comparison.[15] Third, in "context" comparison, we evaluate and measure objects in context by comparison to things around them. Hume suggests that we are deeply influenced by the opinions of others in social contexts, so social referencing plays a large part in the formation of our attitudes, views, and desires.

Some points about reversal comparison, my main interest here, are unexpected. Hume thinks we can experience malice toward *ourselves* in the sense that the thought of past pain is agreeable when we find our present condition satisfying, and the thought of past pleasure makes us uneasy when we find ourselves presently in disadvantageous circumstances by comparison. While it sounds odd to think of these feelings as malice, "The comparison being the same, as when we reflect on

---

[15] Postema (2005: 264–8). However, I don't see these as independent principles, since in Hume's analysis, reversal requires contrast: Hume's explanation why one experiences displeasure at another's good fortune has to do with one's perception of one's own fortune as small in comparison to the other person's.

the sentiments of others, must be attended with the same effects" (T 2.2.8.10). Moreover, the distress of a friend can actually move us to seek displeasure through reversal comparison. The contrast with my friend's dire circumstances might have made me feel even more pleased at my good fortune; yet, Hume says, "as grief is here suppos'd to be the predominant passion, every addition falls to that side, and is swallow'd up in it, without operating in the least upon the contrary affection" (T 2.2.8.11). The same phenomenon accounts for remorse and its effect.

When a criminal reflects on the punishment he deserves, the idea of it is magnify'd by a comparison with his present ease and satisfaction; which forces him, in a manner, to seek uneasiness, in order to avoid so disagreeable a contrast.   (T 2.2.8.11)

Furthermore, envy, for Hume, is explained by the same principles as malice. Envy is excited by some present enjoyment of another, which by comparison diminishes our idea of our own, and malice is an unprovoked desire of evil for another, in order to gain pleasure from the contrast with ourselves (T 2.2.8.12). Finally, in the cases of envy of our inferiors who are approaching or superseding our happiness or status, the effects of comparison are twice repeated:

A man, who compares himself to his inferior, receives a pleasure from the comparison: And when the inferiority decreases by the elevation of the inferior, what shou'd only have been a decrease of pleasure, becomes a real pain, by a new comparison with its preceding condition.
(T 2.2.8.12)

Now I return to the question how sympathy with someone's bad situation gives rise to pity, a form of benevolence, when we might actually despise a person for making us feel uncomfortable (or we might simply turn away to avoid the sympathetic feeling). Hume recognizes the issue himself: "For as pity is an uneasiness, and malice a joy, arising from the misery of others, pity shou'd naturally, as in all other cases, produce hatred; and malice, love. This contradiction I endeavour to reconcile, after the following manner" (T 2.2.9.1). He begins with the crucial point that it is not "the present sensation alone or momentary pain or pleasure, which determines the character of any passion, but the whole bent or tendency of it from the beginning to the end" (T 2.2.9.2). An impression can resemble another in its sensation (pleasurable or painful) but also in the direction each imparts to action, which is the bent or tendency. So, there are two causes from which a transition of passions may arise; one is the double relations of ideas and impressions already explained, and another is a conformity in the tendency and direction of two desires that arise from different causes. Hume's view is that when sympathy with another's uneasiness is weak, it actually *does* produce hatred or contempt, through the double association. The idea of another person's uneasy situation makes me uneasy, and makes me feel displeasure or hatred toward that person, so there are two impressions of displeasure and two associated ideas of the other person. But when sympathy is stronger, it will produce "love or tenderness" by the conformity in the direction of two passions: the sympathetic response and benevolence (T 2.2.9.12). Pity, as we've seen, resembles benevolence, the effect of love, but we feel it when the object is a stranger, rather than someone close to us. Postema makes the best sense of how Hume draws on "the whole bent" of benevolence to explain the effect of sympathy in producing pity:

> The whole bent of benevolence, which one feels towards a family member, loved-one, friend, or partner, consists not merely of unconnected momentary sensations, but also of an extensive pattern of emotionally charged links tracking the fortunes and misfortunes of the beloved as she goes through life. (Postema 2005: 271)

Of course, with strangers we have no such history and connections, so we would expect our momentary engagement with them to result in antagonistic passions. But sympathy can originate pity, for Hume, when the sympathizer has been able to use her imagination to cast a wider net, and experience vividly the person's past, present, and future situation. Hume writes:

> '*Tis* certain, that sympathy is not always limited to the present moment, but that we often feel by communication the pains and pleasures of others, which are not in being, and which we only anticipate by the force of imagination. For supposing I saw a person perfectly unknown to me, who, while asleep in the fields, was in danger of being trod under foot by horses, I shou'd immediately run to his assistance; and in this I shou'd be actuated by the same principle of sympathy, which makes me concern'd for the present sorrows of a stranger ... 'tis evident, that, in considering the future possible or probable condition of any person, we may enter into it with so vivid a conception as to make it our own concern; and by that means be sensible of pains and pleasures, which neither belong to ourselves, nor at the present instant have any real existence. (T 2.2.9.13)

When sympathy is extended in this way, the bent or motive force of benevolence is transferred to the sympathetic person, who thereby feels pity and is moved to give assistance (see also Postema 2005: 271). One crucial feature in determining that pity rather than hatred or aversion is evoked is the liveliness and vivacity of the initial sympathetic response.

> When the present misery of another has any strong influence upon me, the vivacity of the conception ... gives me a lively notion of all the circumstances of that person, whether past, present, or future; possible, probable or certain. By means of this lively notion I ... feel a sympathetic motion in my breast, conformable to whatever I imagine in his. (T 2.2.9.14)

If the vivacity of the first idea is diminished, on the other hand, so is the vivacity of the ideas related to it ("pipes can convey no more water than what arises at the fountain"), and I will not be interested in the well-being of the other person. Thus, whether we experience extended or limited sympathy—and thus whether we experience love or benevolence, on the one hand, or hatred and contempt, on the other—depends upon the vivacity of the sympathetic impression. A great degree of misery or strong sympathy towards it causes benevolence; small misery or weak sympathy towards it produces contempt.

6.4 Strength of Mind

Reference to all these sources of violence and contrariety constitutes evidence that Hume believes our emotional lives are dominated by disorder and internal conflict. I don't think that this represents his entire assessment of the situation, however. While rationalist thinkers appeal to reason as the regulator, Hume argues that sustaining and strengthening the effects of the calm passions is one of the chief remedies to our situation. (This implies, of course, that motivation is not necessarily a function of the violence of a passion). As I've noted, those for whom the calm passions are motivationally stronger than the violent passions possess the virtue of strength of mind. Hume introduces this virtue in the context of a conflict between concern for long-term self-interest and a violent passion (say, a desire for something immediately appealing, but unhealthy in the long run). He notes that some people are not influenced by the notion of their greatest possible good, while others can counter the influence of the violent passions and be undetermined by present uneasiness.

> In general we may observe, that both these principles operate on the will; and where they are contrary, that either of them prevails, according to the *general* character or *present* disposition of the person. What we call strength of mind, implies the prevalence of the calm passions above the violent... (T 2.3.3.10)

In the *Enquiry Concerning the Principles of Morals*, Hume connects strength of mind with happiness, and the lack of strength of mind with misery. Then he remarks that it is our calm passions that specify the priority of objects and give us resolutions for action, but sometimes our resolve is derailed by violent passions provoked by imaginative portrayals of immediate pleasure (EPM 6.15). Only the person of resolute temper, who can keep distant pursuits in focus, has a chance at happiness and honor.

I want to delve more deeply into the matter of the constitution of strength of mind and the question why Hume regards it as an admirable trait before I consider the question whether persons can cultivate it. There are two issues here. The first has to do with the content of strength of mind. It seems as though one might exhibit strength of mind, the prevalence of calm over violent passions, even if the prevailing calm passions are vicious traits of character. While Hume recognizes that most characters are mixtures of virtuous and vicious traits, one implication of his description of strength of mind is that we could admire someone for possessing strength of mind even if that person coolly and consistently exhibits evil traits.

On the other hand, this possibility seems unlikely, in part because sympathy with those who are affected by an agent is the source of moral approval and disapproval, and resolute evil has more devastating effects on others than wavering evil does. Hence, our sympathies would indicate that the person with the former disposition is worse than one with the latter. But given Hume's characterization of strength of mind, how does he rule out the possibility that calming and steadying sinister motivations are to be recommended?

The second issue has to do with the structure of strength of mind. The virtues for Hume are all non-moral motives that garner approval for the effects they tend to produce. Hume states as an "undoubted maxim" in his discussion of morality that *"no action can be virtuous, or morally good, unless there be in human nature some motive to produce it, distinct from the sense of its morality"* (T 3.2.1.7). For instance, relieving the distress of others is morally good because it is done from a motive of benevolence or regard to the good of humanity. But strength of mind is unique in that it is defined in terms, not of a particular motive, but of the causal force (i.e., strength) of any number of motives in competition with others.[16]

I turn to the question of content. On Hume's account, moral admiration is derived from our sympathizing with the effects on others or the agent of the actions caused by the trait in question. Generally, actions motivated by calm passions such as benevolence, love of life, concern for long-term rather than short-term good, settled principles of character, and moral sentiments, have positive consequences of which we approve. However, this seems false when the trait in question is a settled principle of character that also is ordinarily thought a vice, such as malevolence. How can Hume address this matter and maintain a coherent description of strength of mind? Several avenues of reply suggest themselves.

First, Hume might think that vicious motives are rarely, if ever, felt calmly, even when a person has become habituated to act on them. Anger and malice are motives that seem consistently experienced with internal disorder or upheaval. So, perhaps we needn't worry that strength of mind would encompass the prevalence of vices over virtues. On the other hand, it's hard to see why it would be the case that all vices are experienced vivaciously and forcefully when they act as motives. Furthermore, just as one might postpone the fulfillment of immediate desire in order to achieve a long-term but distant good, one might put off the production of near or immediate evil to produce a more lasting but distant devastation. So, strength of mind could theoretically include vicious dispositions that restrain the immediate desires in order to produce a more profound evil. Hence, the suggestion that vicious motives are always violent passions is simply false.

A second, related suggestion is that while vicious motives may be felt calmly, virtuous ones are never violent. So, a vicious motive's taking precedence over a

---

[16] I want to put aside one natural way to think of strength of mind: to regard it as the opposite of weakness of will. Weakness of will, by all standard accounts, Hume's included, is the case of the agent's thinking she ought to do one action, but being moved by a causally stronger motive to do a competing action. But while strength of mind is exhibited when a person overcomes a motive that she feels with some urgency and turmoil, strength of mind is not the same as acting from a sense of duty: that is, from realization that a certain action is the one that ought, morally-speaking, to be done. Strength of mind could *sometimes* involve the motive of duty, as in the case where a moral sentiment (approval or disapproval from the common point of view) overcomes a violent passion like anger in causing action. But since there are many other calm passions besides the moral sentiments, any of their triumphs over the violent passions might constitute strength of mind. Strength of mind also surely includes cases of acting on dispositions for the long-term good over the short.

virtuous one may be a case of one calm passion's exerting causal strength over another. This suggestion seems plausible when the passions under consideration are instincts like benevolence or kindness to children. But as Loeb has argued (1977: 398), all the secondary passions—at least when first acquired—are violent. Various desires that have to do with the good of those we care about might be experienced with violence, as for instance, when a mother's child is threatened by an intruder. Surely these are among the admirable motives, even if experienced with some psychological disturbance. So, it also seems false to say that virtuous motives are never violent.

A third suggestion is that what we admire when we approve of the calm passions' defeating violent ones is the resolve or determination it takes to resist acting on immediate desires, whatever they aim for. So, strength of mind is not actually the prevalence of calm passions over violent passions, but is instead a fortitude that can be valued apart from the other traits that accompany it. Someone who is able to act on calm passions—even if these may be such motives as malevolence or spite—is admirable, not for the calm passion, but for having a certain resolve. Of course, this is not exactly what Hume says about strength of mind, but it is not an implausible way to see it. We might wonder whether it takes a great deal of fortitude to act on entrenched principles, but it sometimes does take fortitude to act in such a way as to turn certain motives that are not customary into habits. While doing so would not be an effort for someone who is naturally disposed to act in these ways—such as a person disposed by their natural desires to care about others—it would take some effort and resolve to turn a miser into a generous person. So, perhaps, fortitude *is* what we admire in the persons who have strength of mind. I'll return to this suggestion later.

A fourth possibility is to say that acting from established vicious dispositions is simply not indicative of strength of mind because strength of mind is not delineated solely by prevailing calm passions, but by the prevalence of calm passions within certain limits. I think this reading gets support from the context in which Hume introduces strength of mind as a virtue. He has been discussing how calm passions, known more by their effects than by how they feel, are frequently mistaken for reason. He says that these desires are of two kinds: certain instincts implanted in our natures and the general appetite to good and aversion to evil. Then he writes that there are certain violent emotions of the same kind. I have quoted the sentence about the instinct of resentment, but it bears repeating—this time, along with what follows it:

> When I receive any injury from another, I often feel a violent passion of resentment, which makes me desire his evil and punishment, independent of all considerations of pleasure and advantage to myself. When I am immediately threaten'd with any grievous ill, my fears, apprehensions, and aversions arrive to a great height, and produce a sensible emotion. (T 2.3.3.9)

So, here we have examples of resentment and love of life as violent passions, even though they are generally calm. Then Hume writes the paragraph, part of which I've already quoted, introducing strength of mind (T 2.3.3.10).[17] He seems to have in mind there two situations under which persons demonstrate possession of this virtue. One is that they have general characters such that they pursue their long-term natural good (pleasure) over their immediate and intensely-felt desires. The other is that they have general dispositions to pursue the ends of morality over other immediate interests. Then he goes on to say that no one is constantly possessed of strength of mind. "From these variations of temper proceeds the great difficulty of deciding concerning the actions and resolutions of men, where there is any contrariety of motives and passions" (T 2.3.3.10). I take it Hume means that we often have a difficult time determining whose character actually embodies this broad virtue.

The context here suggests that strength of mind specifically has to do with pursuing long-term, prudential and moral goods over short-term, self-interested goods. Calm benevolence that manifests itself in a plan of long-term giving is approved over immediate intense feelings of benevolence that, due to a sudden plea, overcome us, causing us to give without consideration to future demands on our resources. Action due to calm, considered resentment is healthier than action due to momentarily provoked resentment. This reading is substantiated by two other mentions of strength of mind in Hume's *Enquiry Concerning the Principles of Morals*. One is in Section 4, "Of Political Society":

HAD every man sufficient *sagacity* to perceive, at all times, the strong interest, which binds him to the observance of justice and equity, and *strength of mind* sufficient to persevere in a steady adherence to a general and a distant interest, in opposition to the allurements of present pleasure and advantage; there had never, in that case, been any such thing as government or political society, but each man, following his natural liberty, had lived in entire peace and harmony with all others. (EPM 4.1)

And later, in Section 6, "Qualities Useful to Ourselves," in an eloquent passage, Hume connects strength of mind with happiness and its lack with misery, there defining it in terms of forgoing short-term pleasures for long-term interest:

All men, it is allowed, are equally desirous of happiness; but few are successful in the pursuit: One considerable cause is the want of STRENGTH of MIND, which might enable them to resist the temptation of present ease or pleasure, and carry them forward in the search of more distant profit and enjoyment. Our affections, on a general prospect of their objects, form certain rules

---

[17] That passage is:

The common error of metaphysicians has lain in ascribing the direction of the will entirely to one of these principles, and supposing the other to have no influence. Men often act knowingly against their interest: For which reason the view of the greatest possible good does not always influence them. Men often counter-act a violent passion in prosecution of their interests and designs: 'Tis not therefore the present uneasiness alone, which determines them. In general we may observe, that both these principles operate on the will; and where they are contrary, that either of them prevails, according to the *general* character or *present* disposition of the person. What we call strength of mind, implies the prevalence of the calm passions above the violent... (T 2.3.3.10)

of conduct, and certain measures of preference of one above another: And these decisions, though really the result of our calm passions and propensities, (for what else can pronounce any object eligible or the contrary?) are yet said, by a natural abuse of terms, to be the determinations of pure *reason* and reflection. But when some of these objects approach nearer to us, or acquire the advantages of favourable lights and positions, which catch the heart or imagination; our general resolutions are frequently confounded, a small enjoyment preferred, and lasting shame and sorrow entailed upon us. And however poets may employ their wit and eloquence, in celebrating present pleasure, and rejecting all distant views to fame, health, or fortune; it is obvious, that this practice is the source of all dissoluteness and disorder, repentance and misery. A man of a strong and determined temper adheres tenaciously to his general resolutions, and is neither seduced by the allurements of pleasure, nor terrified by the menaces of pain; but keeps still in view those distant pursuits, by which he, at once, ensures his happiness and his honour. (EPM 6.15)

Hume mentions both sorrow and shame as the effects of a deficit of this virtue, and both happiness and honor as the effects of its possession. Hence, my view is that strength of mind, for Hume, is not simply any calm passion exercising control of actions over the violent passions. It has to do specifically with those calm passions that have as their aim the long-term interest of the agent, or the goals whose pursuit are approved by the moral sentiments.[18]

As a matter of fact, Hume indicates that living morally and acting for long-term self-interest are connected in an important sense, given what he writes of the circumstances of the sensible knave in Section 9 of EPM. The sensible knave is surely possessed of calm vicious passions in his taking advantage of the system of justice and making himself an exception to the rules when it serves his interest and does no harm to the institution: "a sensible knave, in particular incidents, may think, that an act of iniquity or infidelity will make a considerable addition to his fortune, without causing any considerable breach in the social union and confederacy" (EPM 9.22). Hume admits that some people will not be repelled by the "baseness" demonstrated by such behavior, but he continues with this often-quoted passage:

But in all ingenuous natures, the antipathy to treachery and roguery is too strong to be counterbalanced by any views of profit or pecuniary advantage. Inward peace of mind, consciousness of integrity, a satisfactory review of our own conduct; these are circumstances very requisite to happiness, and will be cherished and cultivated by every honest man, who feels the importance of them. (EPM 9.23)

---

[18] Karl Schafer (2008) maintains that Hume generally approves of strength of mind,
> but this should not be taken to mean that he believes that the calm passions always ought to prevail over the violent ones. Rather, it is simply that he endorses a general tendency for "reason" in this sense (the calm passions) to move one to act in opposition to the violent passions. (207, n. 24)

I here agree with Schafer's point that Hume does not think all calm passions should prevail over violent, but this is because I take strength of mind to encompass the prevalence of only some of the calm passions.

So, when we turn our moral sensibility inward, take stock of our own character, and find it deficient, we'll suffer a loss of the peace of mind necessary to happiness. Lack of strength of mind results in behavior that undermines enlightened self-interest, whether the deficiency be lack of prudential, self-interested sentiments, or of moral sentiments.[19]

This leaves the second puzzle concerning structure: how does strength of mind fit into Hume's theory of the virtues, since it is defined, not as a particular trait, but as the prevalence of certain passions over others? It shares this puzzle with courage, which seems to be characterized as the feature of a person's character that allows that person to confront and overcome fear (see McCarty 2012). The question that both strength of mind and courage raise is just what natural motive we approve when we approve of behavior that exhibits that virtue, given that the defining feature of each is its causal strength to influence action.

One suggestion is that strength of mind might be identified with the trait of prudence, which is typically thought of as concern for one's long-term good. The text, however, does not corroborate this interpretation. Prudence is mentioned several times as a virtue in Book 3 of the *Treatise* (T 3.3.1.24, 3.3.2.11, 3.3.4.4), but strength of mind is never mentioned in Book 3 at all. In the second *Enquiry*, prudence appears in a long list of qualities useful to the self, but strength of mind is not included in that list:

discretion, caution, enterprize, industry, assiduity, frugality, economy, good-sense, prudence, discernment; besides these endowments, I say, whose very names force an avowal of their merit, there are many others, to which the most determined scepticism cannot, for a moment, refuse the tribute of praise and approbation. *Temperance, sobriety, patience, constancy, perseverance, forethought, considerateness, secrecy, order, insinuation, address, presence of mind, quickness of conception, facility of expression*... (EPM 6.21)

Prudence is also called "an intellectual virtue" in Appendix 4 of EPM, but strength of mind is not mentioned in that context (although it surely is also an intellectual virtue). Strength of mind is noted in EPM 4.1 (quoted earlier) as a virtue that, if everyone had it all the time, would make political society unnecessary, and in the passage from EPM 6.15 (quoted earlier) as a trait useful to the self because it is necessary to happiness.

The same kind of argument can be made against identifying strength of mind with perseverance or fortitude. Perseverance appears in the above list of features useful to the self and is mentioned in connection with the virtue of industry in both the *Treatise* and the *Enquiry*: "*Industry, perseverance, patience, activity, vigilance, application, constancy*, with other virtues of that kind...are esteem'd valuable upon no

---

[19] See Immerwahr (1992) for an informative discussion of the effect of calm passions on happiness. Immerwahr says that Hume connects with the prevalence of violent passions all of the following: misery, folly, vice, love, factions, polytheism, and popular religion (1992: 302).

other account, than their advantage in the conduct of life" (T 3.3.4.7). In EPM, Hume cites the example of the industrious tortoise in the fable who "by his perseverance, gained the race of the hare" (EPM 6.10). The conclusion to EPM (Section 9) lists perseverance, along with industry, discretion, frugality, secrecy, order, forethought, judgment (and, Hume says, a long list of other features) as virtues whose tendency to promote the happiness of their possessor is the sole foundation of their merit (EPM 9.12). Strength of mind is not mentioned explicitly in any of the discussions of perseverance, fortitude, or industriousness.

The way to understand strength of mind, I think, is not as any particular motive, but as a constellation of traits comprising certain calm passions: of benevolence, resentment, love of life (self-love), kindness to children, and of the moral and aesthetic sentiments. Someone in whom these qualities manifest themselves in action, overcoming the vivacious passions that prompt immediate and short-term gratification, exhibits strength of mind. Thus, strength of mind is a general disposition we attribute to a person, rather than a single natural motive. It is a disposition that depends on both the presence and the strength of other specific motives. It makes sense to see it this way, since such a conception of strength of mind allows for our imputing specific causes to the action, namely the particular calm passions that motivate, and it allows for attributing a general character assessment to an actor. The broad character assessment is not identified with those individual motivating passions, but is one that refers to an overall tendency in the person. The overall tendency of one's character is defined in terms of the causal strength of the individual motives.

This way of interpreting strength of mind is not inconsistent with Hume's undoubted maxim, as far as I can see. It is not quite like the case of justice, in which the search for an original natural motive to the rule-following behavior demanded by justice either turns up nothing, or else appeals to a complex and transformed self-interest (depending on one's reading). Jane McIntyre (2006b) has argued that strength of mind is a "quasi-artificial" virtue, having features in common with both the natural and the artificial virtues associated with justice in Hume's theory. Strength of mind is like the natural virtues because it is useful to the self, perhaps also immediately pleasurable to self and useful to others. It's like the artificial, she says, in that it does not result in good in every single act, but rather, the praiseworthy ends of acts that exhibit strength of mind are achieved only through adherence to an overall plan, just as in acts of justice. I think, however, that strength of mind is clearly a natural virtue for Hume.

First, there are numerous natural motives we might find behind such behavior. That is, one is in possession of this virtue when any of a number of particular calm motives for distant and long-term goods are strong enough to overcome the violent urges for near and intense momentary goods. Second, while the behavior exhibited by strength of mind requires the postponement of gratification for a longer-term good (for instance, saving one's money for college instead of spending it on eating out at fine restaurants), that such behavior serves the longer-term good is clear. In the case of justice, the agent might very well wonder whether or not following the rules when others are doing the same will make any difference to the effectiveness of the system overall. Thus, the original motive to live according to the rules of justice is harder to find than is the motive to save my money instead of spending it on fine dining. Strength of mind, I think, is no more an artificial virtue than are its cousins—prudence, industry, perseverance, and fortitude—all of which require restraint in fulfilling immediate desires.

Consequently, strength of mind, on my interpretation, is properly considered a natural virtue in Hume's theory. As I noted earlier, Hume writes that a person with strength of mind

> adheres tenaciously to his general resolutions, and is neither seduced by the allurements of pleasure, nor terrified by the menaces of pain; but keeps still in view those distant pursuits, by which he, at once, ensures his happiness and his honour.

The person with such strength behaves in these ways by acting on a calm benevolence or a calm self-interest (love of life), or a calm moral sentiment (among other motives), whose force is greater than the causal force of violently-felt competing motives.

6.5 Moderating the Passions with the Passions

Even though Hume insists that violence is a dimension of a passion different from its causal strength, the two, on his account, are frequently connected. He writes that it is "certain" that if we want to push someone to action, "'twill commonly be better policy to work upon the violent than the calm passions, and rather take him by his inclination, than what is vulgarly call'd his *reason*" (T 2.3.4.1). A variation in the situation of the object relative to the agent will change the calm and violent passions into each other. When a good is viewed from a distance, such as the completion of a marathon considered at the beginning of the race, it produces a calm reaction. When that same good is brought nearer—say, when the runner is 2 miles from the finish—the thought of completion can produce a violent token of that same type of passion and spur the exhausted runner to exert even more force. So, we are likely to increase the violence of passions toward pleasurable objects by bringing them "nearer," and thereby increase a person's motivation toward them (T 2.3.4.1).

However, given this phenomenon, one might wonder how Hume can carve out a practical gap between the motivational strength of a passion and its violence, if violence turns out to be so important to a passion's effect on action. Hume spends five sections (T 2.3.4–T 2.3.8) in Book 2, Part 3, "Of the will and direct passions," on the topic of augmenting and diminishing the motivational strength of the passions. There he writes about several factors that affect motivational force, typically by working on the violence or calmness of the passions (although not in all cases). The impact of custom, of the imagination, and of contiguity and distance in space and time, are each treated in separate sections. Jane McIntyre comments that Hume has a problem substantiating the strength/violence distinction because he offers very little commentary on how to increase the causal strength of passions without working on increasing their violence (see McIntyre 2006b: 397).

I think the question whether Hume is able to carve out the necessary space between motivational strength and violence is even more pressing in light of the following considerations. His reference to the effect of the force and vivacity with which the object of a passion is conceived raises the question how the force and vivacity of a mental state are related to the violence and strength of a passion. I want to take seriously the suggestion that force and vivacity, as invoked in Book 1 of the *Treatise*, are the same phenomenon as violence, as invoked in Book 2. The fundamental difference between impressions (sensations and passions) and ideas is, of course, their relative degrees of force and vivacity. Among ideas, beliefs are more lively and vivacious than ideas that are not believed. Perhaps, then, a violent passion is simply one whose object is represented with a higher degree of force and vivacity than that of a calm passion. In treating the psychological impact that contiguity in space and time has upon our passions for objects, Hume writes:

> Here then we are to consider two kinds of objects, the contiguous and remote; of which the former, by means of their relation to ourselves, approach an impression in force and vivacity; the latter by reason of the interruption in our manner of conceiving them, appear in a weaker and more imperfect light. This is their effect on the imagination.

So far, Hume is talking about the manner in which we conceive the objects, but then he continues:

> If my reasoning be just, they must have a proportionable effect on the will and passions. Contiguous objects must have an influence much superior to the distant and remote. Accordingly we find in common life, that men are principally concern'd about those objects, which are not much remov'd either in space or time, enjoying the present, and leaving what is afar off to the care of chance and fortune. Talk to a man of his condition thirty years hence, and he will not regard you. Speak of what is to happen to-morrow, and he will lend you attention. The breaking of a mirror gives us more concern when at home, than the burning of a house, when abroad, and some hundred leagues distant. (T 2.3.7.3)

So, the force and vivacity of an idea of an object are influenced by the contiguity of the object to the agent, and either because of this fact, or analogously to it, an agent's interest in closer objects is greater than her interest in distant objects. Consequently, the motivational force of her interest varies in proportion to the distance from the object. Hume doesn't actually say that the violence of the passion for the closer object is greater (one might have great concern, but experience it calmly), but it is reasonable to suppose that this is what he means when he writes about "more concern," since he has been discussing in this context the effects of violence on motivation. What he also doesn't say, which is significant to the present topic, is that increased force and vivacity of the passion are responsible for increased motivational effect. His reference in the passage to force and vivacity has to do with the liveliness of the idea of the object of the passion, and how its liveliness varies with distance across space and time.

So, if the violence of a passion is proportionately related to the force and vivacity of its object, as Hume seems to say at T 3.2.7.2, then the problem of distinguishing motivational force from violence is even more pronounced, given his comments about the relation between force and vivacity and motivational strength. I do believe there are good reasons to think that calmness and violence of passions *are* the same features as the force and vivacity of mental states. First, it would be an unduly complicated picture of our mental life to suppose that all mental states vary in force and vivacity, a phenomenal dimension, but that impressions of reflection (the passions) vary in yet another, very similar phenomenal dimension. Rather, it makes best sense of Hume's philosophy of mind to see the characteristic of force and vivacity as a continuum along which fall ideas, beliefs, and impressions, with some impressions having more forcefulness than others. In fact, when Hume describes the distinction between impressions and ideas, which he says at first is a difference between them of "force and liveliness, with which they strike upon the mind," he uses the term "violence" in the next sentence: "Those perceptions, which enter with the most force and violence, we may name *impressions*..." (T 1.1.1.1). So, it would make sense to think that in the case of impressions of reflection, the internal upheaval that is definitive of the violence of a passion *just is* its force and vivacity. Second, Hume makes the comment that the calm passions are often mistaken for reason, saying that "every action of the mind, which operates with the same calmness and tranquility, is confounded with reason by all those, who judge of things from the first view and appearance" (T 2.3.3.8). This can be explained by the fact that reason deals with the logical connections between ideas, and ideas are on the low end of the force and vivacity—or violence—continuum, close to the calm passions.

To return to the question at hand: Does Hume have grounds to make the practical distinction between strength of motivation and violence of a passion? I think he does, in part because he emphasizes that strength of calm over violent passions is never possessed by an agent constantly. That such a state of calm over violent exists, but rarely and not continuously, is consistent with his many claims about the overwhelming motivational effect of violent passions. When he introduces discussion of strength of mind, he does so in the context of a conflict between concern for long-term self-interest and a violent passion (say, a desire for something immediately appealing, but unhealthy in the long run):

Men often act knowingly against their interest: For which reason the view of the greatest possible good does not always influence them. Men often counter-act a violent passion in prosecution of their interests and designs: 'tis not therefore the present uneasiness alone, which

determines them. In general we may observe, that both these principles operate on the will; and where they are contrary, that either of them prevails, according to the *general* character or *present* disposition of the person. What we call strength of mind, implies the prevalence of the calm passions above the violent; tho' we may easily observe, there is no man so constantly possess'd of this virtue, as never on any occasion to yield to the sollicitations of passion and desire. From these variations of temper proceeds the great difficulty of deciding concerning the actions and resolutions of men, where there is any contrariety of motives and passions.
(T 2.3.3.10)

Here Hume describes the will as being determined sometimes by present uneasiness (or easiness), and sometimes by distant good (or bad). The passion or passions that become the more habitual principles of action are the prevailing inclinations, but even these are at times overcome, it seems, by other passions. To say this is consistent with the view that the easiest way to motivate a person *typically* is by augmenting the violence of the relevant passion or desire. The person with strength of mind, however, can be motivated by another kind of appeal, at the times when the person is in possession of that strength.

So, while there is theoretical accommodation for the exercise of strength of mind, how optimistic can we be about the possibility of its cultivation? Hume observes several times that the causes and the effects of both the calm and violent passions are greatly dependent on the "peculiar temper and disposition" of each person. Generally, he says, the violent passions have a greater influence on actions, but "the calm ones, when corroborated by reflection, and seconded by resolution, are able to controul them in their most furious movements" (T 2.3.8.13). So, his theory offers hope for some sort of moderation of the more destructive passions. However, he immediately follows with this caveat:

What makes this whole affair more uncertain, is, that a calm passion may easily be chang'd into a violent one, either by a change of temper, or of the circumstances and situation of the object, as by the borrowing of force from any attendant passion, by custom, or by exciting the imagination. Upon the whole, this struggle of passion and of reason, as it is call'd, diversifies human life, and makes men so different not only from each other, but also from themselves in different times.   (T 2.3.8.13)

Not only are persons different from one another because of their violent passions, but persons are different "from themselves in different times." The passions vacillate so profoundly that the emotional differences seem to constitute different people at different times. This passage highlights the many obstacles to calming the passions, since violence can be heightened by many factors, including the effects of individual temperaments and dispositions, the changing circumstances of the object, other associated passions, custom, and the imagination.

I want to argue, however, that at least three features of Hume's theory of emotional conflict imply that regulation of the passions is possible. While temperaments and dispositions are original to persons, the particular affections, emotions, and passions they experience are a function of their dispositions in conjunction with other factors. Manipulating these factors, I think, allows for the use of some passions to moderate the effects of other passions. The first feature of Hume's account that allows this reading lies in his discussion of custom and calm passions. The second is a key point in his treatment of conflicting passions, the fact that one passion can neutralize another just as an alkaline neutralizes an acid. The third lies in Hume's treatment of a virtue called "greatness of mind," which is connected in an unobvious way to his discussion of the principles of sympathy and comparison. In fact, the principle of sympathy, by itself, is a fourth feature of the passions that plays a crucial role in self-regulation. So, Hume's theory embodies the very view that Senault warned was dangerous—that the passions govern themselves by opposing one passion to another.[20]

6.5.1 Acclimation

How can we cultivate strength of mind? Hume has earlier made the point that the easiest way to motivate a person is by augmenting the violence of the relevant passion or desire, but he also implies that the motivational force of calm passions can be increased by the impact of habit. The more accustomed we become to acting for a long-term good over a short-term one, or to acting from calm benevolence over disgust, etc., the more strongly we are inclined to act on the relevant passion again. Hume writes that custom bestows "a *facility* in the performance of any action or the conception of any object; and afterwards a *tendency or inclination* towards it" (T 2.3.5.1). When we initiate action toward a new object, the effort is difficult but also exciting, and enlivens the mind, producing surprise. Hume thinks that surprise augments both agreeable and disagreeable feelings. But when the motivating passions returns and we act on it repeatedly, the novelty wears off and the passion is calmed. Likewise, the facility with which we so act is increased and becomes a source of quiet pleasure.

> The pleasure of facility does not so much consist in any ferment of the spirits, as in their orderly motion; which will sometimes be so powerful as even to convert pain into pleasure, and give us a relish in time for what at first was most harsh and disagreeable. (T 2.3.5.3)

Furthermore, the imagination can assist the effort to acclimate to certain behaviors. If the desire for a distant good can be made lively or violent, perhaps by imagining its consequences and benefits, and bringing them in picturesque ways before the mind, then it is more likely to have a causal force strong enough to prevail over competing desires. If I can envision the healthy and pleasant consequences of having a regular exercise program, I might be able to overcome the desire to relax on my sofa for the next hour instead of getting out to the gym. If an agent succeeds at this mental

---

[20] See Zimmerman (2007) and Immerwahr (1992) for discussions of how Hume thinks we might increase the strength of calm passions. McIntyre (2006b) has a bit to say about this as well.

maneuver frequently, then this way of behaving can become habitual, and the desire or passion from which she acts will become calm, but effective.

6.5.2 Neutralizing Destructive Passions

Hume's account of the principles at play in the mind's reaction to conflicting passions suggests a strategy for canceling certain passions or their effects. (1) Sometimes a more violent passion will absorb a less violent one, and increase the former's forcefulness (violence) even more. So, if we can bring a good vividly to mind, we might provoke a passion that incorporates another passion we think is noxious for us. So, if I feel envy at my colleague's good fortune, I might focus on the value of her contributions to the university and profession so that I feel gratitude or admiration. If that gratitude or admiration is experienced vividly or forcefully enough, it might consume envy and perhaps intensify the feeling of admiration. (2) When we have conflicting passions resulting from alternate views of an object, Hume observes that the two will neutralize one another, leaving the mind in a state of equanimity. So, if I want to minimize the distress I feel from the prospect of a medical treatment, I might try imagining the beneficial effects of the procedure in order to produce a reaction that annuls the painful one. Of course, the difficulty lies in achieving a reaction forceful and lively enough to counter the fear, but Hume's view leaves open the possibility that we can neutralize negative passions by what we attend to. (3) If the conflict of passions is due to uncertainty about the nature of an object, the passions of joy and sadness will alternate, with their intensity heightened by the insecurity. They eventually blend into a new passion of either hope or fear. These observations suggest that we might push the mix toward hope by concentrating on the possibility that the good will result. Since understanding probabilities is a crucial factor in how and to what degree the passions of joy and sadness alternate, attending closely to the odds of one outcome or another can affect whether the emotion of hope or fear is predominant.

6.5.3 Lessons from Greatness of Mind

In a section of the *Treatise* close to the end of Book 3 ("Of Morals"), Hume discusses a virtue he calls "greatness of mind," and connects it to the principles of sympathy and comparison. He calls greatness of mind "heroic virtue," the sort of trait that prompts acts of courageousness and magnanimity, and says it essentially partakes of proper pride and well-established self-esteem (T 3.3.2.13). To introduce the topic, Hume returns to the principles of sympathy and comparison, which he detailed in Book 2, and comments that since sympathy and comparison are directly contrary, "it may be worth while to consider, what general rules can be form'd, beside the particular temper of the person, for the prevalence of the one or the other" (T 3.3.2.5). Once again, he refers to temperament as a factor in the passions we commonly experience, but implies that there is more at work than simply natural dispositions. He uses an example to draw out the principles underlying the use of sympathy and comparison. If I'm safely on land, I might think of people miserable at sea in a storm, but this idea increases my own happiness by comparison only when the idea of those people suffering out on the ocean is very forceful and lively. The effects of my imagination, however, will never equal that of my actually witnessing (from my safe position on land) the ship at a distance being tossed by the waves and in danger of sinking. Then Hume asks us to suppose

> the ship to be driven so near me, that I can perceive distinctly the horror, painted on the countenance of the seamen and passengers, hear their lamentable cries, see the dearest friends give their last adieu, or embrace with a resolution to perish in each other's arms.

In this case, sympathy is activated and comparison is muted: "No man has so savage a heart as to reap any pleasure from such a spectacle, or withstand the motions of the tenderest compassion and sympathy" (T 3.3.2.5). The general principle at work, he concludes, is that the liveliness of an idea of another's situation determines whether our conception has a sympathetic or comparative effect on us. When too dull, it has no effect. Comparison requires some degree of vivacity, but sympathy, being the conversion of an idea of another's feeling into our own, requires a very lively and striking idea. In fact, his example shows that not only does sympathy require lively ideas of others' conditions, but that such ideas force us to feel sympathetic responses, rather than comparative ones.

In applying these principles to the case of pride, Hume observes that the presence of "a great man" can sometimes cause envy and hatred in us, as we shrink by comparison, but it can sometimes cause respect and esteem through sympathy with his pride. Simply imagining a person of superior qualities doesn't much affect us. However, when a person

> whom we are really persuaded to be of inferior merit, is presented to us; if we observe in him any extraordinary degree of pride and self-conceit; the firm persuasion he has of his own merit, takes hold of the imagination, and diminishes us in our own eyes, in the same manner, as if he were really possess'd of all the good qualities which he so liberally attributes to himself.
>
> (T 3.3.2.6)

Here the conditions are right for comparison to take hold, since the ideas are forceful enough to make us experience resentment. If, on the other hand, we were convinced that the person actually possesses the merit he or she purports to have, the idea is strong enough for sympathy, and we feel admiration. Hume concludes that "an overweaning conceit" of our merits is vicious, because it makes others uncomfortable, while a justified sense of our talents and accomplishments is a virtue. "[N]othing is more useful to us in the conduct of life, than a due degree of pride, which makes us sensible of our own merit, and gives us a confidence and assurance in all our projects and enterprizes" (T 3.3.2.8).

There are a couple of ways in which the lessons from Hume's analysis of greatness of mind can be used to minimize conflict and the experience of stressful passions.

First, if we can fasten onto a firm, but lively idea of another's condition, we might cause ourselves to experience unwavering sympathetic reactions that result in our feeling benevolence, love, or pity, rather than resentment, hatred, or malice by comparison. Of course, sympathetic feelings with others in distress are not pleasurable, and we might prefer to avoid them. However, all things considered, they seem superior to the team of emotions associated with hatred, given that the former are more likely to procure the admiration of others. Furthermore, we will have a much better life if we surround ourselves with those who have a genuine sense of their own merits than if we spend time around those with inflated opinions of their own worth. We will find ourselves frequently sharing in the joy of others and admiring them, rather than feeling resentment and jealousy of others who constantly make us feel less accomplished than we otherwise might feel. More importantly, in order to be productive, ambitious, courageous, or magnanimous, we need to make a fair assessment of our own contributions and take pride in our talents and accomplishments. "Whatever capacity any one may be endow'd with, 'tis entirely useless to him, if he be not acquainted with it, and form not designs suitable to it." Hume thinks that we should know our own strengths, and if we are to err on one side or the other, it should be on the side of overrating our merit. "Fortune commonly favours the bold and enterprizing; and nothing inspires us with more boldness than a good opinion of ourselves" (T 3.3.2.8).

6.5.4 Sympathy and Social Regulation

We live among people and we care deeply about what others think of us. Hume writes, "Our reputation, our character, our name are considerations of vast weight and importance; and even the other causes of pride; virtue, beauty and riches; have little influence, when not seconded by the opinions and sentiments of others" (T 2.1.11.1). We desire to be admired by others, and our self-esteem is influenced by others' attitudes and opinions of us. These psychological tendencies are explained in part by the common desire to be well regarded, but also, again, by sympathy. Sympathy makes it possible for us to absorb and experience the attitude of others toward us, which they pick up on and reflect back to us, and so on: "the minds of men are mirrors to one another, not only because they reflect each other's emotions, but also because those rays of passions, sentiments and opinions may be often reverberated, and may decay away by insensible degrees" (T 2.2.5.21). So, passions are obviously also regulated by the situation of persons in society, where we reflect one another's feelings and are induced to behave in ways conducive to conviviality and sociability.

In a recent article, Jane McIntyre explores what is "new and extraordinary" about Hume's account of the passions, referring to Hume's own phrase from his Abstract of the *Treatise*. In so doing, she examines central themes in the work on the passions in the early modern era and finds two of special interest: (1) the relation of mind and body; and (2) the government of the passions. The first is a concern that emerges from analyses of the passions that emphasize their physiological components (such as those of Descartes and Malebranche). The second theme, she contends, stems from those philosophers whose interest is the passions' relation to morality. She argues that a key feature of Hume's theory is to show, contrary to the rationalists, that norms for the passions are derived from what is natural and useful in human nature. The standards are shared through sympathy, and therefore "the government of the passions takes on an important social component" (McIntyre 2006a: 213). James Harris, continuing McIntyre's project of situating Hume's theory of the passions in the context of the reason-passion debate, remarks that writers in the eighteenth century were "obsessed" with the topic of how the passions can be governed. By then, the passions were seen, not as destructive, but as the locus of the moral life, the "fabric" of society and economy, and the means of having an intimate relation to God (Harris 2013: 270). Harris argues that the accepted view of the role of philosophy in the eighteenth century was that it not only served to analyze the passions, but to restrain and organize them in our lives.[21]

According to Harris, Hume's views on self-regulation should be read with Mandeville as the backdrop. On Mandeville's story, the unsociable passions need to be manipulated by a governing class that will transform a state of nature into an orderly society. Hume, on Harris's interpretation, counters Mandeville by maintaining that governance lies in a social process crucially dependent on sympathy, not on political authority (Harris 2013: 280). After Hume undermines reason as the moderator, the eighteenth-century reader would expect an appeal to outside authority as the solution to the problem how the passions can be governed in a way that leads to healthy activity. Hume, however, introduces the idea that persons regulate one another in the context of a social system (see Harris 2009: 137). Harris says that Hume's account of the passions thus introduces a theory of "sympathetic sociability" as his answer to the problem of passionate regulation (ibid.: 139). "What has always been taken to be a contest between reason and desire is in fact the interaction of a panoply of feelings, some vivid and pressing, others more elusive and reticent" (ibid.: 132). McIntyre's and Harris's analyses emphasize the social aspect of self-regulation and show how it is significant in Hume's theory of the passions. At the same time, I have also illustrated how the principles of individual moderation are available for those who have the constitution to use them.

---

[21] He highlights differences among these thinkers, of course: some invoked religion in the regulation of the passions; others, like Shaftesbury, saw proper governance as a matter of physiological health of the individual and of finding one's proper place in a social and political context. Hutcheson agreed that appropriate management of the passions required finding "a balance of various countervailing forces," rather than a focus on self-interest, and recommends that persons find an impartial perspective on the world that reveals one's place in a larger moral system (Harris 2013: 277).

6.6 Limits to Self-Regulation of the Passions

6.6.1 Intractable Human Nature

I have argued that Hume's theory of the passions embodies psychological principles that make it possible for us to transform some of our passions—to mitigate the force of some of the pernicious motivations and to bolster the causal impact of some of the beneficial ones. I do not want to exaggerate the degree to which Hume's theory allows such control, however.[22] Self-regulation clearly has limits set by entrenched features of human nature. First, of course, Hume emphasizes the role of individual temperament on one's ability to undertake a project of passionate transformation, or to succeed at it. Those who are naturally moderate in food and drink, or who are naturally resolute in seeking long-term goals of lasting benefit, or those in whom certain normal attractions of appetite naturally hold little appeal, will obviously have an easier time acquiring strength of mind than those who have the opposing tendencies. Perhaps there are some agents for whom strength of mind is simply beyond reach. Second, Hume portrays more pessimism about individual control of the passions in his discussion of justice in *Treatise* Book 3 than he does in his Book 2 treatment of the passions. In T 3.2, he underscores the role of personal perspective and proximity of goods (the work of the principle of contiguity again) in magnifying passions for short-term benefits:

> It has been observ'd, in treating of the passions, that men ... proportion their affections more to the light, under which any object appears to them, than to its real and intrinsic value.... Now as every thing, that is contiguous to us, either in space or time, strikes upon us with such an idea, it has a proportional effect on the will and passions, and commonly operates with more force than any object, that lies in a more distant and obscure light. (T 3.2.7.2)

It is important to note that our motivations are not due to deception about the greater good; rather, we simply cannot get our passions to conform to our judgment. Hume continues:

> Tho' we may be fully convinc'd, that the latter object excels the former, we are not able to regulate our actions by this judgment; but yield to the sollicitations of our passions, which always plead in favour of whatever is near and contiguous.

The propensity to prefer the near, but trivial advantage, over the remote, but significant one, Hume calls, "on a cursory view ... incapable of any remedy" (T 3.2.7.4).

But the qualification is telling, since (Harris's view notwithstanding) Hume *seems* to suggest in the discussion of justice that the remedy consists in civil government. He writes:

---

[22] I am greatly indebted to Lauren Kopajtic's excellent discussion (2015), for underscoring the difficulties, on Hume's theory of human nature, of cultivating strength of mind naturally.

Men are not able radically to cure, either in themselves or others, that narrowness of soul, which makes them prefer the present to the remote. They cannot change their natures. All they can do is to change their situation, and render the observance of justice the immediate interest of some particular persons, and its violation their more remote.   (T 3.2.7.6)

These persons, who have no interest in injustice and are satisfied with their present condition, become the rulers; they are motivated to constrain others and inculcate habits of justice in others. But, again, there must be individuals who are naturally motivated "to change their situation," or else the whole system cannot get started. Presumably these are persons within whom the conditions for developing strength of mind are present (if they don't already possess the virtue); and so, these individuals are able to pursue their genuine self-interest without coercion. The thesis I have defended, that there are principles in Hume's psychology that allow for the natural strengthening of calm over violent passions, depending on the nature and dispositions of individuals, is logically consistent with his pessimism in Treatise 3.2. Nonetheless, Hume's warnings about the limits on developing strength of mind are more pronounced there.

6.6.2 Is Reason Doing the Moderating Work After All?

Since the strategies for moderation of passionate conflicts frequently involve bringing ideas to mind with forcefulness, a natural question is whether the work of regulation is actually being done by reason after all. Of course, the practice of moderation requires the use of the understanding and imagination to bring to mind the ideas that provoke the passions we aim to cultivate, but this does not mean that reason works alone. First, reason is *not* deciding what passions are best. As Hume emphasizes, it is our own calm passions that determine our priorities, by reflective approval of various passionate motivations, based on their generally agreeable effects. Second, whether we engage in moderation at all is a function of emotional constitution. As I have suggested, while some people may simply lack the psychological constitution to develop strength of mind, or to arouse ideas vivacious enough to experience sympathetic feelings over comparative ones with any regularity, or to feel the proper pride definitive of greatness of mind, some of us are able to affect our own passions and practice a useful regulation of some passions by others. Since many of the generally calm passions are instinctual, we all experience them to some degree. Third, the impetus to control some passions by other passions depends on the degree to which we can tolerate conflict and upheaval. This varies from person to person, depending not on reason, but, again, on one's affective make-up. Fourth, it's worth noting that the success of the attempt to moderate the passions depends on other background passions inherent in one's nature. That is to say, the outcome is never a product of reason alone; bringing to mind the image of a cliff overlooking an open vista may make you feel exhilarated and make me feel nauseous. Finally, because the means of adjusting the passions is provided by our sympathetic nature, our desire for the good opinion of others, and our desire for the pleasure of self-esteem and pride, reason is not their regulator. Reason, for Hume, works in the service of the passions in the process of self-governance, which allows that our lives are not necessarily dominated by emotional chaos and contrariety.

6.7 The Practical Role of Strength of Conviction

Since being moved to action is dependent on a motivating passion *and* an appropriate belief, a discussion of Hume and competing motives has to include reference to the role of belief in producing action. In CHAPTER 2, I discussed Hume's section "Of the influence of belief," where he writes about the practical effect of belief on action. I have argued that beliefs give us practical information by which we guide our behavior in view of what we want or are attracted to, and they arouse passions we *already* possess when they concern the existence of certain objects toward which those passions might be directed. While they are essential to action and so not subordinate to passion in that way, I take seriously Hume's pronouncement of reason as slave to the passions. I take it to mean that the relevance of a belief to action depends on what passions the person possesses, which are not produced by belief or by reason. I'll admit that "reason as slave to the passions" seems at odds with Hume's writing in the first *Enquiry*:

belief is something felt by the mind, which distinguishes the ideas of the judgment from the fictions of the imagination. It gives them more weight and influence; makes them appear of greater importance; enforces them in the mind; and renders them the governing principle of our actions. (EHU 5.12)

It is significant, however, that Hume does not write that beliefs govern passions, but that they govern action. It makes sense to think that, given that a person's ends are in place, belief governs action by affording the actor enlivened ideas about the nature of objects that might fit the characterization of one of her ends, or ideas about the means to ends—ideas which prompt her to act on the basis of the ends set by her passions.

My claim that we always act on the strongest motive is qualified by an "all-things-being-equal" clause (with "motive"—as I earlier noted—referring to the passion or desire, rather than to its combination with belief, in the way contemporary Humeanism has it). Among those qualified conditions is the strength with which the beliefs that concern the means to the respective ends are held. It makes sense to think that the outcome of competing motives is affected by the degree of conviction one has with respect to the pertinent beliefs. Thus, the action an agent undertakes in a given case can be decided by the strength of belief when the competing desires are of equal force. For instance, Mr. Hume has two desires of equal prominence: he would like to relax this evening, but he also desires to finish the essay he was unable to revise in the afternoon, owing to interruptions. He knows from many past experiences that playing backgammon with his friends will be relaxing, so he has a strong belief about the appropriate way to fulfill his first desire. He is uncertain whether his fatigued mind is clear enough to focus on writing, so he is much less convinced about having the effective means to his second end. It is reasonable to predict that Mr. Hume will therefore play backgammon this evening. Hume's discussion of probability (when he is back to work as a philosopher), following his discussion of the influence of belief, constitutes, I think, his commentary on strength of belief in action. He identifies degrees of evidence and corresponding conviction: knowledge is the result of comparison of ideas (knowledge of necessary truths); proof is causal reasoning that is free of doubt (resulting in beliefs like the sun will rise tomorrow or that all people will die); and probability is evidence "attended with uncertainty" (T 1.3.11.2). Probability is interesting in this discussion, since beliefs of probability can vary in strength depending on one's reaction to the evidence upon which one's beliefs are grounded. Hume divides probability into that which is founded on chance and that which arises from consideration of causes. "Unphilosophical probability," a third sort of probability, is not recognized by philosophers, Hume says, but it is important in a discussion of this sort, since it has to do with features of human nature that affect the degree of conviction with which a belief is held.

Since chance indicates the lack of causes, its prospect leads to indifference. Thus, Hume's discussion of this topic takes up the question how a number of equal chances for different outcomes can operate on the mind to produce belief. His response to it is to show by use of a die that belief in an outcome is fixed only when more than one of its six sides is inscribed with the same number of dots; then the strength of the belief that that number will turn up is a result of the "impulses" of the same-numbered sides uniting into a dominant force. That force, however, is diminished by the impulses produced by contrary numbers on the other sides. "The vivacity of the idea [belief] is always proportionable to the degrees of the impulse or tendency to the transition [from impression to idea]" (T 1.3.11.13). In the case of causal probability, strength of belief is affected in various ways that correlate with the way in which beliefs are acquired—that is, by a constant conjunction of experiences and the mind's relation of the idea of one of those experiences to a present impression of the other. Hume notices, therefore, that probability is affected by a contrariety of events, which interrupts the constancy of the conjunction. "A contrariety of events in the past may give us a kind of hesitating belief for the future after two...ways" (T 1.3.12.6). One way lies in producing an "imperfect" habit, which makes the transition to belief less forceful and steady. The other lies in our taking into account the contrary events and weighing the experiments on each side. The way in which we reason from an interrupted regularity is to "draw together the divided images presented by experience" to entertain an idea about a single future event. When a greater number of images concur on one side than on the other:

These agreeing images unite together, and render the idea more strong and lively, not only than a mere fiction of the imagination, but also than any idea, which is supported by a lesser number of experiments. Each new experiment is as a new stroke of the pencil, which bestows an additional vivacity on the colours without either multiplying or enlarging the figure. (T 1.3.12.11)

So, for instance, people generally came to believe that smoking causes lung cancer, despite the fact that not all who smoke develop the disease. The evidence for the conclusion mounted with each new case, and with the preponderance of cases on the positive side, the belief became widely accepted, and with a high degree of conviction. Obviously, investigations into causes of various diseases and their possible treatments employ probabilistic thinking as Hume describes it, and conclusions are reached with various degrees of confidence depending on the amount of conflicting versus consistent evidence.

Hume's discussion of unphilosophical probability offers additional explanations of the psychological factors that affect the forcefulness of our beliefs. These considerations are less quantifiable than those in philosophical probability and are not recognized as normatively legitimate, but they do nonetheless influence the degree of confidence a believer has in the conclusion she has reached. First, when the memory of the resemblance between the past conjoined experiences is diminished by the passage of time, the evidence is also diminished in our minds and the degree of belief accordingly affected:

The argument, which we found on any matter of fact we remember, is more or less convincing according as the fact is recent or remote; and tho' the difference in these degrees of evidence be not receiv'd by philosophy as solid and legitimate; because in that case an argument must have a different force to-day, from what it shall have a month hence; yet notwithstanding the opposition of philosophy, 'tis certain, this circumstance has a considerable influence on the understanding, and secretly changes the authority of the same argument, according to the different times, in which it is propos'd to us. (T 1.3.13.1)

Second, Hume writes that "our degrees of belief and assurance" are influenced by how recent an experiment relevant to a particular belief took place; we are more forcefully affected by the recent evidence than by an experiment whose results have been obscured by time (T 1.3.13.2).

Third,

when an inference is drawn immediately from an object, without any intermediate cause or effect, the conviction is much stronger, and the perswasion more lively, than when the imagination is carry'd thro' a long chain of connected arguments, however infallible the connexion of each link may be esteem'd. (T 1.3.13.3)

Hume explains this consequence by the fact that the vivacity of the original impression upon which a current belief depends decays in proportion to the distance along which the impression must transfer its force. So, for instance, an arson investigator follows a chain of clues, one event leading to another as its cause, and so on, back to a conclusion about the perpetrator. The longer the chain of events, and so of ideas, from present experience to the idea of its originating cause, the weaker the conviction that the real perpetrator has been identified.[23] Finally, a fourth source of unphilosophical probability is the use of general rules. Some general rules are formed by the mind's seeing as connected what are actually accidental circumstances, and so these result in prejudices and rationally unfounded generalizations, such as "An *Irishman* cannot have wit, and a *Frenchman* cannot have solidity..." (T 1.3.13.7). We find however, that such rules actually run in opposition to other rules, and we learn to discriminate between effective causes and circumstantial ones by noting that an effect is often produced in absence of a circumstance we thought was a cause. So, while general rules at first may prompt the imagination to run to an effect on the occasion of a perception whose idea has been accidentally associated with another idea, the "second effect" of the mind's general rules is to "take a review of this act of the mind, and compare it with the more general and authentic operations of the understanding." Then "we find it to be of an irregular nature, and destructive of all the most establish'd principles of reasoning; which is the cause of our rejecting it" (T 1.3.13.12).[24] Hume adds that this second-order effect of general rules does not prevail in all persons; it depends on characters and dispositions. So, prejudices do exercise an influence on many persons' convictions.

My point in writing about probabilities here is to highlight the fact that Hume recognizes the natural forces that impact the force and vivacity with which beliefs are experienced, and this force and this vivacity, I contend, are correlated with the strength or conviction with which the belief is held.[25] Strength of belief is equal in influence to strength of passion when it comes to the determination of action. Thus, it is actually over-simplistic to say that we always act on the strongest passion; we act on the strongest passion among those in competition when the beliefs about instrumental means to their ends are equally strong. But when beliefs about the means to the ends set by the passions one possesses at a given time are not equal in vivacity—due to some of the circumstances here detailed—the

---

[23] Hume spends some time explaining how this source of probability does not undermine all belief in historical statements, as it might at first glance seem to. He argues that since we rely on texts for history, and these texts are reproduced identically, or are closely resembling, the credibility of statements of history is not undermined by long chains of causes and effects, or chains of human testimony. If we have knowledge of one volume now, we have knowledge of all resembling volumes from the past, and the mind moves along them easily to present belief (T 1.3.13.16).

[24] Hume's authentic operations of the understanding—that is, those that are normative for belief—are spelled out in his section, "Rules by which to judge of causes and effects" (T 1.3.15).

[25] Hume gives a nice summary of the features that impact probability and belief when he writes:

> 'Tis by habit we make the transition from cause to effect; and 'tis from some present impression we borrow that vivacity, which we diffuse over the correlative idea. But when we have not observ'd a sufficient number of instances, to produce a strong habit; or when these instances are contrary to each other; or when the resemblance is not exact; or the present impression is faint and obscure; or the experience in some measure obliterated from the memory; or the connexion dependent on a long chain of objects; or the inference deriv'd from general rules, and yet not conformable to them: In all these cases the evidence diminishes by the diminution of the force and intenseness of the idea. This therefore is the nature of the judgment and probability. (T 1.3.13.19)

resulting action is a function of which instrumental belief one holds with the greatest confidence, given that the strength of competing passions is equal. When both the motivational strength of competing passions and the strength of conviction toward their respective instrumental beliefs are unequal, the resulting action is a product of the relative strength of belief-passion couples.

I have here described strength or degree of conviction of a belief in terms of the usual, "rational" route of inductive reasoning. Hume recognizes, however, that there are also beliefs acquired largely as an effect of surprise, amazement, or astonishment, which get their vivacity from associated passions:

> Admiration and surprize have the same effect as the other passions; and accordingly we may observe, that among the vulgar, quacks and projectors meet with a more easy faith upon account of their magnificent pretensions, than if they kept themselves within the bounds of moderation. The first astonishment, which naturally attends their miraculous relations, spreads itself over the whole soul, and so vivifies and enlivens the idea, that it resembles the inferences we draw from experience. (T 1.3.10.4)

Hume's account of ordinary belief formation does not explain beliefs people sometimes form due to influences exercised on them when they have not had experiences of the purported causes. So, for instance, one may come to believe in a miracle due, not to a constant conjunction of experiences, which would make such beliefs routine, but instead to what Hume identifies as the force of passions like wonder and amazement, which influence the ideas associated with them. Those ideas approach the force and vivacity of beliefs, likely surpassing the liveliness of causally-formed beliefs. They are likely to influence action, depending on other beliefs and passions a person experiences at the same time, since they are felt with an intensity different from regular, causally-formed beliefs, which come over us less forcefully.

This discussion of strength of desire and strength of beliefs raises interesting questions about weakness of will, which is typically defined as an actor's doing what she thinks she ought not to do. The Humean analysis of this phenomenon is easily done in terms of strength of desire, with the stronger desire overtaking the desire otherwise preferred. A discussion of weakness of will for Hume has to be set in the context of his moral theory, since his theory does not evaluate actions for rationality but for virtue, with prudence or regard for long-term self-interest as a part of virtue. But I will note that since strength of belief is also a factor in motivation, one might act on an improper passion which is of equal strength to a proper (virtuous) passion when the confidence in the belief related to the improper passion is greater than the conviction about the means to the proper passion. So a virtuous desire's failing to determine action against another, competing desire, need not be a case of weakness of will.

7
Conclusion
The Passions in Hume's Project

In the beginning of CHAPTER 1, I referred to prominent Hume scholar Norman Kemp Smith's puzzlement at the placement of Hume's presentation of the theory of the passions following the discussion of the understanding in Book 1 of the *Treatise*. Kemp Smith alleges that the discussion of the passions opens up a new set of issues, instead of illustrating the applications of the principles of psychology that Hume develops in Book 1 (Kemp Smith 1941: 160). But other commentators have had a different take on the presentation of the passions between a discussion of knowledge and a discussion of morality. Still others point to Hume's later works, the second *Enquiry* or the *Dissertation on the Passions*, as telling sources for the purpose Hume meant his narrative on the passions to fulfill. In this concluding chapter, I consider interpretations of the significance of Hume's theory of the passions, some of which refer back to topics I have treated.[1] My point in this brief survey is to support the conjecture that the theory of the passions is, for Hume, more significant for its role in motivating, explaining, and regulating action than for its role in any other aspect of Hume's study of human nature. Of course, not all of the passions are themselves causes of action, but even those that are not motives are frequently associated with those that are.

7.1 The Understanding, the Passions, and Morals as a System

Some scholars take seriously the idea that *Treatise* Books 1 and 2 together are meant to constitute a continuous project. They have argued that the theory of the passions is designed to show how the experimental method is to be applied in an elegantly unified study of our intellectual and emotional lives. So, we find John Passmore and Nicholas Capaldi interpreting Book 2 of the *Treatise* as a demonstration of the principles of association of impressions and ideas, as earlier articulated in Book 1 (Passmore 1968: 106). Capaldi writes, "An understanding of the exact nature of

---

[1] Some of this material first appeared in Radcliffe (2015b).

Newton's influence on Hume can serve as the key to understanding Hume's philosophy as a whole, and it can explain why Hume structures the *Treatise* as he does" (Capaldi 1975: 49). He believes that Book 2 "is in many respects the most important for exemplifying the major themes of Hume's philosophy" and that the associative mechanism of the passions serves to confirm Hume's "mechanics of causal belief" (ibid.: 130). Passmore, in his chapter entitled "The Associationist," emphasizes the parallel between the mental principles at play in Hume's epistemology and those in the theory of the passions. He cites as the central psychological problem of Book 2 "to construct the more complicated 'indirect passions' out of the direct passions, with the aid of the associative principles." Later, he writes that this analysis "has the same importance in Hume's theory of the passions as causality has in his theory of the understanding" (Passmore 1968: 124–5). Capaldi believes that it also supports Hume's anti-rationalist morality, and contributes to the discussion of personal identity, or the self.[2]

Many commentators have emphasized that Hume's theory of the passions presents a remedy to the skepticism about the self that emerges from Book 1, where he declares that the idea of the self is a fiction. Other readers see the main thrust of the theory of the passions as looking forward to Hume's moral sentimentalism, and the discussion presented here in CHAPTER 5 shows how the passions are essentially connected to the derivation of morality. Some commentators have accentuated the role of the passions in human sociability, psychological health, and self-regulation, aspects of which I discussed in CHAPTER 6. These three foci have in common the fact that they rely on the practical force of the passions. Hume's theory of the passions addresses the skepticism about the self, makes possible an anti-rationalist moral theory, and explains human sociability and psychological health only because the passions function as motives to action—or so I shall argue here, by looking more closely at these key functions of the passions.

7.1.1 A Solution to the Problem of the Self

Many commentators disagree with Kemp Smith's claim that the discussion of the indirect passions is out of proportion to their importance. For they find in that discussion a resolution to the skepticism about the self presented in Book 1. There, Hume shows that we cannot trace the idea of a self to any simple impression in experience; instead we find a changing string of perceptions:

The mind is a kind of theatre, where several perceptions successively make their appearance; pass, re-pass, glide away, and mingle in an infinite variety of postures and situations. There is properly no *simplicity* in it at one time, nor *identity* in different.   (T 1.4.6.4)

---

[2] Capaldi (1975: 130). Passmore sees Hume's invocation of the self in his analysis of pride and humility as a large problem (see 1968: 126).

He suggests that this idea is instead derived for each of us from mentally grouping or "bundling" perceptions that we associate by causality and resemblance (T 1.4.6). However, in Hume's Book 2 discussion of the indirect passions, it appears that his skepticism about the existence of the self has dropped out. When he explains the nature of sympathy there, he invokes the idea of the self, writing, "'Tis evident that the idea, or rather, impression of ourselves is always intimately present with us" (T 2.1.11.4). To explain this change, readers point to the fact that Hume distinguishes personal identity "*as* it regards our thought or imagination" from personal identity "*as* it regards our passions" (T 1.4.6.5). Some commentators have argued that Hume presents two conceptions of the self, while others have thought that he extends and completes the non-substantial idea of the self from Book 1 of the *Treatise* through his treatment of the indirect passions in Book 2.

In a 1989 article, Jane McIntyre argues that Hume's intellectual conception of the self is incomplete without the passions. Her interpretation finds a coherent idea of the self that is extended through his treatment of our concern with our own motives and actions, explained primarily by sympathy. McIntyre observes that Hume's approach in his Book 1 discussion of personal identity, which makes no reference to action ascription and responsibility, is in contrast to his predecessors Locke, Butler, and Hutcheson, who maintained that an adequate account of personal identity "must explain the effect of the past on our present feelings, and thereby provide a foundation for considering the future in choosing our present actions" (McIntyre 1989: 549). While Butler and Hutcheson thought that self-concern presupposes the existence of a substantial self, Hume held fast to his conclusion in Book 1 that there is no unified self, but only a succession of associated perceptions. So, Hume needed to explain why past thoughts, perceptions, and actions affect my present feelings; and why at times, as McIntyre puts it, I "act out of concern for a future collection of perceptions that will bear to me, now, the relation I bear to my past" (ibid.: 550). The explanation lies in his account of the passions, especially in his discussion of indirect passions and sympathy.

Although on Hume's account of moral judgment we approve or disapprove of others' character traits via our tempered sympathy with the effects of those traits, we are at times also made to scrutinize our own actions and characters (as I've noted previously). Character, composed of a person's passions or motivations, plays a part in the experiences of pride and humility, which are directed toward the self, and in love and hatred, which are directed toward others. Even though I am not a substantial self, the present self is concerned with the past actions and perceptions that are related to it by contiguity and causation, since past actions can provoke the pleasurable feeling of pride or the uncomfortable feeling of humility. Moreover, by sympathy, I share in others' attitudes toward me, which can reinforce my feelings about myself, and support my self-esteem. "Concern with reputation is, therefore, the more public aspect of concern with one's past" (ibid.: 550–2). On McIntyre's interpretation, my engagement with the future is explained by my imagining ideas of future actions that follow from my motives and intentions, rather than from a substance in which my mental states inhere. Sympathy is crucial to explain how the ideas of future actions and their consequences affect my present motivations. Hume writes:

> 'Tis evident, that, in considering the future possible or probable condition of any person, we may enter into it with so vivid a conception as to make it our own concern; and by that means be sensible of pains and pleasures, which neither belong to ourselves, nor at the present instant have any real existence. (T 2.2.9.13)

Thus, McIntyre thinks, the identification of one's interest with the interest of a future person is the result of an extended operation of sympathy. Her interpretation shows how Hume's theory of the passions is critical to his full account of the self as an associated string of perceptions through time.[3]

On another view, Hume's theory of the passions in a sense solves the skeptical problem of the self, not by completing the account, but by presenting an alternative conception, often called "the moral self." Amélie Rorty, for example, seems to identify the self in Book 1 as a metaphysical self. She sees the self of Book 2 as an agent capable of adopting and internalizing the concerns of others, with pride as the key (in a rich account similar to McIntyre's), and by further transformation in Book 3, as a moral self with a sense of justice.[4] Thus, the idea of the self, the idea with which we function, is produced by the passions. In writing of the significance of Hume's theory of the passions, Rorty says:

> [Hume] brought the passions into their own, no longer marks of invasive forces, but our own motivating attitudes. From being merely reactive attitudes, they became, in his hands, the internal sources of action. Perhaps not fully recognising the import of his constructive originality, Hume also marked the social and political contributions to the construction of the complex idea of the self as affected by sympathy, by social patterns of admiration or contempt, and by the political structures that define property. He so enlarged the conception of the passions that he could analyse justice as a cognitively formed motivating sentiment, derived from cooperative activity. And it was Hume, too, who provided the raw materials for a critical evaluation of impoverished or inappropriate ideas of the self. (Rorty 1990: 256)

More recently, others have argued that the self that emerges as the object of pride in Hume's theories of the passions and of morality is a newly-created self.[5] Eugenio

---

[3] McIntyre (1989: 554–6). McIntyre has more recently noted that Hume changes his view in his later works, *EPM* and the *Dissertation*. He no longer relies on sympathy to explain concern for others, which there becomes an original principle: the sentiment of humanity. Thus, he need not invoke the idea of the self in that account (McIntyre 2012: 178–82).

[4] Rorty (1990). Rorty's view is somewhat ambiguous. She may actually agree with McIntyre that Hume is extending the metaphysical idea of the self with his theories of the passions and morality, but she seems to write some of the time as though there are two types of ideas.

[5] See Chazan (1998: 13–30); and Purviance (1997). Terence Penelhum objects, however, that the self cannot be the object of pride or humility if we do not first have a legitimate idea of it. Thus, the indirect passions would simply be directed to an imagined fiction, given Hume's account in Book 1 (Penelhum 1976: 62–4; see also Penelhum 1992b). But Eugenio Lecaldano agrees with Chazan and Purviance on this

Lecaldano also contends that this idea of the self is developed through social interactions; but it is not just a product of pride experienced through sympathetic awareness of others' attitudes—a defect he finds in Rorty's account. Rather, the self is a product of a more resolute consciousness of what one finds morally admirable or disdainful in one's own character.[6]

So, some commentators find one idea of the self, begun in Book 1 and completed in Book 2. Others find an idea of an "intellectual" self in Book 1, and another idea, of a "moral" self, in Book 2. Regardless of which view one favors, a solution to the skepticism of Hume's account of the self requires invoking the practical or motivational features of the passions. Only because (some of) the passions are motives to our actions do we regard them as indicative of character and thus definitive of the self that Hume describes in the discussion of the passions. The pride or humility I experience at my own character, the interest I take in my conception of future passions and their results, and the concern I have for my reputation are dependent upon my passions acting as the sources of the actions attributed to me.

7.1.2 The Entrée to Morality

On a traditional interpretation first offered by Kemp Smith and subsequently adopted by Páll Árdal and Philip Mercer, the content of Hume's theory of the passions serves as an essential part of his moral theory. Also, for Kemp Smith, the account of the passions and morality together inform Hume's epistemology. Kemp

---

point, and in reply to Penelhum, cites Hume, whom he thinks explains how another idea of the self originates in a natural manner: "I find, that the peculiar object of pride and humility is determin'd by an original and natural instinct, and that "'tis absolutely impossible, from the primary constitution of the mind, that these passions shou'd ever look beyond self, or that individual person, of whose actions and sentiments each of us is intimately conscious" (T 2.1.5.3). So, Lecaldano argues that to think that the "reality" of the self must be generated through some intellectual operation occurring prior to the experience of pride is to subscribe to a framework other than Hume's. For Hume, one of the inexplicable principles of the mind is its "recognizing that the reality of the self is, precisely, a matter of passions and sentiments" (Lecaldano 2003: 182).

[6] Lecaldano (2003: 177–8, 189–90). Donald Ainslie actually proposes a more radical view than Rorty's about the composition of the idea of the self from others' attitudes. He suggests that Hume's theory of the indirect passions is designed to solve a slightly different skeptical problem than that of finding a simple substance or self within which our perceptions inhere. Rather, the problem is one of finding qualities that are essential or intrinsic to the persons we are. Just as Hume poses a skeptical problem about necessary connection in causation and presents a sort of solution with the mechanism of the association of ideas conditioned by habit, so, too, he poses an analogous problem about persons, with a parallel solution. In this case, the solution is that "by feeling an indirect passion towards someone that we think of her as more than accidentally related to some quality, such as her country, her riches, her family, or even her character traits" (Ainslie 1999: 470–1, 477–83). In a later piece, Ainslie argues that Hume offers two accounts of the self (even though just one idea): the self "as the locus of experience" and the self "as an embodied person with a distinctive place in the social sphere." (Ainslie 2005: 144). Inspired by Annette Baier, he claims that the perceptions we experience, which enter into the idea of the self, depend on who we are as social beings: the philosopher, for instance, has frequent perceptions of books, lectures, computer screens, and ideas of philosophical inquiry, etc. because of her commitments (Ainslie 2005: 158–9). Åsa Carlson has recently argued that the "two-idea" interpretations of Hume's view of the self are mistaken (Carlson 2009: esp. 174–5).

Smith has long been known as the interpreter of Hume who first argued for a naturalistic, rather than skeptical, interpretation of his philosophy: that Hume offers a theory by which the natural, regular principles of mental operation engender norms for good or bad reasoning and judging. The theme of Kemp Smith's study of Hume's *Treatise* is that his moral theory drives his epistemology:

> it was through the gateway of morals that Hume entered into his philosophy, and...as a consequence of this, Books II and III of the *Treatise* are in date of first composition prior to the working out of the doctrines dealt with in Book I. (Kemp Smith 1941: vi)

So he argues that Hume's sentimentalism about the source of morality is carried into his epistemology and his analysis of belief. On Kemp Smith's view, it is important to realize the subordination of belief and reason to passion, insofar as belief is instinctive or passionate, and so non-rational. Nature sanctions our belief in causal connections because such beliefs are irresistible and a matter of normal human sentiment.[7]

> Only when we have recognized the important functions which Hume ascribes to feeling and instinct, and the highly complex emotions and propensities which he is willing to regard as ultimate and unanalysable, are we in a position to do justice to his new, and very original, conception of the nature and conditions of experience. (ibid.: 154)

Kemp Smith also argues for an intimacy between the passions and morality in that moral sentiments, the feelings of approval or disapproval that we experience toward others in light of their actions, or toward ourselves, in light of our own actions, are direct passions.

Kemp Smith's approach is reflected in Árdal's thesis that "Hume's moral theory is an aspect of the more general account of man's emotional nature" (Árdal 1966: 2). Árdal, however, is interested in the point of Hume's detailed analysis of the indirect passions in the *Treatise*, and claims to find its objective in the moral theory. He writes of the *Treatise*, "If the *Abstract* was written by Hume, as is now commonly thought, then Hume himself thought that the foundation for Book III was laid in Book II" (Árdal 1977: 412). He quotes Hume:

> It may be safely affirmed, that almost all the sciences are comprehended in the science of human nature, and are dependent on it. *The sole end of* logic *is to explain the principles and operations of our reasoning faculty, and the nature of our ideas;* morals and criticism *regard our tastes and sentiments; and* politics *consider men as united in society and dependent on each other.* This treatise therefore of human nature seems intended for a system of the sciences. The author has finished what regards logic, and has laid the foundation of the other parts in his account of the passions. (T Abstract, 3)

Árdal's suggestion is that Hume's lengthy analysis of pride, humility, love, and hatred is meant to set the stage for their role in his conception of morality, in which the

---

[7] For a critical discussion of Kemp Smith's view, see Loeb (2009).

moral sentiments are sometimes identified with those passions (contrary to Kemp Smith). For Árdal, this approach by Hume effectively explains moral judgment without reference to a mysterious moral sense, as Francis Hutcheson had proposed. To approve of another morally is to experience calm love toward that person; to disapprove of another is to experience calm hatred, while moral self-approval and self-disapproval are, respectively, calm pride and humility.[8] Hume provides support for this view when he writes:

> The pain or pleasure, which arises from the general survey or view of any... quality of the *mind*, constitutes its vice or virtue, and gives rise to our approbation or blame, which is nothing but a fainter and more imperceptible love or hatred.   (T 3.3.5.1)[9]

Nonetheless, I have offered reasons for rejecting the identification of the moral sentiments with indirect passions; I think the moral sentiments are instinctual passions, which, for all practical purposes, function like direct passions.[10]

I agree with the general point in Kemp Smith and Árdal that Hume's narrative of the passions and his theory of morality constitute an integrated, mutual-supporting system. On my reading, this is made possible in part by the fact that the moral sentiments, which are the products of the general inclination to good and aversion to evil, can generate motives when natural motives to morality are lacking. Furthermore, as I've argued, the feelings of moral approval and disapproval are instrumental to the production of pride and humility and of love and hatred insofar as moral approval and disapproval enter into the double relation of impressions that produce these indirect passions. Moreover, the principle of sympathy, introduced within the discussion of pride and the effect of others' views of us on our self-image, and on our own passions, explains why the moral distinctions we make reflect the effects of the agents' actions on others.

7.1.3 *Key to Sociability and Psychological Well-Being*

Some recent scholarship has highlighted the unity of Hume's thought and the application of his experimental method, outlined in his epistemology, to his theory of the passions in a slightly different way. An overarching theme of Annette Baier's

---

[8] Árdal (1966: 11, 109–23); Árdal (1977: 407–12). Philip Mercer (1972: 46–58) agrees.

[9] Christine Korsgaard (1991), while acknowledging that there are different ways to read Hume's text on this matter, seems to agree in the end that love and hatred are the same as the moral sentiments.

[10] Rachel Cohon does not necessarily identify the moral sentiments with love and hatred or pride and humility, but she argues that the moral sentiments have the very features that make the four principal indirect passions indirect. First, they take as their intentional object something distinct from their cause. For instance, the relief felt by the poor of Calcutta, with whom I sympathize, makes me approve of Mother Teresa's character and directs my attention toward her. Second, indirect passions are not desire-like; they do not turn the attention of the person who has them toward her own prospective pleasure or pain. The moral sentiments have this feature as well (Cohon 2008a: 174–9). (I want to add that, while most of the indirect passions are not like desires, as I've noted, Hume does define malice and pity, which are indirect, in terms of desire. But since they are desires whose objects are others' pleasurable or painful situations, it is not clear to what degree this consideration affects Cohon's argument.)

book, *A Progress of Sentiments*, is how Hume's study of passions in the second book of the *Treatise* contains within it an answer to his momentous skeptical problem. Of course, I've noted that many other scholars have said the same, but Baier's narrative places special emphasis on the social nature of the passions. The "I" has to step outside the mindset of the Cartesian solitary reasoner, and by attending to my passions and sympathies, I "see myself clearly reflected in [another's] eyes, let her and her views of me as expressed in words, gestures, behavior, help me shape my own self-conception" (Baier 1991: 136). Baier underscores the physical aspect of personal identity—that our minds are expressed through our eyes, hands, voices, and so on. We can be "mirrors to one another" and show sympathy for others only when their passions are exhibited in their behaviors. The discussion of persons in Book 1, Baier notes, is abstracted from the flesh-and-blood nature of persons. But, she argues that Hume, with Book 2, banishes the worries of Book 1 by highlighting the fact that "human persons are essentially incarnate... coming into the world complete with blood ties, and acquiring other social ties as they mature, grow and with others' help acquire self-consciousness" (ibid.: 140). When Hume characterizes the self as in a physical and social world, Baier thinks he can now give realistic answers to the fundamental questions he asked in Book 1, such as the questions, "What am I?" or "How do I believe?" So, Book 2 presents an "enlarged self" (a social self) that includes the body and its perceptions, riches or poverty, successes and failures, memories, mental associations, reputation and self-images, and so on.

Jacqueline Taylor's interpretation of Hume's *Treatise* project of developing a science of human nature with the experimental method of inquiry applied to both the understanding and the passions likewise finds sympathy and sociability at the core of Hume's approach. Taylor argues that at least some of the passions (pride, for instance) are to a great degree socially constructed. Taylor emphasizes an overlooked feature of sympathy in Hume—that not only passions, but also beliefs, are communicated sympathetically. This often happens non-reflectively, as when children "implicitly embrace every opinion propos'd to them" (T 2.1.11.2), but even when we have our own developed beliefs, we can be sympathetically susceptible to the eloquence of others (Taylor 2015b: 194). Since pride centrally involves sympathy with both others' feelings and their beliefs, Taylor emphasizes that the causes of pride, which involve our judgments about the value of the things related to the self, "are shaped by everyday practice and social institutions, and so reflect a particular historical and cultural context" (ibid.: 198). We develop general rules about what qualities are valuable, and these "often reflect the historical and cultural variations in how people recognize, describe, and classify the qualities that they take to be reasons for feeling pride or humility" (ibid.: 199).

Taylor also argues that Hume's theory of the passions in the *Treatise* embodies a social theory of class distinctions, one that can be extracted from his analysis of pride, since sympathy and sympathetic communication of beliefs reinforce the values and beliefs in place in an institution or society (Taylor 2008, 2015a). While she thinks that

Hume has no mechanism for critiquing existing power structures in the *Treatise*'s sympathy-based account of morality, she argues that the revised account of moral judgment in his second *Enquiry* provides the means for such evaluation. There, she argues, he introduces the sentiment of humanity, which some scholarly readers have thought is a version of the moral sentiment of approval in the *Treatise*.[11] However, Taylor's view is that it is a sentiment or moral principle that all have access to, which judges of the overall beneficial or pernicious qualities of actions, people, or institutions. She claims that it allows for a universal morality in the way that the *Treatise* account of moral sentiment, being based on sympathy with particular individual interests, does not.

The "social" interpretation of Hume's approach to the passions, which has sympathy at its core, also relies centrally on the passions' functions as motives. On Taylor's account of Hume's progress in his moral theory from the *Treatise* to the second *Enquiry*, the sentiment of humanity is a sympathy-based response to the impact of someone's character upon those around her. But as Baier says, we can be sympathetic to others only when their feelings are evident in their actions. To be contagious, those socially-oriented passions supported by our public situation with others must be successful as causes of action, since we must infer their presence from what others do.

7.2 The Passions in Relation to Tragedy and Religion

So far, I have concentrated on the purpose of Hume's theory of the passions relative to his epistemology and theory of morality in the *Treatise* and the second *Enquiry*. John Immerwahr has argued that the significance of the *Dissertation on the Passions* has been obscured by comparisons between it and the *Enquiries* (Immerwahr 1994: 226). When it comes to the richness of the exposition, the *Dissertation*, which is an essay-length, shortened version of *Treatise* Book 2, surely wanes in comparison to the other two works.[12] However, in wondering about Hume's intentions for his theory, it is helpful to turn to the *Dissertation*. After all, it was Hume's second attempt to present a psychology of the passions, and he had had many years to reassess the substance of the first presentation and consider the passions' place in his project, as he had done with his presentation of the understanding and morality. The *Dissertation* repeats, often verbatim, passages from the *Treatise*; there is very little reworking, although much cutting. Tom Beauchamp points out that when Hume later expressed dissatisfaction with the *Treatise* (which was a failure as a popular work) and was vexed about some of its errors, he never mentions any disappointment over his treatment of the passions in Book 2. Nor did critics target that part of the *Treatise*.

---

[11] Kate Abramson (2001), for instance, thinks that the sentiment of humanity in the second *Enquiry* is extensive sympathy in the *Treatise*. See also Debes (2007) and Baier (2008b: esp. 309).

[12] The *Dissertation* is about one-sixth the length of *Treatise* Book 2.

Furthermore, Beauchamp notes that the *Dissertation on the Passions* appeared in eight editions whose publication Hume himself supervised (with a ninth after his death) (Beauchamp 2007: xv). So, there is ample evidence that he did not change his mind on matters related to the passions, and that he was happy with the way those ideas were presented in the *Dissertation*.

First, I want to consider the content of the *Dissertation*, which falls into six sections.[13] Section 1 opens with a brief description of how we denominate objects as good or evil, by either an agreeable sensation or a painful one. Then Hume starts with a discussion of the direct passions, with passages taken from *Treatise* 2.3.9 ("Of the direct passions"), with some slight modification, some deletions, and a bit of rearrangement of the order of presentation. So, the first passions that come under consideration are joy and sorrow, fear and hope, desire and aversion. Just as in the *Treatise*, the passions of hope and fear receive the longest treatment of the direct passions, since they are influenced by probabilities and involve more complicated analyses. The section concludes with the discussion of the principles by which contrary passions affect one another (which occurs earlier in the order of discussion in T 2.3.9). Section 2 of the *Dissertation* introduces the indirect passions, with an explanation of the association of ideas and of impressions, and an analysis of the sources of pride and humility. It draws largely upon *Treatise* 2.1 ("Of pride and humility"). Love and hatred are explained in Section 3, with material from *Treatise* 2.2 ("Of love and hatred"), along with several new paragraphs. Section 4 presents further confirmation of the system of the double relation of impressions and ideas, and discusses envy and malice, from *Treatise* 2.2.8 ("Of envy and malice"). Section 5 contains a brief summary of the argument that motivation does not come from reason, but does come from passions, plus the description of strength of mind, with ideas drawn from *Treatise* 2.3.3. ("Of the influencing motives of the will"). The final section examines the causes of violent passions and the means by which violence is augmented, with the discussion taken from analogous sections of the *Treatise* (2.3.4–7).

So, in the *Dissertation*, unlike the *Treatise*, the direct passions are discussed first, before the indirect passions; the discussion of motivation is separated from the analysis of the direct passions; and many topics related to the passions are left out. Perhaps Hume merely thought that the system of the passions was clearer to the reader with the simpler, direct passions first in the order of description. However, if the order of presentation in the *Dissertation* represents what Hume regarded as most important, then he regarded the direct passions as taking precedence over the indirect. I've argued that not all direct passions are motives, but most of them are, and among them are desire and aversion, which are unquestionably motivators. So, perhaps Hume considered the direct passions important for their close

---

[13] I am indebted to Beauchamp's Introduction to the Clarendon Edition in this comparison of the *Dissertation* to the *Treatise*.

connection with action. I have no definitive evidence for this reading, but Immerwahr presents some factors that lend it credence, and which I discuss below. The separation of the discussion of the source of motivation from the discussion of the direct passions makes sense, no matter what one thinks of the change of order in the presentation of the passions, since both direct and indirect passions have among them motives to action.

Next, I want to consider the publication of the *Dissertation*. In 1755, Hume was set to publish four essays ("dissertations") in a collection, which included an essay on the metaphysical principles of geometry. Later convinced of defects in the arguments, he decided to withdraw that particular essay, and asked to publish just the remaining three essays together: on the passions, on the natural history of religion, and on tragedy. The publisher rejected this idea, since the volume would be too short. The three essays were eventually published as *Four Dissertations*, with an added essay on the standard of taste.[14] Immerwahr hypothesizes that Hume's intention to publish the essay on the passions (which in a later edition became "*A Dissertation on the Passions*"), alongside essays on religion and tragedy, suggests that the piece on the passions is meant to support the content of the other two essays. Immerwahr alleges that two themes emphasized in the *Dissertation* are not prominent in Book 2 of the *Treatise*, namely, the doctrine of the direct passions and Hume's treatment of conflicting passions. (As I've noted, those discussions are moved to the front in the *Dissertation*.) Immerwahr argues also that Hume starts with a discussion of the direct passions, and specifically, of hope and fear, as background to his explanation of the origins of polytheism and monotheism in *The Natural History of Religion* (Immerwahr 1994: 230–2). Hume writes: "[I]n order to carry men's attention beyond the present course of things, or lead them into any inference concerning invisible intelligent power, they must be actuated by some passion, which prompts their thought and reflection..." (NHR 2.5). He asks what passion would motivate such an inquiry and dismisses sophisticated ones such as "speculative curiosity" and "pure love of truth." Instead, he alleges that the passions that would be effective in this case are more pedestrian: "the anxious concern for happiness, the dread of future misery, the terror of death, the thirst of revenge, the appetite for food and other necessaries." People agitated especially by fear inquire "with eyes...disordered and astonished" and "see the first obscure traces of divinity" (NHR 2.5). Here the inquiry is prompted by anxiety-generating passions, and the outcome of the investigation is influenced by the same.

In his essay "On Tragedy," Hume confronts the problem of how spectators to a tragic play can feel distressing emotions like fear, anxiety, and sorrow, and yet

---

[14] The situation was actually more complicated than this. Hume added two controversial essays, "On Suicide," and "On the Immorality of the Soul," to make a volume of five dissertations. But those essays proved to be too inflammatory when pre-release copies were circulated, and critics responded. The publisher removed them from the volume, and Hume substituted the essay on taste.

experience aesthetic enjoyment. His answer lies in the phenomenon of "conversion" that I discussed in CHAPTER 6, and treatment of which is moved toward the beginning of the *Dissertation*. The audience undergoes simultaneous and contrary passions, with the inferior adding force to the dominant one. Hume writes:

> The impulse or vehemence, arising from sorrow, compassion, indignation, receives a new direction from the sentiments of beauty. The latter, being the predominant emotion, seize the whole mind, and convert the former into themselves, at least tincture them so strongly as totally to alter their nature. (Essays, "Of Tragedy," 9)

Immerwahr further argues that the *Dissertation* was a technical piece meant to be bookended by two popular pieces, purposely kept short with no introduction or conclusion, which was to be supplied by the other essays (1994: 235–40).

Immerwahr's hypotheses about the *Dissertation* are intriguing. If correct, they add some validation to my proposal that the signature function of the passions is their practical force, since highlighting the direct passions of hope and fear emphasizes two prominent motivating sentiments. Granted, the connection of motivation to the appreciation of tragedy is nebulous, but the principle of conversion, which such aesthetic sentiments draw upon, is instrumental to motivation in ways I have earlier discussed. The principle both explains how we can find beauty in painful circumstances and how force of passions can be augmented by contrary feelings.

7.3 The Passions as an Antidote to Religious Moralizing

Stephen Buckle proposes that past readers have not taken much interest in Hume's theory of the passions in part because they have not understood the genuine intent of it. Its chief point, he argues, is not simply to detail a psychological mechanism, but to undermine religious orthodoxy in morals. Buckle supports this interpretation by pointing out that Hume's psychology is implicitly physicalist, adopting explanations of actions parallel to those offered in Hobbes's mechanistic theory. With passions characterized as impulses to action that do not come under the purview of reason, Hume's view undermines the ordinary religious perspectives that suppose free will and the possibility of rational governance of the passions. Rule by passion was seen as synonymous with vice. However, "Hume's point is not to reject the ideal of the virtuous life, but to offer a new account of how such a life is possible" (Buckle 2012: 206). This understanding, Buckle says, requires a re-appraisal of the moral import of the passions. The passions are not necessarily threats to living a moral life. Rather, passions as "the felt inner motions by which human beings are moved to action, the necessary consequences of causal processes occurring in the human body, must be considered purely as inner mechanisms, entirely neutral" (ibid.: 206–7). One point of special interest, noted by other commentators as well, is that Hume's extensive treatment of pride in the *Treatise*, a Christian vice, shows it to be an innocent pleasure, free of moral stigma. Baier and Buckle both accentuate the point that

Hume's considering proper pride a virtue further supports the theme that his aim is largely an anti-religious one (Baier 1991: 215; Buckle 2012: 210).

If Buckle and Baier are correct about the anti-religious intent of Hume's theory of the passions, we have evidence again that he regards the connection of passions to action as a pivotal feature. Buckle clearly connects the motivating effects of the passions to Hume's rejection of the religious convention in morals:

> Hume's account of the passions aims to show them to be the determinants of human will and action. The human being is fully determined in practical action by the passion-inducing effects of pleasures and pains, with reason reduced to the servant of the passions... The implication is that religious moralists of a traditional stamp... [who] identify the moral life with the life of rational self-government, and who denounce the ungoverned passions as the source of vice, are hopelessly mistaken. All action is passion-driven, so 'ungoverned passion' is not the path to vice; reason and will are not independent judges standing outside of the causal chains that determine human behaviour. Hume's theory of passion as the cause of action is thus... a rejection of the orthodoxies of the religious moralists of his day... (Buckle 2012: 212)

7.4 The Signature Role of the Passions

It is plausible to think that Hume offered his psychology of the passions in the service of all of the goals I have considered here. It is designed to be a study continuous with his examination of the understanding, while also serving as the psychological foundation for his sentimentalist moral epistemology. It embodies a solution to the skepticism about the self that was apparent after the discussion of personal identity in *Treatise* Book 1, and some of its theses serve as central claims in Hume's ethics. The passions are essential to the social relationships fundamental to human wellbeing; their manifestation in behavior is indispensable to the operation of sympathy, which transfers passions between persons and reinforces our healthy feelings of pride. While providing an explanation of sociability, the passions also embody an alternative perspective on morality, replacing the accepted religious moralities of the era and times past with a naturalistic view of the source of action and virtue. We *are* our passions; furthermore, our characters, the objects of moral judgment, are exhibited by those passions that are successful in action. The passionate motivational dynamics that Hume discovers in human nature also serve as explanations of certain paradoxical emotions, such as our taking pleasure in well-portrayed tragedies.

For Hume, the signature role of the passions, then, is practical. While early modern rationalists also regarded the passions as motives, they saw the route to virtue as marked out by reason. On their views, as I've noted, reason often had to redirect the passions, or show them their proper objects, in order to move us to suitable ends. In Hume's theory, by contrast, the passions are not only prompts to action, but also the means of tempering one another, and of developing a virtuous character. For Hume, the practical influence of the passions is integral to our living well, and living morally.

Appendix
The Passions and Reason in Seventeenth- and Eighteenth-Century Philosophy

Here I survey some of the early modern works on the passions and action. I focus on the relation between reason and the passions, as represented by the intellectuals, philosophers, and clergy of the seventeenth and eighteenth centuries. Many offer explanations of just how reason is supposed to manage the passions and transform their effects, but there is no indication among the thinkers here examined that they regarded reason as a motive to action by itself.

A.1 Seventeenth-Century Theories of Passion, Reason, and Action

A.1.1 Early Writers and the Governance of the Passions

The theme that the passions are intimately connected to action and inhabit a part of the soul separate from reason is inherited from Ancient and Scholastic outlooks and is evident in discussions early in the seventeenth century. Thus, the chief purpose of the passions is to motivate, and their treatment implicates the mind-body connection. In 1621, French theologian, Nicolas Coeffeteau, in *A Table of Humane Passions*, defines a passion as "a motion of the sensitive appetite" caused by apprehending good or evil and followed by a bodily movement "contrary to the Lawes of Nature." According to Coeffeteau (1621: Chapter I, 2–3), the passions do not reside in the rational part of the soul because the purpose of that part of the soul has nothing to do with bringing change to the body. In his *Treatise of the Passions and Faculties of the Soule of Man* (first published in 1640), Edward Reynolds (vice chancellor of Oxford University and later Bishop of Norwich) portrays the passions as "natural, perfective" motions that humans receive from their creator for the advancement of their natures. His presumption is that humans have an instilled desire for the good, and the passions enhance human nature by inclining us to good objects or by producing an aversion to noxious ones (Reynolds 1640: Ch. V, 31–2). Reynolds portrays the "dignity" or value of the passions in their being the ministers of reason in the execution of duties, which are to the benefit of our nature (ibid.: Ch. VI, 43–4). The will is a blind faculty on its own, but the understanding serves as its counsellor, either to furnish it with an end upon which to "fasten," or to direct it to the means to that end, all in accord with the rules of "right reason" (ibid.: Ch. XL, 517–18). French philosopher Jean-François Senault (*The Use of the Passions*, 1641) suggests that the Stoics were wrong to advocate relinquishing our passions: the passions are useful, but only when governed, and there is not one passion that cannot become a virtue, since all involve natural inclinations to good and away from evil (ibid.: Fourth Treatise, 126–7). The governance of the passions depends on moderation, but it is dangerous for one passion to moderate another by its opposition (e.g., opposing hope to fear), "fortifying one enemy to destroy another." Moderation instead requires reason, which is "king over Passions...their government is one of her chief Employments" (ibid.: Third Treatise, 117–19). Yet, reason is not sufficient without the aid of God's grace (ibid.; Second Treatise, 66–73).

A.1.2 Descartes and Malebranche: Reason and the Passions' Physiology

Descartes transformed the study of the human passions by proclaiming in a letter prefacing his *Passions of the Soul* (1649) that he planned to examine them as a natural scientist, rather than as a moral philosopher. Descartes recognizes that because the passions are intimately connected to physiological states, their uniformities can be mapped and examined in the same way natural science tracks regularities in its subjects (see Alanen 2006: 179). Unlike philosophers before him, Descartes emphasizes that the soul or self has no parts, and has only one function, which he identifies with thinking. Having this single operation is crucial because Descartes supposes that attributing different functions to the soul destroys its unity (Descartes 1649: art. 17). All perceptions (which are thoughts) are passions in a broad sense. However, some are caused by objects outside us, through the senses, and refer to those objects; some make reference to the body, like hunger, thirst, natural appetites, and "physical" pain; while others, like joy and anger, have no immediate cause to which they refer other than the soul itself. It is only the last set that Descartes regards as "the passions of the soul," strictly speaking (see ibid.: art. 18–27). These passions are representations, and they are thoughts that agitate the soul more strongly than any other. They are confused or obscure representations, and the agent does not know their "proximate cause," and so refers them to the soul (ibid.: art. 28; see also editor's n. 29). Some critics convincingly suggest that this reference to the soul should be understood as a modification, not an attribution of a quality. For instance, when I am afraid of something, I am the subject of the sensation, the one who has the fear; but when I perceive the yellowness of a lemon, I attribute the yellowness to the object (see Brown and Normore 2003: 102). This raises a question about the relationship between a representing passion and its formal object (in the world). Does the passion represent my mind, or does it represent its formal object? If the passions are representing the mind, all passions would then be representations of the same thing. It seems rather that I attribute a quality to the object of the passions, and make a reference to my self. On this reading, for example, my fear of the dark represents the dark as dangerous-to-me; jealousy at my friend's fortune represents her fortune as undeserved-from-my-perspective (see ibid.: 104).

Among the ways that passions originate, for Descartes, are by our decisions to bring certain objects to mind, by the temperament of the body, and by "impressions haphazardly encountered in the brain," as when one feels sad and is unable to say why. With the exception of a very few passions (wonder, esteem and scorn, pride and humility, veneration and disdain), the passions are produced by an object's being characterized as good or bad for us.[1] As Susan James points out, however, the "evaluations of good and harm contained in passions directed

---

[1] Descartes (1649: art. 56–7). Walter Charleton, the seventeenth-century physician who claims Descartes's influence, studied the passions as an inquiry into human health and well-being. He echoes the theme from Senault that the passions can be useful when moderated and directed by reason, but when not, they suggest "false opinions and exorbitant desires." We can achieve internal serenity by directing our desires to things we know through the understanding clearly and distinctly to be good. He argues contrary to Descartes, however, that we possess a rational and a sensitive soul, which explains instances of internal conflict (Charleton 1674, Preface, no page numbers).

to objects outside the mind are... not in the world, waiting to be read." They are like secondary quality perceptions, which may be functions of real (in this case, evaluative) qualities in the world that allow us to make discriminations necessary to our well-being (James 1997: 103). Descartes thinks that the chief effect of the passions is

> that they incite and dispose their soul to will the things for which they prepare their body, so that the sensation of fear incites it to will to flee, that of boldness to do battle, and so on for the rest.[2]

Pertinent to the present topic is the relation between the passions, reason, and the will. While the passions are not under our control, they can be indirectly altered by the representations typically joined with certain passions we will to have:

> Thus, in order to excite boldness and displace fear in oneself, it is not sufficient to have the volition to do so—one must apply oneself to attend to reasons, objects, or precedents that convince [one] that the peril is not great, that there is always more security in defense than in flight, that one will have glory and joy from having conquered, whereas one can only expect regret and shame from having fled, and similar things.   (Descartes, 1649: art. 45)

So, for Descartes, since the passions can sometimes be produced and altered by thoughts, the passions can oppose reason, since such an opposition is really between passionate representations and non-passionate representations. For instance, I have the confused thought of the evil of a severe medical treatment, along with the volition to avoid or delay the treatment (constituting the passion of fear) pitted against the thought that I will be much better off and live a longer life by having the treatment done immediately.[3]

Descartes makes it clear that he thinks the notion of opposition between parts of the soul, as found in the Platonic system and assumed by some of his seventeenth-century predecessors, is mistaken. Because the soul is a unit, it has no higher, rational part to contest the lower, sensitive part, and neither is the will in opposition to appetite. So, the apparent opposition is really a physical struggle. Descartes argues that the movement set up in the pineal gland by the "spirits," which are minute bodies in the blood, can often oppose the movements of volition: the desires prompted by the spirits send the gland in a direction contrary to the direction one's volitions send it. This is what we experience "when what excites fear also makes the spirits enter the muscles that move the legs to flee, and our volition to be bold stops them" (ibid.: art. 47). The person with strength of soul is able to stop the movements that accompany the passions and does so with decisive judgments concerning the knowledge of good and evil, which it has resolved to follow. So, Descartes is convinced that we can control our passions through knowledge and the will. The weakest souls are those who allow passions, often contrary to each other, to drive them this way and that and thus end up in conflict with themselves. For strength of soul, it is important that the judgments about which one is firmly convinced be

---

[2] (1649: art. 40). Lilli Alanen writes, "[P]assions, as Descartes describes them, are experienced as inclinations of the will. They typically present themselves as volitions, as if they were grounded in our own evaluative judgments about their objects and hence as having, true rational grounds" (2003: 122).

[3] Descartes does not necessarily think that passions are false representations. They are representations, but not ones that the person has assented to or denied. "Instead of being formed by the mind's own reflective activity and being based on critical value judgments,... the representations inclining our will in passions are evoked mechanically, by the movements of the animal spirits in the brain..." (Alanen 2003: 123).

true, since regret or repentance will follow upon false judgments, when one discovers the errors (ibid.: art. 48-9).

Malebranche takes over the Cartesian view that willing, imagining, sensing, and so on, are modifications of thought (Malebranche 1674-75: 198). On his theory, God has implanted natural inclinations in our minds, which account for variety among minds, in the way that various motions of matter are needed to determine the fact that matter is not just one indistinguishable mass (ibid.: 265). Among particular inclinations are curiosity, self-love (manifested variously as love of well-being, love of grandeur, the desire for knowledge, the desire to appear learned, inclination for riches, love of pleasure and things that make us happy) and friendship for others (see ibid.: Book IV). While our several inclinations are directed toward God, our will can divert them (ibid.: 267). Yet these various proclivities are aspects of one impulse for or love of the good in general, which is God's end. The mind is directed toward the indeterminate and universal good by its creator; but the mind has freedom, the power to direct its natural inclinations by ordering the understanding to represent particular objects. "A person represents some honor to himself as a good that he might hope for; the will immediately wills this good; that is, the impression toward indeterminate and universal good that the mind is continuously receiving conveys it toward this honor." We do, however, have the freedom to suspend our love of this honor and pursue other goods, understanding that it is not the universal good.[4]

The passions, for Malebranche, are produced by causes other than the natural inclinations; they are livelier and stronger, and they have different objects. Yet, they really are no different in kind from these inclinations, no more than sensation and imagination, which are versions of intellection, are different from the mind itself. Malebranche writes,

The *passions* of the soul are impressions from the Author of nature that incline us toward loving our body and all that might be of use in its preservation—just as the natural inclinations are impressions from the Author of nature that primarily lead us toward loving Him as the sovereign good and our neighbor without regard for our body. (ibid.: 338)

Pure intelligences have inclinations, since they also possess the impulse for the good in general. However, in human beings, who are not "pure spirits," the inclinations are always mixed with "disturbances in the animal spirits"—that is, with passions. So love of truth or virtue is accompanied by a motion in the spirits, a physical change, just as contemplation of abstract truths, in which we employ imagination, is accompanied by a brain change. (This

---

[4] Malebranche writes:

A person represents some honor to himself as a good that he might hope for; the will immediately wills this good; that is, the impression toward indeterminate and universal good that the mind is continuously receiving conveys it toward this honor. But this honor is not the universal good, and is not considered as the universal good by a clear and distinct perception of the mind, for the mind never sees clearly what is not universal, the impression that we have toward the universal good is not brought entirely to rest by this particular good. The mind tends to proceed still further; it does not necessarily and indomitably love this honor, and it is free with regard to it. Now its freedom consists in the fact that not being fully convinced that this honor contains all the good it is capable of loving, it can suspend its judgment and love, and ... by its union with the universal being ... it can think about other things and consequently love other goods. (1674-75: 5)

makes the idea more confused for us, although livelier than it would be without the physical disturbances.[5])

Like many of the philosophers preceding him, Malebranche holds that the passions can distort our perception of good, and his theory offers a physiological explanation of how passions infect our reactions toward related things. Amy Schmitter observes that on Malebranche's account:

Passions invigorate the flow of animal spirits through the brain just as the traces representing the object are called up. Because of their vigor, the spirits are likely to overflow to nearby, related traces of objects (association is here understood in terms of the proximity of brain traces), which then come along for the recollective ride. And so the "dominant passions" we feel will color our thinking about a wide range of objects.   (Schmitter 2016)

Malebranche's account is a precursor to Hume's associationist psychology, which is central to Hume's naturalistic picture of the mind (see Jones 1982, and Kail 2007b, 2008). Malebranche, like Hume, argues that passions can profitably oppose, overtake, and regulate other passions (1674–75: 388). So, his theory is in part a foil for Hume insofar as it retains teleology, and in part an important and productive influence on Hume.

A.1.3 Spinoza: Affective Reason

Spinoza is often mentioned in connection with Hume, with readers noting the two philosophers' thoroughgoing naturalism, mutual rejection of teleological explanations of action, and of divine providence (see Popkin 1979, and Baier 1993). Spinoza's pantheistic metaphysics and rejection of the doctrine of human freedom places him in opposition to various theses in Descartes and Malebranche, and his motivational psychological thesis seems to have more in common with Hobbes's work than with theirs. Pertinent to this discussion is his characterization of passion and its relation to reason. Genevieve Lloyd remarks:

Spinoza ... does stress that we gain freedom from the passions precisely through understanding the necessities that govern them along with the rest of nature. But this is an understanding that transforms the passions into a different kind of emotion—active and rational. And in the

---

[5] See (1674–75: 345). Malebranche distinguishes seven features in a passion, together which appear to constitute his theory of motivation. (1) The mind has a perception, which may be distinct or confused, about the relation of an object to it. (2) When the object appears to be a good, the impulse of the will is determined toward it. Prior to this moment, the will either has an undetermined impulse toward good in general, or an impulse toward some other particular object. When the object appears to be an evil, the mind feels an impulse toward the opposite. (3) A sensation accompanies the intellectual perception of good or evil—either a sensation of love, aversion, desire, joy or sadness, depending on the perception. (4) When we experience a passion, we have a movement of the spirits and the blood toward parts of the body that ready it for motion or cause certain words or cries to be uttered. (5) When we experience a passion, we also have a "sensible emotion of the soul" toward or away from an object, since the soul is joined to the body. (6) We also experience sensations of love, aversion, desire, joy or sadness caused by the disturbance of animal spirits. These are livelier than the earlier named sensations. (7) We experience a sensation of joy or inner delight, which makes all passions pleasant. But it is this delight "that must be overcome by the delight of grace and the joy of faith and reason." Just as we have joy of mind in knowing that we are in the best possible state with respect to what we perceive, so we have false joy with passions, since they present the confused sensation that we are in the best possible state with regard to the objects of sense (see ibid.: 347–9).

process we are given a new form of reason, very different from that associated with the geometry of lines and planes—a form of reason which is itself affective. (Lloyd 1998: 34)

So, Spinoza understands a crucial theme that Hume emphasizes: for reason to control the passions, it must be affective. Of course, Hume thought it was not.

In Spinoza's metaphysics, a human being is a finite mode of the infinite universe, and the human person consists of a mind and a body, which are aspects of the same substance. Spinoza defines the mind as the idea of the body, and the ideas that constitute the mind have intentionality and are ideas of parts of the body. So, for instance, a feeling of physical pain is really the idea of the injured part. Thus, the relation between an idea and its object is an ontological relationship, rather than a representational one.[6] In his motivational psychology, Spinoza sees an individual (each thing) as naturally driven by the endeavor to persist in its being, and the modifications of this fluctuating drive are the affects or emotions, which can either increase or decrease its powers of self-preservation. This endeavor is "will" when it is an impulse of the mind, and "appetite" when it is an impulse of the body (Spinoza 1677: Part Three, Prop. 6-9, 171-2). The passions are the changes or affects induced by factors outside of us (ibid.: Def. 1-3, 164), and desire, which is essential to human beings, is consciousness of appetite. Desires, along with pleasures and pains (passive states wherein the mind passes to a greater or lesser affection, respectively) are the primary emotions: all other emotions arise from these. Love is, for instance, pleasure accompanied by the idea of an external cause; hatred is pain so accompanied by the idea of its cause.[7]

Spinoza undoes the relation between good and desire found in other rationalists and affirms the view found first in Hobbes (and later in Hume): "we do not endeavor, will, seek after, or desire something because we judge it to be good, but on the contrary we judge something to be good because we endeavor, will, seek after, or desire it" (ibid.: Part Three, Prop. 9, 173). Spinoza explains motivation by reference to the striving to keep our powers of self-preservation intact: "The mind endeavours, as far as it can, to imagine those things which increase or help the body's power of acting" (ibid.: Prop. 12, 174). Furthermore, we are affected with the same pleasure or pain by a thought or image of a thing past or future in the way we are affected by the thought of its presence. Thus, we experience emotions of hope and fear, confidence and despair, and so on. This makes us subject to inconstant pleasures and pains: "For hope is simply an inconstant pleasure which has arisen from the image of a thing that is future or past, about whose outcome we are in doubt. Fear, on the contrary, is an inconstant pain, which has also arisen from the image of a thing that is doubtful" (ibid.: Prop. 18, 179).

Spinoza's account of motivation is, of course, descriptive. But the last two parts of his *Ethics* move to a prescriptive account of how we ought best to respond to the situation in which we

---

[6] Steven Nadler writes of Spinoza's theory:

> Unlike Descartes's ideas, however, the relationship between the idea and its object is not an external relationship between two distinct things... the idea and the bodily state of which it is the idea are ultimately identical—they are one and the same thing being expressed through two different attributes. The pain is the expression in Thought of the same thing that is expressed in Extension as an injured body part. This ontological identity, and not what we ordinarily think of as a representational relationship, is what makes an idea the idea *of* a bodily state. (Nadler 2006: 157)

[7] See (1677: Part Three, Prop. 11, 173). Spinoza adds that pleasure is called "joy" or "titillation" "in so far as it is related simultaneously to the mind and the body," and pain "sadness" or "melancholy."

find ourselves: a situation in which we are determined by objects outside our control, of which we have no clear idea, and of whose presence we are doubtful. He finds this an unfortunate state of affairs, like waves on the ocean buffeted about by winds blowing in various directions (see ibid.: Prop. 59, 211-12). We are better off, he argues, to disengage ourselves from the changeable affects by divesting ourselves of the passions and following instead the directives of reason. In so recommending, he seems now to suppose something like an objective ideal for beings of our nature, although he earlier proposed that good is relative to an individual's desires. He supposes that we can use reason to come to understand the nature of God, or the universe, and that we are truer to our own nature in so doing than we are when we seek the nebulous goods which are the objects of our passions (see ibid.: Part Four, Preface, 225-8).

So, while Spinoza sets up an opposition between reason and passion, this opposition is actually between affects. Spinoza writes, "A true knowledge of good and bad cannot, in so far as it is true, restrain any emotion; it can do so only in so far as it is considered as an emotion." And he continues, "The desire which arises from a true knowledge of good and bad can be destroyed or restrained by many other desires which arise from the emotions by which we are harassed" (ibid.: Part Four, Prop. 14-15, 237). So, reason only opposes passion when the state it produces is emotive. Nadler comments: "The clash between knowledge and passions, then, is not a clash between the pure intellect and the emotions... rather, it is an affective struggle, one characterized by competing desires, each of which has a different source" (2006: 223). Unfortunately, rational desires are often overcome by the strength of the passions for objects present and near to us, which signifies that we are often weak-willed and do what we know we ought not to do (see Spinoza, 1677: Part Four, Prop. 17, 248-9). The virtuous person, on the other hand, acts on knowledge of the good, even when passion specifies the same action as reason, because she does the right thing out of an understanding that this action is in her interest, conducive to her survival, rather than from some obscure idea of good. So, this practical use of reason is for Spinoza a manifestation of the natural motivation for self-preservation (see ibid.: Part Four, Prop. 24, p. 243). On Spinoza's theory, the endeavor to persevere is also definitive of an ideal of good for human beings, which Lloyd identifies as Spinoza's *hilaritas*, a reflective pleasure that is a kind of joy that comes from having a well-functioning, thriving mind (see 1998: 40). Here is a case, she argues, of reflection's becoming emotional or affective. The other famous materialist of the century, Hobbes, writing prior to Spinoza (but whom I treat next with Locke), has a very different perspective on reason and on how to deal with the disruptive, but inescapable, passions.

A.1.4 Hobbes and Locke: Reason's Function Separated from the Function of the Passions

In Hobbes's mechanistic universe (*Leviathan*, Hobbes 1651), humans are matter in motion determined by their physiology; and good and evil are defined, respectively, by appetites and aversions, which are a function of each individual person's sources of pleasure and pain. The diverse passions—desire, joy, grief, and so on—derive from these sources, reversing the connection between goodness and motivating states found in previous teleological accounts. Hobbes argues that reason cannot govern the passions, which are exclusively self-interested (ibid.: Chapter 7). He defines reason in terms of its role in deducing the consequences of the words we use; as such, it cannot motivate on its own. But it does serve us practically: it concludes that the creation of an artificial, external authority to referee our passions is the necessary means to fulfill our aims and avoid the conflicts that make life miserable. Accordingly, the function of reason and the function of the passions are separated in Hobbes, as they later are in Hume, and in a way that they are not typically separated in the rationalists. Susan James comments that most commentators until Hobbes thought that various therapeutic techniques could be employed to induce people to use the passions either for their moral improvement or to live well, with reason supplying the insights about what to aim for. Hobbes posed a challenge to the entrenched view that reason could govern passions by arguing that passions alone are the source of the motivation to engage reason (see James 2006: 210–11).

In his *Essay Concerning Human Understanding*, at the end of the century (Locke 1690), Locke's empiricist account of motivation likewise redefines the relation between passions and goodness in hedonistic terms: "Things...are Good or Evil, only in reference to Pleasure or Pain" (Essay: II.XX.2).[8] Locke attributes our ability to move our bodies and our ability to bring up ideas to the perceptions of delight or pleasure attached to certain thoughts or sensations (see ibid.: II.VII.3). Passions, the motivators, are the "internal sensations" that come upon us when we reflect upon our pleasures and pains and their causes.[9] Locke characterizes desire as a state of uneasiness caused by an absent good (although not necessarily all absent goods) (ibid.: II.XXI.31). However, he offers three arguments why contemplation of the missing good by itself is not sufficient to move us, which, he says, is why God made us feel hunger, thirst, and other natural desires. First,

[I]f the bare contemplation of these good ends, to which we are carried by these several *uneasinesses*, had been sufficient to determine the *will*, and set work on us, we should have had none of these natural pains, and perhaps in this World, little or no pain at all.

(ibid.: II.XXI.34)

Locke's second argument, preceded by his acknowledgment of the domination of the rationalist view (as he understands it), a view to which he once subscribed, says:

It seems so establish'd and settled a maxim, by the general consent of all Mankind, That good, the greater good, determines the will, that I do not at all wonder, that when I first publish'd my thoughts on this Subject I took it for granted... But yet, upon a stricter inquiry, I am forced to conclude that *good*, the *greater good*, though apprehended and acknowledged to be so, does not determine the *will*, until our desire, raised proportionably to it, makes us *uneasy* in the want of it. Convince a man never so much, that plenty has its advantages over poverty; make him see and own, that the handsome conveniences of life are better than nasty penury: yet, as long as he is content with the latter, and finds no *uneasiness* in it, he moves not; his *will* never is determined to any action that shall bring him out of it. (ibid.: II.XXI.35)

Third, Locke argues that if the will were determined by thoughts of the good, we would be motivated to pursue the infinitely greatest good all of the time, a future state of infinite pleasure, since it surely outweighs in attraction any pleasures of this world. However, he notes,

---

[8] This and subsequent references to the *Essay* cite Book, Chapter, paragraph numbers. See also my earlier discussion, pp. 126–7.

[9] It's hard to see how the passions are simple modes, which are defined in terms of the collection of multiples of the same simple idea, (here, pleasure or pain). Why Locke thinks they are simple modes becomes more understandable when he considers which ideas represent and what they represent.

it is not the case that we are so motivated; instead, we pursue trivial goods, being motivated by a succession of desires or present uneasinesses (ibid.: II.XXI.38).

In making the case that ideas cannot motivate without feelings of uneasiness, Locke anticipates something like Hume's case for the inertness of reason (depending, of course, upon how Hume's argument is understood). Locke also argues that ideas and sensations of uneasiness cannot be opposed, a thesis which Hume parallels in some respect in his case for the non-opposition of reason and passion. Locke first establishes that only what is present can operate as a cause. Uneasiness at an absent good is present in the mind, but the idea of an absent good is not a good present in the mind, and so is unable to act as a cause of action against uneasiness. Furthermore, the concept of absent good is inert, because it is the product of speculation, which does not move us (he says). Even lively representations of the infinite goods of heaven are not able to move people, who are being prodded by their present feelings of uneasiness about the goods of this world. If those representations give rise to uneasiness, however, then people might be moved by the latter feelings, but Locke seems skeptical that this often happens.[10]

A.1.5 Summary

Most of the seventeenth-century theorists acknowledged that passions were the original motives to action, even though they needed the guidance of reason to succeed at achieving the good. Much of the language in these early discussions of the oversight of the passions is metaphorical: reason is said to govern the passions by showing them the proper ends, but the details of how the passions then adopt those ends is not so clear. In Descartes, the passions are explicitly characterized as representations, and they frequently misrepresent objects as good or evil by their confusedness or obscurity. Reason, on his theory, can alter the passionate representations by bringing to mind genuine depictions of the good, through evoking thoughts of precedents, past experiences, projected consequences, and so on. On Malebranche's theory, motivation originates with our natural inclinations, which are directed by God toward the good, but which can get sidetracked by the passions. The inclinations and passions are intellectual, but the passions also have a physiological component that makes them confused

---

[10] Locke writes:

> The *Idea* of it [absent good] indeed may be in the mind, and view'd as present there: but nothing will be in the mind as a present good, able to counter-balance the removal of any *uneasiness*, which we are under, till it raises our desire, and the *uneasiness* of that has the prevalency in determining the *will*. Till then the *Idea* in the mind of whatever is good, is there only like other *Ideas*, the object of bare unactive speculation; but operates not on the will, nor sets us on work; . . . . How many are to be found that have had lively representations set before their minds of the unspeakable joys of Heaven, which they acknowledge both possible and probable too, who yet would be content to take up with their happiness here? And so the prevailing *uneasiness* of their desires, let loose after the enjoyments of this life, take their turns in the determining their *wills*, and all that while they take not one step, are not one jot moved, towards the good things of another life considered as never so great.
> (1690: II.XXI.37)

One might ask whether Locke's arguments, for the conclusion that the idea of absent good is not a motive and for the conclusion that ideas about the goods of heaven are not motives, are begging the question. Perhaps these observations are better treated as consequences of earlier arguments he has made for the thesis that uneasiness is the only motive to action.

but lively. So. Malebranche offers a physiological explanation of how the passions infect our thinking and the direction of our actions. Spinoza, in making reason affective, commits himself to the thesis that reason can initiate motivation, but the conflict between reason and passion is actually a conflict between competing conations. The seventeenth-century philosophers do suggest that ideas of genuine goodness produced by reason oppose the corrupt notions of goodness promoted by the passions. This survey raises the question, however, whether reason is itself providing an original motive to action, as Hume assumed was the case in the view of many of his rationalist predecessors.[11] The answer appears to be no.

A.2 Eighteenth-Century Theories of Passion, Reason, and Action

James Harris notes of the mixed eighteenth-century perspective, "Writers on the passions were by this time just as likely to assert that the passions are part of God's Providential order... as they were to describe the passions as necessarily a manifestation of sin and a source of corruption" (Harris 2013: 273). At the beginning of the 1700s, English theologians William Ayloffe, Musidoris Burghope, and Francis Bragge continued to promote the thesis that persons' passions, left on their own, have a malignant and destructive effect. In *The Government of the Passions according to the Rules of Reason and Religion* (Ayloffe 1700), Ayloffe repeats several themes from Senault: that while we can use one passion to "repel" another, doing so is "not safe" (ibid.: 50); that only reason with God's grace can restrain the passions, since reason is "obnubulated" by original sin (ibid.: 23); and that the passions are the seeds of virtue (ibid.: 53). My chief interest here is in the way in which the passions receive reason's guidance. Ayloffe says that the soul is slave to the senses, which are deceitful and produce erroneous "knowledge," under whose direction the passions become "irregular" (ibid.: 28–9). "[O]ur Passions are only criminal because they are deceiv'd." Thus, the passions are not in themselves depraved, but reason must show them their objects "in genuine Colours," and it serves to remove the objects that tend to promote rebellion and upheaval (ibid.: 47–51). Burghope, in a sermon preached at the Temple Church, also insists that the passions be fixed on their proper objects, which is to say that the passions are meant to glorify virtue and abhor vice (1701: 4).

Bragge agrees with many previous thinkers that it is neither possible nor desirable "to root out" and destroy any of the passions, which are vigorous tendencies toward what we regard as very good and conducive to our happiness, and aversions to what we take to be very evil and pernicious. Good and evil will always affect us, both in this world and the next (Bragge 1708: 1, 6–8). In this world, the passions are also motives to action, which move us through a strong commotion of "our blood and spirits." In order to be moved in the right way, we must apply reason and religion to rectify our notions of good and evil and make an accurate estimate of the relative worth of goods:

> He that Seriously and often thus employs his Thoughts... will in time become as 'twere Dead and Insensible to all the False Deluding Blandishments of Wealth, and Greatness, and Pleasure, and begot out of Danger of being transported by any Extravagant Degrees, of Passion, in the Pursuit of anything here below. (ibid.:13)

---

[11] For a very helpful overview of the nature of the passions and their role in action in the seventeenth century, see James (2012), "The Passions in Metaphysics and the Theory of Action."

Thus, the use of reason, with God's assistance, will not only enlighten us about what is genuinely good and conducive to our well-being (so that the passions move us according to their intended purpose), but it will also diminish our desires for (or love of) mistaken goods, the petty pleasures of this life.

A.2.1 Cudworth and Clarke and Moral Rationalism

English theologian Ralph Cudworth died in 1688. His *The True Intellectual System of the Universe* was published in 1678, but was also published in several editions in the 1700s. *A Treatise Concerning Eternal and Immutable Morality* was published posthumously, first in 1731, and *A Treatise of Free Will*, not until 1838. For that reason, and because Hume regards Cudworth's views on the origin of morality as significantly similar to Samuel Clarke's, I discuss Cudworth in the context of eighteenth-century thought, along with Clarke. Hume notes in the second *Enquiry* that the view that morality consists in necessary relations discovered by reason was first advocated by Malebranche, and then embraced by Ralph Cudworth and Samuel Clarke (EPM 3.34, n. 12). Hume famously describes Samuel Clarke's moral theory at *Treatise* 3.1.1.4 and then rejects what he takes to be his and Cudworth's moral rationalism by pointing to the inert nature of reason, which guarantees that reason could not be the source of morality, which is motivating or "active" on its own. Interestingly, neither Cudworth nor Clarke actually thought that rational apprehension of necessary relations could move us on its own.

One of the Cambridge Platonists, Cudworth combines mechanistic, corpuscular explanations of nature with Platonic metaphysics, theism, and a defense of free will. His views on reason, passion, and motivation comprise the focus of this discussion, but it's difficult to discern exactly what they are. Because of the content of *Eternal and Immutable Morality* (EIM), Cudworth is and was, by Hume and other early moderns, considered a thorough-going rationalist. Cudworth argues at length in EIM that just as God's arbitrary commands cannot change the nature of a square into that of a circle, so they cannot make something good or bad, just or unjust, that was not so by nature. He also argues that human minds have all ideas innately because they reflect the mind of God. Knowledge is acquired by an active process of cognition that involves recollection of these ideas, but also sense perception, which he says is necessary to acquire knowledge of the order in the external world. Cudworth isn't explicit about how moral knowledge fits into this scheme, but his treatment of morality analogously to geometry in its being composed of necessary, immutable truths implies that they are known in the same way geometrical truths are known: by our clear and distinct conceptions of them. Cudworth has no discussion of whether or how moral knowledge might affect actions, and passions are never mentioned at all in EIM. If we assume that he thought apprehension of morality, which is done by reason, could by itself motivate persons, then we could conclude that he thought reason on its own was motivating. However, the view that demonstrative reason was a motive was unorthodox, and Cudworth makes it clear in other writings that he did not think it. Both John Passmore in his book on Cudworth from the 1950s and contemporary philosopher Michael Gill in his more recent study of Cudworth, contend that he is more aligned with sentimentalism than with rationalism in his motivational theory (Passmore 1951: 52–3; Gill 2006: 38–43).

In his *Sermon Preached before the Honble House of Commons at Westminster* (Cudworth 1647), Cudworth emphasizes the importance of character and internal motivation to living the religious, or the best, life. He writes that knowledge is "more excellent" than riches and outward pleasures; yet, our happiness consists in "a certain divine temper and constitution of soul, which is farre above it" (ibid.: 14). We think it "a gallant thing to be fluttering with our wings of knowledge and speculation," but in fact, what is most important and productive of "sweet delight" is to achieve an inner state of harmony between our will and God's. Later, Cudworth writes of God's effect on us: "[God] is always kindling, cheering, quickening, warming, enlivening hearts" (ibid.: 26). So, there is certainly evidence that Cudworth thought that the motivation to live the best life originated from certain internal sentiments, rather than from knowledge or reason. John Passmore writes about the content of Cudworth's unpublished manuscripts that they show how misleading it is to think of Cudworth as one of Clarke's predecessors, whom Passmore characterizes as having the crudest form of rationalist psychology, with reason acting as "an impersonal arbiter" remote from passion (1951: 52). Reason as intellectual apprehension is not a motive to action, for Cudworth. (As I have suggested and will show shortly, it is not for Clarke, either.) Passmore quotes Cudworth: "the first principle of motion in the soul is not, of course, reason and understanding."[12] Furthermore,

Mere speculative intellection without any inclination to one thing more than another without anything of appetite or volition ... is not the beginning of all actions in the soul, but ... instincts and inclinations are the spring and source of life and activity whence ends are suggested to us that provoke and incite endeavors....[13]

In *A Treatise of Free Will* (1838) (which, along with EIM, was intended as an extension of *The True Intellectual System*), Cudworth puts forward his alternative to faculty psychology with its divided mind. He characterizes the mind as an integration of reason, imagination, passion and appetite, with the contributions from these various sources ordered by the will. Among the features in the soul is an incessant desire, love of good, which is the source of motivation:

that which first moveth in us, and is the spring and principle of all deliberative action, can be no other than a constant, restless, uninterrupted desire, or love of good as such, and happiness. This is an ever bubbling fountain in the centre of the soul, an elater or spring of motion ...
(Cudworth 1838: 173)

The will is free, but it does not decide actions blindly and fortuitously; it is not indifferent to the alternative objects' various degrees of goodness and evil and so it decides on the basis of deliberation and reasoning (see ibid.: 176–7). Affirming Descartes's view that the will is the source of error when it doesn't wait for clear and distinct conception before affirming a proposition, Cudworth says that a person may "upon slight considerations and immature deliberations ... choose and prefer that which is really worse before the better, so as to deserve blame thereby" (ibid.: 179). Contingency in choice derives from the power to consider and deliberate more or less, not in the ability to act against our best judgment. Unlike the divided soul view promulgated earlier in the seventeenth century, in the contest between dictates of conscience and the lower appetites, "there is no necessary understanding ... coming in to umpire between them." Instead, Cudworth says that the soul has a hegemonic, self-governing

---

[12] Passmore (1951: 52); see also Cudworth, *Collection of Confused Thoughts, Memorandums relating to the Eternity of Torments collected out of my little Book* (manuscript fragments).

[13] Passmore (1951: 53); see also Cudworth, *On Liberty and Necessity* (manuscript).

power, which involves among other things, self-recollection, self-attention, heedfulness, and circumspection (see ibid.: 183).

In his Boyle Lectures of 1704, *A Demonstration of the Being and Attributes of God*, Samuel Clarke (1705) presents his argument for the necessary existence of God and his description of God's attributes; his defense of free will against Hobbes and Spinoza is also a prominent theme. In his 1705 lectures, *A Discourse Concerning the Unchangeable Obligations of Natural Religion*, Clarke (1706) discusses the source and nature of morality, which seems to situate him close to Cudworth in that arena. According to Clarke, "there is a Fitness or Suitableness of certain Circumstances to certain Persons, and an Unsuitableness of others, founded in the nature of Things and the Qualifications of Persons, antecedent to all positive appointment whatsoever..." (ibid.: 4). These fitnesses determine truths of morality, such as that we should honor and worship God, that we should not defraud our neighbors, and that we should preserve the life of an innocent man. These truths are, as in Cudworth's theory, necessary and accessible by reason. For reasonable persons, their discernment of these fitnesses also directs their wills, when they are not corrupted by passions:

And by this Understanding or Knowledge of the natural and necessary relations, fitnesses, and proportions of things, the Wills likewise of all Intelligent Beings are constantly directed, and must needs be determined to act accordingly, excepting those only, who Will things to be what they are not and cannot be; that is, whose Wills are corrupted by particular Interest or Affection, or swayed by some unreasonable and prevailing Passion. (ibid.: 11)

Of rational beings whose actions are not regularly governed by reason and by the difference between good and evil, but who instead allow lusts, passions, pride, self-interest, and sensual pleasures to move them, Clarke writes: "These, setting up their own unreasonable Self-will in opposition to the Nature and Reason of Things, endeavour (as much as in them lies) to make things be what they are not, and cannot be" (ibid.: 12). Consequently, it is as though we signify what is not the case when we act contrary to reason.[14]

Clarke acknowledges, then, a conflict between reason and passion in suggesting that when we act contrary to reason and so contrary to moral duty, it is because we are diverted either by "negligent" misunderstanding or by passions like lust or greed. However, human understanding of demonstrative truths does not by itself lead to action, with no contribution from the passions. In his sermon, "The Government of Passion," (delivered in 1710 or 1711[15]), he says that, in God, there is no room for passion, because reason and understanding are perfect and therefore perfectly influence God's actions (Clarke 1724: 143-4). In non-rational beasts, passions and appetites, are the only motivators. Human beings have a middle nature between the two, possessing both passions and reason. Passions and appetites "*excite* and stir them ['men'] up to Action, where their bare abstract *Understanding* would leave them too *remiss*" (ibid.: 144). It is human persons' duty, however, to govern the passions with reason, where, when left alone, the passions would hurry them on to "exhorbitant and unreasonable" things.

---

[14] In a similar vein, William Wollaston, another target of Hume's, held the view that actions are tacit speech and that immorality consists in conveying through one's actions what is not the case. For instance, if I steal someone's gold watch and use it, I am saying that it is mine. See Wollaston (1724).

[15] The discrepancy reflects the difference in the civil calendar and the church calendar. The sermon is subtitled, "Preach'd before the Queen, at St. James Chapel, on Sunday, the 7th of January, 1710-11." The sermon is one of a collection published in 1724.

So, following the theme in earlier writers, Clarke thinks the passions are useful when properly directed and make us diligent in pursuit of "those Actions of Life which Reason *directs* and the Passions *execute*" (ibid.: 145).

Unlike Cudworth, Clarke insists on free will as the ability to choose to act against our best judgment.[16] In *A Demonstration of the Being and Attributes of God*, he is interested in showing that God's actions are neither necessitated (contrary to Hobbes and Spinoza) nor arbitrary (contrary to voluntarist views), but also done freely from reasons. Human freedom is a reflection of God's freedom. While the understanding may be determined to assent to a proposition perceived to be true, such assent is not a volition or cause of volition; it is a reason, rather than a cause, and to think otherwise is a confusion of "moral motives" with "physical efficients":

For the true, proper, immediate, physical efficient cause of action, is the power of self-motion in men, which exerts itself freely in consequence of the last judgment of the understanding. But the last judgment of the understanding, is not itself a physical efficient, but merely a moral motive, upon which the physical efficient or motive power begins to act.

The necessity, therefore, by which the power of acting follows the judgment of the understanding, is only a moral necessity; that is, no necessity at all ...[17]

Clarke exemplifies his thesis by pointing to the man free from pain and psychological disorder, who judges it unreasonable to hurt or kill himself and so is morally necessitated to preserve his health, even though he is physically free to do otherwise.

Clarke was pressed in correspondence by the Cambridge intellectual, John Bulkeley, on the matter why our assent or dissent from practical propositions should be any different from assent or dissent to speculative propositions. The latter is necessary, so, why should the former, "by which the man is determined to act" not be equally necessary, and this, even though persons' practical judgments may be at odds? For instance, a person judges it good to act for his present pleasure and another to act for his long-term happiness. Clarke's reply is worthy of note:

Judging is one thing, and *acting* is another. They depend upon principles totally different from each other, and which have no more connection than activeness and passiveness. Neither God nor man can avoid seeing that to be true which they see to be true, or judging that to be fit and reasonable which they see is fit and reasonable. But in all this, there is no action ... The sum is: there is no connection between *approbation* and *action*, between what is passive and what is active.   (Clarke 1716–17: 126)

So, a rational judgment of goodness or truth, which is compelled by perception, is inert, while the will is active, and it makes no difference what the subject of judgment is. This point is evocative of Hume's view about reason's impotence, even though Hume drops the will out of action and attributes the impetus to passion. In sum, Clarke's view attributes the execution of action to the passions, which can and ought to be guided by the judgments of reason. No one, however, is necessitated to behave as they do, and we are always free to do that for which we

---

[16] See Harris (2005: Chapter 2) for a discussion of Clarke's difficulties with free will.
[17] Clarke, *Demonstration* (1705: 54, 73); see also, Vailati's editorial "Introduction," (ibid.: xxi).

find no reason at all. Clarke's psychological theory, with specific roles delegated to reason and passion, is appreciably different from Cudworth's idea of the soul as self-directing whole.

A.2.2 Hutcheson on Human Nature, the Passions, and Reasonable Action

In 1704, Bernard Mandeville published his infamous poem, *The Grumbling Hive, or Knaves Turn'd Honest*. It later became a part of his work, *The Fable of the Bees: or, Private Vices, Public Benefits* (1714). There he defends the theses that human beings are naturally egoist and that self-interested motivations produce vices useful to a productive and thriving economy. For instance, the (Christian) vice of pride is a crucial impetus to actions performed to gain public honor, and such actions usually produce great social benefits. Developing orthodox virtues, like benevolence and honesty, in fact, remove competitive motivation and lead to economic collapse. One of the targets of Mandeville's *Fable* was Lord Shaftesbury, whose *Characteristics of Men, Manners, Opinions, Times* (1711), argues for the claim that persons are naturally benevolent and sociable. Shaftesbury thinks that we flourish by maintaining proper order among our individual passions and by finding our proper place in society and among the whole of "mankind," giving neither private nor social matters too much emphasis. Francis Hutcheson takes up the defense of natural benevolence and the critique of Mandeville's portrayal of human nature as entirely self-centered. Hutcheson also presents a view of the role of reason in action that is relevant to this discussion, arguing that reasonable action is rooted in the passions and affections, contrary to his rationalist predecessors. For both Shaftesbury and Hutcheson, motivation springs from passions, not from reason alone.[18]

Hutcheson's psychology of motivation, presented in his *Essay on the Nature and Conduct of the Passion and Affections* (1st ed., 1728), has it that the passions and affections divide into four types, all of which are motives: desires and aversions, which are the "pure" affections; affections in a wider sense, which include calm or reflective passions; non-reflective passions; and propensities of instinct, or natural propensities.[19] These desires, passions, and instincts can be managed in several ways to produce the balance that Hutcheson, like Shaftesbury, thought would lead to a happy existence. For instance, we are advised not to attach undue significance to particular desires and find ourselves narrowly devoted to the pursuit of such things as luxury and money. Rather, we are to cultivate reflective passions and to make calm universal benevolence superior to all particular passions. How we are to do this is not, strictly speaking, by exercise of reason, but by "a calm *Attention* of Mind, an habitual *Discipline* over our selves, and a fixed *Resolution* to stop all Action, before a calm *Examination* of every Circumstance attending it" (Hutcheson 1728: 110). James Harris comments:

What Hutcheson constantly enjoins is the adoption of a particular kind of perspective on the world, a maximally impartial perspective, a point of view which reveals one's place in the larger moral system. The point of philosophy is to enable one to take up that perspective.

(2013: 278)

---

[18] Although he was contemporary to Hume and they exchanged ideas in letters well known to scholars, there is debate over the influence of Francis Hutcheson's philosophy on Hume's. It is hard to believe, however, that Hutcheson's arguments on reason and motivation, given their content, were not significant in the development of Hume's theory. For opposing views, see Moore (1995) and Norton (2005).

[19] For a descriptive overview of these passions, see Radcliffe (2004). For other discussions of Hutcheson on motivation, see Jensen (1971); Bishop (1996); and Darwall (1995: Chapter 8, 207–43).

In the *Illustrations on the Moral Sense*, which appeared along with the *Essay on the Passions*, Hutcheson evaluates the view from Clarke and Gilbert Burnet that the criterion of goodness in an action is a matter of rational relations. There Hutcheson offers a passion-based account of practical reason. Anticipating Hume's description of reason, he defines reason as "our *Power of finding out true Propositions*" and reasonableness as "*Conformity to true Propositions, or to Truth*" (Hutcheson 1728: 137). However, since as many true propositions can be uttered about vicious actions as can be about virtuous, Hutcheson concludes that virtue cannot consist in conformity to true propositions. He advances an important distinction: a motivating reason is a description of the qualities that move an agent to do one action over others, and a justifying reason refers to the features that make an act morally justified. According to Hutcheson, justification requires approval, so a justifying reason is a description of the qualities in the action that makes one approve of it. One of Hutcheson's main theses is that justifying reasons presuppose a moral sense. Another is that all motivating reasons presuppose instincts and affections (ibid.: 138–9).

[N]o end can be intended or desired previously to some one of these Classes of Affections, *Self-Love*, *Self-Hatred*, or desire of private Misery (if this be possible), *Benevolence* toward others, or *Malice*: All Affections are included under these; no *end* can be previous to them all... (ibid.: 139)

In considering the view espoused by some of his contemporaries, that no action is good or reasonable to which we are not prompted by reason apart from affections, Hutcheson responds, "As if indeed *Reason*, or the Knowledge of the Relations of things, could excite to Action when we proposed no *End*, or as if *Ends* could be intended without *Desire or Affection*" (ibid.: 139). According to Hutcheson, the view of some rationalists that the intellect not only contemplates, but that it desires and prosecutes action as well, ignores the role of the will. Furthermore, those who argue that we can give reasons for the ends we pursue ignore Aristotle's arguments that reasons for actions require aims or ends, and that reasons for aims or ends must appeal to other ends served, until the justification eventuates in ultimate ends we desire for themselves, or else the reason-giving goes on infinitely.

Even though motivation depends ultimately on passions and affections and justification on sentiments, reason evaluates ends in a certain respect—that is, certain ends can be reasonable relative to other, ultimate ends that the agent holds. Hutcheson writes in correspondence with Gilbert Burnet that reason can be practical when it discovers "what objects are naturally apt to give any person the highest gratifications, or what means are most effectual to obtain some objects."[20] Then:

To a being which acts only for its own happiness, that end is reasonable which contains a greater happiness than any other which it could pursue; and when such a being satisfies itself with a smaller good for itself while a greater is in its power, it pursues an unreasonable end...
But if there are any beings which by the very frame of their nature desire the good of a community or which are determined by kind affections to study the good of others and have withal a moral sense which causes them necessarily to approve such conduct in themselves or others... to such beings that end is reasonable which contains the greatest aggregate of public

---

[20] Burnet (1735: 209). This particular correspondence, from which I cite several points, is dated 12 and 19 June, 1725. Hume, by the way, could agree with this characterization, since these discoveries are discoveries of reason as he sees it, and calling them "practical" simply means that they are relevant to action, even though they are products of theoretical reason.

happiness which an agent can procure... If these beings also have self-love... and at the same time find that their highest happiness does necessarily arise from kind affections and benevolent actions, that end which would appear reasonable would be universal happiness... for both desires are at once gratified as far as they are capable of doing it by their own actions.

(Burnet and Hutcheson 1735: 209–10)

Consequently, practical reasonableness in action is relative to the passionate constitution or nature of the beings whose actions are under assessment.

To the question whether private or public good is the more reasonable aim, however, Hutcheson replies that the answer depends on the dispositions of the judge who is assessing the two general ends. A being who is entirely self-interested (although Hutcheson, I think, believes there are none) will judge his or her own actions according to whether they are conducive to his own pleasure and others' actions according to whether they are conducive to those agents' pleasure. This person may understand what public good is, but would not use it as a measurement of the rationality of anyone's actions (ibid.: 210). To the question whether there are grounds for arguing that virtuous actions are always reasonable ones, Hutcheson responds that "these... natures without a moral sense would see nothing reasonable in the good affections of one man towards another abstractly from considerations of the advantage of virtue to the virtuous agent" (ibid.: 211). On the other hand, if that same question, whether public or private good is most reasonable, were posed to beings who have "a moral sense of excellence in public affections and a desire of public good" (ibid,: 210), they would answer that "it is reasonable that smaller private good should yield to greater public good, and they will disapprove of a contrary conduct" (ibid.: 210). Apart from having a moral sense or benevolent affection, Hutcheson sees no explanation why anyone would approve of actions that pursue public good over private interest; so, there is no other sense in which virtuous actions could be thought reasonable but that in which they appeal to the sensibilities of those with public affections. This does not make them reasonable in themselves. Hutcheson uses this point to answer Clarke's argument that morality of actions derives from their fitness or unfitness to the rational order, since the fitness of actions can only be relative to the ends that agents embrace by their affections (ibid.: 211–12).

A.2.3 Summary

The eighteenth-century saw development of the theme that cultivation of certain passions is essential to human well-being. Some of the thinkers early in the century urged persons to draw on the grace of God and on reason to regulate the passions and develop the ones that promote the genuine good over trivial pleasures. Cudworth and Clarke, who are among the moral rationalists Hume clearly opposes, agree with each other (and with Hume) that the operation of pure intellect, without appetite or feeling, will never produce action. While Cudworth and Clarke disagree over the nature of free will and over the integration of reason and passion within the self, neither regards reason apart from the passions as an active force. Hume was justified in arguing against them that reason cannot regulate passion or oppose passion over the direction of action. But the idea that reason motivated on its own is one that they explicitly denied. A bit later, Hutcheson offers his distinction between motivating reasons and justifying reasons and defends the notion of a moral sense tied to the latter. He recognizes the practicality of reason in a way that Hume would call "loose" and "informal," but Hutcheson and Hume ultimately agree about the importance of the calm passions in living well. Virtually all of the early modern thinkers, then, regarded the passions as a prerequisite to action and the proper passions as essential to human happiness.

Bibliography

Historical Sources

Ayloffe, William (1700). *The Government of the Passions according to the Rules of Reason and Religion.* London: Printed for Knapton.
Bragge, Francis (1708). *A Practical Treatise of the Regulation of the Passions.* London: Printed by J.M. for John Wyat.
Burghope, M. (1701). *The Government of the Passions. A sermon preach'd in the Temple Church, on Midlent Sunday, March the 30th, 1701.* London.
Burnet, Gilbert and Hutcheson, Francis (1735). *Letters Between the Late Mr. Gilbert Burnet, and Mr. Francis Hutcheson, concerning the true Foundation of Virtue or Moral Goodness.* In *Illustrations on the Moral Sense.* Bernard Peach (Ed.). Cambridge, MA: Harvard University Press, 1971, pp. 197–247.
Charleton, Walter (1674). *Natural History of the Passions.* London: printed by T.N. for James Magnes in Ruffell-Street.
Clarke, Samuel (1705). *A Demonstration of the Being and Attributes of God.* In *A Demonstration of the Being and Attributes of God and Other Writings.* Ezio Vailati (Ed.). Cambridge: Cambridge University Press, 1996, 3–92.
Clarke, Samuel (1706). *A Discourse concerning the Unchangeable Obligations of Natural Religion.* In *The British Moralists.* L.A. Selby-Bigge (Ed.). Oxford: Clarendon Press, 1897.
Clarke, Samuel (1716–17). "Clarke's Answer to Bulkeley's First Letter." In *A Demonstration of the Being and Attributes of God and Other Writings.* Ezio Vailati (Ed.). Cambridge: Cambridge University Press, 1996, 125–6.
Clarke, Samuel (1724). The Government of Passion, A Sermon Preach'd before the Queen, at St. James Chapel, on Sunday the 7th of January, 1710-11. In *XVII Sermons on Several Occasions.* London: printed by William Botham, for James Knapton.
Coeffeteau, Nicolas (1621). *A Table of Humane Passions.* London: Printed by Nicolas Oakes.
Cudworth, Ralph (1647). *Mr. Cudworth's Sermon Preached before the Honble House of Commons at Westminster, March 31st, 1647.* Cambridge: Reprinted for J.T. Wheeler, 1852.
Cudworth, Ralph (1678). *The True Intellectual System of the Universe.* Facsimile. Stuttgart: Friedrich Frommann Verlag, 1964.
Cudworth, Ralph (1731/1838). *A Treatise concerning Eternal and Immutable Morality with A Treatise of Freewill.* Sarah Hutton (Ed.). Cambridge: Cambridge University Press, 1996.
Cureau de la Chambre, Marin (1658). *The Characters of the Passions.* Paris.
Descartes, René (1649). *Passions of the Soul.* Stephen Voss (Ed. and Trans.). Indianapolis, IN: Hackett Publishing, 1989.
Hobbes, Thomas (1650). *Human Nature.* In D. D. Raphael (Ed.), *British Moralists 1650–1800.* Indianapolis, IN: Hackett Publishing, 1991, Vol. 1, pp. 3–17.
Hobbes, Thomas (1651). *Leviathan.* Richard Tuck (Ed.). Cambridge: Cambridge University Press, 1996.

Hutcheson, Francis. (1728). *An Essay on the Nature and Conduct of the Passions and Affections, with Illustrations on the Moral Sense*. Aaron Garrett (Ed.). Indianapolis, IN: Liberty Fund, 2002.

Locke, John (1664). *Essays on the Law of Nature*. W. von Leyden (Ed.). New York: Oxford University Press, 1954.

Locke, John (1690). *An Essay Concerning Human Understanding*. P.H. Nidditch (Ed.). Oxford: Clarendon Press, 1975.

Malebranche, Nicolas (1674–75). *The Search after Truth*. Thomas M. Lennon and Paul J. Olscamp (Trans. and Eds.). Columbus, OH: Ohio State University Press, 1980.

Reynolds, Edward (1640). *A Treatise of the Passions and Faculties of the Soul of Man*. London: Printed by R.H. for Robert Bostock.

Senault, Jean-François (1641). *The Use of the Passions*. Henry, Earl of Monmouth (Trans.). London: Printed for J. L. and Humphrey Moseley.

Shaftesbury, Lord (Anthony Ashley Cooper) (1711). *Characteristics of Men, Manners, Opinions, Times*. Lawrence Klein (Ed.). Cambridge: Cambridge University Press, 2000.

Spinoza, Baruch (1677). *Ethics*. G.H.R. Parkinson (Ed. and Trans.). New York: Oxford University Press, 2000.

Wollaston, William (1724). *The Religion of Nature Delineated*. 2nd ed. Delmar, NY: Scholars' Facsimiles & Reprints, 1974.

Contemporary Sources

Abramson, Kate (2001). "Sympathy and the Project of Hume's Second *Enquiry*." *Archiv für Geschichte der Philosophie*, 83: 45–80.

Ainslie, Donald (1999). "Scepticism about Persons in Book II of Hume's *Treatise*." *Journal of the History of Philosophy*, 37: 469–92.

Ainslie, Donald (2005). "Sympathy and the Unity of Hume's Idea of Self." In Joyce Jenkins, Jennifer Whiting, and Christopher Williams (Eds.), *Persons and Passions: Essays in Honor of Annette Baier*. Notre Dame, IN: University of Notre Dame Press, pp. 143–73.

Ainslie, Donald (2015a). "Hume and Moral Motivation." In Donald Ainslie and Annemarie Butler (Eds.), *The Cambridge Companion to Hume's* Treatise. Cambridge: Cambridge University Press, pp. 283–300.

Ainslie, Donald (2015b). *Hume's True Scepticism*. Oxford: Oxford University Press.

Alanen, Lilli (2003). "The Intentionality of Cartesian Emotions." In Byron Williston and Andre Gombay (Eds.), *Passion and Virtue in Descartes*. Amherst, NY: Humanity Books, pp. 107–27.

Alanen, Lilli (2005). "Reflection and Ideas in Hume's Account of the Passions." In Joyce Jenkins, Jennifer Whiting, and Christopher Williams (Eds.), *Persons and Passions: Essays in Honor of Annette Baier*. Notre Dame, IN: University of Notre Dame Press, pp. 117–42.

Alanen, Lilli (2006). "The Powers and Mechanisms of the Passions." In Saul Traiger (Ed.), *Blackwell Guide to Hume's* Treatise. Oxford: Blackwell, pp. 179–98.

Anscombe, G.E.M. (1957). *Intention*. Oxford: Basil Blackwell.

Árdal, Páll (1966). *Passions and Value in Hume's* Treatise. Edinburgh: Edinburgh University Press.

Árdal, Páll (1977). "Another Look at Hume's Account of Moral Evaluation." *Journal of the History of Philosophy*, 15: 405–21.

Árdal, Páll (1989). "Hume and Davidson on Pride." *Hume Studies*, 15: 387–95.
Audi, Robert (1989). *Practical Reasoning*. London: Routledge.
Baier, Annette (1991). *A Progress of Sentiments*. Cambridge, MA: Harvard University Press.
Baier, Annette (1993). "David Hume, Spinozist." *Hume Studies*, 19: 237–52.
Baier, Annette (2008a). "Hume's Post-Impressionism." In *Death and Character: Further Reflections on Hume*. Cambridge, MA: Harvard University Press, pp. 237–56.
Baier, Annette (2008b). "*Enquiry Concerning the Principles of Morals*: Incomparably the Best?" In Elizabeth S. Radcliffe (Ed.), *A Companion to Hume*. Malden, MA: Blackwell, pp. 293–320.
Barnes, W. H. F. (1933). "A Suggestion About Value." *Analysis*, 1: 45–6.
Beauchamp, Tom (2007). "Introduction: A History of Two Dissertations." In Tom Beauchamp (Ed.), *David Hume: A Dissertation on the Passions; The Natural History of Religion*. Oxford: Clarendon Press, pp. xi–cxxxv.
Bell, Martin (2002). "Belief and Instinct in Hume's First *Enquiry*." In Peter Millican (Ed.), *Reading Hume on Human Understanding*. Oxford: Clarendon Press, pp. 175–85.
Bishop, John D. (1996). "Moral Motivation and the Development of Francis Hutcheson's Philosophy." *Journal of the History of Ideas*, 57: 277–95.
Bittner, Rüdiger (2001). *Doing Things for Reasons*. New York: Oxford University Press.
Blackburn, Simon (1980). *Spreading the Word*. Oxford: Clarendon Press.
Blackburn, Simon (1993). *Essays in Quasi-Realism*. New York: Oxford University Press.
Blackburn, Simon (1998). *Ruling Passions*. Oxford: Clarendon Press.
Blackburn, Simon (2000). "Kant versus Hume on Practical Reasoning." In D. P. Chattopadhyaya (Ed.), *Realism: Responses and Reactions: Essays in Honour of Pranab Kumar Sen*. New Delhi: Indian Council of Philosophical Research, pp. 462–80.
Botros, Sophie (2006). *Hume, Reason, and Morality*. London: Routledge.
Brandt, Richard (1979). *A Theory of the Good and the Right*. Oxford: Clarendon Press.
Brett, Nathan and Paxman, Katharina (2008). "Reason in Hume's Passions," *Hume Studies* 34: 43–59.
Bricke, John (1996). *Mind & Morality: An Examination of Hume's Moral Psychology*. Oxford: Clarendon Press.
Broackes, Justin (2002). "Hume, Belief, and Personal Identity." In Peter Millican (Ed.), *Reading Hume on Human Understanding*. Oxford: Clarendon Press, pp. 187–210.
Brown, Charlotte (1988). "Is Hume an Internalist?" *Journal of the History of Philosophy*, 26: 69–87.
Brown, Deborah and Normore, Calvin (2003). "Traces of the Body: Cartesian Passions." In Byron Williston and Andre Gombay (Eds.), *Passion and Virtue in Descartes*. Amherst, NY: Humanity Books, pp. 83–106.
Buckle, Stephen (2001). *Hume's Enlightenment Tract: The Unity and Purpose of* An Enquiry concerning Human Understanding. Oxford: Oxford University Press.
Buckle, Stephen (2012). "Hume on the Passions." *Philosophy*, 87: 189–213.
Capaldi, Nicholas (1975). *David Hume: The Newtonian Philosopher*. Boston, MA: Twayne.
Carlson, Åsa (2009). "There Is Just One Idea of Self in Hume's Treatise." *Hume Studies*, 35: 171–84.
Chazan, Pauline (1998). *The Moral Self*. New York: Routledge, 1998.
Cohon, Rachel (1994). "On an Unorthodox Account of Hume's Moral Psychology." *Hume Studies*, 20: 179–94.

Cohon, Rachel (2008a). "Hume's Indirect Passions." In Elizabeth S. Radcliffe (Ed.), *A Companion to Hume*. Malden, MA: Blackwell, pp. 159–200.

Cohon, Rachel (2008b). *Hume's Morality: Feeling and Fabrication*. New York: Oxford University Press.

Cohon, Rachel (2012). "Evaluations and Urges: Hume on the Indirect Passions and the Moral Sentiments." In Lorenzo Greco and Alessio Vaccari (Eds.), *Hume Readings*. Rome: Edizioni di Storia e Letteratura, pp. 233–50.

Cohon, Rachel and Owen, David (1997). "Representation, Reason, and Motivation." *Manuscrito*, 20: 47–76.

Collier, Mark (2011). "Hume's Science of Emotions: Feeling Theory without Tears." *Hume Studies*, 37: 3–18.

Costelloe, Timothy M. (2013). "The Faculty of Taste." In James Harris (Ed.), *The Oxford Handbook of British Philosophy in the Eighteenth Century*. Oxford: Oxford University Press, pp. 430–49.

Dancy, Jonathan (2000). *Practical Reality*. Oxford: Oxford University Press.

Darwall, Stephen (1995). *The British Moralists and the Internal 'Ought': 1640–1740*. Cambridge: Cambridge University Press.

Davidson, Donald (1976). "Hume's Cognitive Theory of Pride." *Journal of Philosophy*, 73: 744–56.

Debes, Remy (2007). "Humanity, Sympathy, and the Puzzle of Hume's Second *Enquiry*." *British Journal for the History of Philosophy*, 15: 27–57.

Dretske, Fred (1988). *Explaining Behavior: Reason in a World of Causes*. Cambridge, MA: MIT Press.

Eskine, J.K., Kacinik, A.N. and Prinz, J.J. (2011). "A Bad Taste in the Mouth: Gustatory Disgust Influences Moral Judgment." *Psychological Science*, 22: 295–9.

Falk, W.D. (1947–48). "'Ought' and Motivation." *Proceedings of the Aristotelian Society*, 48: 492–510. Reprinted in W.D. Falk (1986). *Ought, Reasons, and Morality*. Ithaca, NY: Cornell University Press, pp. 21–41.

Fieser, James (1992). "Hume's Classification of the Passions and Its Precursors." *Hume Studies*, 18: 1–17.

Foot, Philippa (1978). "Hume on Moral Judgment." In *Virtues and Vices and Other Essays in Moral Philosophy*. Berkeley, CA: University of California Press, pp. 74–80.

Frank, R.H. (1988). *Passions Within Reason*. New York: WW Norton.

Garrett, Don (1997). *Cognition and Commitment in Hume's Philosophy*. New York: Oxford University Press.

Garrett, Don (2006). "Hume's Naturalistic Theory of Representation," *Synthese* 152: 301–19.

Garrett, Don (2015). *Hume*. New York: Routledge.

Gill, Michael B. (2006). *The British Moralists on Human Nature and the Birth of Secular Ethics*. New York: Cambridge University Press.

Greene, J.D., Sommerville, R.B., Nystrom, L.E., Darley, J.M., and Cohen, J.D. (2001). "An fMRI Investigation of Emotional Engagement in Moral Judgment." *Science*, 293: 2105–8.

Hampton, Jean (1995). "Does Hume Have an Instrumental Conception of Practical Reason?" *Hume Studies*, 21: 57–74.

Harris, James (2005). *Of Liberty and Necessity: The Free Will Debate in Eighteenth-Century British Philosophy*. Oxford: Clarendon Press.

Harris, James (2009). "A Compleat Chain of Reasoning: Hume's Project in *A Treatise of Human Nature*, Books One and Two." *Proceedings of the Aristotelian Society*, 109: 129–48.

Harris, James (2013). "The Government of the Passions." In James Harris (Ed.), *The Oxford Handbook of British Philosophy in the Eighteenth Century*. Oxford: Oxford University Press, pp. 270–88.

Hearn, Thomas Jr. (1973). "Árdal on the Moral Sentiments in Hume's *Treatise*." *Philosophy*, 48: 288–92.

Heekeren, H., Wartenburger, I., Schmidt, H., Schwintowski, H., and Villringer, A. (2003). "An fMRI Study of Simple Ethical Decision-Making." *Neuroreport*, 14: 1215–19.

Immerwahr, John (1992). "Hume on Tranquillizing the Passions." *Hume Studies*, 28: 293–314.

Immerwahr, John (1994). "Hume's *Dissertation on the Passions*." *Journal of the History of Philosophy* 32: 225–40.

Inoue, Haruko (Unpublished). "The Ambiguity in Hume's Distinction between the Calm and the Violent Passions." Presented to the 39th International Hume Society Conference. University of Calgary, July 2012.

James, Susan (1997). *Passion and Action: The Emotions in Seventeenth-Century Philosophy*. Oxford: Clarendon Press.

James, Susan (2006). "The Passions and the Good Life." In Donald Rutherford (Ed.), *The Cambridge Companion to Early Modern Philosophy*. New York: Cambridge University Press, pp. 198–220.

James, Susan (2012). "The Passions in Metaphysics and the Theory of Action." In Daniel Garber and Michael Ayers (Eds.), *The Cambridge History of Seventeenth-Century Philosophy*. Cambridge: Cambridge University Press, pp. 913–49. Available from Cambridge Histories Online http://dx.doi.org/10.1017/CHOL9780521307635.029[Accessed 23 January 2015].

Jensen, Henning (1971). *Motivation and the Moral Sense in Francis Hutcheson's Ethical Theory*. The Hague: Martinus Nijhoff.

Jones, Peter (1982). *Hume's Sentiments: Their Ciceronian and French Context*. Edinburgh: Edinburgh University Press.

Kail, P.J.E. (2007a). *Projection and Realism in Hume's Philosophy*. New York: Oxford University Press.

Kail, P.J.E. (2007b). "On Hume's Appropriation of Malebranche: Causation and Self." *European Journal of Philosophy*, 16: 55–80.

Kail, P.J.E. (2008). "Hume, Malebranche and 'Rationalism'." *Philosophy*, 83: 311–32.

Karlsson, Mikael (2000). "Rational Ends: Humean and Non-Humean Considerations." *Sats-Nordic Journal of Philosophy*, 1: 15–47.

Karlsson, Mikael (2001). "Cognition, Desire and Motivation: 'Humean' and 'non-Humean' Considerations." *Sats-Nordic Journal of Philosophy*, 2: 30–58.

Karlsson, Mikael (2006). "Reason, Passion, and the Influencing Motives of the Will." In Saul Traiger (Ed.), *The Blackwell Guide to Hume's* Treatise. Malden, MA: Blackwell, pp 235–55.

Keltner, Dacher and Haidt, Jonathan (1999). "Social Functions of Emotions at Four Levels of Analysis." *Cognition and Emotion*, 13: 505–21.

Kemp Smith, Norman (1941). *The Philosophy of David Hume*. London: Macmillan and Co.

Kopajtic, Lauren (2015). "Cultivating Strength of Mind: Hume on the Government of the Passions and Artificial Virtue." *Hume Studies*, 41: 201–29.

Korsgaard, Christine M. (1991). "The General Point of View: Love and Moral Approval in Hume's Ethics." *Hume Studies*, 25: 3–41.
Korsgaard, Christine M. (1986). "Skepticism about Practical Reason." *Journal of Philosophy*, 83: 5–25. In Christine Korsgaard (1996). *Creating the Kingdom of Ends*. Cambridge: Cambridge University Press.
Kydd, Rachel (1946). *Reason and Conduct in Hume's Treatise*. London: Oxford University Press.
Lance, Mark and McAdam, Matthew (2005). "Review of Dancy, Jonathan, *Practical Reality*." *Ethics*, 115: 393–6.
Lecaldano, Eugenio (2003). "The Passions, Character, and the Self in Hume." *Hume Studies*, 28: 175–93.
Lloyd, Genevieve (1998). "Rationalizing the Passions." In Stephen Gaukroger (Ed.), *The Soft Underbelly of Reason: The Passions in the Seventeenth Century*. London: Routledge, pp. 34–45.
Loeb, Louis (1977). "Hume's Moral Sentiments and the Structure of the *Treatise*." *Journal of the History of Philosophy*, 15: 395–403.
Loeb, Louis (2002). *Stability and Justification in Hume's Treatise*. Oxford: Oxford University Press.
Loeb, Louis (2009). "What is Worth Preserving in the Kemp Smith Interpretation of Hume?" *British Journal for the History of Philosophy*, 17: 769–97.
Mackie, J.L. (1980). *Hume's Moral Theory*. London: Routledge & Kegan Paul.
Magri, Tito (2008). "Hume on the Direct Passions and Motivation." In Elizabeth S. Radcliffe (Ed.), *A Companion to Hume*. Malden, MA: Blackwell, pp. 185–200.
Marušić, Jennifer Smalligan (2010). "Does Hume Hold a Dispositional Account of Belief?" *Canadian Journal of Philosophy*, 40: 155–83.
McCarty, Richard (2012). "Humean Courage." In Ilya Kasavine and Evgeny Blinov (Eds.), *David Hume and Contemporary Philosophy: Legacy and Prospects*. Newcastle upon Tyne: Cambridge Scholars Publishing, pp. 277–87.
McIntyre, Jane L. (1989). "Personal Identity and the Passions." *Journal of the History of Philosophy*, 27: 545–57.
McIntyre, Jane L. (2000). "Hume's Passions: Direct and Indirect." *Hume Studies*, 26: 77–86.
McIntyre, Jane L. (2006a). "Hume's 'New and Extraordinary' Account of the Passions." In Saul Traiger (Ed.), *The Blackwell Guide to Hume's Treatise*. Oxford: Blackwell, pp. 199–215.
McIntyre, Jane L. (2006b). "Strength of Mind: Problems and Prospects for a Humean Account." *Synthese*, 152: 393–401.
McIntyre, Jane L. (2012). "The Idea of the Self in the Evolution of Hume's Account of the Passions." *The Canadian Journal of Philosophy*, 42: 171–82.
Mele, Alfred R. (2003). *Motivation and Agency*. Oxford: Oxford University Press.
Mercer, Philip (1972). *Sympathy and Ethics*. Oxford: Clarendon Press.
Merivale, Amyas (2009). "Hume's Mature Account of the Indirect Passions." *Hume Studies*, 25: 185–210.
Millgram, Elijah (1995). "Was Hume a Humean?" *Hume Studies*, 21: 75–94.
Millican, Peter (2002). "The Context, Aims, and Structure of Hume's First *Enquiry*." In Peter Millican (Ed.), *Reading Hume on Human Understanding*. Oxford: Clarendon Press, pp. 27–65.
Moll, J., de Oliveira-Souza, R., Eslinger, P.J., Bramati, I.E., Mourao-Miranda, J., Andreiuolo, P.A., et al. (2002). "The Neural Correlates of Moral Sensitivity: A Functional Magnetic

Resonance Imagine Investigation of Basic and Moral Emotions." *Journal of Neuroscience,* 22: 2730–6.

Moore, James (1995). "Hume and Hutcheson." In Stewart, M.A. and Wright, John (Eds.), *Hume and Hume's Connexions.* University Park, PA: Pennsylvania State University Press, pp. 23–57.

Nadler, Steven (2006). *Spinoza's Ethics: An Introduction.* New York: Cambridge University Press.

Nagel, Thomas (1970). *The Possibility of Altruism.* Oxford: Clarendon Press.

Nesse, R. (1990). "Evolutionary Explanations of Emotions." *Human Nature,* 1: 261–89.

Nichols, S. (2002). "How Psychopaths Threaten Moral Rationalism: Is It Irrational to be Amoral?" *The Monist,* 85: 285–304.

Norton, David Fate (1982). *David Hume: Common Sense Moralist, Skeptical Metaphysician.* Princeton, NJ: Princeton University Press.

Norton, David Fate (2000). "Editor's Introduction." In David Fate Norton and Mary J. Norton (Eds.), David Hume, *A Treatise of Human Nature.* New York: Oxford University Press, pp. *I*19–*I*99.

Norton, David Fate (2005). "Hutcheson and Hume: The Question of Influence." *Oxford Studies in Early Modern Philosophy,* 2: 211–56.

Norton, David Fate and Norton, Mary J., (Eds.) (2007). David Hume, *A Treatise of Human Nature, A Critical Edition,* Vol. 1. Oxford: Clarendon Press.

Ogden, C. K. and Richards, I. A. (1923). *The Meaning of Meaning.* New York: Harcourt, Brace & Jovanovich.

Owen, David (1999). *Hume's Reason.* New York: Oxford University Press.

Owen, David (2016). "Reason, Belief and the Passions." In Paul Russell (Ed.), *The Oxford Handbook of David Hume.* New York: Oxford University Press, pp. 133–55.

Passmore, J.A. (1951). *Ralph Cudworth: An Interpretation.* Cambridge: Cambridge University Press.

Passmore, J.A. (1968). *Hume's Intentions.* Rev. Ed. New York: Basic Books.

Paxman, Katharina (2015). "Imperceptible Impressions and Disorder in the Soul: A Characterization of the Distinction between Calm and Violent Passions in Hume." *Journal of Scottish Philosophy,* 13: 265–78.

Penelhum, Terence (1975). *Hume.* Basingstoke: Macmillan.

Penelhum, Terence (1976). "Self-Identity and Self-Regard." In Amelie Oksenberg Rorty (Ed.), *The Identities of Persons.* Berkeley, CA: University of California Press: 253–80. Repr. in T. Penelhum, *Themes in Hume: The Self, the Will, Religion.* Oxford: Clarendon Press, 2000, pp. 61–87.

Penelhum, Terence (1992a). *David Hume: An Introduction to his Philosophical System.* West Lafayette, IN: Purdue University Press.

Penelhum, Terence (1992b). "The Self of Book 1 and the Selves of Book 2." *Hume Studies,* 27: 281–91. Reprinted in T. Penelhum, *Themes in Hume: The Self, the Will, Religion.* Oxford: Clarendon Press, 2000, pp. 88–98.

Pigden, Charles (2009). "If Not Non-cognitivism, Then What?" In C. Pigden (Ed.), *Hume on Motivation and Virtue.* New York: Palgrave Macmillan, pp. 80–104.

Popkin, Richard (1979). "Hume and Spinoza." *Hume Studies,* 5: 65–93.

Postema, Gerald (2005). "'Cemented with Diseased Qualities': Sympathy and Comparison in Hume's Moral Psychology." *Hume Studies,* 31: 249–98.

Prinz, Jesse (2015). "An Empirical Case for Motivational Internalism." In Gunnar Björnsson, Fredrik Björklund, Caj Strandberg, John Eriksson, and Ragnar Francén Olinder (Eds.), *Motivational Internalism*. New York: Oxford University Press, pp. 61–84.

Purviance, Susan M. (1997). "The Moral Self and the Indirect Passions." *Hume Studies*, 23: 195–212.

Qu, Hsueh (2012). "The Simple Duality: Humean Passions." *The Canadian Journal of Philosophy*, 42: 98–116.

Radcliffe, Elizabeth S. (1996). "How Does the Humean Sense of Duty Motivate?" *Journal of the History of Philosophy*, 34: 47–70.

Radcliffe, Elizabeth S. (1997). "Kantian Tunes on A Humean Instrument: Why Hume Is Not Really a Skeptic About Practical Reasoning." *The Canadian Journal of Philosophy*, 27: 247–69.

Radcliffe, Elizabeth S. (1999). "Hume on the Generation of Motives: Why Beliefs Alone Never Motivate." *Hume Studies*, 25: 101–22.

Radcliffe, Elizabeth S. (2004). "Love and Benevolence in Hutcheson's and Hume's Theories of the Passions." *British Journal for the History of Philosophy*, 12: 631–53.

Radcliffe, Elizabeth S. (2006). "Moral Internalism and Moral Cognitivism in Hume's Metaethics." *Synthese*, 152: 353–70.

Radcliffe, Elizabeth S. (2008). "The Humean Theory of Motivation and its Critics." In Elizabeth S. Radcliffe (Ed.), *A Companion to Hume*. Malden, MA: Blackwell, pp. 477–92.

Radcliffe, Elizabeth S. (2012a) "Hume and the Passions as Original Existences." In Lorenzo Greco and Alessio Vaccari (Eds.), *Hume Readings*. Rome: Edizioni di Storia e Letteratura, pp. 211–31.

Radcliffe, Elizabeth S. (2012b). "The Inertness of Reason and Hume's Legacy." *The Canadian Journal of Philosophy*, 42 (supplement 1): 117–33.

Radcliffe, Elizabeth S. (2015a). "Strength of Mind and the Calm and Violent Passions." *Res Philosophica*, 92: 1–21.

Radcliffe, Elizabeth S. (2015b). "Hume's Psychology of the Passions: The Literature and Future Directions." *Journal of the History of Philosophy*, 53: 565–606.

Radcliffe, Elizabeth S. (2017). "Alcali and Acid, Oil and Vinegar: Hume on Contrary Passions." In Alix Cohen and Robert Stern (Eds.), *Thinking about the Emotions: A Philosophical History*. Oxford: Oxford University Press, pp. 150–71.

Rorty, Amélie Oksenberg (1990). "'Pride Produces the Idea of Self': Hume on Moral Agency." *Australasian Journal of Philosophy*, 68: 255–69.

Sandis, Constantine (2012). "Action, Reason, and the Passions." In Alan Bailey and Dan O'Brien (Eds.), *The Continuum Companion to Hume*. New York: Continuum, pp. 199–213.

Sayre-McCord, Geoffrey (2008). "Practical Morality and Inert Reason." In Russ Shafer-Landau (Ed.), *Oxford Studies in Metaethics*. Oxford: Oxford University Press, 299–320.

Schafer, Karl (2008). "Practical Reasons and Practical Reasoning in Hume." *Hume Studies*, 34: 189–208.

Schmitt, Frederick (2014). *Hume's Epistemology in the Treatise: A Veritistic Interpretation*. Oxford: Oxford University Press.

Schmitter, Amy M. (2009). "Making an Object of Yourself: On the Intentionality of the Passions in Hume." In Jon Miller (Ed.), *Topics in Early Modern Philosophy of Mind*. Dordrecht: Springer, pp. 223–40.

Schmitter, Amy M. (2016). "17th and 18th Century Theories of Emotions." In Edward N. Zalta (Ed.), *The Stanford Encyclopedia of Philosophy* (Winter 2016 Edition). Stanford, CA: Stanford University Press. URL <https://plato.stanford.edu/archives/win2016/entries/emotions-17th18th/>.

Schnall, S., Haidt, J, Clore, G., and Jordan, A. (2008). "Disgust as Embodied Moral Judgment." *Personality and Social Psychology Bulletin*, 34: 1096–109.

Schroeder, Mark (2007). *Slaves of the Passions*. New York: Oxford University Press.

Selby-Bigge, L. A. (1975). "Introduction." In L. A. Selby-Bigge (Ed.), David Hume, *Enquiries concerning Human Understanding and concerning the Principles of Morals*. 3rd ed., P.H. Nidditch (Rev.). Oxford: Clarendon Press, pp. vii–xxi.

Sinhababu, Neil (2009). "The Humean Theory of Motivation Reformulated and Defended." *The Philosophical Review*, 118: 465–500.

Sinhababu, Neil (2013). "The Belief-Desire Account of Intention Explains Everything." *Nous*, 47: 680–96.

Sinhababu, Neil (2017). *Humean Nature: How Desire Explains Action, Thought, and Feeling*. Oxford: Oxford University Press.

Smith, Michael (1994). *The Moral Problem*. Oxford: Blackwell.

Sobel, David and Copp, David (2001). "Against Direction of Fit Accounts of Belief and Desire." *Analysis* 61: 44–53.

Solomon, Robert (1990) *A Passion for Justice*. Reading, MA: Addison-Wesley.

Stevenson, C. L. (1944). *Ethics and Language*. New Haven, CT: Yale University Press.

Stroud, Barry (1977). *Hume*. London: Routledge & Kegan Paul.

Sturgeon, Nicholas (2008). "Hume's Metaethics: Is Hume a Moral Noncognitivist?" In Elizabeth S. Radcliffe (Ed.), *A Companion to Hume*. Malden, MA: Blackwell, pp. 513–28.

Sturgeon, Nicholas (2015). "Hume on Reason and Passion." In Donald Ainslie and Annemarie Butler (Eds.), *The Cambridge Companion to Hume's Treatise*. Cambridge: Cambridge University Press, pp. 252–82.

Tangney, J. P., Miller, R. S., Flicker, L., and Barlow, D. H. (1996). "Are Shame, Guilt, and Embarrassment Distinct Emotions?" *Journal of Personality and Social Psychology*, 70: 1256–69.

Taylor, Jacqueline (2008). "Hume's Later Moral Philosophy." In David Fate Norton and Jacqueline Taylor (Eds.), *The Cambridge Companion to Hume*, 2nd ed. Cambridge: Cambridge University Press, pp. 311–40.

Taylor, Jacqueline (2015a). *Reflecting Subjects: Passion, Sympathy and Society in Hume's Philosophy*. Oxford: Oxford University Press.

Taylor, Jacqueline (2015b). "Sympathy, Self, and Others." In Donald Ainslie and Annemarie Butler (Eds.), *The Cambridge Companion to Hume's Treatise*. Cambridge: Cambridge University Press, pp. 188–205.

Traiger, Saul (1987). "Impressions, Ideas, and Fictions." *Hume Studies*, 13: 381–99.

Traiger, Saul (2005). "Reason Unhinged." In Joyce Jenkins, Jennifer Whiting, and Christopher Williams (Eds.), *Person and Passions: Essays in Honor of Annette Baier*. Notre Dame: University of Notre Dame Press, pp. 100–16.

van Roojen, Mark (1995). "Humean Motivation and Humean Rationality." *Philosophical Studies*, 79: 37–57.

van Roojen, Mark (2015). "Moral Cognitivism vs. Non-Cognitivism." In Edward N. Zalta (Ed.), *The Stanford Encyclopedia of Philosophy* (Fall 2015 Edition). Stanford, CA:

Stanford University Press. URL <http://plato.stanford.edu/archives/fall2015/entries/moral-cognitivism/>.
Weller, Cass (2002). "The Myth of Original Existence." *Hume Studies*, 28: 195–230.
Weller, Cass (2004). "Scratched Fingers, Ruined Lives, and Acknowledged Lesser Goods." *Hume Studies*, 30: 51–85.
Wheatley, T. and Haidt, J. (2005). "Hypnotically Induced Disgust Makes Moral Judgments More Severe." *Psychological Science*, 16: 780–4.
Wiggins, David (1995). "Categorical Requirements: Kant and Hume on the Idea of Duty." In Rosalind Hursthouse (Ed.), *Virtues and Reasons: Philippa Foot and Moral Theory*. New York: Clarendon Press, pp. 297–330.
Williams, Bernard (1979). "Internal and External Reasons." In Ross Harrison (Ed.), *Rational Action*. Cambridge: Cambridge University Press, pp. 17–28. Repr. in B. Williams, *Moral Luck*. Cambridge: Cambridge University Press, 1981, pp. 101–13.
Zimmerman, Aaron (2007). "Hume's Reasons." *Hume Studies*, 33: 211–56.

Index

abstract (general) ideas 140–1
action(s):
  belief as a disposition to 79–80
  belief as a motive to 2–3, 39–50, 50–9, 84
  effect of strength of belief on 178–82
  and feeling of volition 27
  irrational, unreasonable 87–8, 104–11
  morality as a motive to 11, 112–19
  necessity of passion to 6, 27, 59–64, 89–93
  reasonable 11, 16, 104–11
  reason as motive to 5, 8–9, 30–3, 34–8, 85–8
  responsibility for 7
  as a result of competing motives 10, 16, 28, 146–51
  and the self 185–7
  as signs of character 119, 124, 191
  theory of reasons for 15–16
  see also belief-desire model; Moral-Discernment Interpretation; motives; motivation; Natural-Motive Interpretation
acclimation of passions 171–2
active principles 37, 49, 52, 62–3
Ainslie, Donald 17n6, 123n14, 187n6
Alanen, Lilli 103–4, 101n11, 199n2, 199n3
annexing 76–7
Anscombe, G. E. M. 81
approbation and disapprobation:
  as moral sentiments 60, 122
  as motives 122–3, 128–33
  as pleasure and pain, respectively 126–8
  as sentiments 78
Árdal, Páll 102n13, 131n22, 149nn5,6, 156, 187–9
Aristotle 4, 212
association of ideas and impressions 20, 151, 183, 192, *see also* double relation (association) of ideas and impressions
association of impressions and ideas,
  see association of ideas and impressions
Ayloffe, William 4, 30, 51, 113, 206

Baier, Annette 2n2, 4nn6,7, 29, 93, 100, 108, 146, 152, 189–91, 194–5
Barlow, D.H. 94n3
Beauchamp, Tom 191–2
belief:
  dependence upon impressions 78–9
  as dispositional 79–80
  formation, causes of 68–72, 145
  Hume's Theory of 10
  liveliness, force, vivacity of 68, 72–80, 95
  as a manner of conception 76–7
  objects of 86
  as representation 68
  as sentiment 35, 42, 72–9
  see also conviction
belief and custom (habit) 69–74
belief and desire 81–4
belief-desire model 1, 12, 29, 39, 43, 81–3, 88n21, 137, 143
belief and motivation 39–64, 77–8
beliefs:
  about good and evil 41
  inactive alone 50–9
  moral 12, 138, 142–3, 145
  as motives 2–3, 8–9, 39–50
  non-inferential 40–1, 43n15
  as products of reasoning 41
Bell, Martin 75
besires 82n18
Bittner, Rüdiger 81, 85–7
Blackburn, Simon 138n25
Botros, Sophie 34, 38
Bragge, Francis (Vicar of Hitchin) 4, 30–1, 51, 113, 206
Brandt, Richard 127n20
Brett, Nathan 37n6
Bricke, John 10, 15n3, 24, 29, 81, 94–6
Brown, Charlotte 124n15
Buckle, Stephen 75n13, 194–5
Burghope, M. 113, 206
Burnet, Gilbert 212–13
Butler, Bishop Joseph 4, 185

calm passions 12, 17–18, 147–51, 167–78, 189
  in Hutcheson 211
  mistaken for reason 21, 110, 148, 151
  and moral sentiment 126
  and strength of mind 110–11, 146–7, 160–7
  see also violent passions
Capaldi, Nicholas 183–4
Carlson, Åsa 187n6
causal reasoning 8, 17–18, 33–9, 44n16, 48n22, 68–72, 74–5, 79, 91, 142
character 110, 119, 124–5, 127–8, 132–4, 139, 142–5, 185, 187
character deficiency and motivation 127–30, 132–4
Charleton, Walter (M.D.) 4, 198n1
Cicero, four primitive passions 18

Clarke, Samuel 4, 6, 31–2, 51, 63, 114, 117n9, 209–11
Coeffeteau, Nicolas 4, 197
cognitivism, moral 11–12, 137–8, 143
Cohon, Rachel 22n12, 41, 43n15, 44n16, 45, 100, 101n10, 189n10
Collier, Mark 99n8
common point of view 2, 112, 137, 140
comparison 155–9, 173
  and greatness of mind 171–3
contrariety of passions 152–5
conversion of passions 152
conviction:
  degree of 47–8
  strength of 178–82
Copp, David 82n19
copy(ing) 66–8, 95
Costelloe, Timothy 60n31
courage 165
Cudworth, Ralph 6, 31, 38, 50, 63, 113, 207–9
Cureau de La Chambre, Marin 4
custom (habit) and belief 69–74

Dancy, Jonathan 43n15
Darwall, Stephen 117
Davidson, Donald 103
deliberation 31, 50, 85, 134, 208
demonstration, demonstrative reasoning 8, 33–6, 38
Descartes, Rene 4, 5, 50, 70, 113, 198–200
desire(s) 6–7, 9n11, 17
  and causal strength 46–9
  in Cudworth 208
  definitive of motives in Hume 10, 14, 15n3, 24–7, 128–30, 189n10
  in Descartes 198n1, 199
  and direction of fit 81–4
  as a direct passion 19, 21, 24, 189n10, 192
  in Hobbes 127
  in Hutcheson 211–13
  Locke's characterization of 126–7, 204–5
  in Malebranche 200, 201n5
  mistaking one's own 97
  and pleasure (natural good) 18, 39–43, 48–9, 51–5, 59–60, 62–4, 153
  and representational content 94
  in Reynolds 197
  second-order 128
  in Spinoza 202–3
  see also belief-desire model, direction of fit
direct passions 7, 9n11, 18–24
  as motives 10, 24–8
direction of fit 11, 81–4, 94
disapprobation, see approbation and disapprobation
discernment, moral 121–4, 128, 142
dispositions 31, 35, 37, 54n26, 55–62

Dissertation on the Passions 60–3, 183, 191–4
double relation (association) of ideas and impressions 19–20, 102, 131–2, 149, 192
double relation (association) of impressions and ideas, see double relation (association) of ideas and impressions
Dretske, Fred 99
duty (sense of) 116, 118–20, 124, 127–9, 134, 137, 161n16

envy 158
evaluation, moral 121
evidence, moral 116–17
existence (agent) internalism 117–22
extensive sympathy 135–6, 191n11
externalism, moral 116, 124–5, see also internalism, moral

faculty psychology 208
fear 100
fictions 143–5
Fieser, James 149n7
Flicker, L. 94n3
Foot, Philippa 123n13, 138n25
fortitude 162, 165–6
Frank, R.H. 94n3

Garrett, Don 59n30, 67–8, 78n16, 95n5, 140
general point of view, see common point of view
Gill, Michael 207
good and evil 22–3, 41–2, 47–9, 54n26, 56–7, 60–3
good:
  and desire in Locke 204–5
  and desire in Spinoza 202–3
  general appetite for 21–4, 28, 52, 54, 126, 148–9, 189
  God-instilled proclivity to (in rationalism) 30–2, 50, 63, 197, 200, 201n5, 206, 208
  greater and lesser 48, 107–10
  inclination or instinct to 23–4, 28, 31–2
  of others 155–8, 161, (in Hutcheson) 212–13
  passions as representations of 5, 15, 49n24, 50, 51, 89–90, 93, 111–13
  pleasure as appearance of (Hobbes) 127n20
  proximity of and effect on motivation 146, 151–3, 154, 161, 163–70, 172–4
  role in producing passions 18, 21–2, 26, 60–2, 151–4, 198
  see also pleasure and pain; prospect of pleasure
governance of the passions 4, 31, 194, 197–8, see also moderation (regulation) of the passions; self-regulation of the passions

greatness of mind 171–2
Grove, Henry 4

Haidt, Jonathan 93n3
Harris, James 4n5, 175, 206, 210n16, 211
hatred, *see* love (and hatred)
Hearn, Jr., Thomas 131n22
Hobbes, Thomas 4, 6, 7, 7n10, 92, 116, 118, 127, 203–4
human nature 3, 9, 13–14, 19, 35, 43, 49, 51, 59, 62, 69, 71, 72, 116, 119–21, 124, 139, 144, 155, 157, 161, 175, 176–7, 179, 183, 188, 190, 195, 197, 211
Humean Theory of Motivation 1, 15, 39, 42, 128, *see also* belief-desire model
Humeanism 16
humility, *see* pride, humility
Hutcheson, Francis 6, 126, 147, 175n21, 185, 211–13

ideas 39–42, 44, 47–8, 50–6, 61
  association of 20, 151, 192
  of morality 3, 12, 138–45
  see also abstract (general) ideas
imagination 144, 153–4
Immerwahr, John 165n19, 171n20, 191, 193–4
impressions:
  association of 20, 151, 192
  of reflection 7n10, 17–20, 39–42, 51–6, 66, 99
  as representations 67–8
  of sensation 7n9, 17–18, 53, 67–8, 88, 99–100, 129n21, 144
imprudence 109–10
indirect passions 10–11, 14, 18–21, 93, 184
  and calm-violent distinction 149
  in the *Dissertation* 192–3
  and moral sentiments 131–2, 188–9
  as motives 24–8
  and the self 184–6
  structural conception of 101–3
Inoue, Haroku 150n8
instincts:
  natural 18, 21–4
  as passions 48, 51–5, 59–63, 148
internalism, moral 115–34, *see also* judgment (appraiser) internalism; existence (agent) internalism

James, Susan 4n5, 198–9, 204, 206n11
joy 133
judgment (appraiser) internalism 117, 122
judgments, moral 121, 137, 142
justice:
  and limits to self-regulation 176–7
  virtue of 116, 118, 125, 127, 134–6

Kail, P.J.E. 41, 45–6, 47–8, 54n26
Kant, Immanuel 3
Karlsson, Mikael 42–3
Keltner, Dacher 93n3
Kemp Smith, Norman 14, 131n22, 149n5, 183, 184, 187–9
knave, sensible 164
Kopajtic, Lauren 176n22
Korsgaard, Christine 116, 118, 189n9
Kydd, Rachel 34, 37–8

Lance, Mark 43n15
Leibniz, Gottfried Wilhelm 4
Lecaldano, Eugenio 186–7
Lloyd, Genevieve 201
Locke, John 4, 6, 70, 79, 92, 114, 126, 127n19, 185, 204–5
Loeb, Louis 79, 83, 131n22, 147n3, 149, 188n7
love (and hatred) 102, 131, 156, 158, 189
  as reactive attitudes 28

Mackie, J.L. 123n13, 138n25
Magri, Tito 27
Malebranche, Nicolas 4, 5, 6, 50, 200–1
malice 156–7
Mandeville, Bernard 4, 175, 211
Marušić, Jennifer Smalligan 79–80
maxim, Hume's (undoubted) 119, 121, 124, 161, 166
McAdam, Matthew 43n15
McCarty, Richard 165
McIntyre, Jane 4n5, 166, 168, 174–5, 171n20, 185–6
Mele, Alfred 82n19
Mercer, Philip 155n13, 187
Merivale, Amyas 101n12
Mill, John Stuart 116
Miller, R.S. 94n3
Millican, Peter 75n13
mind, strength of, *see* strength of mind
moderation of the passions, *see* regulation (moderation) of the passions
moral beliefs 3, 12, 138–42
moral concepts 3, 139–45
moral discernment 121–4, 128, 142
Moral-Discernment Interpretation 121–37
moral internalism, *see* internalism, moral
moral sense 125–6, 136, 189
  and Hutcheson 212–13
moral sentimentalism 2, 11–12, 137–8, 142, 184
moral sentiments 2, 112, 115
  as direct passions 132
  and indirect passions 131–2, 188–9
  as motivating 118–23, 125–9, 131–5, 137, 143
  as source of moral ideas 138–43
morality, rationalist view of 30–2, 63–4

Motivation Argument 1, 2, 11, 49, 112–15, 119, 122–3, 128, 135, 143
motivation:
  and belief 39–64
  and causal strength 46–9, 146–7, 168–9
  and degree of conviction 47
  Hume's reference to 35
  moral 137
  and moral discernment 128
  and pleasure and pain 39, 126–30
  source of 61
  see also action(s); desires, definitive of motives in Hume; Motivation Argument; motivational dynamics; motives; passions; prospect of pleasure (and pain)
motivational dynamics 3, 146–7, 195, *see also* acclimation of passions; calm passions; comparison; contrariety of passions; conversion of passions; conviction; governance of the passions; greatness of mind; neutralizing passions; regulation (moderation) of the passions; self-regulation of the passions; strength of mind; sympathy; violent passions
motives:
  as causes 15–16
  and passions 24–8
  and reasons 15–16, 29–30

Nadler, Steven 202n6, 203
Nagel, Thomas 115–16, 118
Natural-Motive Interpretation 119–21
nausea 92–3
Neo-Kantians 90
Nesse, R. 94n3
neutralizing passions 172

obligation, sense of 118–19, 122
original existences 11, 32, 84–5, 89–93
Owen, David 41–2, 44–5, 48n23, 69n5

passions:
  caused by impressions or ideas 100
  and comparison 155–9
  Hume's theory of 17–21
  and imagination 153–4
  mechanistic account of 5
  motivating 128
  as motives (conations) 15, 24–8, 68
  object-directedness (intentionality) of 93, 96, 99, 101–2
  as original existences 90–2, 95–6
  as phenomenal 96–101
  potential to become virtues 30–1
  and reason 12–13, 32, 177, 209
  reasonableness of 104–10
  as sensations 96–101

  signature role of 195
  Stoic classification of 18
  strength of 147–51, 168–9
  structural conception of 99, 101–4
  and understanding 152–5
  violence, force of 168–9
  see also calm passions; contrariety of passions; conversion of passions; direct passions; governance of the passions; indirect passions; primary and secondary passions; regulation (moderation) of the passions; self-regulation of the passions; violent passions
Passmore, John 183–4, 207, 208
Paxman, Katharina 37n6, 151n9
Penelhum, Terrence 93, 102n13, 149n5, 186n5
personal identity 20n9, 184–5, 190, 195, *see also* self, problem of
Pigden, Charles 41
pity 135, 156–7
Plato on desire and reason 88n21
pleasure, prospect of, *see* prospect of pleasure
pleasure and pain:
  and motivation 39
  as motives 126–30
  as sentiments 52
  see also prospect of pleasure
politician(s) 125, 136, 152
Postema, Gerald 156–7, 159
practical reason, reasoning 3, 15, 16, 38, 43n14
  in Hobbes 203–4
  in Hutcheson 147, 212–13
  in Spinoza 203
pride, humility 102, 131–3, 173, 187–91
  as moral sentiments 131–2, 188–9
  and the self 19–20
  as reactive attitudes 28
  see also indirect passions
primary and secondary passions 150
Prinz, Jesse 117n7
probability 179–81
propositions, as objects of reason 84–5
prospect of pleasure (and pain) 15, 22, 33, 43n14, 51–5, 97, 100, 109, 128
  in Locke 127n19
prudence 165

Qu, Hsueh 103n15

rationalists 15, 32, 44, 49–51
reactive attitudes 25
reason:
  as calm passion 110, 148, 151
  as discovery of truth or falsity 91
  faculty of 41–2, 44–6, 91
  and impulses to action 8, 90
  inertness of 1, 2, 10–11, 33–8, 41, 46, 205

in moderating the passions 177–8
never opposed to passions 8, 11
objects of 84–6
and passion 8, 11, 36
practical 15
probabilistic 8, 69n5, 78
propositions as objects of 84–6
as slave to the passions 178
as source of Good 111
see also causal reasoning; demonstration, demonstrative reason
reasons and motives 15–16, 33–8
reflection, impressions of 7n10, 17–20, 66
reflexion 17n6, 147n4
regulation (moderation) of the passions 4–6, 146–7, 167–78, 197–8, *see also* governance of the passions; self-regulation of the passions
religion 193–4
religion and morality 194–5
representation(s):
    beliefs as 9, 59, 65–7, 88
    of good (rationalists) 50–1, 63, 82n18, 111
    ideas as 39, 65–7, 138
    impressions of sensation as 67–8
    of morality 114–15, 143
    not a function of passion 32, 89, 90–3, 95–6, 100–1, 103n14
    not motivating 61, 88
    passions as (rationalists' view) 5–6, 11, 31, (Baier's view) 93, 198–9, 205
resemblance 66–7
Reynolds, Edward 4, 5, 6, 51, 146, 197
Rorty, Amélie 186

Sandis, Constantine 42, 48n23, 50
Sayre-McCord, Geoff 115n5
Schafer, Karl 164n18
Schmitt, Frederick 83n20
Schmitter, Amy 103n14, 201
self:
    Descartes on 198
    and indirect passions in general 25, 93, 99
    and pride or humility 20–1, 102–3, 125, 131–3, 185–7
    problem of 13, 143–4, 184–7, 190, 195
    qualities useful to 165–6
    and sympathy 155n13
self-approbation:
    and motivation 133–7
    and pride 131–3
self-disapprobation:
    and humility 131–3
    and motivation 125–33
    as self-hatred 125–6
self-esteem 133n23, 172–4, 185
self-hatred 124–6, 129

self-interest 110, 115–16, 123, 129, 135, 140, 146, 151, 160–7, 169, 177, 182
    Clarke on 31, 51, 209
    Hobbes on 203
    Hutcheson on 211–13
    Malebranche on 200
    Mandeville on 211
self-love 141, 166
self-regulation of the passions 50, 171, 175–8, *see also* governance of the passions; regulation (moderation) of the passions
self-survey 125
Senault, Jean-François 4, 30–2, 146, 171, 197
sense of duty, *see* duty, sense of
sentiment of humanity 2, 141
sentiment(s) 2, 3, 12, 51, 59–64, 78, 98
    and Cudworth 208
    see also pleasure and pain; moral sentiments; sentiment of belief
sentiment as a capacity 35, 61
sentiment of belief 10, 42, 65, 72–9, 84–5
sentimentalism, *see* moral sentimentalism
Shaftesbury, Lord (Anthony Ashley Cooper, 3rd Earl of) 4, 6, 175n21, 211
Smith, Michael 29, 81, 97, 137
Sobel, David 82n19
Solomon, Robert 94n3
Spinoza, Baruch 4, 5, 6, 201–3
strength of mind 12, 111, 146–7, 160–4
    fit with Hume's theory of the virtues 165–7
    how to cultivate 170–7
Stroud, Barry 42, 79, 84, 97–9
Sturgeon, Nicholas 43n14, 138n25
surprise 58–9
sympathy 112, 155–6
    as basis of moral sentiments 2, 112, 134, 160, 189
    and comparison 156–7
    and greatness of mind 172–4
    and justice 134–5
    and pity 25, 135, 158–9
    and the self 184–7
    and the sentiment of humanity 141, 186n3, 190, 191n11
    in social regulation 174–5, 189–91, 195
    see also extensive sympathy

Tangney, J.P. 94n
taste:
    as internal sentiment 83, 121n12, 141, 188
    as source of motivation 52, 59–64, 83, 90
    and sympathy 135
Taylor, Jacqueline 155n13, 190–1
teleology 5, 10, 30
tragedy 193–4
Traiger, Saul 58n29, 144

van Roojen, Mark 82n18, 138n26
violent passions 12, 17–18, 54n26, 110, 126, 146–59, *see also* calm passions
virtues and vices:
    artificial and natural 118–19
    distinguished by impressions 138
    distinguished by taste 83
    and fictions 44–6
    in Hutcheson's theory 211–13
    ideas of 139–43
    and justice and injustice 76, 113n2, 134–6
    and the Moral-Discernment Interpretation 121–3, 128–30
    as motives 11, 112, 137
    and the Natural-Motive Interpretation 114–21
    as passions 30, 112, 197, 206
    and pride, humility, love, and hatred 20, 131–3
    and the sense of duty 124–5, 129
volition 26–7

weakness of will 161n16, 182
Weller, Cass 94–5, 101n10, 107n16, 110n17
will:
    Clark on 6, 31–2, 117n9, 209–10
    Cudworth on 50–1, 63, 207–8
    Descartes on 199
    Hume's conception of 7–9, 27, 30n2
    Hutcheson on 212
    Locke on 204, 205n10
    Malebranche on 200–1
    and moral rationalists 5, 15, 89, 194
    Reynolds on 197
    Spinoza on 202–3
willing, false sensation of 27
willful murder 122
Williams, Bernard 29
Wollaston, William 114, 209n14

Zimmerman, Aaron 171n20

There is no basis — minus the incorporation of the K'al term betw S+R to use them ... have Costs + Expenses were not necessary. Costs include dissolving vate — saturation — crystalization.